ESSAYS IN
ROMANTIC LITERATURE

ESSAYS IN
ROMANTIC LITERATURE

BY

GEORGE WYNDHAM

EDITED

WITH AN INTRODUCTION BY

CHARLES WHIBLEY

Essay Index Reprint Series

BOOKS FOR LIBRARIES PRESS
FREEPORT, NEW YORK

First Published 1919
Reprinted 1968

809.914
w 99 e
65539
april 1969

LIBRARY OF CONGRESS CATALOG CARD NUMBER:
68-54370

PRINTED IN THE UNITED STATES OF AMERICA

CONTENTS

GEORGE WYNDHAM

THERE never was a time in George Wyndham's life when he did not take delight in books. Neither the army nor politics availed to kill the student that was born within him. A subaltern in barracks, he taught himself Italian, and filled his leisure with the reading of history and poetry. ' The two worlds of dreams and books ' were always very real to him. The present adventure most vividly recalled to his mind the glory of the past. When, in 1885, he set sail for Egypt, ' I do not suppose,' he wrote, ' that any expedition since the days of Roman governors of provinces, has started with such magnificence; we might have been Antony going to Egypt in a purple-sailed galley.' A sojourn in Alexandria after the campaign and the prospect of Cyprus awoke in his mind visions of St. Louis and of the Turks' assault upon Famagusta. When he went to South Africa, Virgil was in his haversack, and he found in the *Heims Kringla* a means of escape from the tedium of speech-making. His taste in literature was catholic, his enthusiasms were tireless. The joy he took in *Gil Blas* did not disturb his sincere appreciation of Chaucer. And though he never lost the faculty of looking back to the remote past, as if he were a part of it, or of welcoming the bravery of a new experiment, he was gradually finding out where his true sympathies lay. At the age of twenty-five he was deep in the study of

Ronsard and the Pléiade, eagerly seeking the best editions of their works, and making the translations which he presently gathered together in a memorable book. Meanwhile he had found out for himself the fierce and haunting beauty of Villon. ' Villon's " Rondeau to Death," ' he wrote, ' is colossal in ten lines. . . . Death strides about inside those ten lines, as if he had all the world to live in. If you know where to put the candle you can throw a large shadow on the sheet.'

Thus, in a spirit of banter, he described himself as ' an archaistic barbarian, wallowing in the sixteenth century, hankering after the thirteenth, and with a still ruder relish for the pagan horseflesh of the Sagas.' Living in the stress of politics, he wrote verses to his friends, and took refuge in a remote period of the past from the havoc of warring parties. In his mind action and reflection were always mingled, and were all the stronger and clearer for their close companionship. He at any rate had no need to echo Coleridge's lament that ' we judge of books by books, instead of referring what we read to our own experience.' Experience was for George Wyndham always the touchstone of literature. He did many things, and he did them well, and he took joy in them all. With the same zest that he read and discoursed upon *A Winter's Tale* or *Troilus and Cressida*, he rode to hounds, or threw himself with a kind of fury into a ' point-to-point,' or made a speech at the hustings, or sat late in the night talking with a friend. For him one enterprise helped another. He had a better understanding of books, because he was doing a man's work in the world. He served his country with greater wisdom, because he had learned from books the sane and sound lessons which history has to teach, because he had let his fancy drink deep at the pure well of poetry.

His speeches, delivered within and outside the House of Commons, are eloquent witnesses of the value of a literary training. He preserved even on the platform a respect for English words and phrases, to which our legislators are unaccustomed, and he won a tribute from Hansard, which, I believe, is unique. The index to the Parliamentary Reports does not err on the side of humanity, and yet you may find under the date of 1st February 1900, when George Wyndham defended the army in South Africa with a fine energy and in a noble style, this solemn entry : ' Wyndham's, Mr., " Brilliant " Defence of the War Office.' And when he sat him down to write, nothing that he had learned in the field or the House of Commons came amiss to him. Gibbon once made confession that ' the Captain of the Hampshire Grenadiers had not been useless to the historian of the Roman Empire.' In all humility George Wyndham might have boasted that the panegyrist of Plutarch owed not a little to the subaltern of the Coldstream Guards. Nevertheless he knew well that life was the substance, not the art, of literature. To do what is worth the doing does not ask the same qualities as to tell the news. And in reviewing Stephen Crane's *Red Badge of Courage*, George Wyndham admitted the general failure of gallant soldiers to reproduce in words the effect of war. ' Man the potential Combatant,' he wrote, ' is fascinated by the picturesque and emotional aspects of battle, and the experts tell him little of either. To gratify that curiosity you must turn from the Soldier to the

Artist, who is trained both to see and tell, or inspired, even without seeing, to divine what things
have been and must be.' If only men of action
had always understood these simple truths, from
how many bad books should we have been saved !

II

Until 1892 George Wyndham had served no
rigid apprenticeship to literature. Hitherto he
had amused his leisure with making verses, and
had discovered for himself in which provinces of
the past he might wander at his ease. He had not
learned the value of discipline and self-criticism.
And then there began the friendship with W. E.
Henley, which completely changed his outlook upon
letters. The friendship was well matched, and fortunate for them both. George Wyndham brought
to Henley, condemned perforce to a life of physical
inactivity, something of the outside world—the strife
of parties and the hopes, too often remote, of sound
government. He confronted the settled wisdom of
forty-three with the inspiring vitality of eight-and-
twenty. Henley, on the other hand, with his ready
gift of sympathy, received the new-comer enthusiastically. He did far more than this. He opened
to him, generously, the stores of his deep and wide
knowledge. He accepted him, so to say, as a pupil
in letters. He showed him short cuts to the right
understanding of poetry and of prose, which he had
reached for himself by toiling along the stony, tedious
high road of experiment. He advised him what to
read ; he lent him books ; he corrected his taste,
where he thought it needed correction ; and he

proved of what value apprenticeship may be, even in the craft of letters. Thus he gave aim and purpose to George Wyndham's desultory studies, and the letters, which they exchanged, show how swiftly their accidental acquaintance grew into an equal and lasting friendship.

It was Henley who took the first step. He wrote from the office of *The National Observer*, hoping, as an editor and a stranger, that, since the party was in opposition, George Wyndham might have leisure to contribute from time to time to the journal. The response came (on 22nd October 1892), in an article criticising Mr. Morley and Lord Rosebery, and called ' Whistling for the Wind.' Henceforth George Wyndham was of the inner council of *The National Observer*, which he aided not only with his pen but with the sound advice of a practical politician; and he was amply repaid by the training, which taught him to surrender his love of ' ancient artifice ' to the necessity of a plain statement. When *The National Observer* passed into other hands, and was succeeded by *The New Review*, of which its contributors at least possess the happiest memory, George Wyndham embraced the venture with an ardour of enthusiasm. He kept a sanguine eye upon the triumphant success, in which he had a simple faith, and which never came. He performed all the duties of a director with unfailing zeal; he touted for ' copy,' like an old hand; having come under the spell of Cecil Rhodes in South Africa, he did his best to help the two causes of Imperialism and *The New Review*, whose Editor preached the doctrine pure and undefiled, by persuading the South Africans to set forth their views in its pages. More than this : he dared to desert, now and again, the stony

ground of politics for the garden of verse, and to
show the specimens of his gathering in the pages of
the review. Thus he proved himself a good comrade, full of hope always and fertile in resource, as
those who worked with him will not forget. And
it was not his fault nor Henley's that the readers
of the 'nineties found things better suited to their
taste than *The New Review*.

III

But Henley did George Wyndham a far greater
service than give him an insight into the triumphs
and failures of periodical literature. In November
1894 he set him to work upon an introduction to
North's *Plutarch*. He could not have designed for
him a happier enterprise, and George Wyndham
buckled him to the task with a delight not un-
mingled with misgiving. He knew well the difficulty of the undertaking. ' Somebody has truly
said,' he had written just before in a letter, ' that
no one can write Poetry after they are forty, nor
Prose before it.' And here he was at thirty embarked upon a sea of prose, not knowing when and
how he would come to port. The gift of expression was always his, even though hitherto in his
full life he had left it untutored, and he sat himself down resolutely to the ungrateful task of casti-
gation. ' The art of writing has to be learned,'
said he, ' like everything else, by practice.' And
the conquest which he made of a stubborn medium
is all the more to his credit, because he had no
natural love of prose. ' I have never cared much for
prose, however excellent,' he told Mr. Wilfrid Blunt,

when the work was done, ' which does not abound
naturally in vivid images. . . . My delight in the
Elizabethan and in some modern French writers,
is largely derived from their use of imaginative
colour.' But he tackled his new task with the same
zeal wherewith he addressed sport or politics, and
he was rewarded by finding as many chances as
he could wish for the use of the colour which he
loved.

Scholarship is largely a matter of temperament,
and George Wyndham, though he had left Eton
early to go into the army, could not expel the
temperament, which nature had implanted within
him. He had but to call upon a reserve of strength,
half-suspected, to be generously answered. With un-
tiring diligence he read the *Lives* in Amyot's French as
well as in North's English. To trace Shakespeare's
debt in *Coriolanus*, *Cæsar*, and *Antony* was a task
very near to the heart of one whose love of Shakespeare was not greater than his understanding. So
he pegged steadily at Plutarch, ' in growing terror
at his increasing size,' and like all good workmen
found a real joy in the work. ' He is a very
jolly fellow to live with,' he wrote, ' and I shall be
sorry to say " Good-bye." '

Meanwhile Henley was always at his side with
encouragement and good counsel. When George
Wyndham complained that he lacked learning, ' In
any case,' replied Henley, ' it isn't learning (so-
called) that is wanted. It is instinct and it is brain.'
So Henley liked ' his idea no end,' and told him it
was perfectly plain sailing. ' 'Tis as easy as lying,'
said he. And then he showed irresistibly the
advantages George Wyndham would reap from
the field of letters. ' You 'll not make the worse

Prime Minister or even Irish Secretary,' he wrote,
' for having done a good piece of critical literature.'
And again he asked : ' How do the wrestlings
go ? It is good to see you at it ! It means, I
think, a style, which is a thing worth having, at
whatever cost ! ' Indeed it meant a style, and
much else besides—an increased and reasoned understanding of men and books.

It was not all praise that Henley gave to George
Wyndham. He knew how to mingle with the
praise salutary warnings. ' You have the writing
instinct,' he wrote in February 1895, ' but you have
not fostered and developed it, on the one hand ;
on the other, you have more or less deboshed it by
hallooing and singing of anthems ; that is, by public
speaking and making verses. You love a phrase
like pie, and are all for altisonancy and colour. But—!
You forget to " jine your flats." You write at a
heat, and don't concern yourself enough with the
minutiae—the little foxes whose absence spoils the
vineyard's whole effect—by which the good stuff is
made to show in its goodness.' Here is a sound lesson
in style, imparted with a certain heat, which Henley
himself was quick to mitigate. ' I fear,' he added,
' I have played the schoolmaster too fiercely and
with too much passion.' But when the work was
finished, and on the eve of publishing, Henley has no
doubt as to its success. ' I can't help thinking,'
he said, ' this is going to be a pleasant experience
for you—(it has been that already)—and to give
you a reputation outside politics. We shall see—
that also.'

That the essay on Plutarch gave George Wyndham
a reputation outside politics is certain. It has stood
the test of twenty years, and seems a better piece

of work to-day even than it did when it was first
submitted to the eye of the reviewers. Whether its
publication aided its author's career is a question
not so easily answered. Politics, for the very reason
of her dulness, is a jealous mistress, and frowns
disapproval upon those who are unfaithful for an
hour to her solemn blandishments. There can be
no doubt about the cordial reception of the work.
George Wyndham's friends (and the Press) were
unanimous in appreciation, and George Wyndham
took a frank delight in the world's approval. He
sunned himself in the warmth of the applause.
' " Bis das, imo decies et centies," ' he wrote to
Mr. Wilfrid Blunt, ' I am overwhelmed by your
praise : of course it is excessive, but I have not
the false modesty to deny that I rejoice in having
won such praise from you. It pleases me the more
in that you select for praise the very field in which
I care most to conquer. . . . I can't thank you
enough for having written your first impression,
for even if you revise it, it is everything to know that
I exacted it once.' That was the just spirit in
which George Wyndham received the plaudits of
his friends. The work was done, and the doing
of it had brought him what was better worth than
those plaudits—the discipline and self-criticism,
which hitherto had been absent from his gay facility.

                         IV

George Wyndham was by character and training
a romantic. He looked with wonder upon the
world as upon a fairyland. It was fortunate for
him, therefore, that in dealing with Plutarch, he

dealt not with the Greek text, of which he knew nothing, but with North's incomparable version. Now the *Lives*, in travelling by a roundabout road from Greek to English, forgot their origin. They are like a beautiful rose, grafted on a briar-stock. Amyot is joined to the Greek by the link of a Latin translation. North knew no version save Amyot's, and had he been suddenly enabled to read the original, he would not have recognised it. As Shakespeare, in *Troilus and Cressida*, turned Homer's heroes into the rufflers of his own time, so North gave to the men of Plutarch's *Lives* the gait and seeming of true Elizabethans. And George Wyndham envisaged North's version as an English book of the sixteenth century, a book lavishly over-laid with all the vivid colours of speech which he loved well. He felt an instant sympathy with North, because ' he offers Plutarch neither to philo-sophers nor grammarians, but to all who would understand life and human nature.' This likewise was the purpose of Plutarch, in whom the dramatic sense never slumbered. But he was a clumsy writer of Greek, and had not his work been happily trans-muted by Amyot and North, he would hardly have kept a secure hold upon the imaginations of wise men. Shakespeare would not have rifled, Montaigne would not have chosen for his ' breviary,' the book of a writer, of whom a professor might say with truth that his language is deficient not only in Attic purity, but even in rhetorical and grammatical skill, that he constantly impedes his readers with difficulties, ' occasioned, not by great thoughts struggling for expression,' but by ' carelessness.'

However, George Wyndham was unconscious of Plutarch's faults. He knew only the magnificent

works composed by Amyot and North on Plutarch's
theme; and his enthusiasm flew upon a stronger
wing than it would have, had he studied only
the prose that came from Chæroneia.   Above all,
he detected in North an essentially English quality,
of which he cherished a heart - whole admiration.   'There was ever in the English temper,' says
he, 'a certain jovial forwardness, by far removed
both from impertinence and bluster, which inclined
us, as we should put it, to stand no nonsense from
any body.   This natural characteristic is strongly
marked in North.'   Indeed it is, and North was not
merely inclined to stand no nonsense in his prose;
he was ready, if need be, and here again George
Wyndham was on his side, to fight for his country.
It is true that in his work he was an accomplished
translator, but he was a knight also, who captained
his three hundred men in the Armada year, and
who certainly 'had the pull' in scenes of battle
over the Bishop.   This combined love of action and
of letters chimed perfectly with George Wyndham's
temper.   With a natural agreement he quotes
Plutarch's admirable saying, that 'he understood matters not so much by words, as he came
to understand words by common experience and
knowledge he had in things.'   Perhaps Plutarch
never came truly to understand words; assuredly
he never came to love them as North and George
Wyndham loved them; but all three shared a love
of action and swift movement.

George Wyndham's essay, then, is purely romantic
in style and purpose.   He uses the language of
chivalry for Plutarch's heroes.   Of Alexander and
Demetrius, of Pyrrhus and Eumenes, he says: 'All
are shining figures, all are crowned, all are the

greatest adventurers in the world ; and tumbling
out of one kingdom into another, they do battle
in glorious mellays for cities and diadems and
Queens.' For this very reason that he looked upon
his own life as romance, he uses the language
of chivalry, and tests his author by his own
experience. He brings whatever knowledge he had
gained of politics and warfare to the task of interpreting North's *Plutarch*. He selects there-
from whatever agrees with his own humour—by
no means a bad method of commentary, especially
upon such a writer as Plutarch. For there is something in Plutarch which is a touchstone of him
who reads. In turning over the pages of the *Lives*,
a man may try his own character, may discover
his own preferences. Or to choose another image,
Plutarch's book is a mirror of truth, which clearly
reveals the face of him who looks therein. Such
was the road of criticism which Montaigne trod. In
talking upon paper about Plutarch, as to the first
man he met, Montaigne began to sketch himself,
and at length succeeded in drawing a full-length
portrait of an intimacy which has seldom been
surpassed. And George Wyndham, following the
same path, humbly and (I think) unconsciously,
arrived at the same end of self-portraiture.

In other words, he took the study of the *Parallel
Lives* as an opportunity of explaining the views of
the soldier and the statesman that he was : he found
in North's *Plutarch* the reflection of his own mind.
He insists upon the political importance of Plutarch ;
he will have none of the paradox which denies
him political understanding ; and he insists upon
this more gladly, because he looks out upon men
and their actions from the same watch-tower as

Plutarch himself. 'Plutarch's methods,' says he, 'at least in respect of politics and war, are not those of analysis or argument, but of pageant and drama, with actors living and moving against a background of processions that live and move.' That is what he too saw in life—pageant and drama and processions, in which he was intent to take his place. With what gusto does he quote from the *Lycurgus*, the passage which follows : ' He that directeth well must needs be well obeyed. For like as the art of a good rider is to make his horse gentle and ready at commandment, even so the chiefest point belonging to a prince is to teach his people to obey!' Here the doctrine and the image are equally near to George Wyndham's heart, and wisely does he comment upon Plutarch's words. ' They set forth his chief political doctrine,' he says. . . . ' That the horse (or the man) should play the antic at will is to him plainly absurd : the horse must be ridden, and the many must be directed and controlled. Yet, if the riding, or the governing, prove a failure, Plutarch's quarrel is with the ruler or the horseman, not with the people or the mount. For he knows well that a ragged colt oftimes proves a good horse, especially if he be well ridden and broken as he should be." '

Never has the part which should be played by the aristocrat in politics been better defined. If George Wyndham found it in Plutarch's pages, perhaps because he sought it diligently, it was most intimately his own. ' This need of authority,' he wrote, ' and the obligation of the few to maintain it—by " a natural grace," springing, on the one hand, from courage combined with forbearance ; and leading, on the other, to harmony between the

rulers and the ruled—is the text, which . . . is
illustrated throughout the *Parallel Lives.*' It was
the text also, which George Wyndham himself illustrated both by doctrine and by example. None
knew better than he the obligation of gentleness.
Destiny, he thought, had conferred upon him duties
as well as privileges, and he esteemed the privileges more lightly than the duties. But who to-day
will preach to such a text, whose very meaning
is obscured in the welter of party interests, of
party feuds, of all the uglinesses, that cloud the
sky of politics ? If only our statesmen would still
remember Plutarch's sound doctrine, enunciated
by George Wyndham, of harmony between the
rulers and the ruled, the darkest problem which
confronts us would be solved, and England would
recover at last something of her natural grace.

Thus George Wyndham, living fiercely in the
present, sought confirmation and support in
the annals of the past. And comparing past and
present, he noted a double contrast between the
England of his day and the world of Plutarch's
heroes. These heroes, said he, extreme in action,
were all for compromise in theory. ' They are
ready to seal with their blood such certainty as
they can attain.' How different was the character
which he gave, with perfect justice, to his own
countrymen ! ' Ever extreme in theory,' he wrote,
' we are all for compromise' in fact ; proud on the
one score of our sincerity, on the other of our common-
sense. We are fanatics, who yet decline to persecute, still less to suffer, for our faith. And this
temperance of behaviour, following hard upon the
violent utterance of belief, is apt to show something
irrational and tame.' With a rare insight, then, he

discovers the essential contrasts in ancient and modern politics, supplies the analysis and the argument, which he says, truly enough, Plutarch sometimes lacks, and then willingly draws the conclusion from his author's narrative that 'theories and sentiments are in politics no more than flags and tuckets in a battle.'

Yet George Wyndham would never frown contemptuously upon flags and tuckets. He loved whatever was sumptuous and decorative in war or in politics as warmly as he loved life itself. So that, if he praised Plutarch as the 'dramatist in politics,' the 'unrivalled painter of men,' he praised him yet more highly as the painter of battle pieces. The backgrounds of the *Lives* reminded him of those pictures of a bygone mode, in which 'armies engage, fleets are sunk, towns are sacked, and citadels escaladed.' He applauds the art of Plutarch in selecting the dominant facts : 'the proportion of the two armies and the space between ; the sun flashing on the distant shields ; the long suspense ' ; and declares that 'there have been few between Plutarch and Tolstoi to give the scale and perspective of battle by observing such proportion in the art.' Nor does it escape him that Plutarch could be, when he chose, a very Greek in restraint. He could keep the action off the stage, and employ the artifice of the messenger as skilfully as the best of the tragedians. He could contrive 'the reverberation and not the shock of fate.' As Thackeray showed us Waterloo, not in the field but in Brussels, so Plutarch painted Leuctra, unerringly, in its effect upon Sparta. But nowhere does George Wyndham use the experience which he had won as a soldier in Egypt to better purpose, than in his comment upon Plutarch's picture of the Roman soldiers after Pydna. He recognises with the eye and ear of one who has shared the joys and labours of the field, the groups round the camp-fires, the lights crossing and recrossing, the songs of the merry soldiers, and then speaks, as his memory bids him. 'It is hard,' says he, 'to analyse the art, for the means employed are of the simplest ; yet it is certain that they do recall to such as have known, and that they must suggest to others who have not, those sights and sounds and sensations, which combine with a special enchantment about the time of the fall of darkness upon bodies of men who have drunk excitement and borne toil together in the day.' That is sincerely observed and rightly said, and the sincerity and the rightness prove that when a man who has felt the stress of life learns to write he makes discoveries which elude the cloistered craftsman. The merit of George Wyndham's essay on Plutarch owes much to the fact that it is the work of one who was a soldier and a politician as well as a writer, who was not merely a Combatant but an Artist.

v

And all the while George Wyndham was constant to the study of French poetry. The sixteenth century held him as firmly in France as in England, and he turned, by a natural sympathy, to Ronsard and the Pléiade. In this avowed preference he was a pioneer of taste, at any rate among his own countrymen. Ronsard had suffered the same fate which has since overtaken Victor Hugo : he had been buried beneath the vast

monument of his own majestic verse. And posterity, envious always, thinking that he, who was
acclaimed the Horace or the Pindar of his age,
deserved the chastening rod, took a fierce revenge
upon the poet for the generous praise lavished upon
him in his lifetime. To-day Ronsard belongs no
longer to antiquity, but to the present world of men
and poets. The enthusiasm of Barbey d'Aurevilly,
the admiration of Gautier, Banville and Heredia,
the loyal acknowledgment, made by the Disciple
Moréas, of the Master Ronsard, have had their
due effect. In England, not Pater himself has
written with a wiser understanding of the great
French poet than George Wyndham. With careful
appreciation he marks his place in the Pléiade,
discovers his sources, praises his sense of beauty.
With the devotion of a pilgrim he ·visited the castle
of Ronsard's father, and transcribed the Latin
mottoes incised upon the door. By a fortunate
accident, he happened upon the ruined Priory of
St. Cosme, whither Ronsard, finding his life a continual death, retired from Court to die, and marked
the Gothic door, through which Ronsard passed,
from which he never emerged. ' A rose-tree grew
up one of the jambs,' wrote George Wyndham, ' and
a vine had thrown a branch across the grey, worm-
eaten panels. When I returned next year the door,
with its time-worn sculpture, was gone.' What
better illustration could be found than this of
Ronsard's text:

> ' Tout ce qui est de beau ne se garde longtemps
> Les roses et les lis ne régnent qu'un printemps ' ?

While George Wyndham extols at its proper worth
the work of the Pléiade, he sees plainly enough

whither its rules, too rigidly interpreted, would
lead. A chain, though it be woven of roses, is irk-
some to bear, and perfection itself, solemnly ordained,
may be a tyranny. Mallarmé has pointed out
that the rules formulated by the successors of the
Pléiade would enable anybody to make a verse
to which none could object. ' But,' says George
Wyndham, ' that savours of deportment rather
than of poesy.' He recognises it as ' an admirable maxim . . . for the genteel mob of eighteenth-
century couplet-mongers, but a useless counsel and,
so, an impertinence to the leader of a revel or a
forlorn hope.' Thus he makes plain, in criticising
others, his own ambition. He cared not which
he led—a revel or a forlorn hope in life or letters.
Each of them suited the temper of his mind. He
was content to be joyous with those who smiled,
or to die in the last ditch for a losing cause. And
in Ronsard, I think, he loved the gay valour of the
man as much as he loved his sentiment of beauty.
He liked to remember his spacious life at the Court,
the favour shown him by Elizabeth and Mary
Stuart, the silver Minerva, which he won at the
Floral Games of Toulouse. But most of all he
reverenced him because he ' was every inch a man,
who stood four-square to the whole racket of his
day.' It was not for Ronsard, for all his love of
roses and lilies, to pass his time idly in an enchanted
garden. ' Here,' says George Wyndham, ' is a
citizen and a soldier, a man who takes a side in
politics and religion, who argues from the rostrum
and pommels in the ring, delighting in all the treasures garnered into the citadel of the past, and ready
to die in its defence.' In sketching thus the ideals
of Ronsard, George Wyndham sketched his own.

VI

When his essay on Plutarch was finished, a
friend demurred to his spending his time upon such
toys of criticism. 'I know that you think I should
be better employed on original work. But I find
that I have a gift of keen imaginative appreciation
combined with another of seeing the past as a whole
philosophically, which enables me, as a critic, to
say things which strike people as original.' Thus he
wrote in defence of himself, and he wrote truly.
It was no vain boast that he possessed the gift
of imaginative appreciation, and having it he
would have been untrue to himself had he cast it
away. And he might have gone further, and urged
that the art of criticism, as he saw it, was creative
also. To rescue from the past the fading figures
of great men, to select from the annals such facts
as shall give truth to portraiture, to set dead
heroes in the light of day—this surely is an act of
creation. Moreover, George Wyndham knew well
that original work, in the higher sense, was out of
his reach, so long as he was immersed in politics.
No man shall serve God and Mammon, and the
Mammon of politics stands in stern opposition to
the God of originality. We cannot picture to ourselves a great poet sitting in the seat of a Prime
Minister, and they who in the House of Commons
have written fine prose may be counted on the fingers
of a hand. George Wyndham, in truth, had obeyed
the call of what he deemed to be duty ; he had
taken (and was taking) his share in the government
of the country, and so long as he did this, he could
count neither upon the leisure nor upon the egoism,

which is necessary for the doing of 'original work.'

Meanwhile he indulged his gift of imaginative appreciation, and proved that he had the rare faculty of placing on their feet before us the straylings of the past. In an essay, entitled *The Poetry of the Prison*, for instance, he has sketched Villon lightly and with a loyal sympathy. 'He writes of his shames,' says he, 'as an old soldier of his scars.' Thus is Villon's character revealed in a phrase. Without a hint of irrelevant censure, George Wyndham describes those shames as he knew them, and acclaims the great poet, 'whose verse is bitter with the bitterness, glad only with the insolence' of his age. By way of contrast turn to R. L. Stevenson's essay on Villon—surely a sad aberration in criticism. Stevenson judges Villon as the Elders of the Scottish Church judged Burns, and cannot contemplate him without a reproof upon his tongue. He tells us that Villon's 'sentiments are about as much to be relied upon as those of a professional beggar,' and proceeds to find in his work 'an unrivalled insincerity.' Unrivalled insincerity! You rub your eyes as you read the words, applied to a poet who in every word that he wrote was emotionally sincere. Still worse, Stevenson says contemptuously, 'it shall remain in the original for me,' of a poem, in which Matthew Arnold, no condoner of insincerity, finds the 'σπου-δαιότης, the high and excellent seriousness which Aristotle assigns as one of the grand virtues of poetry,' the quality which Arnold himself perceives only in Homer and Dante and Shakespeare. Thus, while Stevenson dismisses Villon as 'the sorriest figure on the rolls of fame,' George Wyndham remembers that he 'writes of his shames, as an old soldier of

his scars'; and who shall say that George Wyndham
has not the better of it?

With an equally keen perception of life, George
Wyndham has drawn a sketch of Shakespeare's father.
Acting upon a hint, thrown out by R. L. Stevenson
in talk with Henley, he ascribes to John Shakespeare
something of the whimsical temperament which belonged to the father of Charles Dickens.   He paints
him as a kind of Micawber, perplexed always by 'a
happy-go-lucky incuriousness,' a man of that sanguine temper that is sure always that 'something
will turn up' either in town or country, prosperous
to-day, penniless to-morrow, immersed in lawsuits,
crippled by mortgages, yet resolute in pride, and
appealing always to the College of Heralds for a
grant of arms.   At last we see him 'coming not to
church for fear of process for debt'; and the essential
truth of the portrait helps to explain something of
Shakespeare's own experience, especially his knowledge of law and heraldry.   Indeed, throughout
George Wyndham's essay on the Poems of Shakespeare, the reader will find a rare combination of
research and understanding.   He had read the texts
with a discerning mind.   He had discovered early in
his quest, as all discover who study a literature, deeply
and at first hand, ' that the critics who have written
of it, have never read it, but merely handed on traditional judgments, for the most part astonishingly
incorrect.'   But it was not merely the texts that he
was busied with.   A quick perception brought the
London and the life of Elizabeth's age clearly before

him. He could see it in his mind's eye, because he went wandering into the past, and knew what he himself would have felt in the cross-currents of that busy, turbulent time. 'All the talk was,' he was sure, 'of sea-fights and new editions: Drake and Lyly, Ralegh and Lodge, Greene and Marlowe and Grenville were names in every mouth.' There was nothing in the babbling activity of the eager town that did not appeal to the lust of the eye and the pride of life. Poets and nobles were alike fervent worshippers of the stage, and gladly did George Wyndham picture Shakespeare as the friend of Herbert and Southampton.

His criticism of the Poems is far divorced from any sort of pedantry, as well it might be, since it was written 'in the midst of engrossing duties.' 'In the character of " Johannes Factotum," ' he wrote in November 1895, 'I am at Aldershot doing some cavalry drill; next week I make political speeches. . . . But all the time I am writing an introduction to Shakespeare's *Poems*.' The diversity of interest is shown in the work, not in any weakening of the interest, but in a resolute avoidance of irrelevant, conventional criticism. He cares not for the foolish problems which are wont to perplex the critics of the Sonnets. Mr. W. H. is not of supreme importance to him. He brushes Mr. Tyler's case aside, because it 'cannot be argued without the broaching of many issues outside the sphere of artistic appreciation.' In truth, he follows his quest not as a student of history but as a lover of art. He refrains from seeking parallels to Shakespeare's verse, for that method 'discovers not Shakespeare's art, but the common measure of poetry in Shakespeare's day.' What he sought in

Shakespeare's Poems was the wealth of his imagery, the perfect beauty of his verbal melody.

Even while he sketches in brilliant colours the poet's environment, even while he sets in array the combatants on either side of the Poetomachia, he firmly detaches the Poems from Shakespeare's personal experience, and proves that they owe little enough to the poet's career. What he looked for was 'lyrical discourse'; what he found—in Sonnet 90 —was 'the perfection of human speech.' His letters, written while the Essay was in progress, are packed with enjoyment. 'What stuff it is! "Lucrece" and all '—thus he writes, ' I had really never read " Lucrece," but just listen to this :

> " For sorrow, like a heavy hanging bell,
>   Once set on ringing, with his own weight goes."

Only William could have written that, and this must be driven into the people who glibly quote Hazlitt's *Ice-houses*, and wearily repeat that a lady in Lucrece's unfortunate predicament is little likely to apostrophize Time, Opportunity, Eternity, Sorrow and any other abstractions that suggest a good tirade.'

To this theme, then, he is constant : that Shakespeare is not a Rousseau, not a metaphysician, but a poet, who aims in his Poems at music and beauty; not at self-revelation or the betterment of others. But now and again he deserts the high-road of his argument for the by-paths of ingenious discovery. He suggests that the open-air effects of *Venus and Adonis* are taken one and all from Arden. He marks how the day waxes and wanes from dawn to eve, how even the weather changes, so that pausing at any stanza you might name the hour ;

and thereto he adds according to his wont a luminous
comment from his own experience :   ' A month
under canvas,' says he, ' or, better still, without
a tent, will convince any one that to speak of the
stars and the moon is as natural as to look at your
watch or an almanack.'   Thus once more the
Cheshire Yeoman came to the aid of the critic of
literature, and spoke with an authority denied to
the scholar in his library.

VIII

In life and in letters, as I have said, George Wyndham esteemed most highly ' the leader of a revel
or a forlorn hope.'   In 'The Springs of Romance
in the Literature of Europe ' he essayed to lead
both.   It was an address delivered to the Students
of the University of Edinburgh, and it dealt with
a subject which had long been in George Wyndham's
mind.   More than two years before he was Lord
Rector he had made the design, and even filled in
many of the details.   'The idea is,' he wrote to his
mother, ' Where did romance come from ?   There
was none among our Northern ancestors of the ninth
century.   It came from contact of East and West
—contact with the East owing to the conflict between
Christendom and the Paynim from Roncesvalles onward—contact with the West, from the Geraldines'
transit through Wales into Ireland.'   The idea was
fantastic and difficult to make a reality, as George
Wyndham acknowledged.   'In conclusion,' he wrote,
' I can say with Malory, " Now all was but enchantment " ; and invite you to be enchanted.'
The question which he put in the letter quoted
above, he answered in the address.   ' When, then,

and where does Romance arrive in Europe ?   The
answer to the first question is, not before the second
half of the eleventh century, and, to the second,
probably in Great Britain.'   So he begins with the
Chanson de Roland, which he thinks was retouched
after Henry II. of England ' had, by conquest and
marriage asserted a shadowy overlordship from the
Grampians to the Pyrenees.'   He insists upon the
importance, for his argument, of Eleanor's marriage
with Henry of Anjou.   ' It is when they married (in
1152), and where they married, that most of the
springs of romance commingle in the literature of
Europe.'   And then, aiming at a definition, he
asserts that Romance is welcoming the strange—the
strange in legend, in allegory, in symbol, and in
scenery.   'The reaction of the mind,' says he,
' when confronted with the strange, is, in some sort,
a recognition of ignored realities.   Romance is an
act of recognition.'

It is an ingenious argument, ingeniously con-
ducted, and illustrated with a wealth of erudition.
Of George Wyndham's fancy and courage in its
conduct there can be no doubt.   But there is always
a danger of dogmatising as to times and places,
a danger of which the writer himself was fully
conscious.   If we admit that Romance came into
Europe in the second half of the eleventh century,
and was fully grown, so to say, a hundred years
later, we must discard the whole of Classical
literature from our view. (Fully prepared for the
encounter, George Wyndham advanced the 'disputable proposition,' that the classics are not
romantic.) He makes certain concessions to the
' heckler ';   he gives him Nausicaa and Medea,
Dido and Camilla ;   finally, he throws to his possible

opponents the whole body of Apuleius. But he
seems to miss one point. If he makes a single
exception, he gives up his argument. If there was
Romance among the Greeks and Romans, then
Romance did not come to efflorescence in the
Court of Henry II. and Eleanor, his queen.

Truly the proposition is 'disputable.' (No definition of Romance can exclude from the enchanted
kingdom a vast deal of Greek and Latin literature.)
It is not Nausicaa alone in the *Odyssey* that is
romantic. Romance is in the *Odyssey's* very texture and essence. The return of the wanderer, who
after many years of miraculous dangers comes back
to his wife and home is the theme of high romance.
The hair of Odysseus is wet with the salt sea spray.
Far-distant havens and gallant ships have delighted
his vision. The palace of Alcinous, in whose garden
pear upon pear waxes old, and apple on apple and
cluster ripens upon cluster of the grape, and fig upon
fig, is in fairyland. And what a marvellous tale
Odysseus has to tell! There is the story of Poly-
phemus, the giant who has but a single eye in the
middle of his forehead, and who devoured two of the
hero's companions at a meal. And the bewitchings
of Circe and the siren's song, and the soul-destroying
lotus, and the dark house of Hades itself—these
are the very stuff of which romance is made. Nor
does Homer stand alone. Virgil and Ovid were in
the Middle Ages the great quickeners of romance.
From them the romancers of the Middle Ages borrowed their passion ; to them the ladies of high
romance owed allegiance. And is not Lucian's 'True
History' romantic, and 'Daphnis and Chloe?'
And were there not witches in Thessaly when
Apuleius wrote ?

For me, indeed, classic and romantic are terms which express neither time nor place. The two modes of thought, the two states of mind have lived, side by side, since the beginning of time. They were born, both of them in the Garden of Eden, and the Serpent was the first romantic. But if, as I think, George Wyndham has not brought his good ship Romance into port, he has taken us a joyous voyage among the islands of fancy, shown us many a noble sight, and left us careless of our harbourage. In truth, the address given at Edinburgh ˙is like good talk, set in a formal shape as becomes ink and paper, but good talk all the same, happy, voluble, and sometimes controversial. Even when a friend may disagree with him, what would that friend not give to face him once more across the hearth, and to hear his voice, gay in tone, large in utterance, confronting him ! Above all, when George Wyndham set out to find the hallowed spot, where the springs of romance commingle, he set out upon an adventure. And as his friend, W. P. Ker, told him in a letter, urging him to ' go on,' ' nothing good is done except by adventurers—in that branch of learning anyhow.'

IX

It is characteristic of George Wyndham that if he accepted W. P. Ker's eulogy as ' the tribute of a sportsman to a poacher,' he took a natural pride in the praise that was worth having ; and with the printing of ' The Springs of Romance ' a sudden thought came to him. ' I remembered with regret,' he wrote to his mother, ' the big book I meant to write about romantic literature, with a leaning

towards the French. Then I began to remember
all the things I have written, which I had forgotten.
They are hidden away in *The New Review* (extinct)
. . . and in introductions to books which are out
of print, or don't sell. Then it suddenly flashed on
me that, without knowing it, I have written two-
thirds or three-fourths of my book! And I see
exactly what remains to be written. *The Springs*
is the first chapter. I never thought of that. . . .
Chap. II.—not written—will be *The Chroniclers
and the Crusades.* It is not written, but I have
all the stuff and many notes. That takes me right
through the thirteenth century. It may become
two chapters in order to bring in Dante and the
Spaniards. . . . But after that it is nearly all finished.
IV. or V. is my old Poetry of the Prison, about
Charles d'Orléans and Villon (*New Review*, out of
print); V. or VI. is Chaucer (not written); VI. or
VII. North's *Plutarch*, written—indeed I must cut
it down ; VII. or VIII. is Ronsard, written, . . .
VIII. or IX. is Shakespeare, written, and must be
cut down; IX. or X. is Elizabethan Mariners in
Elizabethan literature, written in the *Fortnightly*
twelve years ago ; X. or XI. is Scott, written; XI.
or XII. is the new French Romantics—not published,
but almost all written, with many translations.'

Such was the book as George Wyndham had
planned it, and would that he had lived to match
the perfecting with the plan! Alas, for the gaps,
which never will be filled! Few men of our time
were better fitted than he by sentiment and knowledge to write about Chaucer. I would give a
wilderness of modern books to hear him discourse
of the Chroniclers and the Crusades. Who the new
French Romantics are I know not, and what he wrote

of them has not come to light.   For the rest, I have
put the book together, as (I think) he would have
wished it done.   All the finished chapters will be found
between these covers, which he marked as portions
of the book which he had written 'without knowing
it.'   In the letter I have quoted he proposed to
cut down the essays on Plutarch and Shakespeare.
This is a task too delicate for friendship to perform, and I have left them precisely as they came
from his hand.   Here, then, is a book planned by
George Wyndham himself, marred by *lacunae*, which
he would have filled up, but none the less complete
in itself, and a fair picture of his mind and art.

George Wyndham possessed, in full measure, what
Mallarmé once called *la joie critique*.   Literature
was for him no πάρεργον, no mere way of escape
from politics.   If he was an amateur in feeling, he
was a craftsman in execution.   He loved books,
and he wrote of them as though he loved them.
His enthusiasm kept pace with his passion of
discovery.   He combined with what Hazlitt called
' gusto ' a marvellous patience.   If he wrote with
excitement, he deemed that no labour in the collecting of facts went unrewarded.   A new ' find '
or a new ' theory ' warmed him like wine.   He
would turn it over in his mind enthusiastically and
furiously discourse upon it.   And sitting himself
down, with pen and paper, he would test it and
check it by all the means within his reach.   When he
first designed his *Springs of Romance*, he sketched
what he would put into it.   ' I shall stick it full of
all I like,' he said, ' the " Regina Avrillosa " and the
Border Ballads ; The Castle of Clerimont, and the
Lady of Tripoli, The Song of Roland and the Fall
of Constantinople, Marco Polo, and Antoine Galand.'

As he came to the writing, he contracted his
scope, but the design was grandiose, and the
Address, which was its result, was all the better
for the knowledge of many books, which he had read
and did not quote. He worked all the more wisely
because he had something in reserve. Moreover,
as I have said, he brought a whiff of the open air
into criticism. If he was happy among his books,
he was happy also riding across country. And on
hunting days he neither read nor wrote.

x

It may seem something of a paradox that George
Wyndham, keenly alive as he was to all the changing
controversies of the hour, should yet have found a
lasting solace in the past ; and yet the paradox
soon disappears in the light of his character and
his upbringing. He had a simple faith in the
force of tradition ; he was acutely conscious of the
heritage that was his. ' This autumn I addict
myself to Politics,' he wrote to a friend in 1907,
' beginning at Perth, on October 18th, and continuing at Hexham, Birmingham, Dover, Manchester,
York, and Leicester. . . . I do this from a sense of
duty. The Gentry of England must not abdicate.'
There was his creed in a phrase : ' The Gentry of
England must not abdicate,' for the very reason
that the gentry had its roots in the past, that it
received from the past its duties and its privileges.
He had not a profound belief in platform discourse,
but it was the means, nearest to his hand, of carrying
on the work which had been bequeathed to him by
his ancestors. He knew that he was but a lantern-
bearer, and he was resolved that his lantern should

be handed to those who came after him, still alight
and clear-burning. Even fox-hunting, in his eyes,
was a glory of tradition. 'The hounds meet here
to-morrow,' he wrote to his father from Saighton on
the Christmas Day of 1907. 'Twenty-eight persons
are coming out from Eaton. . . . And the local lights
will try to hold their own against the paladins of
Leicestershire and Meath. It is interesting—apart
from the fun of it and the sport—to see this when
political changes may abolish the gentry and their
pursuits. Personally I back the gentry.' There is
George Wyndham's view made clear as crystal. He
felt within him that he 'came from afar,' that it
was his first duty to defend the traditional order
of things, and he accepted the existing plan of
political warfare, with a full determination to make
the best of it. And let it be remembered of him
that his mind merged what is in what was, that he
looked upon the past with the eye of the living
present.

A man holding such a creed could not help
finding his keenest interest in bygone times. Gladly
he turned from the racket of the hustings to the
calm of the settled past which yielded its secrets
to his imagination. He delighted, as I have said,
to be thought an 'archaistic barbarian.' He con-
fessed, as we have seen, 'a ruder relish for the pagan
horseflesh of the Sagas.' And gladly would he have
gone back, if he could, still further into the childhood of the world. It was not mere propinquity
which inspired him with a passion for Stonehenge.
When he visited Wells, it was not the cathedral,
not the library, with its Jensen's *Pliny* and the
autograph of Erasmus, that held him most closely
in thrall, it was Wookey Hole, that strange cavern

of the Mendips, out of which flows the river Axe, and which was a place of refuge for our remote forefathers. Its corridors and galleries, its vast chambers, 'like chapter-houses,' filled him with an ecstatic wonder. It delighted him to think that there the Britons hid and defended themselves against the beasts of the fields and other foes, when the lake-village of Glastonbury was destroyed, that there in the soil their combs and their pottery, their coins and their needles and their bones were found. In a moment his fancy was at work. With the help of the excavator he was busy putting the past together from the poor fragments that remain, and divining the habits and ambitions of the ingenious lake-dwellers, who, I think, made but a poor exchange when they left their free homes in the marshes of Glastonbury for the dim-lit caves of Wookey Hole. And, when the excavator showed him a *denarius* of 124 B.C., he was all excitement. ' Now perpend,' said he, ' how is that ? The Roman Conquest was in A.D. 70. I plumped at once for the theory that it has filtered through the dim, but civilised, Europe of which Morris tells his tales.' Here the archæologists are on his side, for Sir Arthur Evans is persuaded by the relics of the fen-settlement at Glastonbury to conclude that ' the more luxurious arts of the classical world were already influencing even the extreme west of our island in pre-Roman times,' that the little ' Western Venice ' of Glastonbury ' may claim some direct heritage from a still older Venetian culture.'

XI

Since George Wyndham felt the ardent curiosity of the archæologist, since in politics he was a stout champion of tradition, since he knew well that we are but lantern-bearers, it is not strange that he turned his critical eyes towards the past, that he was intimately at home in the thirteenth century, that he bade his research halt at the first half of the seventeenth. His only outpost in the modern world was Sir Walter Scott, and Sir Walter was the great reviver of antiquity in our land. It is easy, therefore, to detect a unity of purpose in George Wyndham's work, and this unity prompts the question what more he would have done had a longer span of life been allotted to him. He died in the fulness of his strength and courage. His accession to an estate had filled him with new hopes and new ambitions. He had been disillusioned by politics. The old order, for which he had fought, was fast changing. The passage of the Parliament Bill and the method of its passage had persuaded him, as well they might, to take a grave view of the future. He knew that war was coming with Germany, and he knew that little or nothing was being done to meet the surely impending danger. Above all, he disliked the internationalising of our politics. He feared what he called ' the Ortolan brigade.' He saw that the cause of Progress and of 'the People versus the Peers' was led by ' E——, curly-haired C——, "dear old chappie" D——, and all the other bounding brothers of cosmopolitan finance and polyglot "Society," dining off truffles,' and imitating 'the Yiddish pronunciation of the letter R with a guttural growl. "That's the dog's letter," as Shakespeare says.' And yet he saw clearly enough that English life, with its hunting and its soldiering and its literature, would still go on, and prove 'far more substantial' than the intrigues of Party Politics or the more grasping dreams of Socialism. What, then, would he have done in what seemed to him a disjointed world? He had many projects, half thought out, in his busy mind. There was a life of Bolingbroke which he had reserved for his age, and though Bolingbroke lay far out in the wilds of the eighteenth century, which was no century for him, the modern half of his soul sympathised warmly with Bolingbroke's ideals of a patriot king and a contented people. And there was his estate to manage and to restore to the prosperity which it had enjoyed two hundred years or more before. In a letter, one of the last he wrote, which was actually delivered to Mr. Wilfrid Ward after his death, he admitted that he was absorbed in two subjects: 'Rural England and his library.' Truly they were subjects worthy to absorb him. It was not for him to shirk the duties of the countryside, and the beautiful library at Clouds, already fashioned to his will, was fast being filled with beautiful books. ' "We know what we are, but we do not know what we may be," ' he told Mr. Ward. 'I may— perhaps—take office again. But I doubt it. *Inveni portum.*' Had he? Even if he had found a harbour, it was still restless with the swell of the ocean. His eager mind was discovering new duties, not discarding old ones. · 'Some people inherit an estate,' he wrote in the letter to Mr. Ward, from which I have already quoted, ' and go on as if nothing had happened. I can't do that. . . .

Suddenly I find myself responsible for farming two
thousand four hundred acres, and for paying sums
that stagger me by way of weekly wages and repairs.
So I ask myself " What are you going to do ? " I
mean to use all my imagination and energy to get
something done that should last and remind.' That
he would have done that is certain. He would have
done that and much more besides. Had the call
come, he would, I believe, have returned with fresh
vigour to politics, in spite of partisan intrigues
and the selfishness of Socialism. ' The gentry of
England must not abdicate,' he had said, and he
would not have abdicated. A year after his death
came the war, which he had long foreseen and
pondered, and the war would have aroused him in
a moment from his pleasant dreams of fields and
books. Assuredly he would have played his part
in the defence of his native land, and I think
that it would not be displeasing to him that his
essays in the art of letters should be gathered
together and given to the world in this year of
England's gallantry and high endeavour.

CHARLES WHIBLEY.

BIBLIOGRAPHICAL NOTE

The Springs of Romance in the Literature of Europe was delivered, as Lord Rector's Address, to the students of the University of Edinburgh in October 1910, and was published as a pamphlet in the same year. ' The Poetry of the Prison ' made its first appearance in *The New Review*, March 1895. ' Ronsard and the Pléiade ' served as a preliminary essay to selected translations from their poetry, published in 1906. ' North's *Plutarch* ' formed an introduction to the reprint of North's version in W. E. Henley's series of Tudor Translations, 1895. ' The Poems of Shakespeare ' appeared in 1898 as a preface to an edition of the Poems. ' Elizabethan Adventure in Elizabethan Literature ' was contributed to *The Fortnightly Review* in November 1898. And *Sir Walter Scott* was a speech, proposing the Toast of Honour, delivered at the Fourteenth Annual Dinner of ' The Edinburgh Sir Walter Scott Club ' on November 29, 1907. It was published separately in 1908.

THE SPRINGS OF ROMANCE IN THE LITERATURE OF EUROPE

An Address delivered to the Students of the University of Edinburgh, October 1910

A

'It is not the contexture of words but the effects of action that gives glory to the times. . . .'

'It is but the clouds gathered about our owne judgement that makes us think all other ages wrapt up in mistes, and the great distance betwixt us, that causes us to imagine men so farre off to bee so little in respect of ourselves. . . .'

'It is not bookes but onely that great booke of the world and the all-over-spreading grace of heaven that makes men truly judicial. . . .'

S. DANIEL, *Defence of Rhime*, 1603.

THE SPRINGS OF ROMANCE IN THE LITERATURE OF EUROPE

IT was not easy to choose a theme for an address to Edinburgh University. Your unbounded belief in Rectorial discretion permits a latitude that is almost embarrassing. For guidance I had nothing but a sense of my own limitations and a prospect of the scene that confronts me. These suggested a search over the vast province of learning for some plot, not wholly unexplored by your Rector, that should also be linked with the fame of your ancient city. The world allows, and Scott's monument attests, that, from Edinburgh, and by his genius, 'impulse and area' were added to the great movement of the last century which we call the Romantic Revival. That movement changed the literature, architecture, painting, and furniture of Europe, and reversed the attitude of scholarship towards the Middle Ages ; a fact of world-wide importance : incidentally it renewed the bond between Scotland and France ; a fact of peculiar interest to the capital of your country. It so happens that, long before I ever dreamed of the honour you have conferred, the phrase—Romantic Revival—made me wonder, what was revived. 'What,' I asked myself, 'is Romance ? ' Unable to answer, I turned to another question—' When did Romance first come into the literature of Europe ? '—and spent some time in pursuit of so elusive a quarry. My choice of a theme was decided by Edinburgh's connection with the revival of Romance, and my guesses at its origin. I must speak of Romance.

Some may feel that a definition of Romance should precede any survey of its inception and character. I respectfully demur. A definition of Romance would be easy if there were general agreement on the meaning of the word. Unfortunately there is not. Most people if asked, ' What is Romance ? ' would answer, as Augustine did of Time, ' I know when you do not ask me.' When dealing with the dimly apprehended we must discover before we can define. Columbus had no map of America.

One way of discovery would be to select an example of obvious, though undefined, Romance, and then to analyse its contents. But that plan if applied, for instance, to Ariosto's *Orlando Furioso* will be found to lead away from definition rather than towards it. Analysis of extreme romantic types yields a jumble of mythologies, refracted through several layers of history, all more or less distorted and opaque. There is plenty of fighting and love-making, a good deal of scenery and weather ; and, apart from human interest, there are troops of animals and some strange inhuman forces masquerading as giants and dragons and warlocks. From such confusion a definition does not readily emerge. A better way of discovery is called, I believe—rather pompously—the historic method. It amounts to this. If you can establish When and Where a thing happened you may be able to guess Why it happened and, even, What it was. Let us, then, post-

pone analysis of Romance, and set out by weighing
the question with which the Cardinal of Este greeted
Ariosto's presentation of his masterpiece. (1510.)
The prelate asked the poet, ' quite simply,' ' where
he had been for all that rot.' That is what I shall
try to discover. If we begin by detecting when,
and where, Romance first appeared in Europe we
may be able to say why it appeared, and even to
hazard a surmise at its nature. But the last is a
fearsome enterprise, trenching on metaphysics, as
the way is with all inquiry if you push it any distance.
I shall seek in the main for origins, and call my
address ' The Springs of Romance in the Literature
of Europe.'

You can look for the advent of Romance either
in literature that remains and can be studied; or
else, in the theories of learned men who infer the
pre-existence of earlier literature, that has certainly
perished, and may never have been written. They
cite the songs in which, Tacitus tells us, the
Germans extolled the founders of their race; or
the didactic poetry of the Druids, which the Druids
were forbidden to write; or they point in later
versions to a barbarous handling of stories treated
with relative urbanity in earlier versions, and infer
from the discrepancy a common origin for both of
a more primitive character than either reveals.
These deductions from contemporary references to
songs that are lost, and from antique touches in
later documents, are always ingenious and often
delightful. But they present two difficulties. In
the first place, hypothetical literature affords a
foundation too insecure for the erection of theory
that must itself partake of conjecture. In the
second place, it is by no means certain that barbarous

legends are romantic to the races who invent them. I shall return to that view before I conclude. At the outset I must look for the advent of Romance in writings that still form part of the literature of Europe.

THE ADVENT OF ROMANCE

Keeping, then, to literature that remains, I advance the disputable proposition that the writings preserved from Greece and Rome are not romantic ; briefly, that the classics are not romantic. If time permitted I could, I think, sustain that thesis, with qualifications, of course, and concessions to any who disputed its truth. I would readily admit that the Greeks were more romantic than the Romans. I would certainly concede Nausicaa in the *Odyssey* and Medea in the *Argonauts* ; Dido and Camilla in the *Æneid*. But, excepting Virgil, whose peculiar romantic note caught the ear of the Middle Ages, I should point out that my concessions were mainly in respect of the earliest and latest poems of the Classic world, and that, including even the *Æneid*, all such touches of romance as do faintly transfigure the classics are to be found in stories of wandering through strange lands, and of encounters with alien customs and superstitions. I would give my ' heckler ' the *Golden Ass* of Apuleius, and cut the argument short by taking refuge in the considered opinion of Professor W. P. Ker. He writes (*The Dark Ages*, p. 41) : ' Classical literature perished from a number of contributory ailments, but of these none was more desperate than the want of Romance in the Roman Empire, and especially in the Latin language.'

The Latin world of the fifth century was unromantic, and notably so in northern Gaul, the
most Roman, because the least invaded, province
of the Western Empire. Latinised Gauls led an
ordered existence of unchallenged convention, re-
volving round garrisons, townhalls, and schools.
Their life was military and municipal; their
literature, an affair of grammar and rhetoric,
written in classical Latin which had diverged from
vulgar Latin, so widely as to be unintelligible to
all but the learned. From the people's Latin,
spoken throughout the country, almost every trace
of Celtic words and Celtic beliefs had been elimi-
nated. We possess nothing that can be called
Romance in either of these languages. Yet Latin
Gaul was to be the nursery-garden of the first
seedling of romantic literature, and that earliest
growth was not to flourish until it had been trans-
planted. When, then, and where, does Romance
arrive in European literature. The answer to the
first question is, not before the second half of the
eleventh century, and, to the second, probably in
Great Britain. The first piece of obvious Romance
in literature that remains is the ' Song of Roland,'
as we have it in the Oxford MS. (Bodleian, Digby,
23). The composition of the poem is attributed
to a Norman, and the date of it placed between the
Norman conquest of England in 1066 and the
Crusaders' conquest of Jerusalem in 1099. The
handwriting, as distinguished from the composition,
is dated about 1170. Romance arrives six centuries
after the overthrow of the Western Empire, and
appears where a province had been torn from it
long before the Latin Gauls had ceased to speak
or write in languages derived from Rome. We

know when and where Romance appeared. To understand why it came, and to surmise at what it was, we must sketch in the events of those six centuries which preceded and—as I shall urge— prepared for the Advent of Romance after 1050 A.D., and for its rapid development a hundred years later.

In the fifth century two things happened which began the preparation of Gaul to be the nursery-garden of Romance. A Celtic people established themselves in the north-west of Gaul, thenceforward to be called Brittany, where their language is still spoken by the Bretons. They came in numbers, and the territory which they occupied ceased to be Latin. We are told that they sang lays to a little harp, called the rote. But none of their songs appears in literature for centuries. Again in the fifth century, a Teutonic nation, the Francs, invaded the north-east of Gaul, and soon ceased, for the most part, to be German. They were few in number, and their ambition was to be like the Latin aristocracy. Their mother-tongue, after a brief interval, contained more words of Latin than of Teutonic derivation. Their laws were written in learned Latin. Their religion, after 496 A.D., was orthodox Latin Christianity. Clovis, or Chlodoweg—if you like that name better—preferred his title of a 'Roman patrician' to the glory of his conquests. We are told that the Francs sang the deeds of their kings in poems, accompanied on harps. It may well be so. But none of these poems have ever appeared in literature. They may, or may not, have been romantic. We have no record of Frankish verse, save one. There are eight Latin lines in the life of a saint composed in the ninth century. They refer to a legendary action of King Clotair in the seventh century. The author presents them as excerpts translated from a song which, he tells us, was popular at that time. We have nothing else. To reconstruct these non-existent effusions by inference, and even to cite them by name as the panegyric of this or that Frankish king, the song of Clotair, or of Chlodoweg, is, in the word of an eminent French scholar, ' a triumph of scientific hypothesis.' In the fifth, sixth, and seventh centuries France was still Roman and unromantic, but not Teutonic, and with Celts on one flank.

In the eighth century a third event continued the preparation for Romance. The Arabs, after conquering Spain, invaded the south of France and were defeated at the battle of Tours by Charles Martel on the 10th October 732. We know that the Arabs sang songs, for we possess seven odes written by them in ' the days of ignorance ' before Mahomet. And we know that, in the ninth century, they brought into Southern Europe the viol, or fiddle, conveyed from Persia, upon which Jongleurs were, much later, to accompany the Romances of Europe. But the early influence of the Arabs produced no romance. On the contrary, it produced dry translations of the least romantic works of the Greeks. Even the epoch-making contest at Tours bequeathed no legacy to romantic literature. Charles the Hammer never appears as one of its heroes. It was his grandson, Charlemagne, who became all but the greatest of romantic figures. His legendary exploits overshadowed his achievements, and were sung for centuries in every language of Europe. Yet the first legend, that we still possess, was not written until some two hundred and seventy years after his death.   Two other events were needed to complete the preparation.   Despite the lays of the Bretons, the songs of the Francs, the odes of the Arabs, accompanied by rotes, harps, and viols, it is not until after the Normans had established themselves in France at the beginning of the tenth century, and conquered the English in the second half of the eleventh century, that we find the advent of Romance in European literature.   The placid province of Latin Gaul was modified by the juxtaposition of Bretons, the absorption of Francs, the expulsion of Arabs, the absorption of Normans, and the conquest of England, before the 'Song of Roland' appears.

THE SONG OF ROLAND

The ironical adage *Post hoc ergo propter hoc* may be discounted at once, for the song reveals the influence of all those five events, and, but for their happening, could not be what it is.   It is written in French ; because Latinised Gaul, having ceased to be Celtic, never became German, but became France. Its hero, Roland, is the Count of the Marches of Brittany, and it teems with praise of the Bretons :

> ' Icil chevalchent en guise de baruns
> Dreites lur hanstes, fermez lur gunfanuns ' (l. 3054),
>
> These ride with the high air of fighting-men,
> Their spears erect, and battle-pennons furled ' ;

because France was in contact with Celtic Brittany. Its action, in defiance of history, consists of conflicts with Saracens ; because such conflicts in the eighth, ninth, and tenth centuries held the imagination of Europe with a growing horror, that culminated when the Turks took Jerusalem from the Arabs, to profane her shrines and persecute their pious visitors. It is written by a Norman ; because the author dis-covered, in the legendary feats of Roland, a parallel to the historic conquests of his race. But he found it difficult to harmonise the two. So Normandy, though conquered, in his song is still ' la franche ' —the free (l. 2324). Duke Richard is one of Charlemagne's twelve peers, and his Normans are picked from all nations for the highest praise :

> ' Armes unt beles e bons chevals curanz ;
> Ja pur murir cil n'ièrent recreant ;
> Suz ciel, n'ad gent ki durer poissent tant ' (l. 3047).

> ' Handsome their weapons and their coursers strong ;
> Never for death will they admit the wrong ;
> No other nation can endure so long.'

The reference to England, on the other hand, is in the scornful tone of one who had himself followed William to Hastings and Westminster ; because the song was written after, and not before, the conquest of England. To that opinion, at any rate, the weight of French scholarship inclines, as I hold conclusively. When the death-stricken Roland recites the countries he has won for Charles with his sword Durendal, his slighting reference to England—

> ' E Engletere que il teneit sa cambre ' (l. 2332),

> ' And England which he kept for his own room,'

finds no counterpart in any allusion to other legendary conquests. The Saracen is detested, but the Englishman is despised, whilst other nations, although defeated, are hailed as honoured vassals who follow the oriflamme to war. Finally, this song, and no other, won a way for Romance in the literature of Europe ; because northern French, by becoming the Royal language of England, attained a position which Latin, for lack of general comprehension, could no longer hold. Northern French became the tongue common to many nations, and was adapted, as Latin never had been, to the expression of Romance. Here I must note a possibility of misconception. It is urged that some features in the song we possess are earlier than the date attributed to it. Again, we know that the Jongleur, Taillefer, sang some other song of Roland as he rode in front of the Norman advance at Hastings, tossing his sword in the air and catching it by the hilt. But these considerations do not affect my argument. None of the romantic features in the song can be earlier than the Celtic and Saracenic influences ; most of them must be later than the Norman influence, and that influence did not carry Romance into literature until after the Conquest.

The view that the ' Song of Roland ' could not have been written until after the events I have enumerated, or be what it is but for their happening, is confirmed if we glance at the historic fact on which it is based, and compare the song with the account written at the time. For the song reveals the influence of all these events, and the contemporary account shows scarce a trace of any one of them.

On the 15th of August 778, Charlemagne's army had retired from Spain into France over the Pyrenees in safety. But his rear-guard was ambushed by the Basques in a closely-wooded defile and killed out to the last man. That is the historic fact. Now turn to the contemporary account. Charlemagne's secretary, Eginhard, describes the tragedy (*vita et gesta Caroli cognomento Magni*, etc., cap. ix.) in seventeen and a half lines of prosaic Latin. There is no word of the Saracens. Three of the slaughtered chieftains are named, and of these the third, apparently in order of importance, is Rutlandus, the præfect of the frontier of Brittany (*Rutlandus Britannici limitis prœfectus*). That is all that history tells us of Roland. He is not even in command, and sounds no

> ' blast of that dread horn
> On Fontarabian echoes borne,'

that caught the ear of Walter Scott as he was writing *Marmion*.

We hear no more of him in any written word that remains until his romantic glory is unrolled in the four thousand and two ringing lines of the *Chanson de Roland*. Thenceforward it reverberates through literature, expanding into the stupendous cycle of Carlovingian romances, and their derivatives, down to the day on which Ariosto presented the Cardinal of Este with his poem ' of ladies and of knights, of battles and loves, of courtesies and of daring adventures ' :

> ' Le Donne, il Cavalier, l'Arme, gli Amori,
> Le Cortesie, l'audaci Imprese io canto,
> Che furo al tempo che passaro i Mori
> D'Africa il mare, e in Francia nocquer tanto,
> Sequendo l'ire e i giovenil furori
> D'Agramante lor Re che si diè vanto
> Di Vendicar la morte di Trojano
> Sopra Re Carlo Imperator Romano.'

Incidentally the story of Roland gave proverbs to the people—a Roland for an Oliver—and their name to our peers, of whom we still hear so much, even now, when Roland is almost forgotten.

This comparison between the song and the account written at the time exhibits—to adopt a Hibernicism—a ' dry source ' in the brief Latin original ; a long silence ; and, then, the sudden advent of unmistakable Romance, full of the wonders and legends of many lands. Scenery plays her part in human emotion. The mountains are filled with menace :

> ' Halt sunt li p̄ui e tenebrus e grant
> Li val parfunt e les ewes curanz ' (l. 1830).

> ' High are the peaks, and shadow-gloom'd, and vast,
> Profound the valleys where the torrents dash.'

We are told the name of each champion's horse and sword, and their marvellous qualities.

The theory that Romance arrived as a result of the events I have enumerated is still further confirmed, if we proceed from the advent to the huge development of Romance which flooded Europe a hundred years later. For that development follows immediately on a renewal and multiplication of the same or similar influences. Literature is transfigured into Romance by the twilight of the West, the mirage of the East, and the uncouth strength of the North, in direct proportion to the commingling of West and East and North in the politics of the eleventh and twelfth centuries.

I would even dare to suggest that our first version of the ' Song of Roland ' received some later touches, here and there, during the twelfth century, after those influences had been multiplied, *i.e.* at a time more nearly approaching the date, 1170, attributed to the handwriting of the MS. (Bodleian, Digby

23).   One argument for that view is rather technical.
French scholars date the composition of the song
before the conquest of Jerusalem in 1099, because it
nowhere mentions that event.   This, however, involves the difficulty of accounting for the mention of
a valley in Cappadocia, called Butentrot, through
which the Crusaders did actually march.   How comes
it, we may ask, that the first column of the Saracen's
legendary army in the song (l. 3220) is said to have
been recruited from that place ?   May not the
positive inclusion of Butentrot outweigh the negative
omission of Jerusalem ?   And the more, since the
author, who swears he is telling the truth, might
conceivably borrow local colour from Butentrot for
an imaginary picture of the eighth century, but
would scarcely insert the most resounding event of
his own age, 321 years before it happened.

Another argument may be put in this way.

The song in the Oxford MS. contains three
catalogues of nations, viz.—the conquests recited
by Roland before he dies, the divisions in Charlemagne's avenging army, and the judges summoned
to try the traitor, Ganelon.   The judges include
Bretons, Normans, and Poitevins (l. 3702).   The
fifth, sixth, and seventh divisions of the avenging
army (l. 3027) are recruited from Normans, Bretons,
and Poitevins.   The conquests (l. 2322) include
Brittany, Normandy, Poitou, Maine, Aquitaine, and,
you will be surprised to hear, Scotland, Wales,
Ireland, and England.

> ' Jo l'en cunquis Escoce, Guales, Irlande
> E Engletere que il teneit sa cambre.'

Looking to literature, excepting the ' Song of
Roland,' no other poem about Charlemagne—and

there are many—attributes to him any one of these
conquests.   Looking to history, no king ever led all
these nations in war, or accepted homage from their
sovereigns, except Henry of Anjou, who became
Henry II. of England, and married Eleanor of Poitou
and Aquitaine.   For further significance, Anjou,
his ancestral fief, is added to these conquests in
other foreign MSS. and omitted from the Oxford MS.
I suggest that the MS. was retouched, in respect of
these names, after Henry had, by conquest and
marriage, asserted a shadowy over-lordship from the
Pyrenees to the Grampians.   The singular ascription
of such conquests to Charlemagne, and the army-list
of his forces, would have lacked all approach to
likelihood except to audiences familiar with the
short-lived climax of Henry's political career.

Even if this suggestion be scouted, the catalogues
of nations in the ' Song of Roland ' are relevant to
my theme.   They illuminate the theory that Romance
sprang from a mingling of Western and Eastern
influences, at a time when the races of Europe
were bracketed together by the conquests and
marriages of northern leaders.

THE DEVELOPMENT OF ROMANCE

That theory is, once more, confirmed by the
great romantic development of the twelfth century ;
and no illustration of it can, I submit, be more
convincing than the facts of Henry's political career.
They constitute a renewal and multiplication of the
influences which preceded the advent of Romance,
and were immediately followed by a development
of Romance that, from 1150 onwards, flooded the
whole area of mediæval literature.   If we take the

most important of these renewals, and then the most renowned Romances of the Middle Ages, we can, I believe, establish a direct connection between the two.

The Eastern, Saracenic, influence was renewed by Henry's marriage with Eleanor—Alienor or Ænor—a most remarkable woman, to whose memory scant justice is done if we associate it exclusively with Fair Rosamund and Woodstock. Omitting— with regret—most of the sensational adventures in her long life of eighty-two years, we must, for our purpose, recall that she was the granddaughter of William of Poitou, who fought in the First Crusade, and was himself the earliest troubadour, or poet of southern France. He wrote, ' I will make a new song ' :

' Farai chansonetta nova,'

and so he did. That song is more closely related to modern poetry than any masterpiece in the classics (W. P. Ker, *Dark Ages*). Its reiterated rhymes thrill down the ages till they wake an echo from the lyre of Robert Burns. Eleanor, the wife of two kings, the mother of two kings and of two daughters, married to great vassals whose songs are still remembered, is responsible for a good deal of romance. Thanks to her, St. George became, in the words of Caxton, ' patrone of ' the ' royame of Englond and the crye of men of warre.' For that was the battle-cry of her grandfather before the walls of Jerusalem. It descended to her, together with his love of poetry and his love of crusading. She accompanied her first husband, the king of France, to the Second Crusade, in 1147 ; was divorced in 1152, and, within two months, married Henry of

Anjou, the king to be of England, bringing with her ' St. George for England ' and the dower of Poitou and Aquitaine. But these were not all that she bestowed. The troubadours of southern France, after attending her to the East, followed in her train ; reinforced by trouvères, the poets of northern France. She brought to Great Britain, with signal results in literature, the artists who were to fashion the romantic material of many voyages into the great romances of Europe.

The Western, Celtic, influence was renewed when Henry became suzerain of Brittany. It was multiplied when his motley array of vassals, drawn from one-half of France, and, accompanied by Eleanor's poets, were brought into contact with the legends of Wales. The historic Henry, as Count of Anjou, Maine, Touraine, and Poitou, Duke of Normandy and Aquitaine, suzerain of Brittany, king of England and overlord of Wales, had received the homage of the king of Scotland in 1157, and connived ten years later at the departure, through Wales, of the pioneers in the conquest of Ireland. He, like the legendary Charlemagne, was the war-lord of many nations who had crossed swords with Saracens and Celts and listened to Norman translations of their strange songs. No sovereign, we may add, except, perhaps, his consort, Eleanor, was better equipped for turning political adventure to political advantage. His earliest tutor, Master Peter of Saintes, was ' learned above all his contemporaries in the science of verse.' Henry himself ' loved reading only less than hunting.' His hands, it was said, ' were never empty,' always holding ' a bow or a book.' He spoke French and Latin well, and knew something of every tongue from

the Bay of Biscay to the Jordan.   This great lover of
learning and adventure was, for a time, ' the virtual
arbiter of Western Europe ' (*Dictionary of National
Biography*).   The lives of Eleanor and Henry were
potent factors in the renewal of the influences that
preceded the advent of Romance.

Let us now turn to the earliest and most renowned among the poems that mark its development.   We shall find that, like the ' Song of Roland,'
most of them derive from a short, unromantic
original in Latin ; that all were written in northern
French, and many of them in England, in the
second half of the twelfth century, and that all
elaborate themes made vivid by the contact of
northern armies with Celts and Saracens.

THE ROMANCE OF ALEXANDER

The ' dry source ' of the Romance of Alexander
is a Latin abridgment (eighth century) of an earlier
Latin translation (fourth century) from a Greek
forgery (second century).   It produces no effect
for centuries.   Only after the First Crusade had
renewed contact with the East, is it translated into
a French dialect and transfigured.   The ' Milites '
become ' chevaliers,' and Alexander a king surrounded by his barons.   Of this version little
remains.   But after the Second Crusade, in which
Eleanor took part, and her marriage with Henry,
the poets of their continental dominions begin the
portentous expansion of the tale and embroider it
with oriental marvels.   We get the ' Fountain of
Youth,' ' Gog and Magog,' and the oracular

> ' . . . Trees of the Sun and Moon, that speak
> And told King Alexander of his death.' [1]

---

[1] Brome's *Antipodes*, in Lamb's *Specimens*.

' " Signor," fait Alixandre, " je vus voel demander,
Se des merveilles d'Inde me saves rien conter."
Cil li ont respondu : " Se tu vius escouter
Ja te dirons merveilles, s'es poras esprover.
La sus en ces desers pues ii Arbres trover
Qui c pies ont de haut, et de grossor sunt per.
Li Solaus et La Lune les ont fait si serer
Que sevent tous languages et entendre et parler." ' [1]

In a thirteenth-century version, we witness the first appearance of ' The Nine Worthies '—Joshua, David, and Maccabæus, for the Jews ; Hector, Alexander, and Cæsar, for the Heathen ; Arthur, Charlemagne, and Godfrey of Bologne, for the Christians. They made their last bow to the public, so far as I know, in Shakespeare's *Love's Labour's Lost*. Meanwhile they bulk largely in literature, and were painted by Perugino. A hundred years before the antics of Holophernes, Caxton, in the beautiful Preface to his *Life of Godefrey of Boloyne*, beseeched Almighty God that Edward the Fourth of England might deserve the tenth place by launching yet another Crusade, but in vain, for it never set sail. To these fabulous expansions the French Alexandrine owes its name, and, until Plutarch was translated at the Renaissance, they moulded the popular conception of Alexander the Great.

THE ROMANCE OF TROY

The ' dry source ' of the Romance of Troy is once more a prosaic Latin abridgment of Greek forgeries, impudently fathered on a supposititious defender of Troy, Dares Phrygian, and a non-existent besieger, Dictys Cretensis. It produces no

[1] Chanson d'Alixandre, ed. 1861, Dinan, p. 357 ; Yule's *Marco Polo*, i. 122.

effect till, in 1160, one of Eleanor's poets, Benedict of Sainte More, dedicates to her his expansion, which reaches the respectable length of over thirty thousand lines. He asserts the unimpeachable testimony of Dares and Dictys at Homer's expense :—

'Ce que dist Daires et Ditis
I avons si retrait et mis.'

And away goes the development of Romance, till the love of Troilus and Briseîda, which Benedict invented, after figuring in Boccaccio, supplies the theme of Chaucer's great romantic poem, and of Shakespeare's play. In the course of the transition Homer's Briseis becomes Shakespeare's Cressida.

'The skilful painting made for Priam's Troy,'

which Shakespeare weaves into Lucrece (ll. 1366-1559), and the speech required by Hamlet from the players, and Lorenzo's ecstasy (*Merchant of Venice*, v. 1),

'The moon shines bright :—In such a night as this,
When the sweet wind did gently kiss the trees,
And they did make no noise,—in such a night
Troilus, methinks, mounted the Troyan walls,
And sigh'd his soul toward the Grecian tents,
Where Cressid lay that night,'—

are derived from Benedict's expansion no less than from Virgil, and not from Homer. The Romance of Troy left a deep impression in European literature, largely because of what a French scholar has called 'the monomania for Trojan descent.' Shortly after its appearance, no one in France or Great Britain, with pretensions to birth, cared to trace his pedigree from any ancestor less remote than Æneas. So, in close succession to the Romance of Troy, we get a romantic Æneid (*Roman d'Enée*), attributed by Gaston Paris to the same author, and by others to Marie de France, a poetess, who also wrote in England under the auspices of Henry and Eleanor. In it the lordship of the world is promised to the heirs of Rome and descendants of Æneas, who are none other than the nations over whom Henry held sway—

> ' Rome fut grant et bien enclose
> A mervelle fu puis grant cose
> Trestot le *munt* ot en baillie   *world*
> Li *oir* en orent signorie   *heirs*
> Qui d'Enéas descentu sunt
> Signor furent par tot le munt.'

THE ROMANCE OF THEBES

About the same time, and, as some hold, again from the prolific pen of Benedict, we get the Romance of Thebes. The ' dry source ' is a Latin abridgment of Statius. In the expansion we read—of the daughters of Adrastus—that their laughter and kisses outweighed the worth of London and Poitiers, the capitals of the realms of Henry and Eleanor,

> ' Mieuz vaut lor ris et lor baisiers
> Que ne fait Londres ne Peitiers.'

The Castle of Montflor is besieged by a thousand knights, and Saracen Almoravides (Almoraives) from the Crusades take part in an ambush of Hippomedon. The Romance of Thebes furnished titles to romantic versions of Byzantine stories which the Crusaders brought back from the East. Parthenopeus, one of the seven against Thebes, becomes Partonopex of Blois in a fairy tale of singular beauty, that recalls the story of Cupid and Psyche, but with

:he parts reversed, for it is the knight who is for-
)idden to look at the lady.

I am no more concerned, than I am qualified,
;o obtrude an opinion when scholars dispute the
ittribution of the ' Thebes ' to the author of the
' Troy,' or when they differ on points of priority,
interesting in themselves, but immaterial to this
argument. It suffices that, but for the Crusades,
the three romances—of Alexander, of Troy, and
of Thebes—would not have been written to compete
in popular favour with the romances of Charlemagne. They are what they are, because of events
among which the most typical, and probably the
most important, is that Eleanor played the part—
it may be in more senses than one—of a Damozel
Errant in the East. They produced the development of Romance because others, but Eleanor above
all, attracted troubadours, the masters of rhyme,
and trouvères, the masters of narrative, to display
these oriental wares in French, the Royal language
of England, and common tongue of every Court in
Western Europe. Amid a maze of dates we can put
our finger on the year 1147, in which Eleanor set
out for Palestine, and say, with confidence, that here
is a renewal of Eastern influence : and, I would add,
thanks to troubadours, the triumph of rhyme ;
thanks to trouvères, the art of telling a story.

THE ARTHURIAN ROMANCES

But if we do put our finger on that year, we
shall find that we have also covered the source
from which a renewal of Western influence inun-
dated all Europe with the legends of Arthur and
his knights ; incidentally submerging the fame of

Charlemagne and the twelve peers. In the same year, 1147, Geoffrey of Monmouth dedicated the *Historia Regum Britanniæ* to Robert, Earl of Gloucester, the uncle of Henry of Anjou, who directed the first steps of his nephew's dazzling career. It is a short book written in Latin by a Welshman. But it is the 'dry source' of many a river of song. Arthur and Guunhumara, or Guenever, are here introduced for the first time into literature that remains. Let no one suppose, for a moment, that Geoffrey invented the legends which enchanted Europe for so long, and have now renewed their spell through the art of Tennyson and Swinburne and Wagner. He found them: but whether in Wales, or in the 'very old book' —*librum vetustissimum*—brought, so he says, out of Brittany by Walter, Archdeacon of Oxford, is quite beside the mark. What Geoffrey did was to capture the world of letters. His prosaic handling of Celtic mythology in a learned tongue imposed on the clerks of Europe. They received it for history, and were amazed at the close fulfilment of Merlin's prophesies down to the very year in which Geoffrey began to write (1135). We need not intervene when scholars, inspired by local patriotism, dispute the racial extraction of this or that matter involved ; nor attempt to decide whether the Christian graal was a Pagan caldron, or even, as some have it, a stone. It is sufficient to discover what happened in literature. For until these legends won their way into literature they could not produce a romantic effect, and may, for all we can tell, have been destitute of any tinge of romance.

Geoffrey's book was forthwith translated into French poems written by Anglo-Normans, and,

apart from its contents, gave a general impulse to
the production of verse spun from the legends of
Brittany and Wales. In 1150 Marie de France,
who lived in England, begins to write her fifteen
lays. About the same year we get the first story
of Tristan and Yseut from Beroul, who wrote it in
England. Unless we realise that the author staged
his legend in the England of his day, without a
care for anachronisms, we shall be surprised to find
the cathedral cities of Ely and Durham in the
kingdom of Cornwall :

> ' N'a chevalier en son roiaume
> Ne d'Eli d'antresqu' en Dureaume ' (l. 2199).

In 1155 Wace, an Anglo-Norman writing in
England, expands Geoffrey's *History* into a long
French poem. He introduces the ' Round Table '
into literature. ' Arthur,' he says (l. 998), ' made
the round table, of which Bretons tell many fabulous
stories ; the vassals sat down to it all chivalrously
and all equal in degree ' :

> ' Fist Artus la Roonde Table
> Dont Breton dient mainte fable :
> Iloc séoient li vassal
> Tot chievalment et tot *ingal*.'   *equal*.

In another passage (l. 10, 560) the three Arch-
bishops of London, York, and Carleon dine at the
same legendary board ; for to Wace it is a British
institution. Whether it hails, as a legend, from
Brittany, from Wales, or from Arthur's Seat by
Edinburgh, it certainly arrives in literature under the
auspices of Henry. Wace writes of him, ' I find no
more benefactors except the king, Henry the Second,
who has given me a canonry and many other gifts.
May God repay him.' Eventually it was exhibited

as a piece of furniture in Winchester, where Henry
had been crowned in 1154. At Winchester, as at
Glastonbury, Henry's magnetic power polarised the
legends of his Western dominions, and attracted
French artists to sing them from all the realms
bracketed together by his political ambition.
Wace's poem, for the first time, weaves the story
of Tristan into the story of Arthur, and is named,
by a similar process, from Brutus, the imaginary
descendant of Æneas, the ancestor of all the French
and the British nations. This romantic descent was
' the kind of thing that everybody could enjoy,' and
most people did up to the end of the sixteenth
century. It inspired Ronsard's *Franciade*. I once
found it set out in a nobleman's commonplace
book together with other practical hints, such as
the right dishes for a banquet and the proper instruments for concerted music. So late as 1605,
Verstegan devotes a stout volume to destroying
the myth under the imposing title, *A Restitution of
Decayed Intelligence in Antiquities*.

In 1170 we get the second song of Tristan from
Thomas, another Anglo-Norman. In the same year
Christian of Troyes introduces, for the first time,
the love of Lancelot and Guenever. He was not
an Anglo-Norman, but the story was supplied to
him by Eleanor's eldest daughter. In 1175 Christian introduces Perceval and the Graal from a book
lent by the Count of Flanders, who had spent some
months (1172) in England. After that, for fifty
years Arthur and Guenever and Lancelot, Tristan
and Yseut, the Round Table and the Holy Graal,
are translated into every Western tongue, and interlaced with every other story that seemed true. A
continuous legend of Western conquerors was woven

together, reaching right down from the Argonauts who sought the Golden Fleece, through the defenders of Troy, and the founders of Rome, to the champions who had recovered Jerusalem. Such Romances of chivalry stood side by side with the ' new ' classics on the shelves of Mary Stuart's library. Then they disappear into dusty cupboards, to be released again after the Romantic Revival.

Just as the advent of Romance sprang from early contacts with Celtic mythology and Saracenic marvels, so did the development expand when those contacts were renewed and multiplied. Both found their first expression in French poems, written for the most part in England, because the conquest of England exalted that tongue into the position held by Latin through the Dark Ages. But Latin was for the learned alone ; whereas French, for many reasons, appealed to the nations of Europe. To the Celts it was the language of those who had defeated their Saxon oppressors ; and to all Christian people the language of those who had delivered Jerusalem. It was written by poets who welcomed the legends which the Latins had rejected. Every nation saw its folk-lore embellished by consummate artists, and their eponymous heroes glorified with pedigrees from the warriors who had redressed the fall of Troy by erecting the walls of Rome. In the French romances of the twelfth century Europe ' found herself.'

Two Objections

Here let me anticipate some of the criticism which I am conscious of provoking. It may be said that I have ignored the Teutonic Romances.

In reply, I would submit that Teutonic Romance branched off when the empire of Charlemagne was divided between his successors, only to return into the main channel of European literature after the Romantic Revival.

The Sagas and the Nibelungenlied, and the early English Beowulf, were not European romances before the last century. Sigfried, originally a Frankish hero, who picked up Burgundian attributes and echoes of conflicts with the Huns, counts for nothing in the Middle Ages by comparison with Roland or Arthur. The dwarf Alberich creeps through a French romance, *Huon of Bordeau*, to emerge as Oberon in Shakespeare's *Midsummer Night's Dream*. But that may have been because of his diminutive size. There was no room for Teutonic gods and giants in a literature already crowded with colossal characters. Yet the influence of the North is not absent from European romances. On the contrary, since it was the Normans who launched them, the uncouth strength of the North accounts for as much in Romance as the glamour of the West, to the mirage of the East. Perhaps it accounts for more than either, and explains why all three were condemned together as ' Gothic ' during the classical interregnum between the two Romantic periods.

It may be said that I have exaggerated the importance of Eleanor's marriage with Henry of Anjou. On that issue I ' stick to my guns.' They married (1152) five years after St. Bernard launched the Second Crusade from Vezelay, at the moment when Geoffrey of Monmouth published the *History of the Kings of Britain*. Their marriage united the influences attracted by those two events from the

East and West.   It is when they married, and where
they married, that most of the Springs of Romance
commingle in the literature of Europe.   Nor were
the results of that commingling accidental.   They
were produced by design ; and the designers were
largely the poets of Henry's and Eleanor's cosmopolitan court.   Mythological legends from the West,
and miraculous stories from the East, were guided
into one channel by the science of troubadours—
the gay science of courteous love—and by the sterner
skill of northern trouvères.   The design was literary ;
but it was also political.   Henry, an upstart and
a stranger to his Normans, Bretons, and Poitevins,
Gascons, Saxons, and Welshmen, found it convenient
to exploit the imaginary achievements of Arthurian
knights.   None could be jealous of such shadows,
and, the less, since all were assured a common
descent from the defenders of Troy, and shown a
common foe in the assailants of Jerusalem.   Henry
took the cross for the Third Crusade (1187) as a
desperate expedient to save his work of unification
on the eve of its collapse.   His work, akin as it is
to the work of contemporary sovereigns, affords
the most salient example of a vast attempt at
unification prosecuted throughout the politics and
literature of Europe ; and that effort of comprehension reveals, so I believe, the reason why Romance
captured the imagination of Europe in the middle
of the twelfth century.

WHAT IS ROMANCE ?

I have done what I could to discover When and
Where and Why Romance came into European
literature.   But what is Romance ?   Are we any

nearer a definition ?   Here is a power which produced great changes in Europe from 1100 to 1550,
and reproduced them from 1800 until now.   Through
all those centuries there must have been something
in the mind of Europe which needed Romance and
sustained it.   The unromantic interval shrinks to
the relative proportions of an episode in our Western
civilisation.   Clearly, Romance is not a tangle of
absurdities to be dismissed as ' rot ' by the Cardinal
of Este, or despised as ' Gothic ' by the imitators
of classic models.   ' Imitation will after though it
break her neck ' (S. Daniel, *Defence of Rhime*, 1603).
But Romance is a tissue.   In the twelfth century,
when it took hold of the Middle Ages, Romance
displays a deliberate weaving together of many-
coloured strands.   Celtic glamour, the uncouth
strength of the North, and marvels from the fabulous
East, are interlaced in one woof which unfolds a
continuous story of Europe, from the Argonauts'
quest of the Golden Fleece, by way of the fall of
Troy, and the foundation of Rome, to the conquest
of Jerusalem by Crusaders.   An examination of
these strands reveals that the earliest and most alien
are largely mythological.   They consist of many
attempts made by many races, in different ages and
distant countries, to express in symbols their guesses
at the origin and destiny, the hopes and fears, of
man.

May we, then, infer that Romance is comparative mythology ?   In a sense that is true.   Its
elements are largely mythological.   But that view
will not yield a definition of Romance.   If it did,
all mythologies would be obviously romantic.   But
are they ?   There is nothing romantic in a savage's
belief that the Creator of the World is a great hare,

or in a Greek legend that men and women sprang from stones thrown behind them by Deucalion and Pyrrha. These explanations are not romantic so long as they satisfy the curiosity of their authors. They only begin to be romantic—either when they cease to offer a tolerable answer to the riddle of the universe ; or, in a greater degree, when they confront the mind of another civilisation which has explained the universe by a wholly different imaginative process. Mythologies begin to be romantic when they become strange by reason of their antiquity or alien character. Breton and Welsh legends were not romantic to the Celts, when they conceived them. Nor were the sagas romantic to the Icelanders. On the contrary, their rugged strength reproduced a rugged reality. Nor is magic romantic in the East ; it is familiar there. These strands in the fabric of romance became romantic when they struck more modern, and wholly alien, modes of thought by their strangeness. Even this impact of the strange in mythology will not wholly account for the nature of romance. If it did, Latin literature would have been romantic. The Romans, no less than the Normans, were confronted by Celts and Teutons and the fabulous East, yet the impact of outlandish legends produced but little romance in Latin literature. Our search for the nature of Romance must be directed not only to the strange in mythology, but, more closely, to the reaction produced in the minds that were startled by that strangeness. If we find that the attitude towards strange mythologies of periods called Classic differs profoundly from the attitude of periods called Romantic, we may discover a clue to the nature of Romance in the contrast so revealed. And that is what we do find. Classic periods repudiated strange mythologies and Romantic periods welcomed them. Both aimed at unity in their order of thought and, so far as the Romans were concerned, in their order of the world's government. But the Classic world aimed at unity by exclusion, and the Middle Ages at unity by comprehension.

The Greeks stood for understanding the universe by reducing it to the terms of their lofty intelligence, expressed in terms of their all but perfect language. The Romans stood for governing the world by reducing it to one august state with one Imperial religion. To the Greeks the Barbarian was unintelligible ; to the Romans, ungovernable. So both repelled him, and all his strange imaginations, as tending to disturb the pursuit of lucidity and order. It is not the goal of unity, but the method chosen for reaching that goal, which stamped its exclusive character on the Classic world, and sterilised classic literature to romance, save for some faint touches in the earliest and latest poems that dealt with wandering, and sometimes paused to wonder. Even in their own mythology the Greeks got rid of their Titans at the beginning of the world ; whereas the uncouth North kept its giants at endless war against its gods ; and the Persians retained Ahriman in perpetual conflict with Ormuzd ; and the Celts were uncertain whether their Arthur would ever return from the twilight of Avalon.

On the other hand, if we turn to the first Romantic period, we find the most striking characteristic of the twelfth and thirteenth centuries in a huge attempt at unity, throughout politics and literature, prosecuted by an all but universal comprehension. In that age political actors strove to weld Europe into one, assisted by literary authors who sought to correlate with that policy every known record of the Drama of Mankind. Nothing came amiss to them. The political actors repudiated no race, however foreign, and the literary authors, no legend however ancient or far-fetched. Rather did they embrace the strange, seeming to recognise in it something lacking from their own conventions, but akin to a common humanity. They aimed at unity by comprehension, and that method, at least in the domain of literature, was resumed after the Romantic Revival. Walter Scott and Victor Hugo, no less than Benedict of Sainte-More and Christian of Troyes, were eager to welcome the strange from the East, the West, or the North. We may say of each,

'nexuque pio longinqua revinxit.'

I am not concerned to exalt the Romantic above the Classic method in Literature. Both have their several glories, and peculiar seeds of decay. When Romantic interlacing of many themes degenerates into a love of intricacy for its own sake, Romance becomes trivial, and tedious. It is then replaced by classic admiration for the noblest models. But when that degenerates into a love of imitation for its own sake, the classic method becomes slavish, and tedious in its turn. Then we note a Romantic Revival. I am solely concerned to discover a distinction between periods called Classic, and periods called Romantic, which may yield a clue to the mystery of Romance. Such a distinction is I believe, disclosed in the diversity of their attitudes towards the strange and, specially, towards the strange in mythology. It is all but impossible to analyse a reaction of the mind. We cannot put emotions in a crucible. Yet, guided by this profound distinction, we may, perhaps, say that Romance results from welcoming the strange, and specially from welcoming the symbols, perforce fantastic, in which foreign lands and far-away ages have sought to express their ' intimations of immortality ' and doubtful wonder at ' that perpetual revolution which we see to be in all things that never remain the same.'

Romantic Scenery

We get a tentative definition, if we say that Romance is not simply the strange, but a result of welcoming the strange, instead of excluding it. Let us test that definition by seeing if it applies to things generally called romantic. Take a hackneyed illustration—mountain scenery. Since the Revival of Romance, and the novels of Walter Scott, most people agree that mountain scenery is romantic. The definition applies to that view, and goes some way to explain it. Mountain scenery is not romantic, or even strange, to the mountaineer who wrests a hard-won livelihood from its crags and heather. It was strange, but not romantic, to the cultured sybarite of the eighteenth century who describes it in his journal as a ' horrid alp.' It is romantic to the ' heart city-pent ' of the age in which we live, and only because its strangeness is welcome.

ALLEGORY

' Ci est le Romant de la Rose
Ou l'art d'Amors est tote enclose.'

Reverting to the earlier Romantic period, this definition will, I believe, throw a light on one of its features ; the labyrinthine development of Allegory. Assuming that an author seeks a welcome for something novel and strange, he must express the new matter by images that are obvious to his audience ; otherwise it remains unintelligible, and unwelcome. In order to establish the coherence of his novelties with the life to which all are accustomed, he personifies his sentiments in characters with whom all are familiar ; and that is allegory. Take a capital example, the *Romance of the Rose*, which shaped and coloured European literature in the thirteenth century, and for long afterwards. The author of the first part (Guillaume de Lorris, 1237) turns the new sentiments of ' courteous love ' into the usual inhabitants of a mediæval castle, and illustrates the course of love ' which never did run smooth ' by the ups and downs to which life in a fortress was exposed. For that was the kind of thing which any ' fellow could understand.' The author of the first part sought a welcome for a new kind of love, differing, in its delicacy, from the romping of ' Floralia ' and May Games, sung in rustic ditties ; and, in its mysticism, from the stark passion depicted in classic literature. The author of the second part (Jean de Meun, 1277) sought a welcome for a new kind of fun, differing, in its whimsical satire, from the blunt predicaments of Plautus, and the banter of Horace. The new love, and the new fun, were made familiar by allegory to secure a welcome for their strangeness.

FABLES

Will a welcome of the strange account for another feature in mediæval Romance : the revival of Fables in which animals have most of the speaking parts ? I think it will. If you except the animals of Æsop, the dog of Odysseus, the charger of Alexander, and Lesbia's sparrow, there are not many animals in the classics. Man dominates the scene. On the other hand, there is an irruption of animals into the first Period of Romance. To secure a welcome for these intruders the earlier romantics had recourse to Æsop—Ysopet as they call him— who had brought them, long before, from the East, where animals have ever been revered. Marie de France ushers them in under the auspices of an imaginary emperor, called Romulus, and dedicates her Fables to William Longsword, the natural son of Henry II.

> ' Ci cummencerai la première
> Des Fables K'Ysopez escrit.'

But the animals soon made themselves at home by the charm of their own half-strangeness to man. We know the names of the horses of nearly all the heroes of Romance. In the thirteenth century, without any aid from heroes, Reynard the Fox, Bruin the Bear, Chanticleer the Cock, ' came to stay,' till the classical interregnum. After the revival of romance they returned ; so that, now, in the Jungle of Kipling and the Farmyard of Rostand, they occupy the whole of the stage.

Fantastic Symbols

It is the note of Romance to welcome in literature much else beside man : with delight when that
is possible, and, when it is not, with courage. In
Romance man disputes his place with other living
beings and elemental forces without life. He receives the impression of scenery, and guesses at
dim ' dominations and powers ' that baffle his mun-
dane progress and cloud his longing for eternity.
All these Romance accepts for their strangeness ;
and, I would add, for their truth.

When their strangeness is exorbitant, Romance,
in order to make their truth intelligible, resorts to
allegory and fable, and even to fantastic symbols
that seem ludicrous. We laugh, with Cervantes, at
the giants and dragons and warlocks of Romance.
It is our human privilege. Man is divided by
laughter from all that surrounds him. When we
have done laughing, we detect in these symbols an
attempt—frantic if you please—to explain realities
that are coeval with man ; that, indeed, preceded
his origin and may outlast his existence. Man's
domination, even of this earth, is more partial than
would appear from the unromantic presentment of
his case. There are forces in nature, by comparison with whose gigantic strength man's efforts
are puny. There are enemies to his well-being
that, like dragons, are not only dangerous but
loathsome. There are subtleties in the universe
that, like wizards, bewilder and deride his intelligence. Even to-day, enlightened as we are by
popular science, we may recall, without contempt,
the wild allegories by which other men, in other
ages, tried to explain the overpowering, and grisly,

and inscrutable ; we may remember with human
kindness that those who invented the symbols of
horror, invented also a vague belief that horror
can be conquered by a charm in the hand of the
little child.

Universal Affinity

The reaction of the mind, when confronted
with the strange, is, in some sort, a recognition
of ignored realities. Romance is an act of recognition. When Shakespeare attacks the reality of
Time, as if suggesting that, round Time, there is
Eternity, in which all things and all men are co-
existent and co-eternal, we feel that a rare mind is
soaring through a rarer atmosphere to the extreme
verge of the comprehensible. When Tennyson
makes Ulysses say, ' I am a part of all that I have
met,' we feel that this is a dark saying. Yet there
are moments when it seems true of each one of us.
Its truth strikes as a forgotten face strikes by its
strange familiarity. At such moments we understand that darker utterance, ' The Kingdom of God
is within you.' A sense of universal affinity comes
into literature when men are no longer content
with the mythologies, or philosophies, of their own
time and people. Then they turn, with a kindly
curiosity, to other nations and other ages.

> ' Than longen folk to goon on pilgrimages
> To ferne halwes couthe in sondry londes.'

Romance revives, and, extending her welcome to
the strange, discovers in it something which has
always been latent in man's mind, although starved
by convention. The old northern mythology, with
its twilight of the gods, and ceaseless battle against

a doom of eternal cold, is not so absurd in the
twentieth century as amid the certainties of two
hundred years ago.   We are taught to expect that
catastrophe by popular science, the mythology of
our day.   But our day is also the day of the
Romantic Revival, and in it we imitate, unconsciously, the attitude adopted towards the strange
by our forefathers in the first Romantic epoch.   We
turn, as they did, to all mankind's imaginings,
not for comfort, but for human fellowship, in the
great Romance of Man's adventure through the
Universe.   We take our part in that quest, with a
brave astonishment.   In Romantic literature we
listen to the camp-songs of our comrades, and

' Greet the unseen with a cheer.'

THE POETRY OF THE PRISON

THE POETRY OF THE PRISON

THERE is a great gulf fixed between 1450 and 1550, the last watch of the Middle Age and the full flush of the Renaissance. You pass it insensibly, by the way of the years ; but to look backward after those same years is to see, as beyond a bridge that has crumbled, the old social life completely severed from the new, with its conditions all changed for all classes. And nowhere is this contrast more deeply marked than in the lives of poets ; for the change from desultory invasion to world-wide diplomacy commuted the conditions under which in France all, and in England many of, the writers we care to recall, were moved to produce, or did produce, their work. During the Hundred Years' War every man of standing in both countries had to play his part. Of the English in the great expedition under Edward III. ' there was not knight, squire, or man of honour, from the age of twenty to sixty years that did not go ' ; [1] and the burden upon France was aggravated by civil war between the feudatories of the Crown. And thus it came about that Geoffrey Chaucer, entering the customary career of an English gentleman, suffered its common accidents. He joined Edward's expedition in November, 1359, and was taken in a skirmish near Rheims. [2] In *The Knight's Tale*, therefore, we have the poetry, echoed

---

[1] Johnes' *Froissart*, bk. I. c. 206. *See* Rev. W. W. Skeat's *Complete Works of Geoffrey Chaucer*, vol. i. p. xviii. [2] *Ibid.*

45

later in *The Two Noble Kinsmen*, of one who added
the sharp savour of personal suffering to his treatment of materials common to an age when every
house was a fortress and every fortress a gaol. For
Chaucer's experience was one general in the Middle
Age—was the lot of most whose lives were more
precious than their deaths could be : of Richard
Cœur-de-Lion, troubadour and king ; of Enzo of
Sardinia, a poet-king, the son of a poet-emperor, yet
a prisoner to the Bolognese from his twenty-fifth
year to his death, a caitiff for three-and-twenty years ;
of James I. of Scotland, the sweetest singer in
Chaucer's choir ; of Charles D'Orléans, the father
of a king, taken at Agincourt, a stripling of twenty-
five and the first prince in France, to be caged in
England until he was fifty ; of Jehan Regnier, the
precursor of Villon ; of Villon, the last great singer
of the Middle Age—in whose case the doom was,
indeed, for crime, yet for crime only probable in a
society shattered by war ; of Clement Marot, the
sole star in the night between Villon and the Pleiad,
carried first with his king a prisoner of war to Spain,
and twice afterwards imprisoned at Paris for offences
against the law.

The poetry of the Middle Age is so much the
poetry of the prison that, even if the poet escape,
his plot must still be laid between four walls. The
Roman de la Rose, translated by Chaucer and copied
by all, was a chief and pattern poem. Only the
books of Homer have dictated the plan and supplied
the poetic material for a greater city of verse . it is
a Coliseum out of whose ruins many cities have been
quarried. Now in the *Roman de la Rose* all the
allegory is of incarceration and release ; and it is
an allegory which none ever wearied of repeating.

Even as every Arabic poem, on theology or another theme, needs must open with a lament over the wasted camp from which the Beloved has been ravished, so the symbols of mediæval verse are all of castles and surprises, of captivity and escape. And the perennial image of Arabic song became an obvious convention ; not so the mediæval allegory. The tedium of durance, the hope of release, the prospect of ransom, the accident of communication with the world without, were too near to life for that. These had been the personal note of trouvères and troubadours ; and, later, they were the personal note of Charles D'Orléans and Villon and many another. I have named Jehan Regnier. Villon borrowed from him freely ; and, indeed, he is a poet whose realism and pathos have somehow been overlooked. But, for the moment, I shall consider only the master-theme of his songs, which are to be read in a little volume, intituled *Les Fortunes et Adversités de feu noble homme Jehan Regnier*.[1] He was a Burgundian, and being taken by the King's party in 1431, he was imprisoned at Beauvais. Again and yet again in the current forms of ballade, rondel, lay, he sets forth the actual sorrows of the practical captive : his weariness, his ' annoy ' and disgust ; his long parting from his wife ; the silence of his friends, the hopes that depart him where he lies, the messenger who returns no more. To turn his pages is still to read ' un autre balade que ledit prisonnier fit ' ; to find him imploring his wife never to forget, even as he will never forget :—

' My princess of the Heart I beg of thee
That thou nor I forget not thee nor me,

---

[1] Réimpression textuelle de l'édition originale, par Paul Lacroix ; Genève, 1867. Only three copies of the said original are known.

> But let us ever hearken to our love,
> And pray to God and to the maid Mary
> That He will grant us patience from above.
>
> Ma princesse du Cueur je vous supplie
> Que vous ne moy lung lautre si noublye
> Mais noz amours tenons en audience
> Et prions Dieu et la Vierge Marie
> Que il nous doint a tous deux pacience '—

to hear him thank her for her loyalty :—

> ' Ma douce maitresse
> Qui m'a donné de sa largesse
> *Le fleur de ne m'oubliez mie.*'

And she was loyal indeed ; for at the end of two years, and after paying two thousand crowns, she won leave to play the hostage with her son, the while her husband travelled to raise the rest of his ransom.   To pass the long days and nights of those two years, he wrote ballades for his fellow-prisoners, for his gaolers even.   I have said that he was a Burgundian, so that, naturally, among the former were certain Englishmen, allies of his master the duke.   For one of these he made a ballade :—

> ' François parler il ne sçavoit
> A peine ne mot ne demy
> En anglois tousjour il disoit
> *God and o ul lady helpëmy !* '

Thus to us out of the mediæval twilight, rendered as only a Frenchman can render English, comes the cry of a countryman who knew no French. ' God and our Lady help-ë me ' : the grotesque pathos of it ! Regnier could not sleep for the man's •complaining : he moaned on through the night over his wounded hands and feet—' *my fiet and my handez* '—into which the shackles had

eaten. He wailed of it ever, and Regnier lay
awake, listening :—

> ' Oncques je ne dormy
> Mais son refrain toujours estoit
> *God and o ul lady helpëmy !* '

It is the unchanging burden of his lament; so
Regnier, whose art has a good basis of reality, takes
it for his refrain, and knits up his every stave with it.

In truth, the prison and its passion were too near
to life for Regnier and those others ever to be con-
ventionalised out of reality. Conventions they had :
of May mornings, for instance, and the coming of
spring. Yet even these were less conventional than
they seem. The matter was felt and observed under
its traditional phrasing. Where every house was a
moated gaol with never a road to it in winter, there
needed no contrasts, of turnkeys or besieging
trenches, to flush the enlargement brought round by
the spring. For then, in the ' golden morning,'
men came forth from the half-light of loopholed cells
and the stench of rotting rushes, and rode out over
the fields in their new apparel, seeing and smelling
the fresh flowers, and hearkening to birds singing
in the brakes.

> ' The year hath flung his cloak away
> Of wind and cold and rainy skies,
> And goeth clad in broideries
> Of sun-gleams brilliant and gay : '—

thus Charles D'Orléans, in one of the most famous
of his rondels. And thus, through another, not so
famous, he runs a natural and familiar fancy of the
coming of summer :—

> ' King Summer's harbingers are come
> To place his palace in repair,
> And have spread out his carpet-ware
> Woven of greenery and bloom.

Laying the green woof of their loom
Over the country, here and there,
King Summer's harbingers are come
To place his palace in repair.

Hearts long benumbed with weary gloom,
Thank God, are whole again and fair ;
Winter, begone some other-where,
You shall delay no more at home,
King Summer's harbingers are come.'

It is charming, and—what is as much to the purpose,
if not more—it is, as the French say, *vécu*. But,
for all that, it profited its author little. For Charles
had long since come to know by experience—none
better !—that hearts once benumbed with weary
gloom can no more be quite whole, can never be
again in perfect accord with the renewing year.
He wrote these rondels, I doubt not, at Blois, in the
languid liberty of his old age, recalling, with vain
regret, those long years of his wasted manhood,
wherein the banishment of winter and the release
of spring still found him in a northern prison. But
they were the toys of his second childhood. His
Poème de la Prison, written in England, was the
capital piece, even as his imprisonment in England
was the chief feature, of his life.

Like Villon's poem, engendered of a kindred misfortune, it is excellent in art ; like Villon's, too, it
has an interest apart from art. We are often
tempted to fix our looks on the lives of the great
actors in an age : to exaggerate, within these lives,
the salience of certain immortal deeds, and then to
stamp a nation, or an epoch, with such same dies
of individual worth. To yield to that temptation
is to misread history, for the contours of an age may
far more surely be traced in the lives of those who

have suffered their impress than in the valour of those who have sought to change their shape. Now, Charles D'Orléans and François Villon were not great actors : were scarce actors at all. But, while essentially passive, they were yet not dumb. Each of them received the impress of his age upon his life, and each revealed it, a little transfigured by personal reaction, in his song. The imprisonment of Charles, and its effect on his life, the life of Villon, and its result in his imprisonment, show the very image of the Middle Age after the vanishing of its soul. Their poetry is as it were the mask from a dead face.

The son of an Italian mother, Valentina Visconti, Charles D'Orléans was born in the midst of the Hundred Years' War (1391). Doubtless this parentage affected his personal taste, and lent a gracious refinement to the turn of his French ballades and rondels. Doubtless, too, when a hundred years later, Louis XII., the child of his old age, came to the throne, by conferring on that king a claim to the Duchy of Milan it led to a further expansion of Italian influence in France. Yet during his life it was powerless to push on the hands of time. It could not change the necessity of his own or his country's misfortune. He was yet a boy when his father's murder by the Duke of Burgundy fastened an hereditary quarrel on him, and divided the great feudatories of France into the historic factions of Armagnac and Burgundian : so that thenceforward there could be nothing **but** that blind frenzy of civil war, which led to Agincourt and the English occupation. And at Agincourt Charles was caught up out of the strife to be a captive for a quarter-century, an idler growing old in idleness even while

his own party grew to be the national party—
became, indeed, the nation itself, brought to this
late birth by the last and longest agony of feudalism.
From his prison in England he might hear of victory
or of defeat, of the capture of his own town by the
English or of its delivery by Joan of Arc, of the
crowning of an English king in Paris or of a French
king's return to his capital. But for year after
year and decade after decade he could hear little
of ransom, and nothing at all of peace. During this
spell of lost life it was that he made that series of
ballades set in a framework of allegory, which, after
M. Charles d'Héricault—who bases his opinion on
certain MSS. bearing the note, ' Ici finit le livre que
Monseigneur d'Orléans écrit dans sa prison,' and on
many very obvious references to exile, to imprisonment, to the hopes of ransom—I have called his
Poème de la Prison.

The two series of ballades and the setting in which
they are placed form one work of art. Throughout,
the elaborate machinery of allegorical abstraction,
first employed in the *Roman de la Rose*, is most
dexterously imitated and sustained. But what a
difference in the informing spirit of the two poems !
The *Roman de la Rose*, for all the irony of the second
and longer part, does at least show the final con-
summation of Desire. And, again, the enemies that
for a time debar the lovers from enjoyment, are far
from subtle : they are but Danger, Shame, Fear, and
Slander, which every young heart must expect to
face, and may hope to outwit or to overthrow. Now
the later poem opens, likewise, with the glorious
morning of a young life. But the brave heart is
soon ' vestu de noir ' : he languishes in distress ;
the ship of ' Good News,' for which he desires a fair

wind, never comes for all his calling ; if Fortune
turn her wheel in his favour, soon she turns it back ;
and the Beloved of the allegory, who should save
him, dies. So the hope is never achieved, and the
high heart is conquered. Yet not by Danger nor
Fear. The new and victorious enemies of manhood's
endeavour are Melancholy and Weariness. They
were first noted by Charles in his northern prison ;
but they are many since his time who have seen the
sun of their life's promise ' stealing, unseen, to west
with this disgrace.' Merencolie, Ennuy, and, at
last, Nonchaloir, the apathy of a heart ' tout en-
rouillé '—eaten with rust : that is his rendering of
the Preacher's lament.

It is not alone that the cast of the allegory re-
appears, but also all the current forms of French
mediæval verse are with it. And all are changed,
are coloured from within by a charge of personal
sorrow. ' Le premier jour du mois de May ' comes
round again and again : but it is an English May
reflecting the troubled passion of his heart, and it
is utterly unlike the May he remembers. It is

> ' Troublé plain de vent et de pluie :
> Estre souloit tout autrement
> Ou temps qu'ay congneu en ma vie.'

In another ballade he writes of the ' Flower and the
Leaf,' and chooses the leaf for his wear ; but not
on the moral grounds given in the innumerable
versions of this mediæval allegory. He chooses it
because of his personal sorrow :—

> ' Entièrement de sa partie ;
> Je n'ay de nulle flour envie,
> Porte la qui porter la doit,
> Car la fleur, que mon cueur aimoit
> Plus que nulle autre créature,
> Est hors de ce monde passée.'

Who was this flower, the Beloved, the Princess, mistress, sole friend, of the poem ? Some have said his wife, Bonne D'Armagnac, others France, or his liberty, or the memory of the women who had loved him when he was young. Yet, as I think, since the poem is but one sustained allegory, it is all these and more. It is the spirit of his youth : it is all of love, ambition, and hope, that was in him on the fatal morning of Agincourt. Anyhow, the Beloved dies. In Ballade LV. news reaches him : she is dangerously ill. In the next she recovers. In the next she is no more. He used to think, ' at the beginning of the year,' of what gift he could give his lady, ' la bien aimée,' and now death has laid her in the grave ; so at last, in Ballade LXIX., he celebrates her obsequies :—

> ' I made my lady's obsequies
>   Within the minster of desire,
> And for her soul sad *diriges*
>   Were sung by Dule behind the choir ;
>   Her sanctuary was one fire
> With many cierges lit by grief ;
> And on her tomb in bold relief
>   Were painted tears, hemmed with a girth
> Of jewelled letters all around
> That read : ' Here lyeth in the ground
>   The treasure of all joys on earth.'
>
> A slab of gold upon her lies
>   With saphirs set in golden wire ;
> Gems that are loyalty's devise,
>   And gold well known for joy's attire.
>   Both were the handmaids of her hire ;
> For joy and loyalty were chief
> Among the virtues God was lief
>   To show in fashioning her birth,
> That to his praise it might redound,
> She being wonderfully found
>   The treasure of all joys on earth.

Say no word more.   In ecstasies
  My heart is raptured to expire,
Hearing the noble histories
  Of deeds she did.   Whom all aspire
  To set on high and ever higher.

God, binding up death's golden sheaf,
Drew her to heaven, in my belief,
  So to adorn with rarer mirth
His paradise where saints stand round ;
For joy there was in her renowned,
  The treasure of all joys on earth.

ENVOY

Tears and laments are nothing worth,
  All soon or late by death are bound ;
  And none for long hath kept and crowned
The treasure of all joys on earth.'

So henceforward he will worship Nonchaloir.   So
after his release he withdraws from the battle of
life to write rondels with his friends, seeking to
forget the old-time tragedy of his youth and the
present misery of his native land.   'I could not
believe,' Petrarch had written, 'that this was the
same France I had seen so rich and flourishing.
Nothing presented itself to my eyes but a fearful
solitude, an utter poverty, land uncultivated, houses
in ruins.   Even the neighbourhood of Paris showed
everywhere marks of desolation and conflagration.
The streets are deserted, the roads overgrown with
weeds, the whole is a vast solitude.' [1]   That was in
1360 ; and eighty more years of invasion and civil
broil had come and gone in the hapless land since
then.

As we have seen, some seeds of the Renaissance
were sown in Charles's parentage, but only to lie

[1] Green, *History of the English People*, i. 438.

dormant through a dateless winter. His kinship
with the South might colour his own taste and shed
a little lustre on his court at Blois : it could not
redeem him from the dark conditions of his age nor
change these sensibly through France. They had
seemed at their darkest when, amid the last spasms
of the war, François Villon was born in a Paris still
held by the English, who that very year (1431)
burned Joan, ' la bonne Lorraine,' at Rouen. But
they grew darker still when the English had departed
the land, for not till after the tide of conquest had
turned was there revealed the full horror—the rot
and stench—of the wreckage it had submerged.
The winter following on Charles VII.'s re-entry into
Paris (1437) was one of pestilence and famine and
unheard-of cold. Wolves prowled in the streets,
attacking grown men.[1] Charles D'Orléans took
refuge from those evil days in the glow of an easy
mind : he shut himself in, as a man on winter even-
ings shuts himself into a little chamber lit with a
cheerful blaze. It was not so with Villon. The
grisly shadows of his childhood crept into his soul,
and from his soul into his song ; so that when most
his verses glitter and ring with tears and laughter,
there shall you look to meet a wolf at any turn.

The record of his manhood opens with a sordid
tragedy, and closes, so far as we know it, with a
blackguardly revenge. Skipping the follies of ' le
petit escolier,' we find him, a young man, sitting, on
a June evening in 1455, after supper under the
clock-tower of Saint Bénoit-le-bétourné. A priest,
one Philippe Sermoise, wronged, it may be, in a

---

[1] ' François Villon d'après des documens nouveaux.'   Marcel Schwob.
Revue des deux Mondes, 15 Juillet 1892.   I am indebted to this article
for the details of Villon's life, there published for the first time.

shameless intrigue, drew near, and after an exchange of insults, pushed him down. It is a note of the time that every bystander slunk forthwith into the shadows, and the two were left alone in the twilight. Then the priest drew a dagger and stabbed Villon in the lip ; but Villon, striking from under his cloak, knifed his antagonist in the groin, and, finally, being disarmed by a newcomer, picked up a heavy stone and pashed in the priest's brain-pan. Banished for this manslaughter, he took to the road, and he travelled the highways of France. They were infested, as ever in the Middle Age, yet more thickly then than ever, by a wandering populace of minstrels, beggars, sham clerks, goliards, broken men, camp-followers, and thieves. For the Hundred Years' War had come to an end with Charles VII.'s entry into Bordeaux in 1453, and this tide of scum was now swollen beyond any previous high-water mark by the disbanding of his army. Within its eddies there existed from that year until its extermination in 1461, the secret society (not unlike the Camorra) of the ' Coquillards,' or ' Companions of the Shell,' with a jargon of its own, with 'prentices, past-masters, and a chief, ' le Roi de la Coquille ' : briefly, a complete hierarchy of blackguardism, with organised departments of brutality or craft, to which each newcomer was detailed according to his natural aptitude for crimes. It is beyond doubt, as M. Schwob has shown, that Villon was received into this association. He wrote six ballades in its slang ; he consorted for years with two notorious ' companions,' Regnier de Montigny and Colin de Cayeux, in whose felonies he lent a hand, and whose deaths he mourned. In 1456 his banishment was remitted, and he returned to Paris with his new-found know-

ledge of the world. Nor was he long in turning it
to account. In the December of the same year you
will find him, with Colin de Cayeux and another,
scaling the high walls of the Collège de Navarre to
pick the common chest of the dons and students in
the Faculty of Theology, the while another rascal
Guy de Tabarie by name, kept watch outside over
the ladder and the cloaks. Villon, for his share of
the plunder, pocketed a hundred gold crowns, and,
as he tells us in the *Petit Testament*, ' about Christmas, in the dead season, when the wolves live on
wind,' he shifted his quarters to Angers. With a
wise prevision, as it turned out ; for when, next
year (1457), the chest was found empty, Tabarie
first blabbed, and then, under torture, gave full
information against his confederates. Villon derides
him in the *Grand Testament* for his habit of telling
the truth, and bequeaths a halter to one of his
examiners, while to another, François de Ferre-
bourg, a sharper vengeance is reserved. But for
the moment the poet could return no more to Paris.
A Companion of the Shell dared hope for little mercy :
three had been boiled alive at Dijon but two years
before, and the society was ever getting thinned by
the axe and the rope. Villon, indeed, was not to
see Paris again until he was amnestied on the accession of Louis XI., in 1461, for yet another crime of
the ' Coquillards,' perpetrated, we know not when,
at Montpipeau : a crime which ended in the hanging
of Colin de Cayeux, and in his own condemnation to
perpetual imprisonment at Meung, in the donjon
of the Bishop of Orléans. We get glimpses of him
at the courts of Charles D'Orléans and of Jean II.
de Bourbon, but soon he wanders out of sight again,
by the ways of those that love darkness, and when

we fish him up again he is in irons at Meung. There, on bread and water, he must have composed the bulk of the great poem which has made him immortal : a work of unfailing execution, of brilliant lines playing like forked lightning over unguessed chasms of awful truth. He writes of his shames in it as an old soldier of his scars : ' Necessité fait gens mesprendre. Et faim saillir les loups des bois.' The worship of the Virgin or the beastliness of the stews ; the old age of the wit told to hold his tongue, or of the harlot heart-sick for lost loveliness ; the fortune of those who fare sumptuously, and, again, of those who beg naked and see bread only through the windows they go by; the passing of renowned ladies and great emperors and saints : all these are as one to his art. The truth of them is there, set down with unfaltering precision, without a trace of effort. He sings the ' snows of yester-year ' in words that haunt the ages, or lightly casts an acrostic of his name into an envoy aching with desolation :—

> ' Vente, gresle, gelle, j'ay mon pain cuict !
> Ie suis paillard, la paillarde me duit.
> Lequel vault mieux ? Chascun bien s'entresuit,
> L'ung l'autre vault : c'est à mau chat mau rat.
> Ordure amons, ordure nous affuyt,
> Nous deffuyons honneur, il nous deffuyt,
>   En ce bourdeau, ou tenons nostre estat.'

So he sings. It is easy as the wind in autumn, and as musical, and—whirling with dead leaves ! With this and the rest of the *Grand Testament* in his pocket he returned to Paris in 1461, and we hear of him but once again, playing a mean part in a squalid brawl. François Ferrebouc, the examiner, his old enemy, knocked up one night after supper by Villon and his friends, was stabbed by an unknown

hand. The record of his manhood ends as it began,
and he passes for ever into utter darkness.

From some lampoons in his work and this last
act of rascality or cowardice, it would seem that he
could never forgive any person concerned in the
criminal investigation of 1457 : the calamity which
made him an outcast. It was in that year, and in
such dubious plight, that Villon drifted to the court
of Charles D'Orléans at Blois. It was a strange
meeting of two poets : the younger, of twenty-six,
a known criminal, a gaol-bird to be ; the elder, of
sixty-six, aged before his time, enfeebled with long
imprisonment in his country's cause, so fallen into
decay that six years later he could no longer even
sign his name. Of the manner of their meeting we
know nothing directly ; but, indirectly, we can
gather enough from significant hints in their writings
and from the shortness of one's stay. There is a
dull official poem by Villon on the birth of Charles's
daughter in December, 1457. It is copied in his
hand into a manuscript containing poems in the
writing of Charles himself and other rhyming friends.
But the fourteen pages following Villon's contribution are blank. An explanation may be found in
his refrain to a ballade, the first line of which, ' Je
meurs de soef auprès de la fontaine,' was apparently
given out by Charles as the text for a poetical tournament. We have the thing done and copied out by
Charles and many of his guests ; but Villon's work
is very different from theirs. The antithesis to be
maintained in every line lent itself perfectly to the
theme of his own false position. The official line
has reminded him of the reservation with which he
was received, of the half-hearted hospitality. He
dies of thirst beside the fountain ; chatters with

cold by the hearth ; is an exile in his own land.   He
laughs through his tears, and expects without hope
—so he leads up to the refrain, ' Bien recueilly,
debouté de chascun '—he is well received, and rejected of all.   To understand this ballade, addressed
to his ' clément Prince,' and the shortness of Villon's
visit, you scarce need the allusions, scattered through
his writings, to the lot of the man who has borne
a reputation for wit in his youth : to the old monkey
whose tricks no longer please : who, if he hold his
tongue, is taken for a worn-out fool and, if he speak,
is told to hold his tongue.   Indeed, we are not left
in doubt by Charles himself as to his impression of
his guest.   He has sketched his Villon in a rondel
and, lest any should fail to recognise the likeness,
assists with an obvious allusion to the author of
the *Grand Testament*.   That poem opens with this
frightful confession :—

> ' " En l'an trentiesme de mon aage
>   *Que toutes mes hontes j'ay beues*." '

The second of these two lines gives the first and
the refrain of Charles's rondel, ' Qui a toutes ses
hontes beues ' :—

> ' He that hath drunken all his shame
>   Cares nothing for what people say ;
>   He lets derision pass its way
> As clouds may go the way they came.
>
> If in the street they hoot his name,
>   He winks and turns to wine and play.
> He that hath drunken all his shame
>   Cares nothing for what people say.
>
> A truffle likes him more than fame ;
>   If folk laugh, he must laugh as they ;
>   But if it comes to blushing—Nay,
> He keeps his countenance the same
> Though he have drunken all his shame.'

So did these poets meet, and so they parted. Both belonged to the last hours of the Middle Age ; both saw the forces of feudalism overthrow the society they had founded ; both lived and died in the wilderness of the ensuing desolation. The one, caught in the catastrophe, became a waif among wolves and robbers ; the other, by a subtler irony, was at once the leader and the idle witness, the ' flag rather than the captain ' of the feudal party which, abjuring its nature, was to found the new order of monarchy and national life. Charles D'Orléans, aloof from his age, confined perforce in a foreign prison, and later, making a lodge, of choice, in the wilderness, distilled into the narrowest vials songs sweet as any, and yet trivial. Of the cup handed him by Destiny he drank one half, and then set it down unfinished. But Villon drained it to the lees ; knew all the life which renders the legends of Louis XI. and Prince Hal intelligible. His verse is bitter with the bitterness, glad only with the insolence, of those days. And yet it is great verse—verse haunted with all their horror, steeped in their infinite sadness.

RONSARD AND LA PLÉIADE

RONSARD AND LA PLÉIADE

IT is bold to select a limited period in the poetry
of one country, for the arts have a continuous
organic life to be traced through many lands back
to origins in distant ages. Yet there are periods,
often long, when the arts simulate death, and periods,
always short, when they seem to be born again.
The greatest of these rebirths took place throughout
Western Europe during the sixteenth century, and
constitutes a feature so striking that the epoch in
which it occurred is often called after it, the Renaissance. We may explain the renaissance of the
arts, but we cannot explain it away. There it is ;
in architecture, in sculpture, in painting, in music,
and perhaps, above all, in poetry. In poetry something happened—not, indeed, altogether without
parallels—in the thirteenth century, and again in
the nineteenth. But the outburst of poetry in
Europe during the Renaissance was greater in
volume, more ingenious in variety, than at any time
before or since. The modern world exploded into
an ecstasy of song.

The poetry of Ronsard and his companions, their
conscious endeavour to re-endow the world with an
all but lost delight, is, in terms of time and place, a
central event of the Renaissance. They wrote in
the middle of the sixteenth century and in the heart
of France.

E

The Age and the Man

I need not dwell on the age in which they wrote. It is enough for my purpose to say that the age of Ronsard exhibited, in the vigour of their prime, new ideas of monarchy, nationality, and religion, which breaking up, and breaking away from, old ideas of feudalism, the empire, and the papacy, induced an era of gorgeous embassies in the place of local war waged under sordid conditions. ' The Alps had been levelled for ever ' when, ' on the last day of the year 1494, the army of Charles VIII. entered Rome.' Thenceforward, until the fatal day of Pavia, Italy was the ring in which the Houses of France and Austria wrestled for the headship of Christendom. Italy, the turning-point in the welter of war and diplomacy, became a vortex, sucking in streams of courage and intellect from all Europe. Never had there been such contact between contemporary civilisations. But this wide embrace of the present was not all. Of modern countries Italy remembered most of the classic past ; had always remembered it, confusedly, as a man dreaming remembers a day of excitement and success. More than a century before the French invasion Petrarch, though he could not read them, had wept with joy over the codices of Homer and Plato. Since then the texts of antiquity had been recovered and printing-presses established, so that between 1494 and 1515, the invasion of Charles VIII. and the victory of François I. at Marignano, the press of Aldus printed in Venice thirty-three first editions of the classics. It was then and there also, in an Italy which riveted the gaze of every cultured mind, that men, having listened once again to the songs of their loveliness, turned to unearth and piece together the broken and buried gods of beauty. The revolution in mediæval politics and religion synchronised with the recovery of classic literature and sculpture.

Now Ronsard, the man apart from the poet, is an embodiment of all the forces and confusions of his time. I shall speak first of him and his companions; next, of the sources of their inspiration and the aim of their art; lastly, of their achievement and influence.

Pierre de Ronsard, son of the Seigneur Loys de Ronsard, the High Steward of François Premier's household, was born in 1525, the year of that king's defeat at Pavia, which decided adversely his duel with the House of Austria. The historian De Thou wrote afterwards that his birth made amends to France for even so great a disaster. He lay in the cradle when his father set out with the king's hostages to suffer duress until the royal ransom should be paid. I visited his father's castle, De la Poissonnière, as a reverent pilgrim, some years ago. It stands, beneath a low cliff of white rock overgrown with ivy, in the gentle scenery, elegiac rather than romantic, to which Ronsard's verse ever returns. Above the low cliff are remnants of the Forêt de Gastine; between the castle and the little river Loir, bedecked with *fleur de lis*, stretch poplar-screened meadows.

The castle is inscribed here and there, indeed everywhere, in the fashion of that day, transitional between Gothic and Renaissance, with Latin mottoes curiously appropriate to Ronsard's temperament and to the alternations of his posthumous fame. Above a door you may read ' Voluptati et gratiis '; about the windows, ' Veritas filia temporis ' and ' Respice finem.' Within, beneath his arms and those of France, sculptured on the apex of the great pyramidal chimney-piece in the hall, there runs the confident legend ' Non fallunt futura merentem ' ; and below, in a deep band, a fence of blossoming roses seems to grow on the surface of the stone. It is a moot point whether he himself added this frieze to symbolise his love for a half-guessed princess, who wore the rose for her emblem, or .whether the very nest in which he was born presaged that lovely accident of his art—the marriage of what Pater has called the *askesis* of stone with the pathetic blossoming and fading of the rose.

But we are not to think that Ronsard, or any of his companions, evaded the conditions of their age to indulge in the languid fallacy of art for art's sake. He was plunged as a child into the unrest of camps and courts, as a youth into travel and diplomacy, and, long years after he had deliberately sought the seclusion of art and study, replunged into the cruel conflicts of religious animosity.

When nine years old he fell ill at the College of Navarre, and was taken by his father to the king's camp at Avignon. There he became page to the Dauphin François, who was poisoned six days later. He found another protector in Charles, Duc d'Orléans, and, at the age of twelve, accompanied Madeleine of France on her journey to wed James of Scotland. Those days were hectic in their precocity.

He passed two years in Edinburgh, and then travelled for six months in England. He could dance and fence well, as was expected, but was given over to solitary wandering and the writing of verses. To prevent such original vagaries the Duc d'Orléans sent him, in 1540, aged fifteen, on a mission to Flanders and on again to Scotland. He was wrecked on the coast, escaped by swimming, and, returning in the same year to Germany in the suite of the French Ambassador, Lazare de Baïf, travelled thence to Turin with Guillaume de Langey, Seigneur du Bellay. Thus it was that he came to know one of his future comrades in the Pléiade, Antoine de Baïf, and to know of another, and greater, Joachim du Bellay, De Langey's kinsman.

At sixteen he spoke English, Italian, and German, and was conversant, in all those tongues, with affairs of State ; but, being stricken by deafness, and so handicapped for a life of action otherwise promising, he turned to letters, learnt Virgil by heart, and read the poetry of Clement Marot and the *Roman de la Rose.* He acquired the dower of mediæval song, the storied legend of Guillaume de Loris and Jehan de Meung, changing from allegorical romance to allegorical sarcasm, and, in Marot, the tired affectations of used formality. The Middle Age, though few felt this, had come to a full close. Ronsard, probably, was conscious of that conclusion, for he had devoured the best of its verse and was still unsatisfied. Then—as the way is with precocious youth—two accidents assailed and redirected his life.

The Court, in which he still held a post, was at Blois. Wandering thence as his wont was, on a certain day (21st April 1541), aged sixteen, he met a girl in the forest with fair hair, brown eyes, and smiling lips. He returned a poet to write his *Amours* in honour of Cassandra, and loved her vainly for seven years. His father, who objected to poetry, being dead in 1544, he began, perhaps because he loved, and love is new, to study Greek,

the new knowledge, stealing off to be taught by
the humanist Dorat with De Baïf, his diplomatic
companion. Ere long the second accident befell.
Wandering with a promising career lost and a
froward mistress discovered, he met at some time
not long before 1547 another young man, Joachim
du Bellay, from whom the high calls of war and
diplomacy had also, oddly enough, been muffled by
the curtain of early deafness. Both were turning for
consolation to the poetry of the ancients. The
meeting was memorable. Out of it sprang the
association of poets and scholars who called themselves at first ' La Brigade,' and afterwards ' La
Pléiade,' in imitation of poets at the court of Ptolemy
Philadelphus. With Ronsard, Du Bellay, Dorat,
and De Baïf, were Estienne Jodelle, Pontus de Tyard,
and Remy Belleau. I must add Olivier de Magny
and, later, many others to fill the places of the dead
—Jean Passerat, Gilles Durant, and Philippe des
Portes. The original confederacy toiled in secret
till Du Bellay brought out, in 1549, their manifesto,
La Défense et Illustration de la Langue Française.
Each guarded his labours so jealously that, when
Du Bellay surreptitiously read the *Odes* on which
Ronsard had been working, nothing but the ardour
of youthful friendship averted a quarrel. This
incident precipitated the publication of their poetry.
Ronsard's first four books of *Odes* appeared in 1550,
and his *Amours* in 1552 ; Du Bellay's *Olive* in 1549,
and his *Regrets* in 1558. I shall not attempt a
bibliography of their poetry, amazing in its amount,
or a nice discrimination of the ladies by whom it
was partly inspired. Louise Labé, the Aspasia of
Lyons, who had ridden to war after the Dauphin,
accoutred as a captain, who played on many musical

instruments, read Greek, and wrote poetry in French
and Italian ; or, again, Diane de Poictiers, actually
mistress to the King, practically a Secretary of State,
and accidentally governess to the Queen's children,
the model for the *Diane Chasseresse* in the Louvre
and châtelaine d'Anêt, with its fanciful traceries
and elaborate *parterres*, are both so typical of that
transitional age that each might exhaust an essay.
Ronsard, alone, sang voluminously to Cassandra,
Marie, Helène ; frequently to Marguerite, Duchesse
de Savoie, and Marie Stuart. And surely Ronsard
loved that queen. Else could he have put into the
mouth of Charles ix. the address to the shade of his
elder brother—

> Ah ! frère mien, tu ne dois faire plainte,
> De quoi ta vie en sa fleur s'est éteinte ;
> Avoir joui d'une telle beauté,
> Sein contre sein, valait ta royauté.

Yet Ronsard loved divine beauty even more ; perhaps loved most, certainly cared most for, the
art by which he expressed his love, and, though
he loved them, cared least for the beautiful women
whose human loveliness helped him to detect Divine
Beauty and braced him to elaborate her ritual. The
last line of his last love sonnet runs :—

> Car l'Amour et la Mort n'est qu'une mesme chose.

He uses his head for the expression of his art, not
for the analysis of his emotion.

Neither shall I seek to follow out their diplomatic
journeys. Briefly, they sojourned often in Italy,
or at Lyons, and spent sweet and splendid days,
described by Brantôme, among the many castles
in the wide valley of the Loire.

Ronsard's *Odes* were at the outset vehemently
attacked, but, first aided by the protection of his

Marguerite, sister to Henri II., and then winning on
their merits, his poetry and the poetry of his companions carried all before it at the court and in the
country.   Ronsard won a greater fame than was
ever accorded to a poet in his lifetime.   He was
acclaimed a Horace, a Pindar, a Petrarch.   The
Academy of the Floral Games at Toulouse sent
him a silver Minerva ; his king must have him
at all times by his side ; our own Elizabeth gave
him a diamond—comparing its water to the purity
of his verse ; and Marie Stuart, when others had
deserted his old age, a buffet worth two hundred
crowns, addressed 'A Ronsard l'Apollon de la source
des Muses.'   Châtelard read his *Hymn to Death*,
and no other office, for consolation on the scaffold.

Montaigne, who could confer dignity beyond
the gift of kings, writes, say in 1575 : ' Since
Ronsard and Du Bellay have raised our French
poetry to a place of honour, I see no apprentice
so little but he must inflate phrases and order
cadences much about as they do.   For the common
herd there were never so many poets, but easy
enough as it is for these to reproduce their rhymes,
they still fall short enough of imitating the rich
descriptions of the one, and the delicate inventions
of the other.'

The striking feature in the lives of Ronsard and
his companions is their rapid recognition ; but this
instant glory was soon followed by sudden eclipse.
The last decade of Henri II.'s reign (1549-1559)
comprises most of the work for which he and his
comrades are famous.   Through these years of poetry
and pageantry, storms, political and religious, were
silently brewing to burst over the head of Henri's
son, and incidentally to turn Ronsard the poet into

a pamphleteer. But whilst they lasted the Pléiade saw crowns of lesser states pushed about like pieces in a game; yet with all Europe for the chess-board, and with players whose gestures and apparel still shine from between the wars of dynasties and the wars of religion, as from a sunny patch between the shadows of two thunder-clouds. Beneath that shaft of light their lives and poetry glisten. They watched the game of high politics, wrote sonnets to the players, and often took a hand in it themselves. Its extension over Europe, demanding long travel and exile abroad, changed the inspiration of their art, and charged it with splendid colours. But, of them all, Ronsard was the only one who lived on into the silence of old age amidst altered and uncongenial surroundings. He saw his companions die; Du Bellay and De Magny in 1560, Jodelle in 1573, Belleau in 1577. His *Franciade* fell dead of its own weight, and was forgotten in the horrors of the St. Bartholomew. Even from as early as 1560 an unmoral delight in mere learning and the love of beauty was no longer possible. His heart, as a patriot, bled for France in her misery of religious war, which ever seemed to him, as a Catholic, wicked and irrational. So he set aside his theories of art, his stately measures and plaintive melodies, and took his stand, like a man, in the midst of his country's dissensions.

This aspect of his life is so rarely considered that I recommend the study of his *Discours*, or poetical pamphlets, to any who would understand the attitude of a liberal and cultivated scholar, who yet struck in, hard, on the side of Royalty and Catholicism, rather because he was a philosophic conservative by temperament than because he held any

precise views on religion or politics.   In his elegy on
the tumult of Amboise, he writes, 1560 :—

Ainsi que l'ennemi par livres a séduit
Le peuple dévoyé qui faussement le suit,
Il faut en disputant par livres le confondre,
Par livres l'assaillir, par livres luy respondre.

But he was not content with diatribes.   According
to De Thou, he placed himself, in 1562, at the head
of the gentry and routed the Huguenot pillagers.
' Quâ ex re commota nobilitas arma subit, duce sibi
delecto, Petro Ronsardo ' (Livre xxx. 1562).

The most interesting account of his way of thinking and living is to be found in his *Response aux
injures et calomnies de je ne sçay quels prédicantereaux
et misnistreaux de Genêve.*

The brutalities of the attack—*Le Temple de
Ronsard*—which he countered in this reply justify
its violence, and challenge his parade of worldly
amenities.   He had been accused of being a turncoat Huguenot, an unavowed Catholic priest, a
pagan who sacrificed a buck in all seriousness to a
heathen god, an evil-liver, and of much else which
cannot conveniently be repeated.   So he describes
himself, without extenuation, in this vein :—

' Waking, I say my prayers ; get up, dress, study,
composing or reading, in pursuit of my destiny for
four or five hours.   When weary I go to church.
There follows an hour's talk and dinner : " Sobre
repas, grace, amuçement."   If fine, I wander in a
wood or village, and seek solitary places.

J'aime fort les jardins qui sentent le sauvage,
J'aime le flot de l'eau qui gazouille au rivage.
La devisant sur l'herbe avec un mien amy
Je me suis par les fleurs bien souvent endormy
A l'ombrage d'un saule ; ou, lisant dans un livre,
J'ay cherché le moyen de me faire revivre.

'In bad weather I go into society, play cards, take part in gymnastics, leaping, wrestling, or fencing, and make jokes—

> et à la vérité
> Je ne loge chez moi trop de sévérité
> J'ayme à faire l'amour, j'ayme à parler aux femmes,
> A mettre par escrit mes amoureuses flammes ;
> J'ayme les bals, la dance, et les masques aussi
> La musique et le luth ennemis de soucy.

'When the dusky night ranges the stars in order and curtains the sky and earth with veils, without a care I go to bed, and there, lifting my eyes, voice, and heart up to the vault of heaven, I make my orison, praying the divine goodness for gentle pardon of my failing.   For the rest I am neither rebellious nor ill-natured.   I do not back my rule with the sword. Thus I live ; if your life be better, I do not envy. Let it be better by all means.'

> Au reste je ne suis ny mutin ny meschant,
> Qui fay croire ma loy par le glaive trenchant.
> Voilà comme je vy ; si ta vie est meilleure,
> Je n'en suis envieux, et soit à la bonne heure.

He explains that he is not a priest ; but, in those places where it is right to display the office and duty of a devout heart, he is a stout pillar of the Church, wearing the proper vestments of the minor orders which he had taken, with certain priories conferred on him for his services, by his king.   With his astounding touch of unconventional admiration for all living creatures, he compares himself in his cope to a snail on an April morning :—

> Par le trou de la chappe apparoit eslevé
> Mon col brave et gaillard, comme le chef lavé
> D'un limaçon d'avril . . .

and discourses of the snail with the fair palace he carries along slimy tracts among the fresh grass and flowers, shooting out his horns, a warrior of the garden, who pastures on the dew with which his house is besprinkled. He attends the services of his priory and honours his prelate. If others had done so, there would have been no civil troubles, the fair sun of the ancient age of Astræa would shine over all France. No ritters from the Rhine would have drunk her vintage and squandered her money. No English would have bought her lands. It is absurd for a Calvinist to judge a Catholic, as though a Jew accused a Turk, or a Turk a Christian ; God only, the unfailing Judge, knows the hearts of all. He goes on :—

' You say my muse is paid to flatter. No prince can boast (I wish he could) of having paid me a salary. I serve whom I please with unfettered courage. I sing the king, his brother, and mother. Of others I am not the valet : if they are mighty lords, I too have a high heart.

' You say I have been a student, a courtier, a soldier. Quite true. But I have never been a street-preacher·or hypocrite (*cafard*), selling my vain dreams to ignorant men. I'd rather row in a galley, or labour with swollen hands in fields that no one has heard of, than cease to be a gentleman in order to become a cheat (*pipeur*). You say it ill becomes me to speak of virtue : Pharisee ! If all the ambrosia and nectar of heaven be yours, still *le bon Dieu* will keep us a little brown bread. If your new sect should carry you to Paradise, our old one will at least see the door, and we, poor banished wretches, by God's goodness, will still find some room in a retired corner of His house, though, as in reason, the

best places must be for you who are children of
grace.   And yet let me remind you of the Pharisee
and the Publican.   After all, virtue cannot be shut
up in Geneva.   She is a winged creature, who passes
over the sea, takes flight to the sky, and traverses
the earth like lightning, the wandering guest of all
the world !

> La vertu ne se peut à Genève enfermer :
> Elle a le dos ailé, elle passe la mer,
> Elle s'envole au ciel, elle marche sur terre
> Viste comme un esclair, messager du tonnerre . . .
> Ainsi de peuple en peuple elle court par le monde,
> De ce grand univers l'hostesse vagabonde.

' You say that in my frenzy I scatter my verses
like leaves to the wind.   I do.   Poetry is an art ;
but not comparable to the fixed arts of preaching
and prose.   The right poets have their hidden
artifice, which does not seem art to verse-mongers,
but fares forth under a free restraint whithersoever
the muse may lead it.   I gather my honey, as the
bees do, from every flower of Parnassus.   I am mad,
if you please, when I hold a pen, but without one,
perfectly sane.   You are like a child who, seeing
giants and chimæras in the clouds, holds the pageant
for truth.   The verses with which I disport myself,
you take in earnest ; but neither your verses nor
mine are oracles.

' You say that the fame I once had is defeated.
Do you really suppose that your sect embraces all
the world ?   You are very much mistaken.   I have
too much fame.   I would rather without noise or
renown be but a shepherd or a labourer.   There is
no happiness in being pointed at in the street.

> Celuy n'est pas heureux qu'on montre par la rue.

'You say that I should die overwhelmed with sorrow did I see our Roman Church fall. I should be unhappy. But I have a stout heart, and that inside my head which, if tempests come, must swim with me through the floods. Perhaps your head, if we do reach an unknown shore, will turn out to be useless.

'No! no! I do not depend on Church revenues or royal favour. I live a true poet and have deserved as well of my country as you, false impostor and braggart that you are.

'All your barking will not strip me of the laurel wreath I have deserved for service done to the French language.

'Undaunted by toil I have laboured for the mother-tongue of France. I have made her new words and restored the old. I have raised her poetry to a level with the art of Rome and Greece. I repent me of the deed if this art is to be used by heretics to serve the ends of shop-boys.

'You—and you cannot deny it—are the issue of my muse. You are my subjects; I your only king. You are my streams. I am your fountain. The more you exhaust me, the more does my unfailing spring cast back the sands and gush forth perpetually to fulfil your rivulets.'

There is more in this haughty strain. But at the last he prays God devoutly that the fearful end of civil strife may be averted, and that the torch of war, like a brand in the fire, may consume itself in smoke.

> Le feu, le fer, le meurtre, en sont le fondement,
> Dieu veuille que la fin en arrive autrement,
> Et que le grand flambeau de la guerre allumée,
> Comme un tison de feu, se consomme en fumée.

I have made this long citation because it reveals the man, more fully than any list, however congested, of names and dates ; and because it supplies a corrective to conventional views based on this or that obvious feature of Ronsard's poetry. It is important to know that a poet chiefly remembered for a few plaintive songs of fading roses, and a deliberate attempt to recast a language and develop the mechanism of verse, was every inch a man who stood four-square to the whole racket of his day.

For this, so far from diminishing the value of his particular love of loveliness, and personal servitude to the machinery of art, tends, on the contrary, to prove the general importance to mankind of these things for which he cared most. It is clear that he cared also, and acutely, for much that other men prize. Here is a citizen and a soldier, a man who takes a side in politics and religion, who argues from the rostrum and pommels in the ring, a conservative with a catholic pleasure in life, delighting in all the treasures garnered into the citadel of the past, and ready to die in its defence. Yet his life-work, for all these distractions, consists in an exaltation of

> Beauty that must die
> And Joy whose hand is ever at his lips
> Bidding Adieu :

consists in that ; and in a curious attention to the formalities of verse, to the artistic liturgy of beauty which affirms, paradoxically, that Beauty, by reason of her certitude, is, despite of death, in some irrational way at once divine and immortal. That mystical message comes from a human, sturdy, God-fearing, battle-stained man with ' accents of dignity that die upon the lips ' of monastic devotees to art cloistered for its own sake.

Little else need be said of his life. After the
death of Charles IX. an immense solitude encom-
passed the man who had taken part in so many
activities. Tasso, it is true, in 1575, submitted to
him at Paris the earlier cantos of his *Jerusalem
Delivered*. But Ronsard retired from the Court of
Henri III. His life had, he writes, become a continual death, so he sought out the Priory of St. Cosme
to die. I strayed to the place by pure accident.
Walking near Plessis-les-Tours one summer evening,
along the dyke constructed by our Plantagenets to
restrain the inundations of the Loire, I saw a cart-
road leading through an avenue of poplars to a
Gothic archway. I followed the track and found,
lit up by the sunset, a stone mansion of the fifteenth
century, neglected and partitioned into the dwellings
of four peasant proprietors. The end gable of the
upper story was attached by a flying gallery to the
ruins of a Gothic church. I was asked if I was
looking for the tomb of Ronsard, and told, with a
grin, that some learned men had failed to find his
grave twenty years earlier, and that I should only
waste my time. I thought otherwise. This was
evidently St. Cosme. There, was the late-Gothic
door, through which Ronsard passed to his death-bed,
still decorated with Renaissance carvings of fruits
and flowers. A rose-tree grew up one of the jambs,
and a vine had thrown a branch across the grey,
worm-eaten panels. When I returned the next year
the door, with its time-worn sculpture, was gone.
But I retrieved parts of it from the wood-heap. The
scene echoed the note on which Ronsard harped with
poignant insistence—

> Tout ce qui est de beau ne se garde longtemps
> Les roses et les lis ne règnent qu'un printemps.

There, he had dictated his last verses—

> L'un meurt en son printemps, l'autre attend la vieillesse,
> Le trespas est tout un, les accidens divers :
> Le vray thresor de l'homme est la verte jeunesse,
> Le reste de nos ans ne sont que des hyvers.—

and, again, with his incongruous mingling of Catholic faith and pagan despair—

> Quoy mon âme, dors-tu, engourdie en ta masse ?
> La trompette a sonné, serre baggage, et va
> Le chemin *déserté* que Jésus-Christ trouva.
> Quand tant mouillé de sang racheta nostre race.

This is the religious verse of a man who, against his will, had seen religion confounded with war ; who had deplored—

> Un Christ empistolé, tout noirci de fumée ;

who almost dreaded that the way of salvation dear to his ancestors was to be obliterated by insurgents against whom he had himself borne arms.

But he died in that way. When asked at the point of death, ' De quelle résolution il voulait mourir ? ' he answered, according to a contemporary, Binet, ' Assez aigrement, qui vous fait dire cela, mon bon amy ? Je veux mourir en la religion Catholique, comme mes ayeulx, bisayeulx, trisayeulx, et comme j'ai tesmoigné assez par mes escrits ! '

He discoursed at length on his life, saying again and again, ' Je n'ay aucune haine contre personne, ainsi me puisse chacun pardonner.' He dictated two more Christian sonnets, and remained a long while with arms extended towards the sky : at last, like one in his sleep, he rendered his spirit to God, and his hands in falling let those present know the moment of his death.

The Priory of St. Cosme was suppressed, and the

only design of Ronsard's shattered monument is
' par suite d'un vol '—so a French archæologist tells
me—now in the Bodleian at Oxford.

SOURCES AND AIMS

Having touched on the age in which the Pléiade
wrote, and dwelt on the personality of their leader, I
come to the *sources of their inspiration and aim of
their art.* Here we must walk warily. From this
point onward I shall rather invite inquiry than seek
to deliver a judgment. There is no final judgment.
Conflicting judgments make the work of the Pléiade
a matter of interest to-day, especially to students
of the Renaissance.

The judgment which stood unchallenged in France
for two centuries averred that having thrown away
the tradition of French poetry, and the French
language after it, the Pléiade invented, *per saltum*, a
new language and a new poetry, awkwardly, and all
but exclusively, imitated from Greek models.

The opposite view, urged tentatively by Sainte-
Beuve in 1828, was emphasised by Pater in his
famous essay on Joachim du Bellay, and can best be
stated in his words :—' In the Renaissance, French
poetry did but borrow something to blend with a
native growth, and the poems of Ronsard, with their
ingenuity, their delicately figured surfaces, their
slightness, their fanciful combinations of rhyme, are
but the correlatives of the traceries of the house of
Jacque Cœur at Bourges, or the Maison de Justice at
Rouen.' Their work, he writes, shows ' a blending
of Italian ornament with the general outline of
Northern design,' and exhibits ' the finest and
subtlest phase of the Middle Age itself.'

The first view makes the Pléiade too Greek and violently prone to innovation ; the second, too French and complacently mediæval, with but a top-dressing of Italian ornament. In truth, their sources were manifold ; to a degree in excess of both theories, taken together. They drew their inspiration from every known fountain of poetry and, consequently, aimed in their art at designing elaborate channels, sufficiently definite to contain, yet numerous enough to display, all the flashing waters they had derived from so many a muse-haunted hill.

Let me enumerate their sources. In the first place, they valued the best of mediæval French verse. They knew their thirteenth century. Ronsard had studied the *Roman de la Rose*. He knew of the romance-cycle of Charlemagne, for he writes in one of his many ' regrets pour Marie Stuart ' : —

> Que ne vivent encor les palladins de France !
> Un Roland, un Renaud ! ils prendroient sa défence
> Et l'accompagneroient et seroient bien heureux
> D'en avoir seulement un regard amoureux.

They knew of the Arthurian cycle ; Du Bellay, in their manifesto, far from proposing a classical subject for an epic poem, writes, ' choose one of those beautiful old French romances *comme un Lancelot, un Tristan, ou autres.*' Ronsard, in his preface to his *Franciade*, when attacking those who sought to write in classic Latin, says, ' Why, it would be better worth your while—*comme un bon bourgeois*—to make a dictionary of the old words of Artus, Lancelot, and Gawain, or a commentary on the *Roman de la Rose.*' They revived the Alexandrine verse of twelve syllables from a very early French poem on the legend of Alexander. But if they knew of the Alexandrian cycle, the Carlovingian cycle, the

Arthurian cycle, and took delight in the *Romance of the Rose*, why, then, they enjoyed the heritage of mediæval French verse, which, as Matthew Arnold has truly said, ' took possession of the heart and imagination of Europe in the twelfth and thirteenth centuries, and taught Chaucer his trade, words, rhyme, and metre.' As Chaucer puts it—with a narrower application which may justly be extended —' The note I trowë makëd was in Fraunce.' They derived from that source their ' fluidity of move-ment ' and the Alexandrine verse, but, so far as I know, nothing else.

In the second place, coming to French poetry which immediately preceded their own, they knew and appreciated Clement Marot, Mellin de St. Gellais, Heroet, and Maurice Scève. Ronsard praises all four. But there are two things to be noticed. They skip over Charles d'Orléans and Villon, springing from the thirteenth century to their immediate predecessors, and from these select only four as bright exceptions. The rest were Court poetasters, recharging the *ballade* and *rondeau*, like old rocket-cases, with a few pinches of dull flattery or indecent wit. The *Chant Royal* had become the exercise of a drudge. The *Blasons* were inanities and brutalities, mere ' gabble of tinkers,' with neither ' wit, manners, nor honesty,' of which it is impossible to speak. Ronsard apostrophises Marot as ' Seule lumière en ses ans de la vulgaire poésie ' (Preface to *Odes*, 1550). Marot's *Hero and Leander* can be read ; his fable of *The Lion and the Rat* is racy ; and some of his *rondeaux* delightful : yet Ronsard's tribute was generous. He must have raged against such pranks in redoubled rhyme, as for example :—

La blanche colombelle belle
Souvent je voys priant, criant,
Mais dessoubz la cordelle d'elle
Me jecte un œil friant, riant, etc. etc.

We may cry out with *Maria*, ' What a cater-
wauling do you keep here ! ' and acknowledge that
the rare art of the Middle Age had declined to
' damnable iteration.'

Whilst the Pléiade did not discard the dower
of mediæval song, or condemn all their immediate
predecessors, it cannot be said that they present in
the main the last phase of the Middle Age, decorated
with Italian ornament.

In the third place, having travelled much in Italy,
they knew Petrarch by heart, and helped themselves, no doubt freely, to his material. But Du
Bellay wrote ' contre les Petrarquistes' ; Ronsard
attacked courtiers ' qui n'admirent qu'un petit
sonnet Petrarquisé ' ; and both were justified in this
repudiation. The method of their verse was distinct
from the method of Italian verse, and, passing from
form to matter, they strike a note of plaintive
mystery, which is not to be heard in Petrarch.

In the fourth place, besides this direct influence
from Italy, they receive an indirect influence already
transfigured by the School of Lyons, and notably by
Maurice Scève, whose *Délie* is rather an anagram
of *l'Idée*, the platonic idea of beauty, than a title
borrowed from the Delia whom Tibullus loved.
Lyons, the city of Grolier, was a centre of sensitive
culture where, to quote Brunetière, ' the natural-
ism of Italy had become enriched, perhaps even
a little over-weighted, by a mystical significance.
Platonism, from being a relaxation of the intelligent,
and matter to put into a sonnet, had been there

transmuted into, as it were, an inward religion, secret and passionate, of beauty.'

In the fifth place, they had all the Latin authors at their finger-ends. Yet they knew them for literary echoes, calling Horace ' the Latin Pindar.' To Du Bellay the *Iliad* is ' admirable,' the *Æneid* ' laborious.' But of the Latins they set Virgil on a lonely eminence.

And so, lastly, they deliberately sought their inspiration in the fullest measure from the Greeks. Ronsard tells us that he once shut himself up for three days to read the *Iliad* at a sitting. But since their main intention was lyric, their chief model was Pindar. I can speak of Pindar only at second-hand. Accepting Professor Butcher for my guide, I learn that Pindar made a twofold claim. On the one hand, he claimed constant inspiration, enthusiasm, and something of a divine importance attaching to lyric poetry as such ; on the other, that lyric poets were the trustees and exponents of an intricate traditional artifice with subtle laws which they alone understood and always obeyed. Now that is precisely the double claim put forward by Ronsard.

After Pindar, among Greek sources, the Pléiade drew largely on Theocritus, Callimachus, Lycophron, and generally on the Alexandrine poets who flourished at the court of the Ptolemies. Brunetière insists on this, and approves their choice, since, being absorbed in remaking a language and designing poetical forms, what they needed were ' writing-masters.' In the great edition of Ronsard's works of 1623, a commentator, Marcassus, refers the reader to Lycophron for the elucidation of classical machinery in the very poem from which I quoted the apostrophe to Roland and ' les palladins de France.' That

illustrates the multiplicity of the Pléiade's sources,
and the impartiality with which they tapped them
even for one poem.   They drew also on the Greek
Anthology, republished at Paris in 1551, so that all
the flowers of Meleager passed into their verse ;
and, later, on the Anacreon, published by Estienne
at Paris for the first time in 1554.

If you except the Troubadours, there is scarce a
stream of lyric verse, ancient or modern, which they
did not sedulously conduct into the swollen river
of their song ; and, apart from literary origins, they
laid much else under contribution : the splendour of
courts, the pageant of embassies, the weariness of
exile, the loveliness of women, the glory of gardens
—much, too, which they accepted frankly from wild
Nature, or went curiously to seek even from among
the appliances of industry in towns.

The aim of their art is declared in Du Bellay's
Défense et Illustration, and in Ronsard's prefaces to
his *Odes* and the *Franciade*.

They did not embark on a wanton quest after
novelty.   Rather, they were confronted by two
real difficulties—the poverty of language and the
degradation of poetry—which had to be surmounted
before French could become a medium for modern
literature.   The French language had never been
amplified and elevated to the pitch required for that
purpose.   French poetry had fallen and shrunk
from the state it once held in the hands of Chaucer's
masters.   The Pléiade found a language too scanty
to convey the new features of Renaissance civilisation, and quite unfitted to express conceptions im-
ported from Greek thought.   For that, in its loftier
and more suggestive phases, poetry, the first and last
mode of speech, is needed ; but their native poetry

was worn down to a jingle.   What was to be done ?
The common view among any who saw the difficulty
and sought a solution, seems to have been that
French did well enough for ordinary business and a
good song ; dog-Latin for law and history ; and
that, for higher flights of poetry or philosophy, there
was no expedient save to master and employ the
vocabularies, syntax, and poetic forms of classic
Latin and Greek.

Against this the Pléiade protested. Du Bellay,
in the first book of his manifesto, defends the French
language. All languages, he argues, are, so to say,
' born equal.'   All were made in the same way, for
the same purpose, viz. by the human fancy to interchange the conceptions of the human mind. New
things must always have demanded new words, and
there is no reason why that process should not be
continued.   French is not a barbarous tongue, nor
so poor as many assert.   In so far as it is poor it is
only so because our ancestors, like the early Romans,
were too busy with war to waste time on words.
The right plan is to follow the example set by the
Romans, that is, to enrich our own vocabulary by
acclimatising classic words, and to give it flexibility
and point by imitating classic models.   In his second
book, passing from the poverty of language to the
abasement of poetry, he urges that French poetry
can be lifted from the rut.   The authors of the
Roman de la Rose ought to be read, not for imitation,
but to secure a first image of the French tongue.   Of
recent poets some have done well, and France is
obliged to them.   But much better may be done.   A
natural gift is not enough.   Forasmuch as our court
poets drink, eat, and sleep at their ease, he who
would be read and remembered must endure hunger

and thirst and long watches. These are the wings
on which the writings of men soar up to heaven.
The poet is to avoid copying mere tricks, to develop
his own individuality, and to imitate those of a
kindred genius, otherwise his imitation will resemble
that of a monkey. He is to read Greek and Latin
authors day and night and to forswear ' Rondeaux,
ballades, vyrelaiz . . . et autres telles épiceries.'
Odes are to be written by setting to work as Horace
did, so as to achieve a standard till then unattempted.
Poetry of this kind is to be distinguished from the
vulgar, enriched and illustrated with appropriate
words and carefully chosen epithets, adorned with
solemn sayings, and varied in every way with poetic
colour and decoration.

Epigrams and satires are deprecated. Sonnets,
the learned and pleasant invention of Italy, are
praised. The long poem is to be essayed, but let
the theme be taken from old French romances.
Idleness and luxury have destroyed the desire of
immortality ; but glory is the only ladder upon
whose rungs mortals may with a light step ascend to
heaven and make themselves the companions of the
gods. Use words which are purely French, neither
too common nor too far-fetched, and, if you like,
sometimes annex some antique term and set it, as
it were a precious stone, in your verse. Rhyme
is of the essence of French verse. It must be rich ;
free rather than constrained ; accepted rather than
sought out ; appropriate and natural ; in short, such
that the verse falling on it shall not less content the
ear than music well harmonised when it falls on a
perfect chord. Blank verse is a more doubtful
matter ; but as painters and sculptors use greater
pains to make nude figures of lovely and good

proportion, so must blank verse be athletic and muscular.

He attacks the court versifiers, prays to Apollo that France may engender a poet whose resonant lute shall silence the wheezy bagpipes of the day, and, after exhorting the French to write in their own tongue, concludes with an eulogy of France.

Ronsard repeats much of this thesis in his prefaces. He dwells on the salient paradox that, whilst the French language was still prattling in infancy, French poetry was languishing and grimacing towards death. But he chiefly insists on the necessity of designing varied metres and rhyme-schemes for lyric poetry, attesting—and the duality of his argument is an index to his aim—first, the example of Pindar, and secondly, the diversity of Nature, which exacts an infinite response to her moods.

For the rest, he makes short work of his critics, saying, in the sturdy vernacular which he could ever command for all his artifice: ' If, reader, you are astonished at the sudden changes in my manner of writing, you are to understand that when I have bought my pen, my ink, and my paper, they belong to *me*, and I may honestly do what I please with my own.'

ACHIEVEMENT AND INFLUENCE

There can be no question of the vast material embraced by the Pléiade, and the high aim envisaged in their attempt to renew language and revive lyrics. But two questions obtrude. What did they accomplish ? What influence did they exert ? Again we have diverse judgments. It is for students of the Renaissance, and, not least, for students of our nation, to seek the final decree. We cannot know

French idiomatically and genetically. But we emancipated ourselves, thirty years before they did, from the tame conclusions of academic art, and are by so much the less afraid to reverse the judgments of the seventeenth and eighteenth centuries.

What, then, did the Pléiade effect ? They settled decisively, and long before we did, that the mother-tongues of Northern Europe, and not Greek or Latin, were to be explored for adequate expression, and exploited for the highest flights of poetry. That new words must be found for new things ; that rhyme is at once a necessity for lyrics in modern languages which have no definite quantities, and a treasure added to the economy of classic verse ; that modern poetry, based on the number, and not on the time-value, of syllables in a line, must be contrived in consonance with the ancient songs and genius of European languages, and not in clumsy reproductions of sapphics or alcaics ; that the lyric must be of endless variety to fit the multitudinous response of human emotion to the infinite appeals of sensation and passion. Finding nothing but worn-out *ballades* and *rondeaux*, they revived the freshness, plaintive or gay, of the song, and invented the stately pro-gression of the ode. Ronsard alone, apart from his Pindaric odes, devised sixty-three lyric metres. They decided that beauty is to be frankly enjoyed for its obvious delight, and humbly adored for its inward mystery ; that the poet's calling is an arduous enterprise comparable to the sculptor's ascetic conflict with marble, and never more so than when he sings the pathos of

> Beauty and anguish walking hand in hand
> The downward slope of death.

All this, I believe, and hope to indicate, was an

effective contribution to England as well as to
France.

They reproduced the sonnet on the exact model
of Petrarch in such numbers and with such ease that
it cannot be called an exotic in French, a feat un-
accomplished in England till Rossetti wrote the
House of Life. But, apart from their general contribution to the renaissance of poetry, they settled
some matters particular to French verse, as the
alternation of masculine and feminine rhymes, and
the sovereignty of the Alexandrine. I use the word
settled advisedly, for I am well aware that experiments in these directions had been made by their
immediate predecessors, just as a dozen sonnets,
and no more, had been hazarded before their time.
I know that they reverted from the Alexandrine,
and that they did not invariably observe the rules
which they had practically established. It was the
volume and the general excellence of their verse,
the dash and cogency of their propaganda, which
prevailed. Indeed, by the irony of fate, their fame
was overthrown for two centuries in France, and their
more varied contributions to poetry obscured, just
because they had carried some few metrical reforms
to a point at which these were usurped by Malherbe
and his successors, and emphasised to the desolating
exclusion of all else.

We cannot speak of tracing their influence con-
tinuously in France. It was sharply rejected early
in the seventeenth century, and accepted again with
diffidence only after an interval of two hundred
years. The story is well known. Malherbe (born
1555), who, but for Ronsard, could never have
written his celebrated *Consolation à M. du Périer*,
after erasing half his master's lines, took up his pen

again and, to show the great critic he was, ruled out the rest. The poetry of the Pléiade was no longer read at court, nor at all, save here and there in the houses of country gentlemen, and by an ever-diminishing band of defenders in the university and local parliaments. It slept in dusty volumes on the shelf, as the Elizabethan poetry of England lay dormant for a somewhat shorter period. In 1754 an anonymous author describes La Pléiade as ' les sept Poëtes fameux qu'on ne peut plus lire,' and sets up others in their place. I do not know his name, but—and this pleases me—he dedicates his anthology to an officer in a Royal Household, member of several academies, and ' ancien Capitaine de Dragons.' The Alexandrine verse and ' classic ' couplet reigned supreme through an age of periwigs and powder, following on an age of full-bottomed wigs and clanking dragoons. The lyric was an outcast.

In poetry—as in architecture—the exuberance of a transitional period is pruned down to classic repose, which, in turn, becomes first puristic, and then, in a sequence of degradation, conventional, respectable, dull, and at last downright ugly and repellent. But the hunger for beauty then becomes clamant, and the desire for manifold expression is again begotten by the love of beauty. So you have a romantic revival of unrestrained abundance, taking its good things from wheresoever they can be found.

This happened in 1828. That great critic Sainte-Beuve produced two works : the *Tableau de la Poésie française du XVIe Siècle* and the *Œuvres choisies de Pierre de Ronsard*. They effected a poetic revulsion and mark an epoch. The degenerate classic was arraigned as a ' Roi fainéant,' and the

romantic ruled in his place. The lyric revived.
The metres of Ronsard were resumed and carried
forward to the ' Strophes frissonnantes ' of Victor
Hugo.   The ode, the sonnet, the song, were multiplied ; and song, since then, has never been silenced
in the native land of the Trouvères and Troubadours.
It breaks out repeatedly, and at each new deliverance
with a bolder rejection of conventional tyranny, a
heartier acclamation of Ronsard, Prince des Poètes
Français.   From 1857 his complete works were republished by M. Prosper Blanchemain.   De Banville,
that exquisite conqueror of metrical difficulty, hails
him in one of his own neglected metres—

> O mon Ronsard, O maître
> Victorieux du mêtre,
> O sublime échanson
> De la chanson !

François Coppée is content to be Ronsard's ' humble
and modest apprentice.'   To Émile Deschamps he
is a ' sublime virtuoso, improvising on an imperfect
instrument.'   Albert Glatigny cries out :—

> Dans tes bras je me réfugie,
> Et veux, divine et noble orgie,
>   Être ivre de rimes ce soir.

Sully-Prudhomme, addressing ' le maître des char-
meurs de l'oreille,' says the last word on the loss and
recovery of the lyric—

> Ah ! depuis que les cieux, les champs, les bois et l'onde
> N'avaient plus d'âme, un deuil assombrissait le monde,
> Car le monde sans lyre est comme inhabité !
> Tu viens, tu ressaisis la lyre, tu l'accordes
> Et, fier, tu rajeunis la gloire des sept cordes
> Et tu refais aux Dieux une immortalité.

Ronsard and du Bellay are now called ' les vrais
classiques ' (*La Lignée des Poètes Français au XIXe*

Siècle, 1902). It is enough to make Boileau turn in his grave.

If, however, instead of reading Ronsard's poetry, or the poetry of poets who recrowned him, you turn to any critical history of French literature, you will find praise doled out still somewhat grudgingly. Critics and compilers of literary manuals cannot bring themselves to believe that the conventional judgments of the eighteenth century have been definitely reversed. The mystery of beauty and exuberance of song do not always appeal to them. That is why students of the Renaissance should prosecute individual research.

Ronsard's poetry was neglected partly because of its volume ; mainly because his immediate successors were preoccupied with their own efforts.   But they urged three excuses for their neglect ;—that his verse was overloaded with excerpts from classic myths ; that his diction included words foreign to the genius of French poetry, inasmuch as they were old-fashioned and colloquial, or new-fangled and out-landish ;   that he invented too many caressing diminutives. These pleas were repeated by suc-cessive generations of critics, who, in the absence of reprints, never read Ronsard's poetry for them-selves. They ought now to be re-examined. It may fairly be said that no one of the features arraigned is typical of Ronsard's art, and that, when taken together, they affect but a small proportion of his seventy or eighty thousand lines.   They are accidents of his day and of the conditions under which he wrote ; obvious to the next ensuing age, but not characteristic for all time. We can now estimate their insignificance.

His allusions to classic mythology are but faded

apparel tricking a fair body. We may reflect that novels, the typical product of our own literature, will suffer just such an eclipse as the lyrics of the sixteenth century. They, too, are voluminous. Their enthusiastic references to an Age of Invention, to railways and motor cars, will some day seem no less superfluous than Renaissance references to an Age of Learning, to Apollo and the muses. Yet things of beauty outlast their contemporary trappings ; and even these—at first a zest, then a bore— become in the end a curiosity, not without charm. The mythology of Ronsard, though faded, has a vague decorative value, as of old tapestry.

Turning to strictures on Ronsard's diction : it is true that he preserved some mediæval terms. ' Spenser in affecting the ancients writ no language,' was Ben Jonson's condemnation of a like accident in the *Faery Queen*. Censure of that kind is the ' common form ' of seventeenth-century criticism on sixteenth-century romance, and should carry but little weight with us who live after the romantic revival. It is true, again, that Ronsard did not reject homely words from high-flown periods. He writes of ' chemises ' and ' chandelles '; things abhorrent to the fastidious pomp of ' Le Roi Soleil,' whose court poets found nothing amiss in a Ramillies wig on the head of a Greek god. L'Abbé de Marolles, in 1675, writes—of a rose !—

> Au moment que j'en parle, on voit que sa *perruque*
> Tombe en s'élargissant, qu'elle devient caduque.

A wig could never be out of place in the eyes of Ronsard's detractors. But candles were too common. The compatriots of Shakespeare who read, with no shock but of joy,—

Though not so bright
As those gold candles fix'd in heaven's air—

need not boggle at Ronsard's ' chandelles.' So, too,
with some of his neologisms ; in our ignorance as
foreigners we may even regret that his ' myrteux '
and ' frétillard ' are obsolete in French.

As for his diminutives, I deny that Ronsard invented them. He took them from old French songs.
In these, the pensive lover ' par ung matinet,' in
the shadow of a ' buyssonnet' is left ' tout seullet'
by ' le doux roussignolet ' (*Chansons du XVe Siècle*,
Gaston Paris). Jehannot de Lescurel (*French
Lyrics*, Saintsbury) has ' doucette, savoureusette,
joliette, bellette, jeunette,' and so on, with a relish-
ing frequency to which Ronsard never approached.
Mythological machinery—archaisms, colloquialisms,
neologisms—caressing diminutives these—were but
trivial excrescences on a rich style ; in its staple
ever fresh and forthright, striking, and sonorous.
Ronsard's immediate successors, who kicked at his
renown, paraded these excrescences to justify their
apostasy, and then annexed his goods under cover of
the derision they had provoked. They ignored the
true characteristics of his art ; but they did not
neglect them. Disguising their debt, they took all
they could carry ; and that was enough to furnish
their stock-in-trade. Excepting the Drama, every
mode of poetic expression exhibited by French
' classic ' authors is, in so far as form is concerned,
to be found in Ronsard, with much else of value
which they did not appraise. The French ' classic '
was disengaged from the labyrinth of the Pléiade's
production. According to Brunetière, Ronsard's
sentiment for the harmonies of the French language
has never been equalled. He invented, or brought

G

into favour, all the combinations of rhythms and
metres of which French is capable. All his inventions have not been adopted, but no new ones
have been made. He determined the essential types
of French lyrics, and fixed the model not only of the
Classic, but even of the Romantic ode. His *Discours*
gave eloquence a place for ever in French poetry.
These were his lasting contributions to art, and the
wealth of them has not, even now, been exhausted.

The Pléiade called into being a paradise, almost a
wilderness of beauty; florid,—I cannot deny it,—intricate and luxuriant in its growth, flaunting its profusion, mad as midsummer is mad : and in the midst
they planted a tree of knowledge. Their successors,
having tasted of that tree, set to work with axe and
bill on the wilderness, lopping it into a formal garden
and, at last, turning it into a public place. Their
rules, as Mallarmé suggests, will enable anybody to
make, with certainty, a verse to which nobody can
object. But that savours of deportment rather than
of poesy. It enjoins a sacrifice of distinction to
avoid a charge of eccentricity ; an admirable maxim
for any who pursue a respectable calling along
a crowded thoroughfare, for the genteel mob of
eighteenth-century couplet-mongers, but a useless
counsel and, so, an impertinence to the leader of a
revel or a forlorn hope. The poets of the French
romantic revival were leaders in both capacities, and
they threw these restraints to the winds. They took
Ronsard for their Bible, and, as Théophile Gautier
puts it, ' burned to go forth and combat *l'hydre
du Perruquinisme.*' The ' wiggery '—the pomp and
punctilio—of ' classic ' artifice are now being relin-
quished, though reluctantly, and, so to say, against the
grain, by the wooden compilers of literary manuals.

Thus it stands with the Pléiade's influence on the French language and French poetry. I have but one other question to propound. What effect did the Pléiade work, by example or precept, on the remaking of the English language and of English poetry ? What degree of influence did they exert on our own Elizabethan revival ? The judgment has stood that their influence was of the slightest ; but I ask for a stay of execution and more evidence. Is it certain that our late sixteenth-century poets drew so much of their inspiration from Italy, and so little of it from France ? Mr. Sidney Lee (*Elizabethan Sonnets*, 1904) has impugned, has, indeed, traversed that judgment. He based his finding on the materials conveniently collected by Edward Arber in his invaluable reprints. These should be examined more exhaustively with a less exclusive attention to the sonnet : and who will say that MSS., and odd volumes in old libraries, which only in 1895 rendered up four lost pearls of Thomas Watson's poetry, do not entice to many another ' adventure of the diver ' ?

The argument may be stated thus : Italian models had been extant since Petrarch, who lived far into the life of Chaucer. Wyat and Surrey, who turned to these Italian models in the earlier years of the sixteenth century, failed to assimilate them, and did little in the way either of remaking the English language or reviving lyrics. The poets who effected these objects for England, as the Pléiade had effected them for France, praised and dismissed Surrey and Wyat, the ' courtly makers,' just as Ronsard had bowed out his precursors of François i.'s court. But they were familiar alike with the Pléiade's practice and with their preaching. They proceeded

to the study of Italian from a knowledge of French,
and received Italian poetry through the medium of
French art. Thus transmuted it could be assimilated,
and this was done by English poets, who echo the
music of the Pléiade's verse and repeat its critical
conclusions in literary manifestoes.

Take the condition of English lyrics during the
last ten years of Henri II.'s reign, the glittering and
august decade of the Pléiade in its prime, which
it fulfilled with infinitely varied lyric forms;
with thousands of sonnets easily written on the
Petrarchan model; and — let it be noted — with
critical manifestoes of sedulous ingenuity. What
had we then in England ? *Tottel's Miscellany* of
1557. Will any one contend that even the verse of
Surrey and Wyat, great though its merit be, is comparable in volume, variety, clarity, and assurance to
the verse of the Pléiade ? No ; Surrey and Wyat
grope after Italian models which could not be wholly
assimilated even by them. The other authors included in that collection are mostly—except Lord
Vaux—reminiscent of country catches and the
'canter canter' of fourteen-syllabled lines. Our
lyrics, stately or melodious, come much later. But
Tottel's Miscellany, Douglas's *Virgil* (1553), Drant's
Horace (1566), Turberville's *Ovid* (1569), reprints
even of *Piers the Plowman's Vision* (1551, 1561),
archaic alike in language and poetic form, comprise,
with the racy doggerel of Skelton and the somno-
lences of Stephen Hawes, all the recent English verse
which Spenser had to read as a boy. Spenser was
born in 1552. It is not, therefore, strange, but it
is significant, to find Spenser in 1569, aged seventeen,
translating Du Bellay's *Vision*.

Take, again, the Epistle prefixed to Spenser's early

anonymous work, *The Shepherd's Calendar* (1579), dedicated to Sir Philip Sidney. It refers, after naming Marot and Sanazarius, to ' *divers* other excellent both Italian and French poets whose footing this authour '—*i.e.* Spenser—' everywhere followeth : yet so as few, but they be well scented, can trace him out.' It does not, however, demand a very keen nose to retrace the *footing* of such a stanza as :—

> Bring hither the pink and purple columbine
> > With gelliflowers ;
> Bring sweet carnations and sops-in-wine,
> > Worn of paramours ;
> Strew me the ground with daffadowndillies,
> With cowslips, and king-cups and loved lilies.
> > The pretty paunce
> > And the chevisaunce
> Shall watch with the fair fleur-de-lice.

That, with its intricate metre, quickly recurrent rhyme, and profusion of flowers, is redolent of the land of the *fleur de lis*, and imprinted by the metrical footing of the Pléiade.

Even so late as in 1591, Spenser, at the age of thirty-nine, translates Du Bellay's *Antiquitez de Rome*, concluding with an envoy to

> Bellay, first garland of *free* Poesie,

in which Spenser declares the French poet's immortality, and awards him a fame ' exceeding all that ever went before.'

Thomas Watson, a contemporary of Spenser and Sidney, may be named with them as a literary renovator of lyrics. He acclaims Spenser :—

> Thou art Apollo, whose sweet hunnie vaine
> Amongst the muses hath the chiefest place.

He sojourned in Paris with Sir Francis Walsingham, Sidney's father-in-law. In his *Eclogue* Sidney is 'Astrophill,' Francis Walsingham 'Melibœus,' and Thomas Walsingham 'Tityrus,' who is made to say of the author, 'Corydon':—

> Thy tunes have often pleas'd mine eare of yoare,
>> When milk-white swans did flocke to heare thee sing,
> Where *Seane* in *Paris* makes a double shoare,
>> *Paris* thrise blest if shee obey her king.

Watson was familiar with the verse of Ronsard, the French king's reigning poet. He declares the use which he made of it in prose prefaces to certain numbers of his Ἑκατομπαθία, *or Passionate Centurie of Loue* (1582), *e.g.* in the preface to xxvii. 'In the first sixe verses of this Passion, the author hath imitated perfectly sixe verses in an ode of *Ronsard*, which beginneth thus: "Celui qui n'ayme est malheureux"; and in the last staffe of this Passion also he commeth very neere to the sense, which *Ronsard* useth in another place, where he writeth to his *Mistresse* in this manner: "En veus tu baiser Pluton,"' etc. He makes similar ascriptions of the numbers xxviii. liv. and lxxxiii. In some Latin verses prefixed to Watson's work by C. Downhalus we read:—

> Gallica Parnasso cœpit ditescere lingua,
> Ronsardique operis Luxuriare novis.

Turning now to Sir Philip Sidney—'The reviver of Poetry in those darke times' (Aubrey's *Brief Lives*)—let us take, as a test, the Alexandrine verse of twelve syllables, a metre peculiarly French, revived by Ronsard from a French trouvère to be the classic metre of France. In 1591, the year of Spenser's envoy to Du Bellay, Sir Philip Sidney,

Spenser's friend and comrade in lyric experiments, published *Astrophel and Stella*. The first sonnet is written in Alexandrine verse. But his very repudiation—in the third sonnet—of Pindar's apes who flaunt

in phrases fine,
Enamelling with pied flowers their thoughts of gold,

is obviously directed at the Pléiade, but only, I would urge, as a rhetorical development of the first sonnet, written in their metre, which ends :—

'Foole,' said my Muse to me, 'looke in thy heart and write.'

When addressing the Lady Penelope, as a lover, Sidney puts aside his literary masters, the more simply to adore her. But when treating of poetry, as a critic, he reveals those masters to be none other than the Pléiade, the apes of Pindar, who filled with their fame the court to which he had been accredited. Sidney had travelled in Italy. But in 1572 he was Gentleman of the Chamber to Charles IX., the king, patron, and intimate friend of Ronsard, whom his sovereign once invited, perhaps in the presence of Sidney, to sit beside him on his royal throne.

Of these three deliberate renovators Mr. Sidney Lee has written :—' It is clear that it was through the study of French that Spenser passed to the study of Italian. . . . Spenser had clearly immersed his thought in French poetry ' ; ' Sidney's masters were Petrarch and Ronsard ' ; and, again, ' Sidney and Watson both came under the impressive influence of Ronsard.' So much for these, but the majority of Elizabethan sonneteers concentrated their attention on contemporary France, and derived their knowledge of Italian work from adaptations by Ronsard and Desportes. Mr. Lee prints five

sonnets of Daniel side by side with their originals by
Desportes, and six sonnets of Lodge side by side
with their originals by Ronsard. He has shown
Chapman's ' Amorous Zodiacke ' to be but a close
and clumsy translation from Gilles Durant. Mr.
Kastner proves Constable's debt to Desportes, and,
since the Pléiade's influence extended to Scotland,
traces seven sonnets of Montgomery to Ronsard.
Drummond of Hawthornden, who studied Ronsard,
Muret, and Pontus de Tyard, did not neglect French
translations of Ariosto, Tasso, and Sanazzaro.

But there is a more subtle debt due from our
Elizabethans to the Pléiade which, though harder
to prove with precision, is yet sensible. Apart from
actual translation, and outside the sonnet-form, we
can—as in the stanza quoted from Spenser—hear
a haunting echo of the Pléiade's music, and see the
very facture which distinguished their lyrics by its
maze of varied metre and richly recurrent rhyme.
This can be detected most readily in those English
authors who set themselves deliberately, and with
ostentation, to the task of constructing lyrics and
vindicating rhyme. Daniel's *Delia* may take its
title from Maurice Scève's *Délie,* but its inspiration
comes certainly from Ronsard.

> When winter snows upon thy sable hairs
>   And frost of age hath nipt thy beauties near ;
> When dark shall seem the day that never clears,
>   And all lies wither'd that was held so dear—

is pure Ronsard. Even when Daniel translates,
openly, from *Marino,* he does it to the lilt and colour
of Ronsard's music—

> Fair is the Lily ; fair
>   The Rose ; of Flowers the eye !
> Both wither in the air,

> Their beauteous colours die ;
> And so at length shall lie,
> Deprived of former grace,
> The Lilies of thy Breasts, the Roses of thy Face.

Daniel's allusion to ' Tyber, Arne, and Po,' the rivers of Italy, is often cited ; but without the further reference to ' Loyre and Rhodanus,' the rivers of the Pléiade. Yet he drank deeply from those streams. Or take Herrick, a graduate of Cambridge, where, I have seen it stated, Ronsard's poetry was studied. Read Ronsard and then listen to—

> W'ave seen the past-best Times, and these
> Will nere return, we see the Seas,
> And Moons to wain ;
> But they fill up their Ebbs again :
> But vanisht, man,
> Like to a Lilly-lost, nere can,
> Nere can repullulate, or bring
> His dayes to see a second Spring
>
> .   .   .   .   .   .
>
> Crown we our Heads with Roses then,
> And 'noint with *Tirian Balme* ; for when
> We two are dead
> The World with us is burièd . . .

or listen to—

> Then cause we *Horace* to be read
> Which sang, or seyd,
> A Goblet, to the brim,
> Of Lyrick Wine both swell'd and crown'd
> A Round
> We quaffe to him.

Herrick, I doubt not, had read Anacreon in Greek : but the Pléiade was the first to translate Anacreon into modern verse, and, what is more, to write anacreontics on a model that could be, and was, easily reproduced in English. Herrick writes *Charon and Phylomel, a Dialogue Sung*. But Olivier de Magny had written a dialogue between a lover and

Charon, long a favourite piece at the French court,
which, Colletet tells us, had been set to music by the
most skilful composers.   The coincidence can hardly
be accidental.

Or, take this track : Du Bellay writes in the metre
of *In Memoriam* ; so does Théophile, the last disciple
of the Pléiade school, unjustly gibbeted by Boileau—

> Dans ce val solitaire et sombre
> Le cerf, qui brame au bruit de l'eau
> Penchant ses yeux dans un ruisseau,
> S'amuse à regarder son ombre—

so does Ben Jonson ; and you have but to glance at
Ben Jonson's lines—

> Though Beauty be the mark of praise
> And yours, of whom I sing, be such,
> As not the world can praise too much,
> Yet 'tis your virtue now I raise—

to guess the, perhaps unconscious, origin of Tennyson's melody.   Ben Jonson, in his Pindaric ode,
improves on Ronsard.   But Ronsard first attempted
a modern reproduction of strophe, antistrophe, and
epode ; and Ben Jonson follows closely in his steps.
Perhaps the most provoking, and yet elusive, echo
rings throughout Wither's *Fair Virtue, The Mistress
of Philarete.*   Compare the *Picture of Fair Virtue*
for the sense to Ronsard's elegy to Janet, the court
painter, and for both sense and rhythm to the twelfth
ode in his fifth book—

> Through the Veins disposèd true
> Crimson yields a sapphire hue,
> Which adds grace and more delight
> By embracing with the white.
> Smooth, and moist, and soft, and tender
> Are the Palms ! the Fingers, slender
> Tipt with mollified pearl :—

Doights qui de beauté vaincus
Ne sont de ceux de Bacchus,
Tant leurs branchettes sont pleines
De mille rameuses veines
Par où coule le beau sang
Dedans leur yvoire blanc,
Yvoire où sont cinq perlettes
Luisantes, claires et nettes,

and on, and on, in a running rivulet of seven-syllabled
verse ; a metre rarely handled with success in
English, but inimitably rendered by Wither to the
very tune of Ronsard.

There is a case for the influence of the Pléiade
on the practice of our Elizabethans and their successors. But practice is not all. The Elizabethans
preached as the Pléiade had preached. The outburst of Elizabethan lyrics came some forty years
after the Pléiade's decade of tumultuous production
(1549-1559), and, precisely as with them, was accompanied by manifestoes on the defects of the
vernacular and the methods of exalting poetry, in
that medium, to the height which it held in Greece
and Rome. The identity of the problems confronting the Elizabethans with the problems solved by
the Pléiade is apparent from Elizabethan criticism of
language and verse. Just as in France a generation
earlier, so then in England, while some were content
with archaic rhythms, others declared that poetry
must be written in classic languages ; and yet others
that, though written in English, it must be crushed,
without rhyme, into the moulds of classic metres.
William Webbe's *A Discourse of English Poetrie*
(1586) shows the extent of the peril to which our
lyrics were exposed. He writes of ' This brutish
Poetrie . . . I mean this tynkerly verse which we
call ryme.' But we must not condemn his error too

harshly.   The fact that he fell into it illustrates the
reality of the difficulty with which the Elizabethans
had to deal ; a difficulty which would not have
existed had Surrey and Wyat, by imitating Italian
models, effected a new departure which could
be followed up.   Indeed, the contrast between the
rhyme-doggerel that prevailed and classic masterpieces, familiar to scholars, goes far to explain his
mistake.   For that contrast was sharply projected
from current translations of the classics into what
passed for English verse.   What could a scholar and
lover of poetry make of Turberville's *Ovid* (1569)?

Penelope opens her Epistle to Ulysses in this
strain :—

> To thee that lingrest all too long
> Thy wyfe (Ulysses) sendes :
> Gayne write not but by quick returne,
> For absence make amendes . . .

and concludes :—

> And I that at thy parture was
> A Gyrle to beholde :
> Of truth am warte a Matrone now,
> Thy selfe will iudge mee olde.

It needs no Holophernes to pronounce, ' For the
elegancy, facility, and golden cadence of poetry,
caret.'   Webbe despaired of such an engine.   He
catches, for a moment, a gleam of the true dawn
from the *Shepheardes Calender*, whose anonymous
author—Spenser—he calls ' the rightest English poet
that ever I read.'   Yet he is not satisfied with
Spenser's muse.   On the contrary, he proceeds to
show how Hobinol's ditty may be civilised by casting
it into ' the Saphick verse '; and this is' what he
makes of the stanza already quoted, which begins

> Bring hither the pink and purple columbine :—

Bring the Pinckes, therewith many Gelliflowers sweete,
And the Cullambynes : let us have the Wynesops,
With the Cornation that among the love laddes
    Wontes to be worne much.

Daffadowndillies all a long the ground strewe,
And the Cowslyppe with a pretty paunce let heere lye.
Kingcuppe and Lillies so belovde of all men,
    And the deluce flowre.

That is where we were in 1586, a generation after
the Pléiade—two generations after Surrey and Wyat
—two hundred years after Chaucer. Webbe per-
petrates this ' Saphick ' outrage *seriatim* on twelve of
Spenser's thirteen stanzas, but, ' by reason of some
let,' defers execution on the last, ' to some other
time, when I hope to gratify the readers with more
and better verses of this sorte.' English poetry
was rescued from such torture by literary renovators
who had studied the Pléiade. The darkness, made
visible by Webbe's lucubration, was illumined with
rays reflected from France. We have *The Arte of
English Poesie*, ascribed to Puttenham, published
in 1589 ; and *An Apologie for Poetrie* by Sir Philip
Sidney, published in 1595, though circulated, unknown to Webbe, in MS., since 1582 (?).

Their manifestoes exhibit two interesting features.
In the first place, they grapple with exactly those
problems which the Pléiade had done much to solve,
and arrive at the same solutions. In the second
place, they disclose an intimate acquaintance with
the rules and genius of the new French poetry which
the Pléiade had created. The Elizabethan essayists
in their turn sought also to renew language and con-
struct lyric metres. For such enterprises the Italians
offered no adequate model. They either wrote, often
very well, in Latin, or else were content to follow

the *lingua toscana* of Dante and the poetic forms of Petrarch.   Their work was beside the mark at which the English renovators aimed.

Sidney, in his *Apologie*, like the Pléiade, finds our mediæval verse ' apparelled in the dust and cob-webs of an uncivil age,' and, like the Pléiade, asks, ' What would it work if trimmed in the gorgeous eloquence of Pindar?'   Apart from this aspiration he is evidently at home in the language on which the Pléiade had laboured, and well aware that it approached more nearly than Italian to English as a medium for modern verse.

He dwells on rhymes ' by the French named masculine and feminine,' claiming a like, indeed a greater, variety for English, and denying it alto-gether to Italian.   He points out that the French have ' the cæsura, or breathing-place, in the middest of the verse,' and that we almost unfailingly observe the same rule, which is unknown to the Italian or Spaniard.   And so, too, with Puttenham. Puttenham, indeed, trounces an English translator for conveying too crudely ' the hymnes of Pyndarus, Anacreon's odes, and other lirickes among the Greeks, very well translated by Rounsard, the French Poet, and applied to the honour of a great Prince in France.'   He objects to the use of French words—*freddon, egar,* etc.—' which have no maner of conformitie with our language.'   But his theories are largely the theories of the Pléiade, and he evinces a peculiar knowledge of their art.   He writes, ' this metre of twelve sillables the French man calleth a verse Alexandrine, and is with our modern rimers most usuall.'   If that was true in 1589, it follows that much English verse has been lost which was modelled on Ronsard's metre.

Puttenham and Sidney were fighting in the 'eighties' of the sixteenth century the battle for the vernacular and modern rhyme which the Pléiade had won in the 'forties.' They use the Pléiade's weapons, which were not to be found in any Italian armoury. And their victory was not assured till Daniel, steeped, above others, in the influence of Ronsard, published his *Defence of Rhime* (1603). That defence fitly concludes the contest for rhyme in English lyrics. The attack, renewed by Milton (1669), on *The Invention of a Barbarous Age* is irrelevant to the issue, and cannot touch Daniel's glorious declaration of the conservative principle underlying all sound progress in the arts: 'It is but a fantastike giddiness to forsake the waye of other men, especially where it lyes tolerable. But shall wee not tend to Perfection ? Yes, and that ever best by going on in the course wee are in, where we have advantage, being so far onward of him that is but now setting forth. For wee shall never proceede, if we bee ever beginning, nor arrive at any certaine Porte, sayling with all windes that blow.'

I have but sketched the outlines of an inquiry which, if prosecuted, may prove that the Pléiade exerted a more active influence on our Elizabethan revival than most of us have hitherto supposed. I believe it was great. The libraries at Petworth and Hatfield suggest the closeness of the literary connection between France and England during the years in which Queen Elizabeth could neither make up her mind to marry the French king's brother, nor to accept his sister-in-law as her successor to the throne. Even the *Cortegiano* of Castiglione, the stock example of Italian influence, was printed by

Wolfe (1588) in three parallel columns—*Italiano*,
François, 𝕰𝖓𝖌𝖑𝖎𝖘𝖍; thus attesting the mediating
influence of French literature at a time when the
Pléiade were the arbiters of its elegance. But,
whether the influence of the Pléiade on our Elizabethans was great or slight, we may, as students
of the Renaissance, ponder the parallel between the
neglect which both endured for so long, and rejoice
at the reparation at last accorded to each by their
countrymen in France, as in England. You may
cavil at that phrase. But there can be no greater
reparation than to accept gifts long proffered and
long neglected, simply and gladly ; gladly, because
they are good—simply, because they are needed.
The lyric gifts of the Elizabethans and the Pléiade
were sorely needed when a Coleridge or a Keats in
England, a Gautier or a Hugo in France said, ' There
they were,' and sang, ' Here they are ! '

The eighteenth century, for all its intellectual
turmoil, in the end produced, like a volcano, but a
thin conclusion of air-blown ashes. The need for
some inward, unseizable satisfaction grew desperate.
Mankind ranged over arid wastes of thought and
action, snatching, like hunger-stricken herds, at
morality, philosophy, revolution, war. But inanity
gnawed at their vitals. The mind of man demands
for its well-being a triple diet of the True, the Good,
the Beautiful, and is famished in plenty if stinted
of but one element in its celestial food. Beauty had
departed as the cult of beauty by the arts declined
from the classic, through the conventional, to the
repellent. Then came revolt. Poets, who are
priests of Beauty, restored the liturgy of song by
retrieving these lost canticles of delight in loveliness.

Reparation was made to the Elizabethans and to the Pléiade by their compatriots.

Non fallunt futura merentem.

Can we make that reparation international ? If the dynastic wars of the fourteenth century and the sectarian diplomacy of the sixteenth century sent Chaucer and Sidney to school in France, may not the democratic understanding embraced in the twentieth century by the two Western Nations lead to a yet larger traffic between their several possessions in ' the realms of Gold ' ?   Let us celebrate our friendship with France by annexing her lyric heritage, and courting 'reprisals on our own. The moment is propitious.   It prompts a renewal of that contact with contemporary endeavour, coupled with a reversion to past achievement, which precipitated the Renaissance.   Let this be done.   Then the poets of the two lands, endowed with the most ancient and glorious traditions of song, may raise again their Hymns to Divine Beauty in conscious antiphonies from either shore.

NORTH'S PLUTARCH

NORTH'S PLUTARCH

I

PLUTARCH was born at the little Theban town of Chæronea, somewhere about 50 A.D. The date of his birth marks no epoch in history ; and the place of it, even then, was remembered only as the field of three bygone battles. The name Chæronea, cropping up in conversation at Rome, for the birthplace of a distinguished Greek lecturer, must have sounded strangely familiar in the ears of the educated Romans whom he taught, even as the name of Dreux, or of Tewkesbury, sounds strangely familiar in our own. But apart from such chance encounters, few can have been aware of its municipal existence; and this same contrast, between the importance and the renown of Plutarch's birthplace, held in the case of his country also. The Bœotian plain—once ' the scaffold of Mars where he held his games ' [1]—was but a lonely sheepwalk ; even as all Greece, once a Europe of several States, was but one, and perhaps the poorest, among the many provinces of the Empire. Born at such a time and in such a place, Plutarch was still a patriot, a student of politics and a scholar, and was therefore bound by every tie of sentiment and learning to the ancient memories of his native land. Sometimes he brooded over her

---

[1] Ἄρεως ὀρχήστραν. (*Marcellus*, 21.) This contrast has been noted by R. C. Trench, D.D., in his *Plutarch*. *Five Lectures*, 1874. An admirable volume full of suggestion.

altered fortunes. Bœotia ' heretofore of old time
resounded and rung again with Oracles ' ; but now
all the land that from sea to sea had echoed the
clash of arms and the cadence of oratory was ' mute
or altogether desolate and forlorn ' : . . . ' hardly
able ' he goes on, '. to make three thousand men for
the wars, which are now no more in number than
one city in times past, to wit : Megara, set forth and
sent to the battle of Platæa.' [1]   At Athens, though
Sulla had long since cut down the woods of the
Academy, there were still philosophers ; and there
were merchants again at Corinth, rebuilded by Julius
Cæsar. But Athens, even, and a century before,
could furnish only three ships for the succour of
Pompey ; while elsewhere, the cities of Greece had
dwindled to villages, and the villages had vanished.
' The stately and sumptuous buildings which Pericles
made to be built in the cittie of Athens ' were still
standing after four hundred years, untouched by
Time, but they were the sole remaining evidence of
dignity. So that Plutarch, when he set himself to
write of Greek worthies, found his material selected
to his hand. Greek rhetoricians, himself among
them, might lecture in every city of the South ; but
of Greek soldiers and statesmen there was not one in
a land left empty and silent, save for the statues of
gods and the renown of great men. The cradle of
war and statecraft was become a memory dear to
him, and ever evoked by his personal contact with
the triumphs of Rome. From this contrast flowed
his inspiration for the *Parallel Lives* : his desire, as
a man, to draw the noble Grecians, long since dead,

---

[1] *Plutarch's Morals.* Philemon Holland, 1657, p. 1078, in a letter
addressed to Terentius Priscus, ' On oracles that have ceased to give
answers.'

a little nearer to the noonday of the living ; his
delight, as an artist, in setting the noble Romans
whose names were in every mouth, a little further
into the twilight of a more ancient romance. By
placing them side by side, he gave back to the
Greeks that touch which they had lost with the living
in the death of Greece, and to the Romans that
distinction from everyday life which they were fast
beginning to lose. Then and ever since, an imaginative effort was needed to restore to Greece those
trivialities of daily life which, in other countries,
an imaginative effort is needed to destroy ; and
hence her hold on the imagination of every age.
Plutarch, considering his country, found her a
solitude. Yet for him the desert air was vibrant
with a rumour of the mighty dead. Their memories
loomed heroic and tremendous through the dimness
of the past ; and he carried them with him when he
went to Rome, partly on a political errand, and partly
to deliver Greek lectures.

In Juvenal's ' Greek city ' he needed, and indeed
he had, small Latin. ' I had no leisure to study and
exercise the Latin tongue, as well for the great business I had then to do, as also to satisfy them that
came to learn philosophy of me ' : thus, looking
back from Chæronea, does he write in his preface to
the *Demosthenes and Cicero*, adding that he ' understood not matters so much by words, as he came to
understand words by common experience and knowledge he had in things.' We gather that he wrote
many, if not all, of the *Lives* at his birthplace, the
' poor little town ' to which he returned : ' remaining
there willingly lest it should become less.' But it
was in Flavian Rome, in the ' great and famous city
thoroughly inhabited ' and containing ' plenty of all

sort of books,' that, 'having taken upon him to write
a history into which he must thrust many strange
things unknown to his country,' he gathered his
materials ' out of divers books and authorities,' or
picked them up, as a part of ' common experience
and knowledge,' in familiar converse with the
cultured of his day.   I have quoted thus, for the
light the passage throws on the nature of his re-
searches in Rome, although the word ' history ' may
mislead.   For his purpose was not to write histories,
even of individuals.   He tells us so himself.   ' I will
only desire the reader,' he writes in his preface to the
Alexander and Cæsar, ' not to blame me though I do
not declare all things at large . . . for they must
remember that my intent is not to write histories but
only lives.   For the noblest deeds,' he goes on, ' do
not always shew man's virtues and vices, but oftentimes a light occasion, a word, or some sport makes
men's natural dispositions and manners appear
more plainly than the famous battles won, wherein
are slain ten thousand men.'   'As painters do take
the resemblance of the face and favour of the
countenance,' making ' no accompt of other parts of
the body,' so he, too, asks for ' leave to seek out the
signs and tokens of the mind only.'   That was his
ambition : to paint a gallery of portraits ; to focus
his vision on the spiritual face of his every subject,
and for every Greek to hang a Roman at his side.
To compass it he set himself deliberately, as an
artist, unconscious of any intention other than the
choice of good subjects and, his choice once made,
the rejection from each of all but the particular and
the significant.   He stood before men's souls to
study ' the singularity each possessed,'[1] as Velasquez

[1] *Paulus Æmilius.*

in a later age before men's bodies; and, even as his
method was allied, so was his measure of accomplishment not less.

But the *Parallel Lives* shows something different
from this purpose, is something more than a gallery
of portraits hung in pairs. Plutarch stands by his
profession. His immediate concern is with neither
history nor politics, but with the ' disposition and
manners ' of the great. He chooses his man, and
then he paints his picture, with a master's choice
of the essential. And yet, inasmuch as he chooses
every subject as a matter of course on political
grounds—as he sees all men in the State—it follows
that his gallery is found, for all his avowed intention,
to consist of political portraits alone. Thirteen,
indeed, of his sitters belong not only to history but
also to one chapter of history—a chapter short,
dramatic, bloody, and distinctly political. This was
the chance. When Plutarch, the lecturer, dropped
into Roman society fresh from the contemplation of
Greece ' depopulate and dispeopled,' he found its
members spending their ample leisure in academic
debate. After more than a hundred years they were
still discussing the protagonists in that greatest of
political dramas which, ' for a sumptuous conclusion
to a stately tragedy,' had ushered in the empire of
the world. Predisposed by contrast of origin and
affinity of taste, he threw himself keenly into their
pastime, and he gives, by the way, some minute
references to points at issue. For instance, when
Pompey and the Senate had deserted Italy at Cæsar's
approach, a stern-chase of ships and swords had
swept round three continents, and thereon had
followed a campaign of words and pens at Rome.
In that campaign the chief attack and reply had been

Cicero's *Cato* and Cæsar's *Anticaton*; and these, he
tells us,[1] had 'favourers unto his day, some defending the one for the love they bare Cæsar, and others
allowing the other for Cato's sake.' We gather
that he and his Roman friends argued of these
matters over the dinner-table and in the lecture-
halls, even as men argue to-day of the actors in the
French Revolution. Now, to glance at the 'Table
of the Noble Grecians and Romanes' is to see how
profoundly this atmosphere affected his selection of
Roman lives. For, excluding the legendary founders
and defenders, with the Emperors Galba and Otho
(whose lives are interpolations from elsewhere), we
find that thirteen of the nineteen left were party
chiefs in the constitutional struggles which ended
on the fields of Pharsalia and Philippi. The effect on
the general cast of the *Lives* has been so momentous
that a whole quarter covers only the political action
which these thirteen politicians crowded into less
than one hundred years. The society of idlers,
which received Plutarch at Rome, was still debating
the ideals for which these thirteen men had fought
and died; it was therefore inevitable that, in seeking
for foreign parallels, he should have found almost as
many as he needed among the actors in that single
drama. As it was, he chose for his greater portraitures all the chief actors, and a whole army of
subsidiary characters for his groups in the middle
distance: as Saturninus and Cinna from one act,
Clodius and Curio from another. Nothing is wanting.
You have the prologue of the Gracchi, the epilogue of
Antony, and between the play from the triumph of
Marius to Brutus in his despair: 'looking up to the
firmament that was full of stars,' and 'sighing' over

[1] *Cæsar.*

a cause lost for ever. And yet it remains true that Plutarch did not make this selection from—or rather this clean sweep of—the politicians of a certain epoch in order to illustrate that epoch's history, still less to criticise any theory of constitutional government. The remaining Romans, howbeit engaged in several issues, and the Greeks, though gathered from many ages and many cities, are all politicians, or, being orators and captains, are still in the same way chosen each for his influence on the fortunes of a State. But they were not consciously chosen to illustrate history or to discuss politics. Thanks, not to a point of view peculiar to Plutarch but to an instinct pervading the world in which he lived, to a prepossession then so universal •that he is never conscious of its influence on his aim, they are all public men. For himself, he was painting individual character ; and he sought it among men bearing a personal stamp. But he never sought it in a private person or a comedian ; nor even in a poet or a master of the Fine Arts. To look for distinction in such a quarter never occurred to him ; could never, I may say, have entered his head. He cannot conceive that any young ' gentleman nobly born ' should so much as wish to be Phidias or Polycletus or Anacreon ; [1] and this from no vulgar contempt for the making of beautiful things, nor any mean reverence for noble birth, but because, over and above the making of beautiful things, there are deeds that are better worth the doing, and because men of noble birth are freer than others to choose what deeds they will set themselves to do. Why, then, he seems to ask, should they seek any service less noble than the service of their countrymen ? why pursue any

---

[1] Preface to *Pericles*.

ambition less exalted than the salvation of their
State ?   For his part, he will prefer Lycurgus before
Plato ; for, while the one ' stablished and left behind
him ' a constitution, the other left behind him only
' words and written books.' [1] His preference seems
a strange one now ; but it deserves to be noted the
more nearly for its strangeness.   At any rate, it was
the preference of a patriot and a republican, whose
country had sunk to a simple province under an alien
emperor,`and it governed the whole range of Plu-
tarch's choice.

   This result has been rendered the more conspicuous by another cause, springing at first from an
accident, but in its application influenced by the
political quality of Plutarch's material.   Lost sight
of and scattered in the Dark Ages, the Parallel Lives
were recovered and rearranged at the revival of
learning.   But just as a gallery of historical portraits, being dispersed and re-collected, will in all
probability be hung after some chronological scheme,
so have the lives been shuffled anew under the influence of their political extraction, in such a sort
as to change not only the complexion but also the
structure of Plutarch's design.   They form no longer
a gallery of political portraits, hung in pairs for
contrast's sake : they are grouped with intelligible
reference to the history of Athens and of Rome.
We know from Plutarch's own statements that he
had no hand in their present arrangement.   He was
engrossed in depicting the characters of great men,
and he wrote and dedicated each pair of lives to
Socius Senecio, or another, as an independent
' book,' ' treaty,' or ' volume.'   It is clear from
many passages that he gathered these ' volumes '

[1] *Lycurgus.*

together without reference to their political bearing
on each other. The *Pericles and Fabius Maximus*,
which is now the Fifth ' book,' was originally the
Tenth ; and the change has apparently been made to
bring Pericles, so far as the Greeks are concerned,
within the consecutive history of Athens : just as
the *Demosthenes and Cicero*, once the Fifth, is now
by much removed so that Cicero may fall into place
among the actors of the Roman drama. So, too, the
Theseus, now standing First, as the founder of Athens,
was written after the *Demosthenes*, now set well-nigh
at the end of the series. And on the same grounds,
evidently, to the *Marius* and the *Pompey*, written
respectively after the *Cæsar* and the *Brutus*, there
have been given such positions as were dictated by
the development of the drama. The fact is, Plutarch's materials, being all political, have settled of
themselves, and have been sorted in accordance with
their political nature : until his work, pieced together by humanists and rearranged by translators,
bears within it some such traces of a new symmetry,
imperfect yet complex, as we detect in the strati-
fication of crystalline rocks. Little has been added
in North's first edition to the substance of Plutarch's
book ; [1] but its structure and, as I hope to show,
some of its colour and surface are the product, not
only of the one mind which created it, but of the
many who have preserved it, and of the ages it has
outworn. The mere changes in the order of the
' books ' have neither increased nor diminished their
contents ; but by evolving, as they do, a more or
less symmetrical juxtaposition of certain elements,

[1] In North's edition of 1579 all is Plutarch, through Amyot, excepting
the *Annibal* and the *Scipio African*, which were manufactured by Donato
Acciaiuoli for the Latin translation of the *Lives* published at Rome by
Campani in 1470.

they have discovered the extent to which the work
is permeated by those elements. As the quartz
dispersed through a rock strikes the eye, when it is
crystallised, from the angles of its spar ; so the
amount of Plutarch's political teaching, which might
have escaped notice when it was scattered through
independent books, now flashes out from the grouping together of the Athenians who made and unmade
Athens, and of the Romans who fought for and
against the Republican Constitution of Rome. For
the Parallel Lives are now disposed in a rough
chronological order ; in so far, at least, as this has
been possible where the members of each pair belong
severally to nations whose histories mingle for the
first time, when the activity of the one ceases and
the activity of the other begins. In earlier days they
had but dim intimations of each other's fortunes :
as when, in the *Camillus*, ' the rumour ran to Greece
incontinently that Rome was taken ' ; and it is only
in the *Philopœmen and Flaminius* that their fates
are trained into a single channel. So that, rather,
there are balance and opposition between the two
halves of the whole : the latter portion being
governed by the grouping in dramatic sequence of
the thirteen Romans who took part in the constitutional drama of Rome ; whereas the earlier is as
it were polarised about the history of Athens. Considering the governing lives in each case, and dis-
regarding their accidental companions, you will find
that in both the whole pageant is displayed. There
are excursions, but in the latter half we live at
Rome ; in the earlier we are taken to Athens : there
to be spectators of her rise, her glory, and her fall.
We listen to the prologue in the *Solon* ; and in the
Themistocles, the *Pericles*, the *Alcibiades*, we contem-

plate the three acts of the tragedy. The tragedy of
Athens, the drama of Rome : these are the historic
poles of the *Parallel Lives* ; while, about half-way
between, in the book of *Philopœmen and Flaminius*,
is the historic hinge, at the fusion of Greek with
Roman story. For Philopœmen and Flaminius
were contemporaries : the one a Greek whom
' Greece did love passingly well as the last valiant
man she brought forth in her age ' ; the other, a
Roman whom she loved also, Plutarch tells us,
because, in founding the suzerainty of Rome, he
founded it on the broad stone of honour. In this
book the balance of sustained interest shifts, and
after it the Lives are governed to the end by the development of the single Roman drama. We may
say to the end : since Plutarch may truly be said to
end with the suicide of Brutus. The *Aratus*, though
of vivid and, with the *Sylla*, of unique interest—for
both are based on autobiographies [1]—belongs, it is
thought, to another book. [2] This, I have already
said, is true of the *Galba* and the *Otho*, dissevered as
they are by the obvious division of a continuous
narrative ; and of the *Artaxerxes*, which, of course,
has nothing to do among the Greek and Roman lives ;
while the *Hannibal and Scipio* (major), included by
North, is not even Plutarch. These lives, then, were
added, no doubt, to complete the defect of those
that had been lost ; as, for instance, the *Metellus*
promised by Plutarch in his *Marius*, and the book of
Epaminondas and Scipio (minor), which we know him
to have written, on the authority of his son.

If, then, ignoring these accretions, we study the

---

[1] Freeman, *Methods of Historic Study*, p. 168. Mahaffy, *Life and Thought*.
[2] A. H. Clough, *Plutarch's Lives*. 1883.

physiognomy of the *Parallel Lives* as revealed in the
' Table,' the national tragedy of Athens and the
constitutional drama of Rome are seen to stand out
in consecutive presentment from its earlier and latter
portions. Each is at once apparent, because each
has been reconstituted for us. But the fact that
such reconstitution has been possible—proving, as
it does, how complete was the unsuspected influence
of Plutarch's political temperament over his conscious selection of great men—puts us in the way of
tracing this influence over his every preference. It
gives a key to one great chamber in his mind, and a
clue which we can follow through the windings of
his book. It makes plain the fact that every one of
his heroes achieved, or attempted, one of four political services which a man may render to his fellows.
Their life-work consisted (1) in founding States ;
(2) in defending them from foreign invasion ; (3) in
extending their dominion ; or (4) in leading political
parties within their confines. All are, therefore,
men who made history, considered each one in relation to his State. In dealing, for instance, with
Demosthenes and Cicero, Plutarch ' will not confer
their works and writings of eloquence,' but ' their
acts and deeds in the government of the commonwealth.' In this manner, also, does he deal even
with his ' founders,' who can scarce be called men,
being but figures of legend and dream. Yet they too
were evolved under the spell of political prepossession
in the nations which conceived their legends ; and
the floating, shifting appearances, the ' mist and
hum ' of them, are compacted by a writer in whom
that prepossession was strongly present. That such
airy creatures should figure at all as historical statesmen, having something of natural movement and

bulk, in itself attests beyond all else to this habit of
Plutarch's mind. Having 'set forth the lives of
Lycurgus (which established the law of the Lacedae-
monians), and of King Numa Pompilius,' he thought
he 'might go a little further to the life of Romulus,' and
' resolved to match him which did set up the noble
and famous city of Athens, with him which founded
the glorious and invincible city of Rome.' He is
dealing, as he says, with matter ' full of suspicion
and doubt, being delivered us by poets and tragedy
makers, sometimes without truth and likelihood, and
always without certainty.' He is dealing, indeed,
with shadows ; but they are shadows projected
backward upon the mists about their origin by two
nations which were above all things political ; and
he lends them a further semblance of consistency
and perspective, by regarding them from a political
point of view in the light of a later political experience. His *Theseus* and his *Romulus* are, indeed, a
tissue woven out of folk-lore and the faint memories
of a savage prime : you shall find in them traces of
forgotten customs ; marriage by capture,[1] for instance, and much else that is frankly beyond belief ;
things which, he says, ' peradventure will please the
reader better for their strangeness and curiosity,
than offend or mislike him for their falsehood.' But
his *Lycurgus*, saving the political glosses, and his
Pompilius are likewise all of legend and romance:
of the days ' when the Aventine was not inhabited,
nor enclosed within the walls of Rome, but was full of
springs and shadowed groves,' the haunt of Picus
and Faunus, and of ' Lady Silence ' ; yet he contrives to cast a political reflection over even this

---

[1] The marriage of Pirithous, p. 62, and the ravishment of the Sabines,
85.

I

noiseless dreamland of folk - lore. Lycurgus and
Theseus, in the manner of their deaths, present
vague images of the fate which in truth befell the
most of their historic parallels. Lycurgus kills
himself, not because his constitution for Sparta is in
danger, but lest any should seek to change it; and
the bones of Theseus, the Athenian, murdered by his
ungrateful countrymen, are magically discovered,
and are brought back to Athens 'with great joye,
with processions and goodly sacrifices, as if Theseus
himself had been alive, and had returned into the
city again.' As we read, we seem to be dreaming
of Cato's death at Utica; and of Alcibiades' return,
when the people who had banished him to the ruin
of their country 'clustred all to him only and . . .
put garlands of flowers upon his head.'

The relation of the *Lives* in the three other categories to the political temper of Plutarch and his
age is more obvious, if less significant of that temper
and its prevalence in every region of thought. Of
the Romans, Publicola and Coriolanus belong also
to romance. But both were captains in the first
legendary wars waged by Rome for supremacy in
Italy; and the lives of both are charged with the hues
of party politics. Publicola is painted as the aristocrat who, by patient loyalty to the Constitution,
lives down the suspicions of the populace; Coriolanus, as a type of caste at once noble for its courage
and lamentable for its indomitable pride. Passing,
after these four, out of fable into history, there
remain six Romans besides the thirteen involved in
the culminating drama. Three of these, Furius
Camillus, Marcellus, and Quintus Fabius Maximus,
were the heroes of Rome's successful resistance
to foreign invasion, and two, T. Q. Flaminius and

Paulus Æmilius, the heroes of her equally successful foreign and colonial policy ; while one only, Marcus Cato, is chosen as a constitutional politician from the few untroubled years between the assurance of empire abroad and the constitutional collapse at home. Turning from Italy to Greece, we find, again, that after the two legendary founders and Solon, the more or less historical contriver of the Athenian constitution, the remainder Greeks without exception fall under one or more of the three other categories : they beat back invasion, or they sought to extend a suzerainty, or they led political parties in pursuit of political ideals. Swayed by his political temperament, Plutarch exhibits men of a like stamp engaged in like issues. But, in passing from his public men of Italy to his public men of Greece, we may note that, while the issues which call forth the political energies of the two nations are the same, a difference merely in the order of event works up the same characters and the same situations into another play with another and a more complicated plot. Rome had practically secured the headship.of the Italian States some years before the First Punic War. Her suzerainty was, therefore, an accomplished fact, frequently challenged but never defeated, before the Italian races were called upon to face any foe capable of absorbing their country. But in Greece, neither before nor after the Persian invasion did any one State ever become permanently supreme. So that, whereas, in Italy, the issue of internal wars and jealousies was decided long before the danger of foreign domination had to be met ; in Greece, overshadowed in turn by the Persian, the Macedonian, and the Roman, that issue was never decided at all. It follows that the history of Italy is the history

of Rome, and not of the Latins or of the Samnites;·
but that the history of Greece is, at first, the history
of Athens, of Sparta, and of Thebes in rivalry with
one another, and, at last, of Macedon and Rome
brooding over leagues and confederacies between the
lesser islands and States. The Roman drama is
single. The City State becomes supreme in Italy;
rolls back wave after wave of Gauls and Carthaginians and Teutons; extends her dominion to the
ends of the earth; and then, suddenly, finds her
Constitution shattered by the strain of world-wide
empire. Plutarch gives the actors in all these
scenes; but it is in the last, which is the most essentially political, that he crowds his stage with the
living, and, afterwards, cumbers it with the dead.
The Greek drama is complex, and affords no such
opportunity for scenic concentration. Even the
first and simplest issue, of repelling an invader, is
made intricate at every step by the jealousy between
Sparta and Athens. Plutarch tells twice over [1] that
Themistocles, the Athenian, who had led the allies to
victory at Salamis, proposed to burn their fleets at
anchor so soon as the danger was overpassed: for by
this means Athens might seize the supremacy of the
sea. The story need not be true: that it should
ever have been conceived proves in what spirit the
Greek States went into alliance, even in face of Persia.
The lives of two other Athenians, Cimon and Aristides, complete Plutarch's picture of the Persian
War; and after that war he can never group his
Greeks on any single stage. Each of them seeks, indeed, to extend the influence of his State, or to
further his political opinions; but in the tangle of
combinations resulting from their efforts one feature

[1] In the *Themistocles* and in the *Aristides*.

remains unchanged among many changes. Through
all the fighting and the scheming it is ever Greek
against Greek. The history is a kaleidoscope, but
the pieces are the same. That is the tragedy of
Greece : the ceaseless duel of the few with the many,
with a complication of racial rivalries between independent City States. There is no climax of development, there is no sudden failure of the heart ; but
an agony of spasm twitches at every nerve in the
body in turn. Extinction follows extinction of
political power in one State after, and at the hands
of, another ; and in the end there is a total eclipse
of national life under the shadow of Rome.

It is customary to date the political death of
Greece from the battle at Chæronea, in which the
Macedonians overthrew the allied armies of Athens
and Thebes. But to Plutarch, who had a better,
because a nearer, point of view, the perennial virulence of race and opinion, which constituted so much
of the political life of Greece, went after Chæronea
as merrily as before. The combatants, whose sky
was but clouded by the empire of Alexander, fought
on into the night of Roman rule ; and, when they
relented, it was even then, according to Plutarch,
only from sheer exhaustion. Explaining the lull in
these rivalries during the old age of Philopœmen,
he writes that ' like as the force and strength of sickness declineth, as the natural strength of the sickly
body impaireth, envy of quarrel and war surceased
as their power diminished.' Of these Greeks, other
than the founders and the heroes of the Persian War,
six were leaders in the rivalry, first, between Athens
and Sparta and, then, between Sparta and Thebes.
Of these, three were Athenians — Pericles, Nicias,
and Alcibiades ; two were Spartans—Lysander and

Agesilaus ; one was Pelopidas the Theban. These
six lives complete Plutarch's picture of the Peloponnesian War. Then, still keeping to Greeks proper,
he indulges in an excursion to Syracuse in the lives
of Dion and Timoleon. Later, in the lives of Demosthenes and Phocion, you feel the cloud of the Macedonian Empire gathering over Greece. And, lastly,
while Rome and Macedon fight over her head for the
substance of dominion and political reform, two kings
of Sparta, Agis and Cleomenes, and two generals of
the Achæan League, Aratus and Philopœmen, are
found still thwarting each other for the shadow.
Plutarch shows four others, not properly to be called
Greeks : the Macedonians, Alexander and Demetrius,
Pyrrhus the Molossian, and Eumenes, born a Greek
of Cardia, but a Macedonian by his career. These
four come on the stage as an interlude between
the rivalries of the Peloponnesian War and the last
futilities of the Achæan League. Alexander for a
time obliterates all lesser lights ; and in the lives of
the other three we watch the flashing train of his
successors. All are shining figures, all are crowned,
all are the greatest adventurers of the world ; and
tumbling out of one kingdom into another, they do
battle in glorious mellays for cities and diadems
and Queens.

Taking a clue from the late reconstitution of the
most moving scenes at Athens and Rome, I follow
it through the *Parallel Lives*, and I sketch the
political framework it discovers. Into that framework, which co-extends with Plutarch's original
conception, I can fit every life in North's first edition,
from the *Theseus* to the *Aratus*. I could not overlook so palpable and so significant a result of Plutarch's political temperament ; and I must note it

because it has been overlooked, and even obscured,
in later editions of Amyot and North. Amyot's
first and second editions, of 1559 and 1565, both end
with the *Otho*, which, although it does not belong to
the *Parallel Lives*, was at least Plutarch. But to
Amyot's third, of 1567, there were added the *Annibal*
and the *Scipion* (major), first fabricated for the Latin
translation of 1470 by Donato Acciaiuoli and translated into French by Charles de l'Escluse, or de la
Sluce, as North prefers to call him. These two lives
North received into his first edition : together with
a comparison by Simon Goulard Senlisien, an in-
dustrious gentleman who, as ' S. G. S.,' supplied him
with further material at a later date.[1] For indeed,
once begun in the first Latin translation, this process
of completing Plutarch knew no bounds for more
than two hundred years. The Spanish historian,
Antonio de Guevara, had perpetrated a decade of
emperors, Trajan, Hadrian, and eight more, and
these, too, were translated into French by Antoine
Allègre, and duly appended to the Amyot of 1567 by
its publisher Vascosan. All was fish that came to
Vascosan's net. The indefatigable S. G. S. concocted lives of Augustus and Seneca ; translated
biographies from Cornelius Nepos ; and, with an
excellent turn for symmetry, supplied unaided all
the Comparisons which are not to be found in Plutarch. The Chæronean either wrote them, and they
were lost ; or, possibly, he paused before the scaling of Cæsar and Alexander, content with the perfection he had achieved. But S. G. S. knew no such

[1] Professor Skeat, in his *Shakespeare's Plutarch*, leaves the attribution
these initials in doubt. They have been taken by many French editors of
Amyot to stand for B. de Girard, Sieur du Haillan, but M. de Blignières
shows in his *Essai sur Amyot*, p. 184, that they stood for Simon Goulard, the
translator of Seneca.

embarrassment; and Amyot's publisher of 1583 accepted his contributions, as before, in the lump. North in his third edition of 1603 is a little, but only a little, more fastidious : he rejects all the Comparisons except, oddly enough, that between Cæsar and Alexander ; but on the other hand, he accepts from S. G. S. the lives of ' worthy chieftains ' and ' famous philosophers ' [1] who—and this is a point— were not, as all Plutarch's exemplars were before everything, public men. Later, the international compliment was returned. The Abbé Bellenger translated into French eight lives—of Æneas, Tullus Hostilius, and so forth—concocted in English by Thomas Rowe ; and these in their turn were duly added, first to Dacier's *Plutarch* in 1734, and afterwards to the Amyot of 1783 : an edition you are not surprised to see filling a small bookcase. Celebrities of all sorts were recruited, simply for their fame, from every age, and from every field of performance —Plato, Aristotle, Philip, even Charlemagne ! [2] And the process of obscuring Plutarch's method did not end with the interjection of spurious stuff. Men cut down the genuine *Lives* to convenient lengths, for summaries and ' treasuries.' The undefeated S. G. S. covered the margin of one edition after another with reflections tending to edification. He and his kind epitomised Plutarch's matter and pointed his moral, grinding them to the dust of a classical dictionary and the ashes of a copybook headline. All these editions and epitomes and maxims, being none of Plutarch's, should not, of

[1] Letter of dedication to Queen Elizabeth.   Ed. 1631, p. 1108.
[2] Fabricated also by Acciaiuoli for Campani's Latin edition of 1470, and attributed to Plutarch by an erudite calling himself Viscellius. Amyot himself fabricated the lives of Epaminondas and Scipio (minor) at the request of Marguerite of Savoye, but never published them as Plutarch.

course, in reason have darkened his restriction on the choice of great men. Yet by their number and their vogue, they have so darkened it ; and the more easily, for that Plutarch, as I have shown, says nothing of the limit he observed. Beneath these additions the political framework of the *Lives* lay buried for centuries ; and even after they had been discarded by later translators, it was still shrouded in the mist they had exhaled. Banish the additions and their atmosphere—fit only for puritans and pedants—and once more the political framework emerges in all its significance and in all its breadth.

From this effect we cannot choose but turn to the *causa causans*—the mind that achieved it. We want to know the political philosophy of a writer who, being a student of human character, yet held it unworthy his study save in public men. And the curiosity will, as I think, be sharpened rather than rebated by the reflection that many of his commentators have, none the less, denied him any political insight at all.[1] Their paradox plucks us by the sleeve. From a soil thus impregnated with the salt of political instinct one would have looked in the harvest for some savour of political truth ; yet one is told that the *Lives*, fruitful of all besides, are barren of this. For my part, I must believe that Plutarch's commentators have been led to a false conclusion along one of two paths : either they have listened too innocently to his avowed intention of

[1] *Plutarch. Five Lectures*, p. 89. Paul-Louis Courier and many others have written to the same effect, questioning Plutarch's accuracy and insight. On the question of accuracy, I am content to quote Ste.-Beuve, *Causeries du Lundi*, vi. 333 : ' Quand on a fait la part du rhéteur et du prêtre d'Apollon en lui, il reste une bien plus large part encore, ce me semble, au collecteur *attentif et consciencieux des moindres traditions* sur les grands hommes, au *peintre abondant et curieux* de la nature humaine ' : and to refer to Freeman, *Methods of Historical Study*, pp. 167, 168, 184.

portraying only character, and have been confirmed
in their error by the indiscriminate additions to his
work ; or, perceiving his exclusive choice of politicians, they have still declined to recognise political
wisdom in an unexpected shape. In a work which
is constituted, albeit without intention, upon lines
thus definitely political, one might have looked for
many direct pronouncements of political opinion.
Yet in that expectation one is deceived—as I think,
happily. For Plutarch's methods, at least in respect
of politics and war, are not those of analysis or of
argument, but of pageant and of drama, with actors
living and moving against a background of processions that move and live. With all the world for
his stage, he shakes off the habit of the lecture-hall,
and it is only now and again that, stepping before
the curtain, he will speak a prologue in a preface, or
turn chorus to comment a space upon the play.
Mostly he is absorbed in presenting his heroes as they
fought and as they fell ; in unfolding, in scene after
scene, his *theatrum* of stirring life and majestical
death. I cannot deny his many digressions on
matters religious, moral, philosophical, and social ;
and it may be that their very number, accentuat-
ing the paucity of his political pronouncements, has
emphasised the view with which I cannot concur.
Doubtless they are there ; nor can I believe that any
would wish them away. It is interesting to hear
the Pythagorean view of the solar system ; [1] and it
is charming to be told the gossip about Aspasia [2]
and Dionysius [3] after his fall. In the *Pericles,* for
instance, Plutarch pauses at the first mention of

---

[1] *Numa Pompilius*: marred in North by a mistranslation. In the
original it approximates to the Copernican rather than to the Ptolemaic
theory.   [2] *Pericles.*   [3] *Timoleon.*

Aspasia's name : 'thinking it no great digression of
our storie,' to tell you 'by the way what manner of
woman she was.'   So he tells you what manner, and,
after the telling, excuses himself once more ; since,
as he says, it came ' in my minde : and me thought
I should have dealt hardly, if I should have left it
unwritten.'   Who will resent such compassion ?
Who so immersed in affairs as to die in willing ignorance of the broken man who seemed to be a ' starke
nideotte,' with a turn for low life and repartee ?
Plutarch carries all before him when he says : ' methinks these things I have intermingled concerning
Dionysius, are not impertinent to the description of
our *Lives*, neither are they troublesome nor unprofitable to the hearers, unless they have other
hasty business to let or trouble them.'   He is irresistible in this vein, which, by its lightness, leads one to
believe that some of the lives, like some modern
essays, were first delivered before popular audiences,
and then collected with others conceived in a graver
key.   There are many such digressions.   But, just
because his heroes are all politicians, of long political
pronouncements there are few : even as of comments
on the art of war you shall find scarce one, for the
reason that strategy and tactics are made plain on a
hundred fields.   His politicians and captains speak
and fight for themselves.   It is for his readers, if they
choose, to gather political wisdom from (say) his lives
of the aforesaid thirteen Romans ; even, as, an they
will, they may deduce from the *Themistocles* or the
Pompey the completeness of his grasp upon the latest
theories on the command of the sea.

Yet there are exceptions, though rare ones, to his
rule ; and in questioning the political bent of his
mind we are not left to inference alone.   In the

Lycurgus, for instance, where the actor is but a walking shadow, Plutarch must needs deal with the system associated with Lycurgus's name : so in this life we have the theory of politics which Plutarch favoured, whereas in the *Pericles* we have the practice of a consummate politician. From the *Lycurgus*, then, we are able to gauge the personal equation (so to say) of the mind which, in the *Pericles*, must have coloured that mind's presentment of political action and debate. Plutarch, like Plato before him, is a frank admirer of the laws which Lycurgus is said to have framed. He delights in that ' perfectest manner of a commonwealth,' which made the city of Lycurgus ' the chiefest of the world, in glory and honour of government, by the space of five hundred years.' He tells of the lawgiver's journey from Crete to Asia, to compare the ' policy of those of Crete (being then very straight and severe) with the superfluities and vanities of Ionia ' ; and you may gather from the context that the one appears to the historian ' whole and healthful,' the others ' sick and diseased.' He seems also to approve Lycurgus's indiscriminate contempt for all ' superfluous and unprofitable sciences ' ; for the devices of ' licorous cooks to cram themselves in corners,' of ' rhetoricians who teach eloquence and the cunning cast of lying,' of goldsmiths and fortune-tellers and panders. Again, it is with satisfaction that he paints his picture of Lycurgus returning ' home one day out of the fields . . . laughing ' as he ' saw the number of sheaves in shocks together and no one shock bigger than another ' ; all Laconia being ' as it were an inheritance of many brethren, who had newly made partition together.' But if Plutarch approves the suppression of luxury and the equal distribution of wealth as ideals, he does not approve the equal distribution of power. He is in favour of constitutional republics and opposed to hereditary monarchies ; though he will tolerate even these in countries where they already exist.[1] But he is for republics and against monarchies only that the man ' born to rule ' may have authority : such a man, for instance, as Lycurgus, ' born to rule, to command, and to give orders, as having in him a certain *natural grace and power to draw men willingly to obey him.'* In any State, he postulates, on the one hand, an enduring Constitution and a strong Senate of proved men ; on the other, a populace with equal political rights of electing to the Senate and of sanctioning the laws that Senate may propose. Yet these in themselves are but preliminary conditions of liberty and order. Besides, for the preservation of a State there are needed rulers few and fit, armed with enough authority and having courage enough to wield it. It is essential that the few, who are fit, shall direct and govern the many, who are not. If authority be impaired, whether by incompetence in the few or through jealousy in the many, then must disaster follow. Now, many who hold this view are prone, when disaster does follow, to blame the folly of the many rather than the unfitness of the few. But Plutarch is distinguished in this : that, holding the view as firmly as any have held it—now preaching the gospel of authority and now exhibiting its proof at every turn—he yet imputes the blame of failure, almost always, to incompetence or to cowardice in the few. ' He that directeth well must needs be well obeyed. For like as the art of a good rider is to make his horse gentle and ready at com-

[1] *Comparison of Demetrius with Antonius.*

mandment, even so the chiefest point belonging to a
prince is to teach his people to obey.' I take these
words from the *Lycurgus*. They set forth Plutarch's
chief political doctrine ; and the statement of fact
is pointed with his favourite image. That the horse
(or the many) should play the antic at will, is to
him plainly absurd : the horse must be ridden, and
the many must be directed and controlled. Yet, if
the riding, or the governing, prove a failure, Plutarch's quarrel is with the ruler and the horseman,
not with the people or the mount. For he knows
well that ' a ragged colt oftimes proves a good
horse, specially if he be well ridden and broken as
he should be.' [1] This is but one of his innumerable
allusions to horse-breaking and hunting : as, for
instance, in the *Paulus Æmilius*, he includes ' riders
of horses and hunts of Greece ' among painters and
gravers of images, grammarians, and rhetoricians,
as the proper Greek tutors for completing the educa-
tion of a Roman moving with the times. And no
one who takes note of these allusions can doubt that,
as one of a chivalrous and sporting race, he was
qualified to deal with images drawn from the *manège*
and the chase. As little can any one who follows
his political drama miss the application of these
images. Sometimes, indeed, his constant theme and
his favourite image almost seem fused : as when he
describes the *natural grace* of his Cæsar, ' so excellent
a rider of horse from his youth, that holding his
hands behind him, he would galop his horse upon
the spur ' ; a governor so ever at one with those he
governed, that he directed even his charger by an
inflexion of his will rather than of his body. This
need of authority and the obligation on the few to

[1] *Themistocles.*

maintain it—by a 'natural grace,' springing, on the
one hand, from courage combined with forbearance ;
and leading, on the other, to harmony between the
rulers and the ruled—is the text which, given out in
the *Lycurgus,* is illustrated throughout the *Parallel
Lives.*

I have said that, apart from the *Lycurgus,* Plutarch's political pronouncements are to be found
mostly in the prefaces to certain 'books' and in
scattered comments on such action as he displays.
And of all these 'books' the *Pericles and Fabius
Maximus* is, perhaps, the richest in pronouncements,
in both its preface and its body, all bearing on his
theory of authority and on its maintenance by
'natural grace.' A 'harmony' is to be aimed at ;
but a harmony in the Dorian mode. Pericles is
commended because in later life 'he was wont . . .
not so easily to grant to all the people's wills and
desires, no more than as it were to contrary winds.'
In Plutarch's eyes he did well when ' he altered his
over-gentle and popular manner of government
. . . as too delicate and effeminate an harmony of
music, and did convert it into an imperious government, or rather a kingly authority.' He has nothing
but praise for the independence and fortitude by
which Pericles achieved Cæsar's policy of uniting
within himself all the yearly offices of the State,
' not for a little while, nor in a gear (fashion) of
favour,' but for ' forty years together.' He compares him to the captain of a ship ' not hearkening
to the passengers' fearful cries and pitiful tears,'
and holds him up for an example, since he ' neither
would be persuaded by his friends' earnest requests
and entreaties, neither cared for his enemies' threats
and accusations against him, nor yet reckoned of all

their foolish scoffing songs they sung of him in the
city.'   So, too, in the same book, when Plutarch
comes to portray Fabius Maximus, he gives us that
great man's view : that ' to be afeared of the wagging
of every straw, or to regard every common prating,
is not the part of a worthy man of charge, but rather
of a base-minded person, to seek to please those
whom he ought to command and govern, because
they are but fools.'   (Thus does blunt Sir Thomas
render Amyot's polite, but equally sound, ' *parce
qu'ils ne sont pas sages.*')   But the independence and
the endurance necessary in a ruler are not to be
accompanied by irritation or contempt.   While ' to
flatter the common people ' is at best effeminate,'
and at worst ' the broad high-way of them that
practise tyranny,'[1] still, ' he is less to be blamed that
seeketh to please and gratify his common people than
he that despiseth and disdaineth them ' ; for here
is no harmony at all, but discord.   The words last
quoted are from the Comparison between Alcibiades
and Coriolanus, two heroes out of tune with their
countrymen, whose courage and independence were
made thereby of no avail.   But in the *Pericles and
Fabius Maximus* Plutarch shows us heroes after his
own heart, and in his preface to their lives he insists
more explicitly than elsewhere on the need of not
only courage and independence but also forbearance
and goodwill ; since without these, their comple-
ments, the other virtues, are sterile.   Pericles and
Fabius, being at least as proud and brave as Alcibiades and Coriolanus, ' for that they would patiently
bear the follies of their people and companions that
were in charge of government with them, were marvellous profitable members for their country.'   He

---

[1] *Furius Camillus.*

returns to this theory of harmony in his preface to the *Phocion and Cato*. In every instance he assumes as beyond dispute, that the few must govern, working an obedience in the many ; but they are to work it by a ' natural grace ' of adaptation to the needs and natures they command. In this very book he blames Cato of Utica, not for the ' ancient simplicity ' of his manner, which ' was indeed praiseworthy,' but, simply because it was ' not the convenientest, nor the fittest ' for him ; for that ' it answered nor respected not the use and manners of his time.'

How comes it to pass that Plutarch's heroes, being thus prone to compromise, yet fight and die, often at their own hands, for the ideals they uphold ? The question is a fair one, and the answer reveals a profound difference between the theory and the practice of politics approved by the ancient world and the theory and the practice of politics approved in the England of to-day. ' The good and ill,' says Plutarch, ' do nothing differ but in mean and mediocrity.' We might therefore expect in his heroes a reluctance to sacrifice all for a difference of degree ; and especially might we suppose that, after deciding an equipoise so nice as that between ' authority and lenity,' his governors would stake little on their decision. But in a world of adjustment and doubt they are all for compromise in theory, while in action they are extreme. They are ready in spite, almost because, of that doubt, to seal with their blood such certainty as they can attain. His statesmen, inasmuch as they do respect ' the use and manners ' of their time, endure all things while they live, and at last die quietly, not for an abstract idea or a sublime emotion, but for the compromise of their day : though they know it for a compromise, and foresee

its inevitable destruction. They have no enthusiasm, and no ecstasy. Uninspired from without, and
self-gathered within, they live their lives, or lay them
down, for the use and wont of their country. In
reading their history an Englishman cannot but be
struck by the double contrast between these tendencies of theory and action and the tendencies of
theory and action finding favour in England now.
Ever extreme in theory, we are all for compromise
in fact ; proud on the one score of our sincerity, on
the other of our common sense. We are fanatics,
who yet decline to persecute, still less to suffer, for
our faith. And this temperance of behaviour, following hard on the violent utterance of belief, is apt
to show something irrational and tame. The actor
stands charged, often unjustly, with a lack of both
logic and courage. The Greeks, on the other hand,
who found ' truth in a union of opposites and the aim
of life in its struggle,' [1] and the Romans, who aped
their philosophy and outdid their deeds, are not, in
Plutarch's pages, open to this disparagement. They
live or die for their faiths as they found them, and
so appear less extravagant and more brave. The
temper is illustrated again and again by the manner
in which they observe his doctrine, that rulers must
maintain their authority, and at the same time
' bear the follies of their people and companions that
are in charge of government with them.' To read the
Pericles or the *Pompeius*, the *Julius Cæsar* or the
Cato, is to feel that a soldier may as well complain
of bullets in a battle as a statesman of stupidity in
his colleagues. These are constants of the problem.
Only on such terms are fighting and ruling to be had.
So, too, with ' the people ' : with the many, that is,

[1] *The Moral Ideal*, Julia Wedgwood, p. 82.

who have least chance of understanding the game, least voice in its conduct, least stake in its success. If these forget all but yesterday's service, if they look only for to-morrow's reward, the hero is not therefore to complain. This short-lived memory and this short-sighted imagination are constants also. They are regular fences in the course he has set himself to achieve. He must clear them if he can, and fall if he cannot ; but he must never complain. They are conditions of success, not excuses for failure ; and to name them is to be ridiculous. The Plutarchian hero never does name them. He is obstinate, but not querulous. He cares only for the State ; he insists on saving it in his own way ; he kills himself, if other counsels prevail. But he never complains, and he offers no explanations. Living, he prefers action before argument ; dying, he chooses drama rather than defence. While he has hope, he acts like a great man ; and when hope ceases, he dies like a great actor. He and his fellows seek for some compromise between authority and lenity, and, having found it, they maintain it to the end. They are wise in taking thought, and sublime in taking action : whereas now, we are courageous in our theories, but exceeding cautious in our practice. Yet who among modern politicians will say that Plutarch's men were in the wrong ? Who, hoarse with shouting against the cataract of circumstance, will dare reprove the dumb-show of their lives and deaths ?

I have shown from the *Lycurgus*, from the prefaces to the *Pericles* and the *Phocion*, and from scattered comments elsewhere, that Plutarch has something to say upon politics which, whether we agree with him or not, is at least worthy our attention. There

is yet an occasion of one other kind—which he takes,
I think, only twice—for speaking his own mind upon
politics.   After the conclusion of a long series of
events, ending, for instance, in the rule of Rome
over Greece, or in the substitution of the Empire for
the Republic, he assembles these conclusions, at first
sight to him unreasonable and unjust, and seeks to
interpret them in the light of divine wisdom and
justice.   Now, he was nearer than we are to the
two great sequences I have denoted, by seventeen
centuries : he lived, we may say, in a world which
they had created anew.   And whereas he took in all
political questions a general interest so keen that it
has coloured the whole of a work not immediately
addressed to politics, in these two sequences his
interest was particular and personal : in the first
because of his patriotism, and in the second because
of his familiar converse with the best in Rome.   We
are happy, then, in the judgment of such a critic
on the two greatest political dramas enacted in
the ancient world.   The human—I might say the
pathetic—interest of the treatment accorded by the
patriotic Greek to the growth of Roman dominion
and its final extension over the Hellenistic East,
will absorb the attention of many.   But it offers,
besides, as I think, although this has been questioned,
much of political wisdom.   In any case, on the one
count or upon the other, I feel bound to indicate the
passages in which he comments on these facts.   We
are not in doubt as to his general views on Imperial
aggression and a ' forward policy.'   After noting
that the Romans forsook the peaceful precepts of
Numa, and ' filled all Italy with murder and blood,'
he imagines one saying : ' But hath not Rome
excelled still, and prevailed more and more in

chivalry ? ' And he replies : [1] ' This question re-
quireth a long answer, and especially unto such men
as place felicity in riches, in possessing and in the
greatness of empire, rather than in quiet safety, peace
and concord of a common weal.' For his part he
thought with Lycurgus,[2] that a city should not seek
to command many ; but that ' the felicity of a city,
as of a private man, consisted chiefly in the exercise
of virtue, and the unity of the inhabitants thereof,
and that the citizens should be nobly minded
(Amyot : *francs de cueurs*), content with their own,
and temperate in their doings (*attrempez en tous leurs
faicts*), that thereby they might maintain and keep
themselves long in safety.' But, holding this general
opinion, and biassed into the bargain by his patriotism, he cannot relate the stories of Aratus and
Philopœmen on the one hand, or of Flaminius and
Lucullus on the other, without accepting the conclusion that the rule of Rome was at last necessary
for the rational and just government of the world ;
and, therefore, was inevitably ordained by the Divine
wisdom. Rome ' increased and grew strong by arms
and continual wars, *like as piles driven into the ground,
which the more they are rammed in the further they
enter and stick the faster.*' [3] For it was by obedience
and self-restraint, by a ' yielding unto reason and
virtue ' that the ' Romans came to command all
other and to make themselves the mightiest people
of the world.' [4] In Greece he finds nothing of this
obedience and this self-restraint ; nothing but
rivalry between leaders and jealousy between States.
Cleomenes, the Spartan king, Aratus and Philopœmen, both leaders of the Achæan League, are among

---

[1] *Comparison of Lycurgus with Numa Pompilius.*
[2] *Lycurgus.*   [3] *Numa Pompilius.*   [4] *Paulus Æmilius.*

the last of his Greek heroes.   He lingers over them
lovingly ;   yet it is Aratus who, in jealousy of
Cleomenes, brings Antigonus and his Macedonians
into Greece ;   and it is Flaminius, the Roman, who
expels them.   In this act some modern critics have
seen only one of many cloaks for a policy of calculated
aggression, but it is well to remember for what it is
worth that Plutarch, the Greek patriot, saw in it
simply the act of a ' just and courteous gentleman,'
and that, according to him, the ' only cause of the
utter destruction of Greece ' must be sought earlier :
when Aratus preferred the Macedonians before allowing Cleomenes a first place in the Achæan League.
In the *Cimon and Lucullus*, even after Greece became
a Roman province, he shows the same rivalries on a
smaller scale.   The ' book ' opens with a story which,
with a few changes, mostly of names, might be set in
the Ireland of a hundred years ago.   One Damon,
an antique Rory of the Hills, after just provocation,
collects a band of moonlighters who, with blackened
faces, set upon and murder a Roman captain.   The
town council of Chæronea condemns Damon and his
companions to death, in proof of its own innocence,
and is murdered for its pains.   At last Damon himself is enticed into a bathhouse, and killed.   Then the
Orchomenians, ' being near neighbours unto the
Chæroneans, and therefore their enemies,' hire an
' informer ' to accuse all the Chæroneans of complicity in the original murder ;   and it is only the just
testimony of the Roman general, Lucullus, who
chances to be marching by, which saves the town
from punishment.   An image is set up to Lucullus
which Plutarch has seen ;   and even to his day
' terrible voices and cries ' are heard by the neighbours from behind the walled-up door of the bath-

house, in which Damon had died. He knows the
whole story from his childhood, and knows that in
this small matter Lucullus showed the same justice
and courtesy which Flaminius had displayed in a
great one. For it is only the strong who can be
just ; and therefore to the strong there falls in the
end, without appeal, the reward, or the penalty,
of doing justice throughout the world. That seems
to be Plutarch's ' long answer ' to those who question
the justice of the Roman Empire. He gives it most
fully in the life of Flaminius, taking, as I have said,
a rare occasion in order to comment on the conclusion of a long series of events. First, he sums
up the results achieved by the noble Greeks, many
of whose lives he has written. ' For Agesilaus,' he
writes, ' Lysander, Nicias, Alcibiades, and all other
the famous captains of former times, had very good
skill to lead an army, and to winne the battle, as
well by sea as by land, but to turn their victories
to any honourable benefit, or true honour among
men, they could never skill of it ' ; especially as,
apart from the Persian War, ' all the other wars and
the battles of Greece that were made fell out against
themselves, and did ever bring them unto bondage :
and all the tokens of triumph which ever were set up
for the same was to their shame and loss.' Having
summed up the tragedy of Greece in these words, he
turns to the Roman rule, and ' The good deeds of the
Romans and of Titus Quintus Flaminius,' he says,
' unto the Grecians, did not only reap this benefit
unto them, in recompense that they were praised
and honoured of all the world ; but they were cause
also of increasing their dominions and empire over
all nations.' So that ' peoples and cities . . . procured them to come, and did put themselves into

their hands'; and 'kings and princes also (which were oppressed by other more mighty than themselves) had no other refuge but to put themselves under their protection, by reason whereof in a very short time . . . all the world came to submit themselves under the protection of their empire.'

In the same way, he, a republican, acquiesced in the necessity for Cæsar. Having told the story of Brutus, the last of the thirteen Romans, he falls on the other of my two occasions, and ' Cæsar's power and government,' he writes, ' when it came to be established, did indeed much hurt at his first entrie and beginning unto those that did resist him : but afterwards there never followed any tyrannical nor cruel act, but contrarily, it seemed that he was a merciful Physician *whom God had ordained of special grace to be Governor of the Empire of Rome, and to set all things again at quiet stay, the which required the counsel and authority of an absolute Prince.*' That is his epilogue to the longest and the mightiest drama in all history ; and in it we have for once the judgment of a playwright on the ethics of his play. Yet so great a dramatist was Plutarch that even his epilogue has not saved him from the fate of his peers. While some, with our wise King James I., blame him for injustice to Cæsar,[1] yet others find him a niggard in his worship of Brutus and Cato. The fact is, each of his heroes is for the moment of such flesh and blood as to compel the pity of him that reads ; for each is in turn the brother of all men, in their hope and in their despair. If, then, the actor chances to be Brutus and the reader King James, Plutarch is damned for a rebel ; but again, if the reader be a

[1] In his interview with Casaubon. See Ste.-Beuve : *Causeries du Lundi.* xiv. 402.

republican, when Servilia's lover wraps him in his cloak and falls, why, then is Plutarch but the friend of a tyrant. Thus by the excellence of his art he forces us to argue that his creatures must reign in his affection as surely as for a moment they can seize upon our own. Take an early hero of the popular party—take Caius Gracchus. We know him even to his trick of vehement speech ; and, knowing him so intimately, we cannot but mourn over that parting from his wife, when he left her to meet death, and she, ' reaching after him to take him by the gown, fell to the ground and lay flatlings there a great while, speaking never a word.' Cato, again, that hero of the other side, lives to be forbidding for his affectation ; yet who but remembers the clever boy making orations full of ' witt and vehemence,' with a ' certaine gravetie ' which ' delighted his hearers and *made them laugh, it did so please them* ' ? One harks back to the precocious youngster, once the hope of the winning party, when Cato, left alone in Utica, the last soul true to a lost cause, asks the dissemblers of his sword if they ' think to keep an old man alive by force ? ' He takes kindly thought for the safety of his friends, reads the *Phœdo*, and dozes fitfully through the night, and behold ! you are in the room with a great man dying. You feel with him that chill disillusion of the dawn, when ' *the little birds began to chirp* ' ; you share in the creeping horror of his servants, listening outside the door ; and when they give a ' shriek for fear ' at the ' noise of his fall, overthrowing a little table of geometry hard by his bed,' it is almost a relief to know that the recovered sword has done its work. And who can help loving Pompey, with his ' curtesie in conversation ; so that there was never man that *requested anything with less*

ill will than he, nor that more willingly did pleasure
unto any man when he was requested. *For he gave
without disdain and took with great honour* ' ? ' The
cast and soft moving of his eyes . . . had a certain
resemblance of the statues and images of King
Alexander.' Even ' Flora the curtisan '—Villon's
' Flora la belle Romaine '—pined away for love of
him when he turned her over to a friend. He is all
compact of courage and easy despair : now setting
sail in a tempest, for ' it is necessity, I must go, but
not to live ' ; and again, at Pharsalia, at the first
reverse ' *forgetting that he was Pompey the Great*,' and
leaving the field to walk silently away. And that
last scene of all : when on a desolate shore a single
' infranchised bondman ' who had ' remained ever '
by the murdered hero, ' sought upon the sands and
found at the length a piece of an old fisher's boat
enough to serve to burn his naked body with ' ; and
so a veteran who had been with him in his old wars
happens upon the afflicting scene ; and you hear him
hail the other lonely figure : ' O friend, what art thou
that preparest the funerals of Pompey the Great ?
. . . Thou shalt not have *all this honour alone* . . .
to bury the only and most famous Captain of the
Romans ! '

There is sorcery in Plutarch's presentments of
these politicians, which may either blind to the
import of the drama they enact, or beguile into thinking that he sympathises by turns with the ideal of
every leader he portrays. But behind the glamour
of their living and the glory of their death, a relent-
less progression of political causes and effects conducts
inevitably to Cæsar's personal rule. In no other book
do we see so full an image of a nation's life, because in
no other is the author so little concerned to prove

the truth of any one theory, or the nobility of any one sentiment. He is detached—indeed, absorbed—in another purpose. He exhibits his thirteen vivid personalities, holding, mostly by birth, to one of two historic parties, and inheriting with those parties certain traditional aspirations and beliefs ; yet by showing men as they are, he contrives to show that truth and nobility belong to many divergent beliefs and to many conflicting aspirations. Doubtless he has his own view, his rooted abhorrence to the rule of one man ; and this persuasion inclines him now to the Popular Party in its opposition to Sulla, and again to the Senate in its opposition to Cæsar. But still, by the sheer force of his realism, he drives home, as no other writer has ever done, the great truth that theories and sentiments are in politics no more than flags and tuckets in a battle : that in fighting and in government it is, after all, the fighting and the governing which must somehow or another be achieved. And, since in this world governing there must be, the question at any moment is : What are the possible conditions of government ? In the latter days of the Republic it appears from the *Lives* that two sets of causes had led to a monstrous development of individuals, in whose shadow all lower men must wither away. So Sertorius sails for the ' Fortunate Islands ' ; Cato is juggled to Cyprus ; Cicero is banished ; while Lucullus, out-metalled by Pompey on his own side, ' lay still and took his pleasure, and would no more meddle with the commonwealth,' and the unspeakable Bibulus ' kept him close in his ' house for eight months' space, and only sent out bills.' At last you have the Triumvirate ; and then, with Crassus killed, the two protagonists face to face : ' whose names the strange

and far nations understood before the name of
Romans, so great were their victories.' Given the
Roman dominion and two parties with the traditions
of Marius and Sulla behind them, there was nothing
for it but that one or other should prove its com-
petence to rule ; and no other way of achieving
this than finding the man and giving him the power.
The Marians found Cæsar, and in him a man who
could find power for himself. The political heirs of
Sulla found Cato and Brutus, and Lucullus and
Pompey ; but none of these was Cæsar, and, such as
they were, the Senate played them off the one against
the other. Bemused with theories and sentiments,
they neither saw the necessity, nor seized the means,
of governing a world that cried aloud for government. In Plutarch you watch the play ; and, whatever you may think of the actors—of Crassus or
Cato, Pompey or Cæsar—of the non-actors you can
think nothing. Bibulus, with his ' bills,' and the
Senate, which bade Pompey disband his troops,
stand for ever as types of formal incompetence.
Plutarch shows that it is wiser and more righteous
to win the game by accepting the rules, even if
sometimes you must strain and break them, than to
leave the table because you dislike the rules. Instead of quarrelling with the rules and losing the
game, the Senate should have won the game, and
then have changed the rules. This Cæsar did, as
Plutarch the republican allows, to the saving of his
country and the lasting profit of mankind. Doubtless he shows the argument in action, and points the
moral only in an epilogue. But living, as we do,
after the politicians of so many ages and so many
parties have laid competing claims to the glory of his
chiefs, this is our gain. Brutus and Cato, heroes of

the Renaissance and gods of liberty a hundred years ago, we are told by eminent historians, were selfish oligarchs: bunglers who, having failed to feed the city or to flush the drains, wrote ' sulky letters ' [1] about the one man who could do these things, and govern the world into the bargain. Between these views it skills not to decide. It is enough to take up the *Lives* and to rejoice that Plutarch, writing one hundred and fifty years after the foundering of the Republic, dwelt rather on its heroes who are for ever glorious than on its theories which were for ever shamed.

In his book are three complete plays : the brief tragedy of Athens—that land of ' honey and hemlock,' offering her cup of sweet and deadly elements to the dreamers of every age ; with the drama of the merging of Greece in the dominion of Rome and the drama of the overthrow of the Roman Republic. And the upshot of all three is that the playwright insists on the culture of the individual for the sake of the State. The political teacher behind the political dramatist inculcates, no theory of politics but, an attitude towards life. Good is the child of custom and conflict, not the reward of individual research ; so he shows you life as one battle in which the armies are ordered States. Every man, therefore, must needs be a citizen, and every citizen a soldier in the ranks. For this service, life being a battle, he must cultivate the soldier's virtues of courage and courtesy. The word is North's, and smacks something more of chivalry than Amyot's *humanité*; yet both may be taken to point Plutarch's moral, not only that victory is impossible without kindness between comrades, and intolerable without

---

[1] Mommsen : he uses the phrase of Cicero.

forbearance between foes, but also, that in every age
of man's progress to perfection through strife these
qualities must be developed to a larger growth
measured by the moral needs of war between nations
and parties.   He insists again and again on this need
of courtesy in a world wherein all men are in duty
bound to hold opposite opinions, for which they must
in honour live and die.   For this his Sertorius, his
Lucullus, and his Mummius, sketched in a passing
allusion, are chiefly memorable ; while of Cæsar he
writes that ' amongst other honours ' his enemies
gave him ' he rightly deserved this, that they should
build him a Temple of Clemency.'   Cæsar, lighting
from his horse to embrace Cicero, the arch-instigator
of the opposition he had overthrown, and walking
with him ' a great way a-foot ' ; or Demetrius, who,
the Athenians having defaulted, gathers them into
the theatre, and then, when they expect a massacre,
forgives them in a speech—these are but two
exemplars of a style which Plutarch ever praises.
And if his standard of courtesy in victory be high,
not lower is his standard of courage in defeat.
Demosthenes is condemned for that ' he took his
banishment unmanly,' while Phocion, his rival, is
made glorious for his irony in death : paying, when
the stock ran out, for his own hemlock, ' sith a
man cannot die at Athens for nothing.'   In defeat
Plutarch's heroes sometimes doubted if life were
worth living ; but they never doubted there were
things in life worth dying for.   Even Demosthenes
is redeemed in his eyes because, at the last, ' sith the
god Neptune denied him the benefit of his sanctuary,
he betook him to a greater, and that was Death.'   So
often does Plutarch applaud the act of suicide, and
so scornfully does he revile those who, like the last

king of Macedon, forwent their opportunity, that
we might easily misconceive his ethics. But ' when
a man will willingly kill himself, he must not do it to
be rid of pains and labour, but it must have an
honourable respect and action. *For, to live or die
for his own respect, that cannot but be dishonourable.*
. . . And therefore I am of opinion that we should
not yet cast off the hope we have to serve our
country in time to come ; but when all hope faileth
us, then we may easily make ourselves away when
we list.' Thus, after Selasia, the last of the kings of
Sparta, who recalled the saying of Lycurgus : that,
with ' great personages . . . the end of their life
should be no more idle and unprofitable then the
rest of their life before.' And this is the pith of
Plutarch's political matter : that men may not with
honour live unto themselves, but must rather live
and die in respect to the State.

II

Side by side, and in equal honour, with Plutarch
the dramatist of politics there should stand, I think
—not Plutarch the moralist but—Plutarch the unrivalled painter of men. Much has been written,
and rightly written, of his perennial influence upon
human character and human conduct; yet outside
the ethics of citizenship he insisted on little that is
not now a platitude. The interest of his morals
springs from their likeness to our own ; the wonder
of his portraitures must ever be new and strange.
Indeed, we may speak of his art much as he writes,
through North, of the ' stately and sumptuous buildings ' which Pericles 'gave to be built in the cittie of
Athens.' For ' it looketh at this daye as if it were

but newly done and finished, there is such a certaine kynde of florishing freshnes in it, which letteth that the injurie of time cannot impaire the sight thereof: as if every one of those foresaid workes had some living spirite in it, to make it seeme young and freshe: and a soul that lived ever, which kept them in good continuing state.' Yet despite this 'florishing freshnes' the painter has been slighted for the preacher, and for this preference of the ethical before the æsthetic element in the *Lives*, and of both before their political quality, Plutarch has mostly himself to thank. Just as he masks a political framework under a professed devotion to the study of individual souls, so, when he comes to the study of these souls, he puts you off by declaring a moral aim in language that may easily mislead. ' When first I began these lives,' he writes in the *Paulus Æmilius*, ' my intent was to profit other : but since, continuing and going on, I have much profited myself by looking into these histories, as if I looked into a glasse, to frame and facion my life, to the moold and patterne of these vertuous noble-men, and doe as it were lodge them with me, one after another.' And again, ' by keeping allwayes in minde the acts of the most noble, vertuous and best geven men of former age . . . I doe teache and prepare my selfe to shake of and banishe from me, all lewde and dishonest condition, if by chaunce the companie and conversation of them whose companie I keepe . . . *doe acquaint me with some unhappie or ungratious touche.*' Now, as matter of fact, he does not keep always in mind these, and these only. Doubtless his aim was moral; yet assuredly he never did pursue it by denoting none save the virtuous acts of the ' most noble, vertuous, and best geven men.' On the contrary, his practice

is to record their every act of significance, whether
good or bad. I admit that he does this ever with a
most happy and most gracious touch ; for his ' first
study ' is to write a good man's ' vertues at large,'
and if ' certaine faultes ' be there, ' to pass them
over lightly *of reverent shame to the mere frayelty of
man's nature.*' [1] He lays the ruin of his country at
the door of Aratus alone ; but ' this,' he adds, ' that
we have written of Aratus . . . is not so much to
accuse him as to make us see the frayelty and weakness of man's nature : the which, though it have
never so excellent vertues, cannot yet bring forth
such perfit frute, but that it hath ever some mayme
and blemishe.' [2] That is his wont in portraying the
ill deeds of the virtuous ; and, for their opposites,
' as I hope,' he writes in the preface to the *Demetrius
and Antonius,* ' it shall not be reprehended in me if
amongst the rest I put in one or two paier of suche, as
living in great place and accompt, have increased
their fame with infamy.'   ' Phisicke,' he submits in
defence of such a choice, ' dealeth with diseases,
musicke with discordes, to thend to remove them,
and worke their contraries, and the great Ladies of
all other artes (Amyot : *les plus parfaittes sciences de
toutes*), Temperaunce, Justice, and Wisdom, doe not
onely consider honestie, uprightness and profit : but
examine withall, the nature and effects of lewdness,
corruption and damage ' ; for ' innocencie,' he goes
on, ' which vaunteth her want of experience in undue
practices : men call simplicitie (Amyot : *une bestise*)
and ignoraunce of things that be necessary and good
to be knowen.' His, then, is a moral standpoint ;
and yet it is one from which he is impelled to study—
(and that as closely as the keenest apostle of ' art

---

[1] Preface to the *Çimon and Lucullus.*   [2] *Agis and Cleomenes.*

for art ')—all matters having truth and significance ; whether they be evil or good. For the sake of what is good, he will neither distort truth nor disfigure beauty. Rather, by the exercise of a fine selection, he will create a harmony between the three ; so that, embracing everything except the trivial, his art reflects the world as it shows in the sight of sane and healthy-hearted men.

His method naturally differs from the method of some modern historians ; but his canon of evidence, too lax for their purpose, is admirably suited to his own. For instance, in telling of Solon's meeting with Crœsus, he will not reject so famous an history on chronological grounds : because, in the first place, no two are agreed about chronology, and in the second, the story is 'very agreeable to Solon's manners and nature.' That is his chief canon ; and though the results he attains by it are in no wise doubt-proof, they yield a truer, because a completer, image than do the lean and defective outlines de-termined by excluding all but contemporary evi-dence. These outlines belong rather to the science of anthropometry than to the art of portraiture ; and Plutarch the painter refuses such restraints. His imagination having taken the imprint of his hero, he will supplement it from impressions left in report and legend, so long, at any rate, as they tally with his own ideal. Nor is there better cause for rejecting such impressions than there is for rejecting the fossils of primeval reptiles whose carnal economy has perished. Given those fossils and a knowledge of morphology, the palæontologist will refashion the dragons of the prime ; and in the same way Plutarch, out of tradition and his knowledge of mankind, paints you the true Themistocles. His, indeed, is the

surer warrant, since there have been no such changes
in human nature as science shows in animal design ;
so that the method is safe so long as a nation's
legends have not been crushed out of shape by the
superincumbent layers of a conquering race. Moreover, Plutarch makes no wanton use of his imagination : give him contemporary evidence, and he abides
by it, rejecting all besides. In his account of
Alexander's death, having the court journal before
him, he repudiates later embellishments : ' for all
these were thought to be written by some, for lyes
and fables, because they would have made the ende
of this great tragedie lamentable and pitifull.'

His results are, of course, unequal. He cannot
always revive the past, nor quicken the dead anew.
Who can ? His gallery includes some pieces done
on a faded convention, faint in colour and angular
in line, mere pretexts for a parade of legendary
names : with certain sketches, as those of Cimon
and Aristides, which are hack-work turned out to
complete a pair. But first and last there stand out
six or seven realisations of living men, set in an
atmosphere, charged with a vivid intensity of expression, and striking you in much the same way as
the sight of a few people scattered through a big
room strikes you when you enter unawares. And
when you have done staring at these, you will
note a half-dozen more which are scarce less vigorously detached. Plutarch's first masterpiece is the
Themistocles, and there is never a touch in it but tells.
Even as you watch him at work, you are conscious,
leaping out from beneath his hand, of the ambitious
boy, ' sodainely taken with desire of glorie,' who,
from his first entry into public life, ' stoode at pyke
with the greatest and mightiest personnes.' But you

soon forget the artist in his creation. You have eyes for nothing but Themistocles himself : now walking with his father by the seashore ; now, after Marathon ' a very young man many times solitary alone devising with himself '—in this way passing his boyhood, for '*Miltiades victory would not let him sleep.*' Then the ambitious boy develops into the political artist ; rivals Aristides, as Fox rivalled Pitt ; and is found loving his art for its own sake, above his country, above his ambition even, wrapt as he is, through good fortune and ill, in the expert's delight in his own accomplishment. Knowing what all men should do, and swaying every several man to do it, he controls both individuals and nations with the inspired prescience of a master conducting his own symphony. He has all the devices at his fingers' ends. In the streets he will ' speake to every citizen by his name, *no man telling him their names* ' ; and in the council he will manage even Eurybiades, with that ' Strike an thou wilt, so thou wilt heare me,' which has been one of the world's words since its utterance. Now with ' pleasaunt conceits and answers,' now—with a large poetic appeal—' pointing ' his countrymen ' the waye unto the sea ' ; this day, deceiving his friends, the next overawing his enemies ; with effrontery or chicane, with good-fellowship or reserve ; but ever with infinite dexterity, a courage that never falters, and a patience that never wearies : he keeps the shuttle of his thought quick-flying through the web of intrigue. And all for the fun of weaving ! Till, at the last, a banished man, being commanded by his Persian master to fight against Greece, ' he tooke a wise resolution with himselfe, to make suche an ende of his life, as the fame thereof deserved.' After sacrificing to the gods, and feasting his friends, he drank poison, ' and so ended his dayes in the cittie of Magnesia, ' after he had lived threescore and five yeres, and the most parte of them allwayes in office and great charge.' Plutarch produces this notable piece, not by comment and analysis but, simply by setting down his sitter's acts and words. It is in the same way that he paints his Alcibiades, with his beauty and his lisp : ' the grace of his eloquence, the strength and valiantness of his bodie . . . his wisdom and experience in marshall affayres ' ; and again, with his insolence and criminal folly to the women who loved him as to the nations he betrayed. He fought, like the Cid, now for and now against his own. But ' he had such pleasaunt comely devises with him that no man was of so sullen a nature, but he left him merrie, nor so churlishe, but he would make him gentle.' And when he died, they felt that their country died with him ; for they had some little poore hope left that they were not altogether cast away so long as Alcibiades lived.'

In the first rank of Plutarch's masterpieces come, with these two, the *Marius*, the *Cato*, the *Alexander*, the *Demetrius*, the *Antonius*, and the *Pompey*. Modern writers have again and again repainted some of these portraits ; but their colour has all been borrowed from Plutarch. These heroes live for all time in the *Parallel Lives*. There you shall learn the fashion of their faces, and the tricks of their speech ; their seat on horseback and the cut of their clothes ; with every tone and every gesture, all the charms and all the foibles that made them the men they were. Marcus Cato is what we call a ' character.' He hated doctors and, no doubt, schoolmasters ; for did he not educate his own son, writing for him 'goodly histories, *in great letters with his oune hande*'? He taught the boy grammar and law, 'to throw a dart, to play at the sword, to vawt, to ride a horse, and to handle all sortes of weapons, . . . to fight with fistes, to abide colde and heate, and to swimme over a swift runninge river.' A 'new man' from a little village, his ideal was Manlius Curius sitting 'by the fyer's side seething of perseneapes,' and he tried to educate everybody on the same lines. Being Censor, he would proceed by way of imprisonment; but at all times he was ready to instruct with apophthegms and 'wise sayings,' and 'he would taunte a marvelous fatte man' thus: 'See, sayd he, what good can such a body do to the commonwealth, that from his chine to his coddepece is nothing but belly?' This is but one of many 'wise sayings' reported of him, whereby 'we may the easilier conjecture his maners and nature.'[1] Even the *Alexander* seems a new thing still; so clear is the colouring, so vigorous and expressive the pose. 'Naturally,' you read, 'he had a very fayre white colour, mingled also with red,' and 'his body had so sweete a smell of itself, that all the apparell he wore next unto his body took thereof a passing delightful savor, as if it had been perfumed.' This was his idea of a holiday: 'After he was up in the morning, first of all he would doe sacrifice to the goddes, and then would goe to diner, passing awaie all the rest of the daye, in hunting, writing something, taking up some quarrell between soldiers, or els in studying. If he went any journey of no hastie busines, he would exercise himselfe by the waie as he went, shooting in his bowe, or learning to get up or

[1] Plutarch's Cato is accepted bodily by Mommsen for a typical 'Roman burgess.' *History of Rome*, vol. ii. pp. 429-432.

out of his charret sodenly, as it ranne. Oftentimes
also for his pastime he would hunt the foxe, or ketch
birdes, as appeareth in his booke of remembrances
for everie daie. Then when he came to his lodging,
he would enter into his bath and rubbe and nointe
himselfe: and would aske his pantelers and carvers
if his supper were ready. He would ever suppe
late, and was very curious to see, that every man at
his bourde were a like served, and would sit longe at
the table, bycause he ever loved to talke.' But take
him at his work of leading others to the uttermost
parts of the earth. Being parched with thirst, in
the desert, ' he tooke the helmet with water, and
perceiving that the men of armes that were about
him, and had followed him, *did thrust out their neckes
to look upon this water*, he gave the water back againe
unto them that had geven it him, and thanked them
but drank none of it. For, said he, *if I drink alone
all these men here will faint.*' What a touch! And
what wonder if his men ' beganne to spurre their
horses, saying that they were not wearie nor athirst,
*nor did think themselves mortall, so long as they had
such a king* '! There is more of self-restraint in
Plutarch's portrait than appears in later copies.
Alexander passes by the ladies of Persia ' without
any sparke of affection towardes them . . . prefer-
ring the beautie of his continencie, before their swete
faire faces.' But he was ever lavish of valour, loving
' his honour more then his kingdome or his life ' ; and
it is with a ' marvelous faier white plume ' in his
helmet that he plunges first into the river at Granicus,
and single-handed engages the army on the further
bank. Centuries later at Ivry, Henri-Quatre, who
learned Plutarch at his mother's knee, forgot neither
the feather nor the act. But the dead Alexander

never lacked understudies. All the kings, his successors, ' did but counterfeate ' him ' in his purple
garments, and in numbers of souldiers and gardes
about their persones, and in a certaine facion and
bowing of their neckes a little, and in uttering his
speech with a high voyce.' One of them is Demetrius
the Fort-gainer,' with ' his wit and manners . . .
that were both fearefull and pleasaunt unto men that
frequented him ' ; his ' sweete countenance . . .
and incomparable majestie ' ; ' more wantonly geven
to follow any lust and pleasure than any king that
ever was ; yet alwayes very careful and diligent in
dispatching matters of importance.' A leader of
forlorn hopes and lewd masquerades, juggling with
kingdoms as a mountebank with knives ; the lover
of innumerable queens and the taker of a thousand
towns ; in his defeat, ' not like unto a king, but
like a common player when the play is done ' ; drinking himself to death for that he found ' it was that
maner of life he had long desired '—this Poliorcetes,
I say, has furnished Plutarch with the matter for
yet another masterpiece, which indeed is one of the
greater feats in romantic realism.

Of the *Antonius* with his ' Asiatic phrase,' it is
enough to say that it is Shakespeare's Antony ; and
at the *Pompey* I have already glanced. The *Cæsar*
is only less wonderful than these because the man is
lost in the leader. Julius travels so fast, that you
'catch but glimpses as he races in his litter through
the night; ever dictating to his secretaries, and
writing by the way. But now and again you see
him plainly—' leane, white and soft-skinned, and
often subject to head-ache ' ; filling his soldiers with
awe, not at his valiantnesse at putting himself at
every instant in such manifest danger, since they

knew 'twas his greedy desire of honor that set him a
fire ' . . . but because he ' continued all labour and
hardnesse more than his bodie could beare.' A
strange ruler of the world, this epileptic, ' fighting
always with his disease ' ! He amazes friends and
enemies by the swiftness of his movements, while
Pompey journeys as in state from land to land.
Pompey was of plebeian extraction, Julius was born
into one of the sixteen surviving patrician *gentes*;
yet Julius burns with the blasting heat of a new man's
endeavour, Pompey as with the banked fires of
hereditary self-esteem. And through all the commotion and the coil he is still mindful of the day of his
youth ' when he had been acquainted with Servilia,
who was extreamilie in love with him. And because
Brutus was boorne in that time when their love was
hottest he persuaded himself that he begat him.' [1]
What of anguish does this not add to the sweep of
the gesture wherewith the hero covered his face from
the pedant's sword ! With the *Cæsar* may stand the
Marius, and the *Sylla* : Sulla the lucky man, *felix*,
Epaphroditus, beloved of all women and the victor
in every fight, who ' when he was in his chiefest
authoritie would commonly eate and drinke with the
most impudent jeasters and scoffers, and all such
rake helles, as made profession of counterfeate mirth.'
He laughed his way to complete political success ;
he was fortunate even in the weather for his funeral ;
and, as he epitaphed himself, ' no man did ever
passe him, neither in doing good to his friends,
nor in doing mischief to his enemies.' Plutarch's
Lucullus, being young and ambitious, marches
further into the unknown East than any Roman
had ventured. He fords the river on foot with the

[1] *Brutus.*

countless hosts of Tigranes on the farther shore,
' himselfe the foremost man,' and marches ' directly
towardes his enemy, armed with an " anima " of
steele, made with scalloppe shelles, shining like the
sunne.' He urges on through summer and winter,
till the rivers are ' congealed with ice,' so that no
man can ' passe over by forde : for they did no
sooner enter but the ise brake and cut the vaines and
sinews of the horse legges.' His men murmur, but
he presses on : till ' the country being full of trees,
woddes and forestes,' they are ' through wet with the
snow that fell upon them,' and at last they mutiny
and flatly refuse to take another step into the unknown. This is a Lucullus we forget. Plutarch
gives the other one as well, and the two together
make for him ' an aunciént comedy,' the beginning
whereof is tedious, but the latter end—with its
' feasts and bankets,' ' masks and mummeries,' and
' dauncing with torches,' its ' fine built chambers and
high raised turrets to gaze a farre, environed about
with conduits of water ' ; its superlative cook, too,
and its ' library ever open to all comers '—is a matter
to rejoice the heart of man. Crassus and Cicero
complete his group of second-bests : Cicero ' dogge
leane,' and ' a little eater,' ' so earnest and vehement
in his oration that he mounted still with his voyce
into the highest tunes : insomuch that men were
affrayed it would one day put him in hazard of his
life.' Here I may pause to note that Plutarch's
references to public speaking are all observed. He
writes from experience, and you might compile a
manual of the art from him. Well did he know the
danger of fluent earnestness. His Caius Gracchus
' had a servant . . . who, with an instrument of
musicke he had . . . ever stoode behind him ; and

when he perceived his Maister's voyce was a little too lowde, and that through choller he exceeded his ordinary speache, he played a soft stoppe behind him, at the sonde whereof Caius immediately fell from his extreamitie and easilie came to himself againe.' Thus, too, his *Demosthenes and Cicero* sets forth full instructions for removing every other blemish of delivery.[1]

The painter of incident is scarce less great than the painter of men. Plutarch's picture of Cicero is completed by a presentment of his death, in which the artist's imagination rises to its full height. Hunted down by Antony's sworders, the orator is overtaken at night in a by-lane ; he stretches out his head from the litter to look his murderers in the face ; and ' his head and his beard being all white, and his face leane and wrinckled, for the extreame sorrowes he had taken, divers of them that were by held their handes before their eyes, whilest Herennius did cruelly murder him.' Then the head was set up by Antony ' over the pulpit for orations,' and ' this was a fearefull and horrible sight unto the Romanes, who thought they saw not Ciceroes face, *but an image of Antonius life and dispositions*' (Amyot : *une image de l'âme et de la nature d'Antonius*). This gift, at times almost appalling, of imaginative presentment, is the distinctive note of Plutarch's art. He uses it freely in his backgrounds, which are animated as are those in certain pictures of a bygone mode ; so that behind his heroes armies engage, fleets are sunk, towns are sacked, and citadels escaladed. Sometimes his effect is produced by a rare restraint. In the *Alcibiades*, for instance, he tells how the Sicilian expedition was mooted which

[1] See also his account of the several manners of Cleon and Pericles.

was to ruin both the hero and his country; and, as
Carlyle might have done, at the corner of every
street he shows you the groups of young men bragging of victory, and drawing plans of Syracuse in
the dust. Sometimes the touch of terror is more
immediate. Take his description of the Teutons
from the *Marius*. Their voices were 'wonderful both
straunge and beastly'; so Marius kept his men close
till they should grow accustomed to such dreadful foes. Meanwhile the Teutons ' were passing by
his campe six dayes continually together ' : ' they
came raking by,' and ' marching all together in good
array ; making a noyse with their harness all after
one sorte, they oft rehearsed their own name,
Ambrons, *Ambrons*, *Ambrons* '; and the Romans
watched them, listening to the monotonous, un-
human call. Here and elsewhere Plutarch conveys,
with a peculiar magic, the sense of great bodies of
men and of the movements thereof. Now and then
he secures his end by reporting a word or twǒ from
those that are spying upon others from afar. This
is how he gives the space and silence that precede a
battle. Tigranes, with his innumerable host, is
watching Lucullus and the Romans, far away on the
farther shore of the river. ' They seemed but a
handful,' and kept ' following the streame to meete
with some forde. . . . Tigranes thought they had
marched away, and called for Taxiles, and sayd
unto him, laughing : " Dost thou see, Taxiles, those
goodly Roman legyons, whom thou praisest to be
men so invincible, how they flie away now ? "
Taxiles answered the king againe : " I would your
good fortune (O king) might work some miracle this
day : for doubtless it were a straunge thing that
the Romanes should flie. They are not wont to wear

their brave cotes and furniture uppon their armour, when they meane onely but to marche in the fieldes : neither do they carie their shieldes and targets uncased, nor their burganets bare on their heades, as they do at this present, having throwen away their leather cases and coveringes. But out of doubt, this goodly furniture we see *so bright and glittering in our faces,* is a manifest sign that they intend to fight, and that they marche towards us." *Taxiles had no sooner spoken these wordes, but Lucullus, in the view of his enemies, made his ensign bearer to turne sodainely that carried the first Eagle, and the bands tooke their places to passe the river in order of battell.'* The proportion of the two armies, and the space between ; the sun flashing on the distant shields ; the long suspense ; the king's laugh breaking the silence, which yet grows tenser, till suddenly the Romans wheel into line : in truth, they have been few between Plutarch and Tolstoi to give the scale and perspective of battles by observing such proportion in their art ! Here Lucullus and a handful of Romans, like Clive and his Englishmen, overthrew a nation in arms ; elsewhere Plutarch gives the other chance, and renders with touches equally subtle and direct the deepening nightmare of Crassus' march into the desert. He tells of the Parthian ' kettle drommes, hollow within,' and hung about with ' little bells and copper rings,' with which ' they all made a noise everywhere together, and it is like a dead sounde.' Does it not recall the Aztec wardrums on the Noche Triste ? Intent, too, on creating his impression of terror, this rare artist proceeds from the sense of hearing to the sense of sight. 'The Romanes being put in feare with this dead sounde, the Parthians straight threw the clothes

and coverings from them that hid their armour, and
then showed their bright helmets and curaces of
Margian tempered steele, *that glared like fire* ; and
their horses barbed with steele and copper.' They
canter round and round the wretched enemy, shooting their shafts as they go ; and the ammunition
never fails, for camels come up ' loden with quivers
full of arrowes.' The Romans are shot through one
by one ; and when Crassus ' prayed and besought
them to charge . . . they showed him their handes
fast nailed to their targets with arrowes, and their
feete likewise shot thorow and nailed to the ground :
so as they could neither flie, nor yet defende them
selves.' Thus they died, one before the other, ' a
cruell lingring death, crying out for anguish and
paine they felt ' ; and ' turning and tormenting
themselves upon the sande, they broke the arrowes
sticking in them.' The realism of it ! And the
pathos of Crassus' speech, when his son's head is
shown to him, which ' killed the Romanes hartes ' !
' The grief and sorrow of this losse (my fellowes),'
said he, ' is no man's but mine, mine only ; but the
noble successe and honor of Rome remaineth still
invincible, so long as you are yet living.' After
these two pictures of confidence and defeat I should
like to give that one of the Romans after Pydna,
where Paulus Æmilius was thought to have lost his
son. It is a wonderful resurrection of departed life.
There are the groups round the camp-fires ; the
sudden clustering of torches towards the one dark
and silent tent ; and then the busy lights crossing
and recrossing, and scattering over the field. You
hear first the droning songs of the tired and happy
soldiers ; then silence ; then cries of anxiety and
mournful echoes ; then, of a sudden, comes the

reappearance, ' all bloudied with new bloude like
the swift-running grey hound fleshed with the
bloude of the hare,' of him, the missing youth,
' that Scipio which afterwards destroyed both the
citties of Carthage and Numantium.'

It is hard to analyse the art, for the means employed are of the simplest ; yet it is certain that they
do recall to such as have known, and that they must
suggest to others who have not, those sights and
sounds and sensations which combine into a special
enchantment about the time. of the fall of darkness
upon bodies of men who have drunk excitement and
borne toil together in the day. How intense, too,
the flash of imagination with which the coming
Africanus is projected on the canvas ! And the book
abounds in such lightning impressions. Thus, Hannibal cracks a soldier's joke before Cannæ ; he
pitches the quip into his host, like a pebble into the
pond ; and the broken stillness ripples away down
all the ranks in widening rings of laughter.[1] Sometimes the sketch is even slighter, and is yet convincing : as when the elder Scipio, being attacked
by Cato for his extravagant administration, declares
his ' intent to go to the wars *with full sayles*.' These
are not chance effects but masterstrokes of imagination ; yet that imagination, vivid and vivifying as
it is, never leads Plutarch to attempt the impossible.
He remains the supreme artist, and is content with
suggesting—what is incapable of representation—
that sense of the portentous, the overpowering,
which is apparent immediately before, or immediately behind, some notable conjunction. Alexander
sounds the charge which is to change the fortunes
of the world, and Arbela is rendered in a few lines.

[1] *Fabius Maximus.*

But up till the instant of his sounding it, you are told
of his every act. Plutarch, proceeding as leisurely
as his hero, creates suspense out of delay. You
are told that Alexander slept soundly far into the
morning, and that he was called three times. You
are told how carefully he dressed, and of each article
of armour and apparel he put on: his 'Sicilian
cassocke,' his ' brigandine of many foldes of canvas,'
' his head peece bright as silver,' and ' his coller
sute like to the same all set full of precious stones.'
The battle has begun between the outposts, and he
is still riding down the lines on a hack : ' to spare
Bucephal, because he was then somewhat olde.'
He mounted the great horse ' always at the last
moment ; and as soone as he was gotten up on his
backe, the trumpet sounded, and he gave charge.'
To-day it is made to seem as if that moment would
never come ; but at the last all things being ready,
' he tooke his launce in his left hande and, holding
up his right hande unto heaven, besought the goddes
. . . that if it were true, he was begotten of Jupiter,
it would please them that day to helpe him and to
incorage the Græcians. The sooth-sayer Aristander
was then a-horsebacke hard by Alexander apparelled
all in white, and a croune of gold on his head, who
shewed Alexander when he made his prayer, an
Eagle flying over his head, and pointing directly
towards his enemies. This marvellously encouraged
all the armie that saw it, and with this joy, the men
of armes of Alexander's side, encouraging one
another, did set spurres to their horse to charge upon
the enemies.' Until the heroic instant you are compelled to note the hero's every deliberate movement. He and the little group of gleaming figures
about him are the merest specks in the plain before

the Macedonian army, itself but a handful in comparison to the embattled nations in front. The art
is perfect in these flash-pictures of great moments
in time : in the Athenians map-drawing in the dust,
in the Romans watching the Ambrons raking by, in
Tigranes' laugh, in Hannibal's joke, in Alexander's
supreme gesture ; and how instant in each the
imaginative suggestion of dragging hours before
rapid and irreparable events ! Equally potent are
the effects which Plutarch contrives by revealing
all the consequences of a disaster in some swift, far-
reaching glimpse. Thus, when Cæsar crossed the
Rubicon, 'Rome itself was filled up with the flowing
repaire of all the people who came thither *like droves
of cattell.*' And thus does Sparta receive the news
of her annihilation :—' At that time there was by
chance a common feast day in the citie . . . when
as the messenger arrived that brought the news of
the battell lost at Leuctres! The Ephori knowing
then that the rumor ranne all about ; that they
were all undone, and how they had lost the signorie
and commaundement over all Grece : would not
suffer them for all this to breake off their daunce in
the Theater, nor the citie in anything to chaunge
the forme of their feast, but sent unto the parentes
to everie man's house, to let them understande the
names of them that were slaine at the battell, they
themselves remaining still in the Theater to see the
daunces and sportes continued, to judge who carried
the best games away. The next morning when everie
man knew the number of them that were slaine, and
of those also that escaped : the parentes and frendes
of them that were dead, met in the market place,
looking cheerfully of the matter, and one of them
embraced another. On thother side the parentes of

them that scaped, kept their houses with their wives, as folk that mourned. . . . The mothers of them, that kept their sonnes which came from the battell, were sad and sorrowfull, and spake not a word. Contrairily, the mothers of them that were slaine, *went friendly to visite one another, to rejoyce together.*' [1] There is no word of the fight. As Thackeray gives you Waterloo in a picture of Brussels, so Plutarch gives you Leuctra, and with more of beauty and pathos, in a picture of Sparta. Of the Roman defeat at Cannæ there is a full and wonderful account ; but what an effective touch is added with ' the Consul Terentius Varro returning backe to Rome, with the shame of his extreame misfortune and overthrowe, that he durste not looke upon any man : the Senate notwithstanding, *and all the people following them, went to the gates of the cittie to meete him, and dyd honourably receyve him* ' !

In these passages Plutarch, following the course of Greek tragedy, and keeping the action off the stage, gives the reverberation and not the shock of fate ; but in many others the stark reality of his painting is its own sufficient charm. He abounds in unfamiliar aspects of familiar places : places he invests with (as it were) the magic born of a wandering son's return. Here is his Athens in her decrepitude. ' The poore citie of Athens which had escaped from so many warres, tyrannies and civil dissensions,' is now besieged by Sulla without, and oppressed by the tyrant Aristion within ; and in his presentment of her condition there is, surely, a foreshadowing of those dark ages when historic sites became the scenes of new tragedies that were merely brutal and insignificant. At Athens ' men were driven for famine

[1] *Agesilaus.*

to eate feverfew that grew about the castell'; also, they 'caused old shoes and old oyle potes to be sodden to deliver some savor unto that which they did eate.' Meanwhile ' the tyrant himselfe did nothing all day long but cramme in meat, drinke dronke, daunce, maske, scoff and flowte at the enemies (suffering the holy lampe of Minerva to go out for lack of oyle).' Is there not a grimness of irony about this picture of the drunken and sinister buffoon sitting camped in the Acropolis, like a toad in a ruined temple, ' magnifying the dedes of Theseus and insulting the priestes'? At last the Roman enters the city about midnight 'with a wonderfull fearefull order, making a marvellous noise with a number of hornes and sounding of trompets, and all his army with him in order of battell, crying, " To the sack, to the sack: Kill, kill." ' [1] A companion picture is that of a Syracuse Thucydides never knew.[2] Archimedes is her sole defence; and thanks to him, the Roman ships are ' taken up with certaine engines fastened within one contrary to an other, which made them turne in the ayer like a whirlegigge, and so cast them upon the rockes by the towne walles, and splitted them all to fitters, to the great spoyle and murder of the persons that were within them.' Elsewhere the Mediterranean pirates, polite as our own highwaymen, are found inviting noble Romans to walk the plank; [3] for Plutarch never misses a romantic touch. Some of his strongest realisations are of moments when fate hangs by a hair: as that breathless and desperate predicament of Aratus and his men on their ladders against the walls of Sicyon; with the ' curste curres' that would not cease from barking; the captain of the watch ' visiting the soldiers with a

---

[1] *Sylla.*   [2] *Marcellus.*   [3] *Pompey.*

little bell ' ; ' the number of torches and a great
noyse of men that followed him ' ; the great grey-
hound kept in a little tower, which began to answer
the curs at large ' with a soft girning : but when
they came by the tower where he lay, he barked out
alowde, that all the place thereabouts rang of his
barking ' ; the ladders shaking and bowing ' by
reason of the weight of the men, unless they did come
up fayer and softly one after another,' till at last,
' the cocks began to crowe, and the country folke
that brought things to the market to sell, began to
come apace to the towne out of every quarter.' [1]
Later in the same life you have the escalading of
the Acrocorinthus : when Aratus and the storming
party, with their shoes off, being lost on the slopes,
' sodainely, even as it had been by miracle, the moone
appearing through the clowdes, brought them to
that part of the wall where they should be, and
straight the moone was shadowed againe ' ; so they
cut down the watch, but one man escaped, and ' the
trompets forthwith sounded the alarom . . . all the
citie was in an uprore, the streets were straight full
of people running up and downe, and of lights in
every corner.' Plutarch's management of light, I
should remark, is always astonishingly real ; he
never leaves the sun or the moon out of his picture,
nor the incidence of clouds and of the dust of battle.
Thus varied his sunshine leaps and wavers on distant armour, or glares at hand from Margian steel ;
or his moonlight glints on a spear, and fades as the
wrack races athwart the sky.

It is all the work of an incomparable painter ;
there is any amount of it in the *Parallel Lives* ; [2] and,

---

[1] *Aratus.*
[2] See the rousing of Greece in the *Philopœmen* ; the declaration of

like his portraits and his landscapes,[1] it has an
æsthetic value which sets it far in front of his moral
reflections.   For value depends, in part, on supply ;
and of this kind of art there is less in literature than
there is of ethical disquisition.   Moreover, in the
Parallel Lives the proportions are reversed, and the
volume of Plutarch's painting is very much greater
than the volume of Plutarch's moralities.   And in
addition to volume, there is charm.   His pictures
have kept their ' flourishing freshness ' untarnished
through the ages ;   whereas his moral sayings, being
sound, have long since been accepted, and, as I
said, are grown stale.   His morality is ours ;   but
he had an unique opportunity for depicting the
politics, the personalities, and the activity of a world
which had passed away.   A little earlier, and he
might have laboured like Thucydides, but only at
a part of it.   A little later, and much would have
perished which he has set down and saved.   He
paints it as a whole, and on that account is sometimes slighted for a compiler of legends ;   yet he had
the advantage of personal contact with those legends
while they were still alive ;   and again and again, as
you read, this contact strikes with a pleasant shock.
To illustrate his argument he will refer, by the way,
to the statue of Themistocles in the Temple of
Artemis ; to the effigies of Lucullus at Chæronea ; to
the buildings of Pericles in their divinely protracted
youth.   The house of Phocion at Melita, and the
' cellar ' in which Demosthenes practised his oratory,

liberty in the *Flaminius* ; the squadron of the Lacedæmonians at Platæa in
the *Aristides* ; the glimpse of Philip at Chæronea gazing at the ' Holy Band
of Thebans all dead on the grounde ' in the *Pelopidas* ; the first ride of
Alexander on Bucephalus in the *Alexander* ; the Macedonians at Pydna in
the *Paulus Æmilius*.

[1] See the country of the Cimbri in the *Marius*, and the campaigns of
Lucullus and Crassus.

were 'whole even to my time.' The descendants of the soldier who slew Epaminondas are, 'to this day,' known and distinguished by the name 'machœriones.'[1] On the battlefield of Chæronea 'there was an olde oke seene in my time which the country men commonly called Alexander's oke, bicause his tent or pavilion was fastened to it.'[2] His grandfather Nicarchus had told him how the defeat of Antony relieved his natal city from a requisition for corn.[3] From his other grandfather, Lamprias, he heard of a physician, his friend, who, 'being a young man desirous to see things,' went over Cleopatra's kitchen with one of Antony's cooks; and there, among 'a world of diversities of meates,' encountered with the 'eight wild boares, rosted whole,' which have passed bodily into Shakespeare. This contact was rarely immediate; but it was personal, and it is therefore quickening. At its touch a dead world lived again for Plutarch, and by his art that dead world lives for us; so that in the *Lives*, as in no other book, all antiquity, alike in detail and in expanse, lies open and revealed to us, 'flat as to an eagle's eye.' We may study it closely, and see it whole; and to do so is to dispossess the mind of many illusions fostered by books of a narrower scope. Juvenal, the satirist, and Petronius, the arbiter of a mode, do not even pretend to show forth the whole of life; yet from their works, and from others of a like purview, men have constructed a fanciful world of unbounded cruelty and immitigable lust. This same disproportion between premise and conclusion runs through the writing of many moderns: just as from the decoration of a single chamber at Pompeii there have been evoked

[1] *Agesilaus.*   [2] *Alexander.*   [3] *Antonius.*

whole cities, each in the image of a honeycomb whose cells are *lupanaria*. Even so some archæologist of the future might take up an obscene gurgoyle, and transfigure Christianity to its image ! This antiquity of cruelty and lust has been evolved for censure by these, and by those for praise ; yet if Plutarch be not the most colossal, taking, and ingenious among the world's liars, we cannot choose but hold that it never existed. For, apart from the coil of politics and the clamour and romance of adventure, his book discovers us the religious and the home lives of old-time Italy and Greece ; and we find them not dissimilar from our own. We see them, it is true, with the eyes of a kindly and a moderate man. Yet he was no apologist, with a case to plead ; and if we may be sure that he was never uncharitable, we may be equally sure that he extenuated nothing. He censures freely conduct which, according to the extreme theory of ancient immorality, should scarce have excited his surprise ; and he alludes, by the way, in a score of places, to a loving-kindness, extending even to slaves and animals, of which, according to the same theory, he could have known nothing, since its very existence is denied. The State was more than it is now ; but you cannot glean that the Family was less, even in Sparta. Shakespeare took from Plutarch the love of Coriolanus for his mother, and found in it a sufficient motive for his play. But Veturia [1] is by no means the only beloved mother in the *Lives*, nor is Coriolanus the only adoring son. Epaminondas thought himself ' most happy and blessed ' because his father and mother had lived to see the victory he won ; [2] and Sertorius, making overtures for peace,

---

[1] Shakespeare's Volumnia.   [2] *Coriolanus.*

said he had ' rather be counted the meanest citizen
in Rome, than being a banished man to be called
Emperor of the world,' and the ' chiefest cause . . .
was the tender love he bare unto his mother.' [1]
When Antipater submitted to Alexander certain well-
founded accusations against Olympia's misgovern-
ment : ' " Loe," said he, " Antipater knoweth not,
that one teare of the mothers eye will wipe out tenne
thousande such letters." ' [2] In face of the parting
between Cratesiclea and her son Cleomenes, one may
doubt if in Sparta itself the love between mother
and son was more than dissembled ; for, on the eve
of his sailing, ' she took Cleomenes aside into the
temple of Neptune and imbracinge and kissinge him ;
perceivinge that his harte yerned for sorrowe of her
departure, she sayed unto him : " O kinge of
Lacedæmon, lette no man see for shame when we
come out of the temple, that we have wept and dis-
honoured Sparta." ' Indeed, the national love of
Spartans for all children born to Sparta seems to
have been eked out by the fonder and the less in-
different affection of each parent for his own. If in
battle Henri-Quatre played Alexander, in the nursery
his model was Agesilaus, ' who loved his children
deerely : and would play with them in his home
when they were little ones, and ride upon a little
cocke horse or a reede, as a horseback.' [3] Paulus
Æmilius being ' appointed to make warre upon King
Perseus, all the people dyd honorably companie him
home unto his house, where a little girl (a daughter
of his) called Tertia, being yet an infant, came weeping unto her father. He, making muche of her,
asked her why she wept. The poore girl answered,
colling him about the necke, and kissing him :—

[1] *Sertorius.*   [2] *Alexander.*   [3] *Agesilaus.*

" Alas, father, wot you what ? our Perseus is dead."
*She ment by it a litle whelpe so called, which was her
playe fellowe.*' Plutarch had lost his own daughter,
and he wrote a letter of consolation to his wife, which
Montaigne gave to *his* wife when she was stricken
with the same sorrow : ' bien marry,' as he says, ' de
quoy la fortune vous a rendu ce present si propre.' [1]
In the *Lives* he is ever most tender towards children,
acknowledging the mere possibility of their loss for
an ever-abiding terror. ' Nowe,' he writes in the
Solon, ' we must not arme ourselves with poverty
against the grief of losse of goodes ; neither with
lack of affection against the losse of our friendes ;
neither with want of mariage against the death of
children ; but we must be armed with reason against
misfortune.' Over and over again you come upon
proof of the love and the compassion children had.
At the triumph of the same Æmilius, through three
days of such magnificence as Mantegna has displayed, the eyes of Rome were all for Perseus'
children : ' when they sawe the poore little infants,
that they knewe not the change of their hard fortune
. . . for the compassion they had of them, almost
let the father passe without looking upon him.' Of
Æmilius' own sons, one had died five days before,
and the other three days survived, that triumph
for which the father had been given four hundred
golden diadems by the cities of Greece. But he
pronounced their funeral orations himself 'in face of
the whole cittie . . . not like a discomforted man,
but like one rather that dyd comforte his sorrowfull
countrymen for his mischance. He told them . . .
he ever feared Fortune, mistrusting her change and

---

[1] Cruserius, who translated the *Lives* into Latin (1561), by a strange coincidence, mourned his daughter's loss and found consolation in his task.

inconstancy, and specially in the last warre.' But
Rome had won ; and all was well, ' saving that
Perseus yet, conquered as he is, hath this comforte
left him : to see his children living, and that the
conqueror Æmylius hath lost his.' This love between children and parents might be expected in
any picture of any society ; yet it is conspicuous in
the *Parallel Lives* as it is not, I believe, in any recon-
struction of the Plutarchian world.   Note, too, the
passionate devotion between brothers, displayed
even by Cato of Utica,[1] to the scandal of other Stoics ;
and note everywhere the loyal comradeship between
husbands and wives.   To Plutarch wedlock is so
sacred that he is fierce in denouncing a certain
political marriage as being ' cruell and tyrannicall,
fitter for Sylla's time, rather than agreable to
Pompey's nature.' [2] Perhaps the commonest view
of antique morality is that which accepts a family
not unlike the family we know, but at the same
time denies the ancients all consideration for their
domestic animals and slaves.   This tendency, it is
thought, is a product of Christianity ; and the
example of the elder Cato is sometimes quoted in
proof of the view.   But in Plutarch's *Cato*, the
Roman's habit of selling his worn-out slaves is given
for an oddity, for the exceptional practice of an
eccentric old man ; and Plutarch takes the occasion
to expound his own feeling. ' There is no reason,'
he writes, ' to use livinge and sensible thinges as we
would use an old shooe or a ragge : to cast it out
upon the dongehill when we have worn it and it can
serve us no longer.   For if it were for no respect els
but to use us alwayes to humanitie, we must ever
showe ourselves kinde and gentle, even in such small

---

[1] *Cato Utican.*   [2] *Pompey.*

poyntes of pitie.   And as for me, I coulde never finde
in my heart to sell my drawt oxe that hadde ploughed
my land a long time, bicause he coulde plowe no
longer for age.'   Here we have a higher standard of
humanity than obtains in living England, and it is a
mistake to suppose, as some have done, that it was
peculiar to Plutarch.   On the contrary, his book is
alive with illustrations of the same consideration for
domestic pets and beasts of service.   A mule employed in building a temple at Athens, used to ' come
of herselfe to the place of labour ' :   a docility,
' which the people liked so well in the poore beast,
that they appointed she shoulde be kept whilest she
lived, at the charge of the town.'   How many
corporations, I wonder, would lay a like load on the
rates to-day ?   In a score of passages is evidence
of the belief that ' gentleness goeth farther than
justice.' [1]   When the Athenians depart from Attica,
the most heartrending picture is of the animals they
leave deserted on the sea-coast.   ' There was besides a certen pittie that made men's harts to yerne,
when they saw the poore doggs, beasts, and cattell
ronne up and doune bleating, mouing, and howling
out alowde after their masters in token of sorrow
when they dyd imbark.'   Xantippus' dog, ' that
swam after them to Salamis and dyed presently,' is
there interred ; and ' they saye at this daye the place
called the Doggs Grave is the very place where he
was buried.' [2]   With like honour the mares of
Cimon, who was fond of racing, are buried at his
side.   Indeed, the ancients, far from being callous,
were, as some would now think, over-sentimental
about their horses and dogs.   Having no slaves of
our own, it is easy for us to denounce slave-owning.

[1] *Cato.*   [2] *Themistocles.*

But this is noteworthy : that while Plutarch, the
ancient, in dealing with the revolt of Spartacus and
his fellow-slaves, speaks only of ' the wickedness of
their master,' and pities their hard lot, North, the
modern, dubs them ' *rebellious rascalls*,' [1] without a
word of warrant either in the nearer French or in the
remoter Greek.

It is, indeed, far easier to pick up points of resemblance than to discover material differences between the social life depicted by Plutarch and our
own ; and the likeness extends even to those half-
shades of feeling and illogical sentiment which often
seem peculiar to a generation. To turn from contemporary life to the *Parallel Lives* is to find everywhere the same natural but inconsequent deference
to birth amid democratic institutions ; [2] the same
belief that women have recently won a freedom
unknown to their grandmothers ; the same self-
satisfaction in new developments of culture ; the
same despair over the effects of culture on a pristine
morality. There are even irresistible appeals to the
good old days. Numa, for instance, ' enured women
to speak little by forbidding them to speak at all
except in the presence of their husbands,' and with
such success, that a woman ' chauncing one daye
to pleade her cause in persone before the judges, the
Senate hearing of it, did send immediately unto the
oracle of Apollo, to know what that did prognosticate
to the cittie.' [3] Here was a beginning ; and the rest
soon followed. Just as Greek historians had branded
the first murderers and parricides by name, even so
' the Romanes doe note . . . that the wife of one
Pinarius, called Thalœa, was the first which ever

---

[1] *Crassus.*   [2] See Themistocles as the rival of Cimon.
[3] *Comparison of Numa Pompilius with Lycurgus.*

brauled or quarrelled with her mother-in-law.' [1]
That was in the days of Tarquin. By Pompey's
time—though he, indeed, was fortunate in a wife
unspoiled by her many accomplishments—the revolution is complete. His Cornelia ' could play
well on the harpe, was skilfull in musicke and
geometrie, and tooke great pleasure also in philosophie, and not vainly without some profit ' ; yet
was she ' very modest and sober in behaviour, without brauling and foolish curiosity, which commonly
young women have, that are indued with such
singular giftes.' Such a woman was the product of
the Greek culture, and for that Plutarch has nothing
but praise.[2] It was first introduced, he tells you,
after the siege of Syracuse ; for Marcellus it was
who brought in ' fineness and curious tables,'
' pictures and statues,' to supplant the existing
' monuments of victories': things in themselves ' not
pleasant, but rather fearfull sightes to look upon,
farre unfit for feminine eyes.' [3] In all this there is
little that differs from the life we know : you have
the same facts and the same reflexions—especially
the same reflexions. For our own age is akin to the
age of Plutarch, in so far as both are certain centuries
in rear of an influx of Hellenic ideas. Those ideas
reconquered the West in the fifteenth century ; and
since this second invasion the results of the first have
been repeated in many directions. Certain phases,
indeed, of thought and feeling in Plutarch's age are
re-echoed to-day still more distinctly than in the
world of his Renaissance translators. For in re-
moteness from the point of first contact with Greek

---

[1] *Comparison of Numa Pompilius with Lycurgus.*
[2] See his defence of it in *Cicero*, his attack on Cato for opposing it, and
passim. [3] *Marcellus.*

influence, and in the tarnish of disillusion which must inevitably discolour any prolonged development, this century of ours is more nearly allied to Plutarch's than the sixteenth was, with its young hope and unbounded enthusiasm. The older activity reminds you of the times which Plutarch painted; the modern temper, of the times in which he wrote.

But in the frail rope which the mind of man is ever weaving, that he may cling to something in the void of his ignorance, there is one strand which runs through all the Plutarchian centuries ; which persists in his own age and on into the age of his early translators ; but which in England has been fretted almost through. Nobody can read the *Parallel Lives* without remarking the signal change which has fallen upon man's attitude towards the supernatural. Everywhere in Plutarch, by way of both narrative and comment, you find a confirmed belief in omens, portents, and ghosts : not a pious opinion, but a conviction bulking huge in everyday thought, and exerting a constant influence on the ordinary conduct of life. Death and disaster, good fortune and victory, never come without forewarning. Before great Cæsar fell there were ' fires in the element . . . spirites running up and downe in the nighte ' and ' solitary birdes to be seene at noone dayes sittinge in the great market-place.' [1] Nor only before a great event, but also after it, occur these sympathetic perturbations in the other world : ' the night being come, such things fell out, as maye be looked for after so terrible a battle.' [2] The wood quaked, and a voice cried out of heaven ! Allied to and alongside of this belief in an Unseen in touch with the living world at every hour of the day-time

[1] *Julius Cæsar.*   [2] *Publicola.*

and night, you have the solemn practice of obscure
rites and the habitual observance of customs half-
insignificant. Some of these are graceful ; others
embarrassing. The divination, for instance, of the
Spartan Ephors must often, at least in August and
November, have shaken public confidence in the
State ; for they 'did sit downe in some open place,
and beheld the stars in the element, to see if they
saw any starre shoote from one place to another,'
and ' *if they did, then they accused their king.*' [1] To
us, this giving of the grotesque and the terrible in
the same breath, without distinction or comment, is
strangely incongruous. Sulla's bloody entry into
Rome was doubly foreshadowed : there was the antic
disposition of certain rats, which first gnawed ' some
juells of golde in a church,' and then, being trapped
by the ' sexton,' ate up their young ; and again,
' when there was no cloude to be seen in the element
at all, men heard such a sharp sound of a trompet,
as they were almost out of their wits at so great a
noise.' [2] No scientific explanation, even if one were
forthcoming, could suffice to lull suspicion in a pious
mind. Æmilius understood as well as any the cause
of the moon's eclipse : ' nevertheless, he being a
godly devout man, so soon as he perceyved the
moone had recovered her former brightness againe,
he sacrificed eleven calves.' [3] To add to the incon-
venience of this habit of mind, there were more
unlucky days in the year than holidays in the mediæval calendar. It was such a day that marred the
prospect of Alcibiades' return : for ' there were some
that misliked very much the time of his landing :
saying it was very unluckie and unfortunate. For
the very day of his returne, fell out by chaunce on

---

[1] *Agis and Cleomenes.*   [2] *Sylla.*   [3] *Paulus Æmilius.*

the feast which they call Plynteria, as you would
saye, the washing day.' [1] Such feasts, with their
half-meaningless customs, accompanied the belief in
portents and ghosts and the ordinary forms of ritual,
being but another fruit of the same intellectual
habit. Some of them seem absurd anachronisms
in the Rome of Julius Cæsar. At the Lupercal, for
instance, even in Cæsar's day, as every one knows
from Shakespeare, young men of good family still
ran naked through the streets, touching brides at
the request of their husbands.[2] Again, on the feast
of the goddess Matuta, ' they cause a chamber mayde
to enter into her temple, and there they boxe her
about the eares. Then they put her out of the
temple, and do embrace their brothers' children
rather than their own.' [3] There is no end to these
customs : customs which are as it were *costumes* of
the mind, partly devised to cover its nakedness, and
partly expressed in fancy. Plutarch tries sometimes
to explain their origin ; but he can only hazard a
guess. Nobody remembers what they mean. They
are, rather, a picturesque means of asserting that
there really is an undercurrent of meaning in the
world.

Beyond and above these mummeries, now so
strange, in a loftier range of Plutarch's thought is
much that is familiar and near. Of some miracles
he writes almost as an apologist. It is said that
' images . . . have been heard to sighe : that they
have turned : and that they have made certen
signes with their eyes.' These reports ' are not,' he
adds, ' incredible, nor lightly to be condemned.
But for such matters it is daungerous to give too
much credit to them, as also to discredit them too

much, by reason of the weaknes of man's nature, which hath no certen boundes, nor can rule itself, but ronneth sometimes to vanitie and superstition, and otherwhile also despiseth and condemneth holy and divine matters.' [1] On such points of belief, as on the immediate inspiration of individuals, ' the waye is open and large': [2] each must decide for himself, remembering that religion is the mean between superstition and impiety.   On the other hand, never once does Plutarch admit a doubt of the Divine Government of the world. He approves his Alexander's saying: ' that God generally was father to all mortall men.' [3] And in a magnificent passage of North's English which might almost have come out of the book of Common Prayer, he upholds the view of Pythagoras : ' who thought that God was neither sensible nor mortall, but invisible, incorruptible and only intelligible.' [4]

III

In substance, then, the book stands alone. Its good fortune has been also unexampled. By a chance this singular image of the ancient world has been happy beyond others in the manner of its transmission to our time. To quote a Quarterly Reviewer : [5] ' There is no other case of an ancient writer—whether Greek or Latin—becoming as well

---

[1] *Furius Camillus.*   [2] *Numa Pompilius.*

[3] *Alexander.* Cf. *Plutarch's Morals*, Phil. Holland, 1657 : the eighth book of *Symposiaques* ; the first question, p. 628.

[4] In the *Brutus* North credits its hero with a declaration of belief in another life.   But this is a mistranslation of Amyot's French.   We know, however, with what passionate conviction Plutarch held this belief in ' a better place, and a happier condition,' from the conclusion of his ' consolatory letter, sent unto his own wife, as touching the death of her and his daughter.'—*Morals*, Phil. Holland, 1657, p. 442.

[5] Vol. cx., No. 220, p. 459, Oct. 1861.   Apparently Archbishop Trench.

known in translations as he was in the classical world, or as great modern writers are in the modern one ' ; and for this chance we have to thank one man, Jaques Amyot. But for his version we should have received none from North ; and without these two, Plutarch must have remained sealed to all but Greek scholars. For the Daciers and the Langhornes could never have conquered in right of their own impoverished prose. They palmed it off on a public still dazzled by the fame wherewith their forerunners had illuminated the *Lives* ; and when these were ousted from recollection, their own fate became a simple matter of time.

The son of a butcher,[1] or a draper,[2] Jaques Amyot was born at Melun in 1513, and was sent as a boy by his parents to study at Paris. You find him there at fifteen, at Cardinal Lemoine's college, and two years later following the lectures of Thusan and Danès. For the University, still hide-bound in scholastic philosophy, was nothing to his purpose of mastering Greek. It was hard in those years, even for the rich, to find books in Greek character,[3] and Amyot must live on the loaves his mother sent him by the river barges, and wait for a pittance on his fellow-students. Yet he toiled on with romantic enthusiasm, reading by the firelight for lack of candles ; till at last he knew all they could teach him, and left Paris to become a tutor at Bourges. There, thanks to Marguerite de Navarre,[4] he obtained a chair in the University, whence he lectured twice a day on Greek and Latin letters during twelve years.

---

[1] Brantôme,
[2] Blignières. According to another, *parentibus honestis magis quam copiosis.*
[3] Before 1530 only a few Homeric *Hymns* and some essays of Plutarch had been published.   [4] The Marguerite of *The Heptameron.*

It was in these years that he began his great work
as a translator: completing in all probability the
Æthiopian History,[1] and the more famous *Daphnis
and Chloe*.[2] But, at the instance of Marguerite's
brother, François I., he also began the *Lives*, receiving by way of incentive the Abbacy of Bellozane;[3]
and to prosecute this purpose, soon after the king's
death, he made a scholar's pilgrimage to Italy. In
the Library of St. Mark at Venice he rediscovered the
Lives of Diodorus Siculus;[4] in the Library of the
Vatican a more perfect MS. of the *Æthiopian History*.
But search as he might during his two years' stay
at Rome, he could never recover the missing lives of
Plutarch. He laboured on the text, but those which
l'injurie du temps nous avoit enviées,[5] were gone past
retrieving. On his return the scholar became a
courtier, in the castles of the Loire, and something of
a diplomat; for he acted as the emissary of Henri II.
at the Council of Trent, playing an inconspicuous
part grossly exaggerated by De Thou. In 1554 he
was appointed tutor to the young princes who were
to rule as Charles IX. and Henri III. In 1559 he
published the *Lives*; the next year, on the accession
of his elder pupil, he was made Grand Almoner of
France; and in 1570 he became Bishop of Auxerre.
In 1572 he published the *Morals*; but this book, like
the *Franciade*, published in the same year, fell com-

[1] Published in 1547 with an interesting passage in the proem: ' Et
n'avoit ce livre jamais esté imprimé, sinon depuis que la librairie du roi
Matthias Corvin fut saccagée, au quel sac il se trouva un soldat allemant
qui mit la main dessus pour ce qu'il le vit richement estofé, et le vendit à
celuy qui depuys le fit imprimer en Allemaigne.'

[2] Published without his name as late as 1559. As tutor to the young
princes he seems to have entertained a certain scruple, which even led him
to suppress one passage in his translation.

[3] 1546. The last benefice bestowed by François.

[4] Of which he translated and published seven in 1554.

[5] Amyot: *Aux Lecteurs.*

paratively dead.   The halcyon days of scholars and
poets ended with the St. Bartholomew ; and thenceforward the darkness deepened over these two and
all the brilliant company which had gathered round
Catherine and Diane de Poictiers.   In 1588 the full
fury of the Catholic League fell upon Amyot, for
standing by his king after the murder of the Guise.
His diocese revolted at the instigation of Claude
Trahy, a truculent monk ; and the last works he
published are his *Apology* and *Griefs des Plaintes.*
In August 1589 he wrote to the Duc de Nivernais :
' Je suis le plus affligé, destruit et ruiné pauvre
prebstre qui, comme je crois, soit en France ' ; in
1591 he was divested of his dignities ; [1] and in 1593
he died.   His long life reflects the changing features
of his time.   In youth he was a scholar accused of
scepticism, in old age a divine attacked for heresy,
and for some pleasant years between, a courtier
pacing with poets and painters the long galleries of
Amboise and Chenonceaux : as we may think, well
within earshot of those wide bay-windows where the
daughters of France ' entourées de leurs gouver-
nantes et filles d'honneur, s'edifioient grandement
aux beaux dits des Grecs et des Romains, rememoriez
par le doulx Plutarchus.' [2]

He was, then, a scholar touched with the wonder
of a time which saw, as in Angelo's *Last Judgment,*
the great works of antiquity lifting their limbs
from the entombing dust of oblivion ; and he
was a courtier behind the scenes in a great age of
political adventure.   Was he also an accurate translator ?   According to De Thou, he rendered his
original ' majore elegantiâ quam fide ' ; according to

[1] Grand Almoner and Librarian of the Royal Library.
[2] Brantôme.

Meziriac,[1] he was guilty of two thousand blunders.[2]
The verdict was agreeable to the presumption of the
seventeenth century, and was, of course, confirmed
by the eighteenth ; but it has been revised. Given
the impossibility of finding single equivalents in the
young speech of the Renaissance, for the literary and
philosophic connotations of a language laboured
during six hundred years ; and given the practice
of choosing without comment the most plausible
sense of a corrupted passage, the better opinion
seems to be that Amyot lost little in truth, and
gained everything in charm.   ' It is surprising,' says
Mr. Long,[3] and his word shall be the last, ' to find
how correct this old French translation generally
is.'   The question of style is of deeper importance.
Upon this Ste.-Beuve acutely remarks [4] that the
subtlety of Plutarch, as of Augustine, and the artless
good-nature of Amyot belong each to its age ; and,
further, are more apparent to us than real in their
authors.   We may say, indeed, without extravag-
ance, that the youth of Amyot's style, modifying the
age of Plutarch's, achieves a mean in full and natural
harmony with Plutarch's matter.   In Amyot's own
opinion, so great a work must appeal to all men of
judgment ' en quelque style qu'il soit mis, pourveu
qu'il s'entende ' ; [5] yet his preoccupation on this
point was punctilious.   He found in Plutarch a
' scabreuse aspérité ' — ' épineuse et ferrée ' are
Montaigne's epithets—yet set himself ' à représenter
aucunement et à adumbrer la forme de style et
manière de parler d'iceluy ' : [6] apologising to any

[1] Who undertook to translate Plutarch, but failed to do so.
[2] *Discours de la Traduction*, 1635 (cf. Blignières, p. 435).
[3] *Plutarch's Lives* ; Aubrey Stewart, M.A., and the late George Long,
M.A., 1880, vol. i. p. xvii.   [4] *Causeries du Lundi*, iv. 469.
[5] Dedication to Henri II.   [6] *Aux Lecteurs.*

who on that account should find his language less
' coulant ' than of yore.   But Amyot was no pedant ;
he would render his original, not ape him ; he would
write French, and not rack it.   He borrowed at need
from Greek and Italian, but he was loyal to his own
tongue.   ' Nous prendrons,' said he—and the canon is
unimpeachable—' les mots qui sont les plus propres
pour signifier la chose dont nous voulons parler,
ceux qui nous sembleront plus doux, qui sonneront
le mieux à l'oreille, qui seront coutumièrement en la
bouche des bien parlants, qui seront bons françois
et non étrangers.'   To render late Greek into early
French is not easy ; so he takes his time.   Not a
word is there save to further his conquest of Plutarch's meaning ; but all his words are marshalled
in open order, and they pace at leisure.   For his own
great reward Montaigne wrote : ' Je donne la palme
avecque raison, ce me semble, a Jaques Amyot, sur
tous nos escripvains François ' ; and he remains the
earliest classic accepted by the French Academy.
But for our delight he found Plutarch a language
which could be translated into Elizabethan English.

If Amyot was the right man for Plutarch, North
was the right man for Amyot.   He was born the
second and youngest son of Edward, first Baron
North, about the year 1535, and educated, in all
probability, at Peterhouse, Cambridge.[1]   His father
was one of those remarkable men of law who, through
all the ranging political and religious vicissitudes
under Henry VII., Henry VIII., Edward VI., Queen
Jane, Mary, and Elizabeth—so disastrous to the
older nobility—ever contrived to make terms with
the winning side ; until, dying in 1564, a peer of the

---

[1] See *Dictionary of National Biography*, which gives fuller information
than I have found elsewhere.

realm and Lord Lieutenant of Cambridgeshire and
the Isle of Ely, he was buried in Kirtling Church,
where his monumental inscription may still be read
in the chancel.   His son Thomas was also entered a
student at Lincoln's Inn (1557), but he soon preferred
letters before law.   He was generally, Leicester wrote
to Burghley, ' a very honest gentleman, and hath
many good things in him, which are drowned only
by poverty.'   In particular, we are told by his great-
nephew, the fourth Baron, he was ' a man of courage,'
and in the days of the Armada we find him taking
command, as Captain, of three hundred men of Ely.
Fourteen years before (in 1574) he had accompanied
his brother Roger, the second Baron, in his Embassy-
Extraordinary to Henri III. : a mission of interest
to us, as it cannot but have encountered him with
Amyot, and may have determined him to translate
the *Lives*.   He was already an author.   In December
1557 he had published, with a dedication to Queen
Mary, his translation of Guevara's *Libro Aureo*,[1] a
Spanish adaptation of the *Meditations* of Marcus
Aurelius ; and in 1570 *The Morall Philosophie of
Doni* . . . ' a worke first compiled in the Indian
tongue.' [2]   For the rest, his immortal service to
English letters brought him little wealth, but much
consideration from his neighbours, his kinsmen, and
his sovereign.   In 1568 he was presented with the
freedom of the city of Cambridge.   In 1576 his
brother gave him the ' lease of a house and household
stuff.'   He was knighted about 1591 ; he received
the Commission of the Peace in Cambridgeshire in
1592 ; in 1601 he got a pension of £40 from the

[1] Subsequent editions, 1568, 1582, 1619.
[2] Second edition, 1601. Reprinted as *The Fables of Bidpai*, with an
Introduction by Joseph Jacobs, 1888.

Queen, duly acknowledged in his dedication of the lives added to the *Plutarch* of 1603. He died, it is likely, before this edition saw the light : a valiant and courteous gentleman, and the earliest master of great English prose.

He also thought the *Lives* a book ' meete to be set forth in English.' [1] Truly : but in what English ? He writes of a Muse ' called Tacita,[2] as ye would saye, ladye Silence.' Should we ? Turning to a modern translation, I find ' Tacita, which means silent or dumb.' The glory has clearly departed : but before seeking it again in North's unrivalled language, I must ask of him, as I have asked of Amyot, Was he an accurate translator ? I do not believe there are a score of passages throughout his 1175 folio pages [3] in which he impairs the sense of his original. And most of these are the merest slips, arising from the necessity imposed on him of breaking up Amyot's prolonged periods, and his subsequent failure in the attribution of relatives and qualifications. They are not of the slightest consequence, if the reader, on finding an obscurity, will rely on the general sense of the passage rather than on the rules of syntax ; and of such obscurities I will boldly say that there are not ten in the whole book. Very rarely he mistakes a word—as ' real ' for ' royal '—and very rarely a phrase. For instance, in the *Pericles* he writes : ' At the beginning there was but a little secret grudge only between these two factions, *as an artificial flower set in the blade of a sworde,*' which stands for ' comme une feuille superficielle en une lame de fer.' In the *Solon* he writes : ' his familier

[1] Dedication to Elizabeth.   [2] In the *Numa*.
[3] The first edition of 1559, compared by me with Amyot's second edition of 1565. I had not the third, of 1567, from which North translated ; but on several points I have referred to the copy in the British Museum.

friendes above all rebuked him, saying he was to be accompted *no better than a beast,*' for ' qu'il seroit bien beste.' Some of his blunders lend power to Amyot and Plutarch both : as in that fine passage of the *Publicola,* wherein the conspirators' ' great and horrible othe, drinking the blood of a man and *shaking hands* in his bowels,' stands for ' touchant des mains aux entrailles.' There is one such error of unique interest. It stands in Shakespeare that

> ' in his mantle muffling up his face,
> Even at the base of Pompey's statua,
> *Which all the while ran blood,* great Cæsar fell ' ;

and we read in North, ' against the base, whereupon Pompey's image stoode, *which ranne all of a goare bloude*' ; but Amyot simply writes, ' qui en fust toute ensanglantée.' The blunder has enriched the world : that is, if it was truly a blunder, and not a touch of genius. For North will sometimes, though very rarely of set purpose, magnify with a word, or transfigure a sentence. ' Le deluge,' for example, is always ' Noe's flood ' ; and in one celebrated passage he bowdlerises without shame, turning Flora's parting caress to Pompey into a ' sweete quippe or pleasant taunte.' [1] Such are the discrepancies which can by any stretch be called blunders ; and the sum of them is insignificant in a work which echoes its original not only in sense but also in rhythm and form. North had the Greek text, or perhaps a Latin translation, before him. In the *Sertorius* he speaks of ' Gaule Narbonensis,' with nothing but ' Languedoc ' in Amyot ; in the *Pompey* he gives the Greek, unquoted by Amyot, for ' let the dye be cast ' ; in dealing with Demosthenes' quinsy, he attempts an

---

[1] Greek ἀδήκτως: Lat., *Ed. Princeps* (1470), ' sine morsu.' Long has another reading and translation, but most will agree that Amyot's is not a blunder but an emendation.

awkward pun, which Amyot has disdained ; and in
the *Cicero* he gives in Greek character the original
for Latin terms of philosophy, whereas Amyot does
not.   These are the only indications I have found
of his having looked beyond the French.   But on
Amyot he set a grip which had its bearing on the development of Tudor prose.   It may even be that, in
tracing this development, we have looked too exclusively to Italian, Spanish, and classical sources.
Sidney read North's book ; Shakespeare rifled it ;
and seven editions [1] were published, within the
hundred years which saw the new birth of English
prose and its glorious fulfilment.   In acknowledging
our debt, have we not unduly neglected the Bishop
of Auxerre ?   Sentence for sentence and rhythm
for rhythm, in all the great passages North's style
is essentially Amyot's. [2]   There are differences, of
course, which catch the eye, and have, therefore, as I
think, attracted undue attention, the more naturally
since they are all in North's favour.   His vigorous
diction puts stuff into the text : he stitches it with
sturdy locutions, he tags it with Elizabethan
braveries.   But the woof and the design are still
Amyot's ; and the two versions may be studied
most conveniently abreast.

In neither writer is the verse of any account.
Indeed, when North comes to an incident of the
Gymnopaedia—'the which Sophocles doth easily
declare by these verses :

'The song which you shall sing shall be the sonnet sayde
By Hermony lusty lasse, that strong and sturdy mayde ;
Which trust her peticote about her middle short
And set to show her naked hippes in frank and friendly sort '—

---

[1] 1579 ; 1595 ; 1603 ; 1612 ; 1631 ; 1657 ; 1676.
[2] Cf. for instance, in the *Antonius*, Cleopatra on the Cydnus ; the death
of Antonius ; and the death of Cleopatra.

you feel that the reference to Sophocles is not only remote but also grotesque. It is very different with their prose. And first, is North's version—the translation of a translation—by much removed from Plutarch ? In a sense, yes. It is even truer of North than of Amyot, that he offers Plutarch neither to philosophers nor to grammarians, but to all who would understand life and human nature.[1] But for these, and for all lovers of language, Plutarch loses little in Amyot, saving in the matter of literary allusion ; and Amyot loses nothing in North, save for the presence of a score of whims and obscurities. On the other hand, we recapture in North an English equivalent for those ' gasconisms ' which Montaigne retained in French, but which Amyot rejected from it. The Plutarchian hues are never lost—they are but doubly refracted ; and by each refraction they are broadened in surface and deepened in tone. The sunlight of his sense is sometimes subdued by a light mist, or is caught in the fantastic outline of a little cloud. But the general effect is touched with a deeper solemnity and a more splendid iridescence ; even where the vapours lie thickest, the red rays throb through.

But the proof of the pudding is the eating. Let us take a passage at random, and compare the sixteenth century renderings with the cold perversions of a later age. For example, Amyot writes [2] that Pythagoras ' apprivoisa une aigle, qu'il feit descendre et venir a luy par certaines voix, ainsi comme elle volait en l'air dessus sa teste ' ; in North this eagle is ' so tame and gentle, that she would stoupe, and come down to him by certaine voyces, as she flewe in

---

[1] Gustave Lanson, *La littérature française* (1894), p. 223.
[2] *Numa Pompilius.*

the ayer over his head ' ; while in an accurate modern
Pythagoras merely 'tamed an eagle and made it
alight on him.' The earlier creature flies like a bird
of Jove, but the later comes down like a brick. The
Langhornes' eagle is still more precipitate, their
Pythagoras still more peremptory. 'That philo-
sopher,' as they naturally call the Greek, 'had so
far tamed an eagle that by pronouncing certain words
he could stop it in its flight, or bring it down.'
Perhaps I may finish at once with the Langhornes by
referring to their description of Cleopatra on the
Cydnus. They open that pageant, made glorious for
ever by Amyot, North, and Shakespeare, in these
terms : 'Though she had received many pressing
letters of invitation from Antony and his friends,
. . . she by no means took the most expeditious
mode of travelling.' Thus the Langhornes ; and
they denounce the translation called Dryden's [1] for
'tame and tedious, without elegance, spirit, or precision ' ! Now, it was a colossal impertinence to put
out the *Lives* among the Greeklings of Grub Street,
in order to 'complete the whole in a year ' ; but it
must be noted that, after North's, this [2] is still the
only version that can be read without impatience.
Dryden's hacks were not artists, but neither were
they prigs : the vocabulary was not yet a charnel of
decayed metaphor ; and if they missed the rapture
of sixteenth-century rhythm, they had not bleached
the colour, carded the texture, and ironed the surface
of their language to the well-glazed insignificance of
the later eighteenth century. Their Plutarch is no

[1] Corrected and revised by A. H. Clough, 1883.
[2] Dryden, in his dedication to the Duke of Ormonde (1683), spoke of
North as ungrammatical and ungraceful. The version he signed was
'executed by several hands'; but with his name on the title-page it dis-
placed North's, which is now for the first time since republished.

longer wrapped in the royal robes of Amyot and
North ; but he is spared the cheap though formal
tailoring of Dacier and the Langhornes.   In our own
time there have been translations by scholars : they
are useful as cribs, but they do not pretend to charm.
Here, for instance, is North's funeral of Philopœmen :
' The souldiers were all crowned with garlandes of
Laurell in token of victory, not withstanding the
teares ranne downe their cheekes in token of sorrowe,
and they led their enemies prisoners shackled and
chained.   The   funeral   pot   in   which   were   Phili-
pœmenes ashes, was so covered with garlands of
flowers, nosegaies, and laces that it could scant be
seene or discerned.'   And here is the crib : ' There
one might see men crowned with garlands but weeping at the same time, and leading along his enemies
in chains.   The urn itself, which was scarcely to be
seen for the garlands and ribbons with which it was
covered,' etc.   Here, too, is North's Demetrius :
' He took pleasure of Lamia, as a man would have
delight to heare one tell tales, when he hath nothing
else to doe, or is desirous to sleep : but indeede when
he was to make any preparation for warre, he had not
then ivey at his dart's end, nor had his helmet perfumed, nor came not out of ladies closets, pricked
and princt to go to battell : but he let all dauncing
and sporting alone, and became as the poet Euripides
saith,

' The souldier of Mars, cruell and bloodie.'

And here is the crib : ' He only dedicated the superfluity of his leisure to enjoyment, and used his Lamia,
like the mythical nightmare, only when he was half
asleep or at play.   When he was preparing for war,
no ivy wreathed his spear, no perfume scented his

helmet, nor did he go from his bedchamber to battle
covered with finery.' ' *Dedicated the superfluity of
his leisure !* ' At such a jewel the Langhornes must
have turned in envy in their graves ! But, apart
from style, modern scholars have a fetish which they
worship to the ruin of any literary claim. Amyot
and North have been ridiculed for writing, in accordance with their method, of *nuns* and *churches*, and
not of *vestals* and *temples*. Yet the opposite extreme
is far more fatiguing. Where is the sense of putting
' chalkaspides ' in the text and ' soldiers who had
shields of brass ' in the notes ? Is it not really less
distracting to read, as in North, of soldiers ' marching with their copper targets ' ? So, too, with the
Parthian kettle-drums. It is an injury to write
' hollow instruments ' in so splendid a passage ; and
an insult to add in a note ' the context seems to
show that a drum is meant.' Of course ! And
' kettle-drums ' is a perfect equivalent for ῥόπτρα,
' made of skin, and hollow, which they stretch round
brass sounders.' But if these things are done in
England, you may know what to expect of Germany.
In the picture of Cato's suicide there is one supreme
touch, rendered by Plutarch ἤδη δ' ὄρνιθες ἦδον ; by
Amyot *les petits oyseaux commençoient desja à
chanter* ; by North, *the little birds began to chirpe*.
But Kaltwasser turns the little birds into crowing
cocks ; and maintains his position by a learned
argument. It was still, says he, in the night, and
other fowls are silent until dawn.[1] If the style of
the eighteenth century be tedious, the scholarship
of the nineteenth is intolerable. The truth is that in
the sixteenth alone could the *Lives* be fitly translated.
For there were passages, as of the arming of Greece,

[1] See *Plutarch's Lives* : Stewart and Long, III. 572.

in the *Philopœmen,* which could only be rendered in an age still accustomed to armour. Any modern rendering, be it by writer or by don, must needs be archaistically mediæval or pedantically antique.

Turning, then, to Amyot and North, the strangest thing to note, and the most important, is that the English, although without a touch of foreign idiom, is modelled closely upon the French. Some explanation of this similarity in form may be found in the nature of the matter. The narration, as opposed to the analysis, of action; the propounding, as opposed to the proof, of philosophy—these are readily conveyed from one language into another, and *Joshua* and *Ecclesiastes* are good reading in most versions of the Bible. But North is closer to Amyot than any two versions of the Bible are to each other. The French runs into the English five times out of six, and in all the great passages, not only word for word but almost cadence for cadence. There is a trick of redundancy in Tudor prose that makes for emphasis and melody. We account it English, and find it abounding in our Bible. It is wholly alien from modern French prose—wholly alien, too, from French prose of the seventeenth century. Indeed, I would go further, and say that it is largely characteristic of Amyot the writer, and not of the age in which he wrote. You do not find it, for instance, in the prose of Joachim du Bellay.[1] But now take North's account of the execution before Brutus of his two eldest sons ; [2] ' which,' you read, ' was such a pitieful sight to all people, that they could not find it in their hearts to *beholde* it, but turned themselves another waye, bicause they would not *see* it.' That effective repetition is word for word in the

---

[1] *Deffense et illustration de la Langue françoise.*   [2] *Publicola.*

French : ' qu'ilz n'avoient pas le cueur de les *regarder*, ains se tournoient d'un austre costé pour n'en
rien *veoir*.'   But, apart from redundancy, the closeness is at all times remarkable.   Consider the phrase :
' but to go on quietly and joyfully at the sound
of these pipes to hazard themselves even to death.' [1]
You would swear it original, but here is the French :
' ains aller posement et joyeusement au son des instruments, se hazarder au peril de la mort.'   The
same effect is produced by the same rhythm.   Or,
take the burial of unchaste vestals : [2] when the
muffled litter passes, the people ' follow it mourn-
ingly with heavy looks and speake never a word ' ;
' avec une chère basse, et morne sans mot dire ' ;
and so on, in identical rhythm, to the end of that
magnificent passage.   I will give one longer example,
from the return of Alcibiades.   You read in North :
' Those that could come near him dyd welcome and
imbrace him : but all the people wholly followed
him : And some that came to him put garlands of
flowers upon his head : and those that could not
come neare him, sawe him afarre off, and the olde
folkes dyd poynte him out to the younger sorte.'
And in Amyot : ' Ceulx qui en pouvoient approcher
le saluoient et l'embrassoient, mais tous l'accom-
pagnoient ; et y en avoient aucuns qui s'approchans
de luy, luy mettoient des chappeaux de fleurs sur
la teste et ceulx qui n'en pouvoient approcher, le
regardoient de loing, et les vieux le monstroient aux
jeunes.'   Here is the very manner of the Authorised
Version : flowing but not prolix, full but not turgid.
Is it, then, fanciful to suggest that Amyot's style,
evolved from the inherent difficulty of his task, was
accepted by North for its beauty, and used by the

---

[1] *Lycurgus.*   [2] *Numa.*

translators of the Bible for its fitness to an undertaking hard for similar reasons and in a similar way ? Amyot piles up his epithets, and links one varied cadence to another : yet his volume is not of extravagant utterance, but of extreme research. He was endeavouring to render late Greek into French of the Renaissance ; and so he sought for perfect expression not—as to-day—in one word but in the resultant of many. And this very volume of utterance, however legitimate, imposed the necessity of rhythm. His innumerable words, if they were not to weary, must be strung on a wire of undulating gold. North copied this cadence, and gave a storehouse of expression to the writers of his time. It seems to me, therefore, not rash to trace, through North, to Amyot one rivulet of the many that fell into the mighty stream of rhythm flowing through the classic version of the English Bible.

But North and Amyot are not men of one trick : they can be terse and antithetical when they will. You read that Themistocles advanced the honour of the Athenians, making them ' to overcome their enemies by force, and their friends and allies with liberality ' ; in Amyot : ' Vaincre leurs ennemies en prouesse, et leurs alliez et amis en bonté ' ! North can play this tune as well as any : e.g., ' If they,' Plutarch's heroes, ' have done this for heathen Kings, what should we doe for Christian Princes ? If they have done this for glorye, what shoulde we doe for religion ? If they have done this without hope of heaven, what should we doe that looke for immortalitie ? ' [1] But he can play other tunes too. Much is now written of the development of the sentence ; and no doubt since the decadence

[1] Dedication to Elizabeth.

advances have been made. Yet, in the main, they are to recover a territory wilfully abandoned. In North and Amyot there are sentences of infinite device—sentences numerous and harmonic beyond the dreams of Addison and Swift. I will give some examples. Amyot : ' S'éblouissant à regarder une telle splendeur, et se perdant à sonder un tel abysme.' That is fine enough, but North beats it : ' Dazeled at the beholding of such brightnesse, and confounded at the gaging of so bottomlesse a deepe.' [1] Amyot : ' Ne plus ne moins que si c'eust esté quelque doulce haleine d'un vent salubre et gracieu qui leur eust soufflé du costé de Rome pour les rafreshir.' And North : ' As if some gentle ayer had breathed on them by some gracious and healthfull wind, blowen from Rome to refresh them.' [2] No translation could be closer ; yet in the first example North's English is stronger than the French, and in the second it flows, like the air, with a more ineffable ease. Take, again, the account of the miracle witnessed during the battle of Salamis. Here is Amyot : ' *que l'on ouit une haulte voix* et grande clameur *par toute la plaine Thrasiene jusques à la mer, comme s'il y eust eu* grand *nombre d'hommes qui ensemble eussent à haulte voix chanté le sacre cantique de Iacchus, et sembloit que* de la multitude *de ceulx qui chantoient il se levast petit à petit une nuée en l'air,* laquelle *partant de la terre venoit à fondre et tumber sur les galeres en la mer.*' And here is North : ' that a lowde voyce was heard through all the plaine of Thriasia unto the sea, as if there had bene a number of men together, that had songe out alowde, the holy songe of Iacchus. And it seemed by litle and litle that there rose a clowde in the ayer from those which sange : that left the

land, and came and lighted on the gallyes in the sea.'
I have put into italics so much of Amyot as North
renders word for word. His fidelity is beyond praise ;
but the combination of such fidelity with perfect
and musical expression is no less than a miracle of
artistry. North, in this passage as elsewhere, not
only writes more beautiful English : he gives, also,
a description of greater completeness and clarity
than you will find in any later version of Plutarch.
The elemental drama transfigures his prose ; but
every fact is realised, every sensuous impression is
set down, and set down in its order. So much may
be said, too, of Amyot ; but in his rendering you are
aware of the words and the construction—in fact,
of the author. In North's there is but the pageant of
the sky ; there is never a restless sound to disturb
the illusion ; the cadence is sublimated of all save a
delicate alliteration, tracing its airy rhythm to the
ear. The work is full of such effects, some of simple
melody, and others of more than contrapuntal in-
volution ; for he commands his English as a skilled
organist his organ, knowing the multitude of its re-
sources, and drawing at need upon them all. Listen
to his rendering of Pericles' sorrow for his son :
' Neither saw they him weepe at any time nor mourne
at the funeralles of any of his kinsmen or friendes,
but at the death of Paralus, his younger and lawful
begotten sonne : for, the losse of him alone dyd only
melt his harte. Yet he dyd strive to showe his
naturall constancie, and to keepe his accustomed
modestie. But as he woulde have put a garland of
flowers upon his head, sorrowe dyd so pierce his
harte when he sawe his face, that then he burst out
in teares and cryed amaine ; which they never saw
him doe before all the dayes of his life.' Yes, the

pathos of the earth is within his compass ; but he
can also attain to the sublimity of heaven : ' The
everlasting seate, which trembleth not, and is not
driven nor moved with windes, neither is darkened
with clowdes, but is allwayes bright and cleare, and
at all times shyning with a pure bright light, as being
the only habitation and mansion place of the eternall
God, only happy and immortall.' [1]

These two passages from the last movement of
the *Pericles* can only be spoken of in North's own
language: they are 'as stoppes and soundes of the
soul played upon with the fine fingered hand of
a conning master.' [2] Yet they are modelled on
Amyot's French. It seems scarce credible ; and
indeed, if the mould be the same, the metal has been
transmuted. You feel that much has been added
to the form so faithfully followed ; that you are
listening to an English master of essentially English
prose. For these passages are in the tradition of
our tongue : the first gives an echo of Malory's
stately pathos, and the second an earnest of our
Apocalypse. In building up these palaces of music
North has followed the lines of Amyot's construction ; but his melody in the first is sweeter, his
harmony in the second peals out with a loftier
rapture.

I have dwelt upon the close relation of North's
style to Amyot's, because it is the rule, and because
it has a bearing on the development of Tudor prose.
This rule of likeness seems to me worthier of note
than any exceptions ; both for the strangeness and
the importance. But, of course, there are exceptions : there are traits, of attitude and of expression,

[1] Amyot : ' Comme estant telle habitation et convenable à la nature
souverainement heureuse et immortelle.'   [2] *Pericles.*

personal to North the man and the writer. He has a
national leaning towards the sturdy and the bluff.
In a sonnet written some twenty years earlier, Du
Bellay, giving every nation a particular epithet,
labels our forefathers for ' les Anglais mutins.' The
epithet is chosen by an enemy ; but there was ever
in the English temper, above all, in the roaring
days of great Elizabeth, a certain jovial frowardness,
by far removed both from impertinence and from
bluster, which inclined us, as we should put it, to
stand no nonsense from anybody. This national
characteristic is strongly marked in North. For
him Spartacus and his slaves are ' rebellious rascals.'
When Themistocles boasts of being able to make a
small city great, though he cannot, indeed, tune a
viol or play of the psalterion, Amyot calls his words
' un peu haultaines et odieuses ' : they are repugnant
to the cultured prelate, and he gives a full equivalent
for the censure of Plutarch, the cultured Greek.[1]
But North will not away with this censure of a bluff
retort : having his bias, he deliberately betrays his
original, making Themistocles answer ' with *great
and stout* words.' There is also in North's character
a strain of kindness, almost of softness, towards
women and children and the pathetic side of life.
In the wonderful passage describing the living burial
of unchaste vestals,[2] where almost every other word
is literally translated, North turns ' la criminelle '
into ' the seely offendour ' : as it were with a gracious
reminiscence of Chaucer's ' ne me ne list this seely
woman chide.' And in the *Solon*, where a quaint
injunction is given for preserving love in wedlock,

---

[1] The Greek epithet is rendered by the word *arrogant* in Clough's revised
Dryden, and by the word *vulgar* in Mr. Stewart's translation.
[2] *Numa.*

Amyot writes that so courteous a custom, being observed by a husband towards his wife, ' garde que les courages et vouluntez ne s'alienent de tout poinct les uns des autres.' (The phrase is rendered in a modern version 'preventing their leading to actual quarrel.') But North lifts the matter above the level of laughter or puritanical reproach : it ' keepeth,' as he writes, ' love and good will waking, that it die not utterly between them.' The beauty and gentleness of these words, in so strange a context, are, you feel, inspired by chivalry and a deep reverence for women. These two strains in North's character find vent in his expression ; but they never lead him far from the French. There is an insistence, but no more, on all things gentle and brave ; and this insistence goes but to further a tendency already in Amyot. For in that age the language of gentlemen received a like impress in both countries from their common standards of courage and courtesy ; and among gentlemen, Amyot and North seem to have been drawn yet closer to each other by a common kinship with the brave and gentle soul of Plutarch. These two qualities which are notable in Plutarch and Amyot in all such passages, lead in North to a distinct exaggeration of phrase, though ever in the direction of their true intent. He makes grim things grimmer, and sweet things more sweet. So that the double translation from the Greek gives the effect of a series of contours traced the one above the other, and ever increasing the curve of the lowest outline.

But North, being no sentimentalist, finds occasion for fifty stout words against one soft saying. The stark vigour of his diction is, indeed, its most particular sign. The profit to the Greeks of a preliminary fight before Salamis is thus declared by

Amyot : it proved ' que la grande multitude des
vaisseaux, ny la pompe et magnificence des pare-
ments d'iceulx, ny les cris superbes et chants de
victoire des Barbares, ne servent de rien à l'encontre
de ceulx qui ont le cueur de joindre de près, et com-
battre à coups de main leur ennemy, et *qu'il ne fault
point faire compte de tout cela, ains aller droit affronter
les hommes et s'attacher hardiment à eulx.*' North
follows closely for a time, but in the last sentence he
lets out his language to the needs of a maxim so
pertinent to a countryman of Drake.   The Greeks
saw, says he, ' that it was not the great multitude of
shippes, nor the pomp and sumptuous setting out of
the same, nor the prowde barbarous showts and
songes of victory that could stand them to purpose,
against noble hartes and valliant minded souldiers,
that durst *grapple with them, and come to hand strokes
with their enemies : and that they should make no
reckoning of all that bravery and bragges, but should
sticke to it like men, and laye it on the jacks of them.*'
The knight who was to captain his three hundred
men in the Armada year, has the pull here over the
bishop ; and on occasion he has always such language
at command.   ' Les autres qui estoient demourez à
Rome ' instead of marching to the war [1] are ' the
home-tarriers and house-doves ' : upbraided elsewhere [2] because they ' never went from the smoke
of the chimney nor carried away any blowes in the
field.'   When Philopœmen, wounded with a dart
that ' pierced both thighes through and through, that
the iron was seene on either side,' saw ' the fight
terrible,' and that it ' woulde soon be ended,' you
read in Amyot ' qu'il perdoit patience de despit,'
but in North that ' it spited him to the guttes, he

---

[1] *Coriolanus.*   [2] *Fabius Maximus.*

would so faine have bene among them.' The phrase
is born of sympathy and conviction. North, too,
has a fine impatience of fools. Hannibal, discovering the error of his guides, ' les feit pendre ' in
Amyot ; in North he ' roundely trussed them up
and honge them by the neckes.' [1] And he is not
sparing in his censure of ill-livers. Phœa, you read
in the *Theseus*, ' was surnamed a sowe for her beastly
brutishe behaviour, and wicked life.' He can be
choleric as well as kindly, and never minces his words.

Apart from those expressions which spring from
the idiosyncrasy of his temperament, North's style
shares to the full in the general glory of Elizabethan
prose. You read of ' fretised seelings,' [2] of words
that ' dulce and soften the hardened harts of the
multitude' ; [3] of the Athenians 'being set on a jolitie
to see themselves strong.' Heads are ' passhed in
peces,' and men ' ashamed to cast their honour at
their heeles ' (Amyot : ' d'abandonner leur gloire ').
Themistocles' father shows him the ' shipwracks and
ribbes (Amyot: ' les corps') of olde gallyes cast here
and there.' You have, ' pluck out of his head the
worm of ambition ' [4] for ' oster de sa fantasie
l'ambition ' ; and Cæsar on the night before his
death hears Calpurnia, ' being fast asleep, weepe and
sigh, and *put forth many fumbling lamentable speeches.*'
But in particular, North is richer than even his
immediate followers in homespun images and pro-
verbial locutions. Men who succeed, ' bear the
bell ' ; [5] ' tenter la fortune le premier ' is ' to breake
the ise of this enterprise.' [6] Coriolanus by his pride
' stirred coales emong the people.' The Spartans
who thwarted Themistocles ' dyd sit on his skirtes ' ;

---

[1] *Fabius Maximus.*   [2] *Lycurgus.*   [3] *Publicola.*   [4] *Solon.*
[5] The old prize for a racehorse.   [6] *Publicola.*

and the Athenians fear Pericles because in voice and
manner 'he was Pisistratus up and downe.' The
Veians let fall their 'peacockes bravery'; [1] and a
man when pleased is 'as merry as a pye.' [2] Raw
recruits are 'fresh-water souldiers.' A turncoat
carries 'two faces in one hoode'; [3] and the
Carthaginians, being outwitted, 'are ready to eate
their fingers for spyte.' The last locution occurs also
in North's *Morall Philosophie* of 1570 : he habitually
used such expressions, and yet others which are
truly proverbs, common to many languages. For
instance, he writes in the *Camillus*, 'these words
made Brennus mad as a March Hare that out went
his blade'; in *Cato Utican* 'to set all at six and seven';
in *Solon* 'so sweete it is to rule the roste'; in
Pelopidas 'to hold their noses to the gryndstone'; in
Cicero, with even greater incongruity, of his wife
Terentia 'wearing her husbandes breeches.' In the
Alcibiades, the Athenians 'upon his persuasion,
built castles in the ayer'; and this last has been
referred to Sidney's *Apologie*; but the first known
edition of the *Apologie* is dated 1595, and it is supposed to have been written about 1581 ; North has
it not only in the *Lives* (1579), but in his *Morall
Philosophie* of 1570.[4] To North, too, we may perhaps attribute some of the popularity in England
of engaging jingles. 'Pritle pratle' and 'topsie
turvie' occur both in the *Lives* and the *Morall
Philosophie*. And in the *Lives* you have also 'spicke
and spanne newe'; [5] with 'hurly burly' and 'pel
mel,' adopted by Shakespeare in *Macbeth* and
Richard III. Since North takes the last from

[1] *Camillus.*   [2] *Ibid.*   [3] *Timoleon.*
[4] *Fables of Bidpai*, 1888, p. 11.
[5] *Paulus Æmilius*; in a gorgeous description of the Macedonian phalanx,
from spick = a spike, and span = a splinter.

Amyot and explains it—' fled into the camp pel mel
or hand over heade '—and since it is of French derivation—*pelle-mesle* = ' to mix with a shovel '—it
is possible that the phrase is here used for the first
time.

Gathered together, these peculiarities of style
seem many ; and yet in truth they are few. They
are the merest accidents in a great stream of rhythm.
That stream flows steadily and superbly through a
channel of another man's digging. For North's style
is Amyot's, divided into shorter periods, strengthened
with racy locutions, and decked with Elizabethan
tags. In English such division was necessary :
the rhythm, else, of the weightier language had
gained such momentum as to escape control. But
even so North's English is neither cramped nor
pruned : it is still unfettered by antithesis and
prodigal of display. His periods, though shorter
than Amyot's, in themselves are leisurely and long.
There is room in them for fine words and lofty
phrases ; and these go bragging by, the one following
a space after the other, like cars in an endless
pageant. The movement of his procession rolls on :
yet he halts it at pleasure, to soften sorrow with a
gracious saying, or to set a flourish on the bravery
of his theme.

IV

The earliest tribute to the language of Amyot and
North was the highest that has ever been, or can
ever be, paid ; both for its own character and the
authority of those who gave it. For Montaigne, the
greatest literary genius in France during the sixteenth century, wrote thus of Amyot : ' Nous estions

perdus, si ce livre ne nous eust tires du bourbier :
sa mercy, nous osons a cette heure parler et escrire ' ; [1]
and Shakespeare, the first poet of all time, borrowed
three plays almost wholly from North.   I do not
speak of *A Midsummer Night's Dream* and *The Two
Noble Kinsmen*, for each of which a little has been
gleaned from North's *Theseus* ; nor of the *Timon of
Athens*, although here the debt is larger.[2]   The wit of
Apemantus, the Apologue of the Fig-tree, and the
two variants of Timon's epitaph, are all in North.
Indeed, it was the ' rich conceit ' of Timon's tomb
by the sea-shore which touched Shakespeare's
imagination, as it had touched Antony's ; so that
some of the restricted passion of North's *Antonius*,
which bursts into showers of meteoric splendour in
the Fourth and Fifth Acts of Shakespeare's *Antony
and Cleopatra*, beats too, in the last lines of his *Timon*,
with a rhythm as of billows :

> ' yet rich conceit
> Taught thee to make vast Neptune weep for aye
> On thy low grave, on faults forgiven.'

But in *Antony and Cleopatra*, as in *Coriolanus* and in
Julius Cæsar, Shakespeare's obligation is apparent
in almost all he has written.   To measure it you
must quote the bulk of the three plays.   ' Of the
incident,' Trench has said, ' there is almost nothing
which he does not owe to Plutarch, even as continually he owes the very wording to Sir Thomas
North ' ; [3] and he follows up this judgment with so
detailed an analysis of the *Julius Cæsar* that I shall
not attempt to labour the same ground.   As regards
the *Coriolanus*, it was noted, even by Pope, ' that the

---

[1] *Essais*, II. iv.
[2] It is founded on one passage in the *Alcibiades* and another in the
Antony.   [3] *Plutarch.   Five Lectures*, p. 66.

whole history is exactly followed, and many of the
principal speeches exactly copied, from the life of
Coriolanus in Plutarch.' This exactitude, apart from
its intrinsic interest, may sometimes assist in re-
storing a defective passage. One such piece there is
in II. iii. 231 of the Cambridge *Shakespeare*, 1865 :

> ' The noble *house o' the Marcians*, from whence came
> That *Ancus Marcius, Numa's daughter's son*,
> *Who, after* great *Hostilius*, here *was king* ;
> *Of the same house Publius and Quintus were*,
> That our *best water brought by conduits* hither.'

The Folios here read :

> ' And Nobly nam'd, so *twice* being *Censor*,
> Was his great Ancestor.'

It is evident that, after ' hither,' a line has been
lost, and Rowe, Pope, Delius, and others have tried
their best to recapture it. Pope, knowing of Shakespeare's debt and founding his emendation on North,
could suggest nothing better than ' And Censorinus,
darling of the people ' ; while Delius, still more
strangely, stumbled, as I must think, on the right
reading, but for the inadequate reason that ' darling
of the people ' does not sound like Shakespeare. I
have given in italics the words taken from North :
and, applying the same method to the line suggested
by Delius, you read : ' And *Censorinus that was so
surnamed*,' then, in the next line, by merely shifting
a comma, you read on : ' And nobly named so, *twice*
being *Censor*.' Had Delius pointed out that he got
his line simply by following Shakespeare's practice
of taking so many of North's words, in their order,
as would fall into blank verse, his emendation must
surely have been accepted, since it involves no
change in the subsequent lines of the Folios ; whereas

the Cambridge *Shakespeare* breaks one line into two,
and achieves but an awkward result :

> ' And [Censorinus] nobly named so,
> Twice being [by the people chosen] censor.'

The closeness of Shakespeare's rendering, indicated
by this use of italics, is not particular to this passage,
but is universal throughout the play. Sometimes
he gives a conscious turn to North's unconscious
humour ; as when, in the Parable of the Belly and
the Members, North writes, ' And so the bellie, all
this notwithstanding laughed at their follie ' ; and
Shakespeare writes in I. i., ' For, look you, I may
make the belly smile As well as speak.'   At others his
fidelity leads him into an anachronism. North
writes of Coriolanus that ' he was even such another,
as Cato would have a souldier and a captaine to be :
not only terrible and fierce to laye aboute him, but to
make the enemie afeard with the sound of his voyce
and grimness of his countenance.'   And Shakespeare,
with a frank disregard for chronology, gives the
speech, Cato and all, to Titus Lartius (I. iv. 57) :

> ' Thou wast a soldier
> *Even to Cato's wish*, not fierce and terrible
> Only in strokes ; but with thy grim looks and
> The thunder-like percussion of thy sounds,
> Thou mad'st thine enemies shake.'

But perhaps the most curious evidence of the degree
to which Shakespeare steeped himself in North is to
be found in passages where he borrowed North's
diction and applied it to new purposes. For instance,
in North ' a goodly horse with a capparison' is offered
to Coriolanus ; in Shakespeare, at the same juncture,
Lartius says of him :

> ' O General,
> Here is the steed, we the caparison.'

Shakespeare, that is, not only copies North's picture, he also uses North's palette. Throughout the play he takes the incidents, the images, and the very words of North. You read in North: ' More over he sayed they nourished against themselves, the naughty seede and cockle of insolencie and sedition, which had been sowed and scattered abroade amongst the people.' And in Shakespeare, III. i. 69 :

> ' In soothing them we *nourish 'gainst* our senate
> *The cockle* of rebellion, *insolence, sedition,*
> *Which* we ourselves have plough'd for, *sow'd and scatter'd.'*

Of course it is not argued that Shakespeare has not contributed much of incalculable worth : the point is that he found a vast deal which he needed not to change. When Shakespeare adds, IV. vii. 33 :

> ' I think he 'll be to Rome
> As is the osprey to the fish, who takes it
> By sovereignty of nature,'

he is turning prose into poetry. When he creates the character of Menenius Agrippa from North's allusion to ' certaine of the plesauntest olde men,' he is turning narrative into drama, as he is, too, in his development of Volumnia, from a couple of references and one immortal speech. But these additions and developments can in no way minimise the fact that he takes from North that speech, and the two others which are the pivots of the play, as they stand. There is the one in which Coriolanus discovers himself to Aufidius. I take it from the Cambridge *Shakespeare*, and print the actual borrowings in italics (IV. v. 53) :

> ' COR. (Unmuffling)   *If, Tullus,*
> *Not yet thou knowest me, and, seeing me, dost not*
> Think *me* for *the man I am, necessity*
> Commands me to name *myself.* . . .

My name is *Caius Marcius, who hath done*
To thee *particularly, and to all the Volsces,*
Great hurt and mischief; thereto witness may
My surname, *Coriolanus : the painful service,*
The extreme dangers, and the drops of blood
Shed for my thankless country, are requited
But with that *surname ; a good memory,*
And witness of the malice and displeasure
Which *thou shouldst bear me : only* that *name remains ;*
The cruelty and envy of the people,
Permitted *by* our *dastard nobles, who*
Have all *forsook me,* hath devour'd *the rest ;*
And suffer'd *me by the* voice of slaves to be
Whoop'd out of Rome. *Now, this extremity*
Hath brought me *to thy hearth : not* out *of hope—*
Mistake me not—*to save my life, for if*
I had fear'd death, of all men i' the world
I would have voided thee ; *but* in mere *spite*
To be full quit *of* those my *banish*ers,
Stand I before thee here. Then *if thou hast*
A *heart* of *wreak* in thee, that wilt revenge
Thine own particular wrongs and stop those maims
Of shame seen through thy country, *speed thee* straight,
And make *my misery serve thy turn : so use it*
That my revengeful *services may* prove
As *benefits to* thee ; for *I will fight*
Against my canker'd country with the spleen
Of all the under fiends. But *if so be*
Thou darest not this *and that to prove more fortunes*
Thou 'rt tired, *then,* in a word, *I also am*
Longer to live most *weary.*'

The second, which is Volumnia's (v. iii. 94), is too
long for quotation. It opens thus :

' Should we be silent *and not speak, our raiment*
And state of bodies would bewray what life
We have led since thy exile. Think with thyself
How more unfortunate than all living women
Are we come hither ' ;

and here, to illustrate Shakespeare's method of
rhythmical condensation, is the corresponding

passage in North. 'If we helde our peace (my
sonne) *and* determined *not* to *speake*, the *state of* our
poore *bodies*, and present sight of *our raiment, would*
easily *bewray* to thee *what life we have led* at home,
since thy exile and abode abroad. But *thinke* now
with thyself, howe much *more unfortunate*ly, *then all*
the *women livinge we are come hether.*' I have indicated by italics the words that are common to
both, but even so, I can by no means show the sum
of Shakespeare's debt, or so much as hint at the
peculiar glory of Sir Thomas's prose. There is no
mere question of borrowed language ; for North
and Shakespeare have each his own excellence, of
prose and of verse. Shakespeare has taken over
North's vocabulary, and that is much ; but it is
more that behind that vocabulary he should have
found such an intensity of passion as would fill the
sails of the highest drama. North has every one of
Shakespeare's most powerful effects in his version
of the speech : '*Trust unto it, thou shalt no soner
marche* forward *to assault thy countrie*, but thy foote
shall *treade* up*on thy mothers wombe, that brought thee*
first int*o-this world* ' ; ' Doest *thou* take *it honourable
for a nobleman to remember* the *wrongs* and injuries
done him ' ; '*Thou hast* not hitherto *shewed thy*
poore *mother any courtesy* ' : these belong to North,
and they are the motors of Shakespeare's emotion.
The two speeches, dressed, the one in perfect prose,
the other in perfect verse, are both essentially the
same under their faintly yet magically varied
raiment. The dramatic tension, the main argument,
the turns of pleading, even the pause and renewal
of entreaty, all are in North, and are expressed by
the same spoken words and the same gap of silence.
In the blank verse a shorter cadence is disengaged

from the ampler movement of prose; here and
there, too, a line is added. ' To tear with thunder
the wide cheeks o' the air,' could only have been
written by an Elizabethan dramatist ; even as

' When she, poor hen, fond of no second brood,
  Has clucked thee to the wars, and safely home,'

could only have been written by Shakespeare. The
one is extravagant, the other beautiful ; but the
power and the pathos are complete without them,
for these reside in the substance and the texture of
the mother's entreaty, which are wholly North's.
It is just to add that, saving for some crucial touches,
as in the substitution of ' womb ' for ' corps,' they
belong also to Amyot. To the mother's immortal
entreaty there follows the son's immortal reply :
the third great speech of Shakespeare's play. It runs
in Amyot : ' " O mère, que m'as tu fait ? " et en luy
serrant estroittement la main droitte : " Ha," dit-il,
" mère, tu as vaincu une victoire heureuse pour ton
païs, mais bien malheureuse et mortelle pour ton
filz : car je m'en revois vaincu, par toi seule." ' In
North : ' " Oh mother, what have you done to
me ? " And holding her hard by the right hand,
" Oh mother," sayed he, " you have wonne a happy
victorie for your countrie, but mortall and unhappy for your sonne ; for I see myself vanquished
by you alone." ' North accepts the precious jewel
from Amyot, without loss of emotion or addition
of phrase : he repeats the desolate question, the
singultus of repeated apostrophe, the closing note of
unparalleled doom. Shakespeare, too, accepts them
in turn from North ; and one is sorry that even he
should have added a word.

What, it may be asked, led Shakespeare, amid all

the power and magnificence of North's *Plutarch*, to
select his *Coriolanus*, his *Julius Cæsar*, and his
Antonius? The answer, I think, must be that in
Volumnia, Calpurnia and Portia, and Cleopatra, he
found woman in her three-fold relation to man, of
mother, wife, and mistress. I have passed over
Shakespeare's *Julius Cæsar*; but I may end by
tracing in his *Antony* the golden tradition he accepted
from Amyot and North. It is impossible to do this
in detail, for throughout the first three acts all the
colour and the incident, throughout the last two all
the incident and the passion, are taken by Shakespeare from North, and by North from Amyot.
Enobarbus's speech (II. ii. 194), depicting the pageant
of Cleopatra's voyage up the Cydnus to meet Antony,
is but North's ' The manner how he fell in love with
her was this.' Cleopatra's *barge* with its *poop* of
gold and *purple sails*, and its *oars* of *silver*, which
' *kept stroke*, after the sound of the musicke *of flutes* ' ;
her own *person* in her *pavilion, cloth of gold of tissue,*
even as *Venus* is pictured ; her *pretty boys* on each
side of *her*, like *Cupids, with* their *fans* ; her *gentle-
women* like the *Nereides, steeri*ng the *helm* and handling the *tackle* ; the ' wonderful passing sweete savor
of *perfumes* that perfumed the *wharfe*-side ' ; all
down to Antony ' left post *alone in the market-place* in
his Imperiall seate,' are translated bodily from the
one book to the other, with but a little added ornament of Elizabethan fancy. Shakespeare, indeed, is
saturated with North's language and possessed by
his passion. He is haunted by the story as North
has told it, so that he even fails to eliminate matters
which either are nothing to his purpose or are not
susceptible of dramatic presentment: as in I. ii. of
the Folios, where you find Lamprias, Plutarch's

grandfather, and his authority for many details of
Antony's career, making an otiose entry as Lamprius,
among the characters who have something to say.
Everywhere are touches whose colour must remain
comparatively pale unless they glow again for us as,
doubtless, they glowed for Shakespeare, with hues
reflected from the passages in North that shone in
his memory. For instance, when his Antony says
(I. i. 53) :

> ' To-night we 'll wander through the streets and note
> The qualities of people,'

you need to know from North that ' sometime also
when he would goe up and downe the citie disguised
like a slave in the night, and would peere into poore
men's windowes and their shops, and scold and brawl
with them within the house ; Cleopatra would be
also in a chamber-maides array, and amble up and
down the streets with him ' ; for the fantastic
rowdyism of this Imperial masquerading is all but
lost in Shakespeare's hurried allusion. During his
first three Acts Shakespeare merely paints the man
and the woman who are to suffer and die in his two
others ; and for these portraits he has scraped together all his colour from the many such passages as
are scattered through the earlier and longer portion of
North's *Antonius*. Antony's Spartan endurance in
bygone days, sketched in Cæsar's speech (I. iv. 59)—

> ' Thou didst drink
> The stale of horses and the gilded puddle
> Which beasts would cough at : thy palate then did deign
> The roughest berry on the rudest hedge ;
> Yea, like a stag when snow the pasture sheets,
> The barks of trees thou brousedst. On the Alps
> It is reported thou didst eat strange flesh,
> Which some did die to look on '—

is thus originated by North : ' It was a wonderful example to the souldiers, to see Antonius that was brought up in all fineness and superfluity, so easily to drink puddle water, and to eate wild fruits and rootes : and moreover, it is reported that even as they passed the Alpes, they did eate the barks of trees, and such beasts as never man tasted their flesh before.'   For his revels in Alexandria, Shakespeare has taken ' the eight wild boars roasted whole ' (II. ii. 183) ; for Cleopatra's disports, the diver who ' did hang a salt fish on his hook ' (II. v. 17). In III. iii. the dialogue with the Soothsayer, with every particular of Antony's Demon overmatched by Cæsar's, and of his ill luck with Cæsar at dice, cocking, and quails ; in III. x. the galley's name, *Antoniad* ; and in III. vi. Cæsar's account of the coronation on a ' *tribunal silver'd*,' and of Cleopatra's ' giving audience ' in the habiliment of the *Goddess Isis*, are other such colour patches.   And this, which is true of colour, is true also of incident in the first three Acts.   The scene near Misenum in II. vi., with the light talk between Pompey and Antony, is hardly intelligible apart from North : ' Whereupon Antonius asked him (Sextus Pompeius), "And where shall we sup ? "   " There," sayd Pompey ;   and showed him his admiral galley . . . " that," said he, " is my father's house they have left me."   He spake it to taunt Antonius because he had his father's house.'   On the galley in the next scene, the offer of Menas, ' Let me cut the cable,' and Pompey's reply ' Ah, this thou shouldst have done and not have spoke on't ! ' may be read almost textually in North : ' " Shall I cut the gables of the ankers ? "   Pompey having paused a while upon it, at length answered him : " thou shouldst have done

it and never told it me." ' In III. vii. the old
soldier's appeal to Antony not to fight by sea, with
all his arguments; in II. xi. Antony's offer to his
friends of a ship laden with gold; in III. xii. his
request to Cæsar that he may live at Athens; in
III. xiii. the whipping of Thyreus, with Cleopatra's
announcement, when Antony is pacified, that ' Since
my lord Is Antony again, I will be Cleopatra—' [1] all
these incidents are compiled from the many earlier
pages of North's *Antonius*. But in the Fourth Act
Shakespeare changes his method : he has no more
need to gather and arrange. Rather the concentrated passion, born of, and contained in, North's
serried narrative, expands in his verse—nay, ex-
plodes from it—into those flashes of immortal speech
which have given the Fourth Act of *Antony and
Cleopatra* its place apart even in Shakespeare. Of
all that may be said of North's *Plutarch*, this perhaps
is of deepest significance : that every dramatic
incident in Shakespeare's Fourth Act is contained in
two, and in his Fifth Act, in one and a half folio
pages of the *Antonius*. Let me rehearse the incidents.
The Fourth Act opens with Antony's renewed
challenge to Cæsar, and is somewhat marred by
Shakespeare's too faithful following of an error in
North's translation.

> ' Let the old ruffian know
> I have many other ways to die '

is taken from North ; but North has mistaken
Amyot, who correctly renders Plutarch's version of
the repartee, that ' he (Antony) has many other ways
to die ' : (' *Cesar luy feit response, qu'il avoit beaucoup
d'autre moiens de mourir que celuy là.*') In North,

[1] One of North's mistranslations : she kept Antony's birthday, not her
own.

this second challenge comes after (1) the sally in
which Antony drove Cæsar's horsemen back to their
camp (IV. vii.); (2) the passage in which he 'sweetly
kissed Cleopatra, armed as he was,' and commended
to her a wounded soldier (IV. viii.) ; (3) the subsequent defection of that soldier, which Shakespeare,
harking back to the earlier defection of Domitius,
described by North before Actium, develops into
Enobarbus's defection and Antony's magnanimity
(IV. v.), with Enobarbus's repentance and death
(IV. vi. and ix.).   In North, hard after the challenge
follows the supper at which Antony made his
followers weep (IV. ii.) and the mysterious music
portending the departure of Hercules (IV. iii.).   The
latter passage is so full of awe that I cannot choose
but quote. ' Furthermore,' says North, ' the self
same night within little of midnight, when all the
citie was quiet, full of feare, and sorrowe, thinking
what would be the issue and end of this warre : it is
said that sodainly they heard a marvelous sweete
harmonie of sundrie sortes of instruments of musicke,
with the crie of a multitude of people, as they had
beene dauncing, and had song as they use in Bacchus
feastes, with movinges and turninges after the
manner of the satyres, and it seemed that this daunce
went through the city unto the gate that opened to
the enemies, and that all the troupe that made this
noise they heard went out of the city at that gate.
Now, such as in reason sought the interpretation of
this wonder, thought that it was the god unto whom
Antonius bare singular devotion to counterfeate and
resemble him, that did forsake them.' [1]   The incident

[1] Translated word for word from Amyot. Any one who cares to pursue
this tradition of beauty still further towards its sources will find that in the
Antonius Amyot was in turn the debtor of Leonardus Aretinus, who did the
life into Latin for the *editio princeps* (1470) of Campani.

is hardly susceptible of dramatic representation, but Shakespeare, as it were spellbound by his material, must even try his hand at a miracle. Follows, in North, the treachery of Cleopatra's troops ; Antony's accusation of Cleopatra (IV. x. xi. and xii.) ; Cleopatra's flight to the monument and the false message of her death (IV. xiii.) ; Antony's dialogue with Eros, the suicide of Eros, and the attempt of Antony (IV. xiv.) ; and the death of Antony (IV. xv.). Every incident in Shakespeare's Act is contained in these two pages of North ; and not only the incidents but the very passion of the speeches. ' O Cleopatra,' says Antonius, ' it grieveth me not that I have lost thy companie, for I will not be long from thee ; but I am sorry, that having bene so great a captaine and emperour, I am in deede condemned to be judged of less corage and noble minde then a woman.' Or take, again, the merciless realism of Cleopatra's straining to draw Antony up into the monument : — ' Notwithstanding Cleopatra would not open the gates, but came to the high windowes, and cast out certaine chaines and ropes, in the which Antony was trussed : and Cleopatra her oune selfe, with two women only, which she had suffered to come with her into these monuments, trised Antonius up. They that were present to behold it, said they never saw so pitiefull a sight. For they plucked poore Antonius all bloody as he was, and drawing on with pangs of death, who holding up his hands to Cleopatra, raised up him selfe as well as he could. It was a hard thing for these women to do, to lift him up : but Cleopatra stooping downe with her head, putting to all her strength to her uttermost power, did lift him up with much adoe, and never let goe her hold, with the helpe of the women beneath

that bad her be of good corage, and were as sorie to
see her labour so, as she her selfe.   So when she had
gotten him in after that sorte, and layed him on a
bed :   she rent her garments upon him, clapping
her breast, and scratching her face and stomake.
*Then she dried up his blood that berayed his face, and
called him her Lord, her husband, and Emperor, forgetting her miserie and calamitie, for the pitie and
compassion she took of him.'*   In all this splendour
North is Amyot, and Amyot is Plutarch, while
Plutarch is but the reporter of events within the recollection of men he had seen living ; so that Shakespeare's Fourth Act is based on old-world realism
made   dynamic   by   North's   incomparable   prose.
Then come Antony's call for wine and his last speech,
which Shakespeare has taken with scarce a change :
' And for himself, that she should not lament nor
sorrowe for the miserable chaunge of his fortune at
the end of his dayes :   but rather that she should
thinke   him   the   more   fortunate,   for   the   former
triumphe and honors he had received, considering
that while he lived he was the noblest and greatest
prince of the world, and that now he was overcome
not cowardly, but valiantly, a Romane by another
Romane.'   In Shakespeare :

> ' Please your thoughts
> In feeding them with those my former fortunes
> Wherein I liv'd : the greatest prince o' the world,
> The noblest : and do now not basely die,
> Not cowardly put off my helmet to
> My countryman, a Roman by a Roman
> Valiantly vanquished.'

To the end of the play the poet's fidelity is as close ;
and North's achievement in narrative prose is only
less signal than Shakespeare's in dramatic verse.

Every characteristic touch, even to Cleopatra's outburst against Seleucus, is in North. Indeed, in the Fifth Act I venture to say that Shakespeare has not transcended his original. There is in North a speech of Cleopatra at the tomb of Antony, which can ill be spared ; since it is only indicated in Shakespeare (v. ii. 303) by a brief apostrophe—

> ' O, couldst thou speak,
> That I might hear thee call great Cæsar ass
> Unpolicied '—

which is often confused with the context addressed to the asp. In North you read : ' She was carried to the place where his tombe was, and there falling downe on her knees, imbracing the tombe with her women, the teares running doune her cheekes, she began to speake in this sorte : " O my deare Lord Antonius, not long sithence I buried thee here, being a free woman : and now I offer unto thee the funerall sprinklinges and oblations, being a captive and prisoner, and yet I am forbidden and kept from tearing and murdering this captive body of mine with blowes, which they carefully gard and keepe, only to triumphe of thee : looke therefore henceforth for no other honors, oferinges, nor sacrifices from me, for these are the last which Cleopatra can geve thee, sith nowe they carie her away. Whilest we lived together nothing could sever our companies : but now at our death, I feare me they will make us chaunge our countries. For as thou being a Romane, hast been buried in Ægypt : even so wretched creature I, an Ægyptian, shall be buried in Italie, which shall be all the good that I have received of thy contrie. If therefore the Gods where thou art now have any power and authoritie, sith our gods

here have forsaken us : suffer not thy true friend
and lover to be caried away alive, that in me, they
triumphe of thee : but receive me with thee, and let
me be buried in one selfe tombe with thee. For
though my griefes and miseries be infinite, yet none
hath grieved me more, nor that I could lesse beare
withall : then this small time, which I had been
driven to live alone without thee." ' Her prayer is
granted. The countryman comes in with his figs ;
and then, ' Her death was very sodaine. For those
whom Cæsar sent unto her ran thither in all hast
possible, and found the souldiers standing at the
gate, mistrusting nothing, nor understanding of her
death. But when they opened the dores, they found
Cleopatra starke dead, layed upon a bed of gold,
attired and araied in her royall robes, and one of
her two women, which was called Iras, dead at her
feete ; and her other woman called Charmion halfe
dead, and trembling, trimming the Diademe which
Cleopatra ware upon her head. One of the souldiers
seeing her, angrily sayd unto her : " Is that well
done, Charmion ? " " Verie well," sayd she againe,
" and meet for a Princes discended from the race of
so many noble kings." She sayd no more, but fell
doune dead hard by the bed.'

I doubt if there are many pages which may rank
with these last of North's *Antonius* in the prose of
any language. They are the golden crown of his
Plutarch, but their fellows are all a royal vesture
wrapping a kingly body. For the *Parallel Lives* is a
book most sovereign in its dominion over the minds
of great men in every age. Henri iv., in a love-
letter, written between battles, to his young wife,
Marie de Médicis, speaks of it as no other such hero
has spoken of any other volume, amid such dire

surroundings and in so dear a context. But if it
has armed men of action, it has urged men of letters.
Macaulay claimed it for his ' forte . . . to give a life
after the manner of Plutarch,' and he tells us that,
between the writing of two pages, when for weeks a
solitary at his task, he would ' ramble five or six
hours over rocks and through copsewood with
Plutarch.' Of good English prose there is much,
but of the world's greatest books in great English
prose there are not many. Here is one, worthy to
stand with Malory's *Morte Darthur* on either side
the English Bible.

THE POEMS OF SHAKESPEARE

THE POEMS OF SHAKESPEARE

I

MODERN critics have found it convenient to preserve the classification of poetry which their predecessors borrowed from the ancients at the Revival of Learning. But, in order to illustrate his theory, each has been forced to define anew such terms as 'lyric,' 'elegiac,' 'epic,' and the terms, in consequence of these repeated attempts, have at last ceased to be definite. Now, despite this shifting indefiniteness, when we say of any poetry that it is lyrical and elegiac, we are understood to mean that it deals with emotion rather than with doctrine or drama; and further, that its merit lies, not so much in the exclusive delineation of any one emotional experience, as in the suggestion, by beautiful imagery and musical sound, of those aspirations and regrets which find a voice but little less articulate in the sister-art of music. Narrowing the definition, we may say that the best lyrical and elegiac poetry expresses, by both its meaning and its movement, the quintessence of man's desire for Beauty, abstracted from concrete and transitory embodiments. The matter in such poetry is of 'Beauty that must die'; the method, a succession of beautiful images flashed from a river of pleasing sound. It is the effect of an art which appeals to the mind's eye with a lovely and vivid imagination, and to the mind's ear with a melody at all times soft and (since Beauty dwells with Sadness) at many times pathetic.[1] To illustrate one art by another is often to lose, in the confusion of real distinction, most of the gain won by comparing justly ; yet, at the risk of that loss, it may be said of lyrical and elegiac poetry that it stands to other poetry, and to all speech, in some such relation as that of sculpture to architecture. And this is particularly true of Shakespeare's Poems. Marble may be used for many ends, and in all its uses may be handled with a regard for Beauty ; but there comes a Phidias, possessed beyond others with the thirst for Beauty, and pre-eminent both in perception and in control of those qualities which fit marble for expressing Beauty to the mind through the eye. He is still unsatisfied by any divided dedication ; and so, in the rhythmic procession of a frieze, he consecrates it to Beauty alone. At other times he may be the first of architects, an excellent citizen at all. The Poems of Shakespeare may be compared to the Frieze of the Parthenon, insomuch

---

[1] Mr. Bagehot seems to deny this when he says (*Hartley Coleridge*) that with ' whatever differences of species and class the essence of lyrical poetry remains in all identical; it is designed to express, and when successful does express, some one mood, some single sentiment, some isolated longing in human nature.' I doubt it. On the contrary the essence of lyrical, certainly of elegiac poetry, consists in the handling of sentiment and emotion to suggest infinity, not unity, not the science of psychology but, the mysticism of desire. The emotion may sometimes be isolated for the sake of more effectively contrasting its definiteness with the vast aspiration it engenders. A lyrical poet, for instance, would be content to echo the single note of a curlew, but only because it suggests a whole moorland : the particular moorland, that is, over which one bird is flying, and therewith the flight of all birds, once a part of religion, over all moorlands in all ages. Such a poem, if it were successful, would give, not only the transient mood of a single listener but, all the melancholy and all the meaning and all the emotion without meaning that have ever followed the flight of a lonely bird over a waste place. Mr. Bagehot knows this, for he goes on thus :— ' Hence lyrical poets must not be judged literally from their lyrics : they are discourses ; they require to be reduced into the scale of ordinary life, to be stripped of the enraptured element, to be clogged with gravitating prose.' And why is this to be done ? ' To judge the poet.' Exactly ! But why judge the poet instead of enjoying the poem ?

as both are works in which the greatest masters of
words and of marble that we know have exhibited
the exquisite adaptation of those materials to the
single expression of Beauty. Other excellences there
are in these works—excellences of truth and nobility,
of intellect and passion ; and we may note them,
even as we must note them in the grander achievement of their creators : even as we may, if we choose,
find much to wonder at or to revere in the lives
of their creators. But in these things of special
dedication we must seek in the first place for the
love of Beauty perfectly expressed, or we rebel
against their authors' purpose. Who cares now
whether Phidias did, or did not, carve the likeness
of Pericles and his own amidst the mellay of the
Amazons ? And who, intent on the exquisite response of Shakespeare's art to the inspiration of
Beauty, need care whether his Sonnets were addressed
to William Herbert or to another ? A riddle will
always arrest and tease the attention ; but on that
very account we cannot pursue the sport of running
down the answer, unless we make a sacrifice of all
other solace. Had the Sphinx's enigma been less
transparent, it must have wrecked the play of
Sophocles, for the minds of the audience would have
stayed at the outset : much in the manner of trippers
to Hampton Court who spend their whole time in the
Maze. Above all, must the mind be disencumbered,
clean, and plastic, when, like a sensitive plate, it is
set to receive the impression of a work of art.

But are Shakespeare's Poems works of art ? Can
the *Venus and Adonis*, the *Lucrece*, and the *Sonnets*
be received together as kindred expressions of the
lyrical and elegiac mood ? These questions will
occur to every one acquainted with the slighting

allusions of critics to the Narrative Poems, or with
the portentous mass of theory and inference which
has accumulated round the Sonnets. For to find
these poems and certain of these Sonnets so received
we must turn back, over three hundred years, to one
of Shakespeare's contemporaries.   Francis Meres,
in his *Palladis Tamia,* a laboured but pleasing
' comparative discourse ' of Elizabethan poets and
the great ones of Italy, Greece, and Rome, wrote
thus :—' As the soule of Euphorbus was thought
to live in Pythagoras, so the sweete wittie soule of
Ovid lives in mellifluous and honey-tongued Shakespeare, witness his *Venus and Adonis,* his *Lucreece,*
his sugred sonnets among his private friends.'
Meres, therefore, was the first to collect the titles
or to comment on the character of Shakespeare's
Poems.   But although, since 1598, he has had many
successors more competent than himself, and though
nearly all have quoted his saying, not one has
followed his example of reviewing the three works
together and insisting on their common characteristic.   The Poems, indeed, have but rarely been
printed hand in hand (so to speak) and apart from
the Plays. This strange omission did not follow,
as I think, on any deliberate judgment : it was,
rather, the accidental outcome of the greater interest aroused by the Plays.   The Poems were long
eclipsed ; and critics, even when they turned to
them again, were still thinking of the Plays—were
rather seeking in the Poet for the man hid in the
Playwright than bent on esteeming the loveliness
of Shakespeare's lyrical art.   For this purpose the
Sonnets showed the fairer promise : so the critics
have filled shelves with commentaries on them,
scarcely glancing at the *Venus* and the *Lucrece* ;

and, even in scrutinising the Sonnets, they have been so completely absorbed in the personal problems these suggest as to discuss little except whether or how far they reveal the real life of the man who, in the Plays, has clothed so many imaginary lives with the semblance of reality. The work done in this field has been invaluable on the whole. It is impossible to over-praise Mr. Tyler's patience in research, or to receive with adequate gratitude the long labour of Mr. Dowden's love. Yet even Mr. Dowden, when he turns from considering Shakespeare's art in the Plays, and would conjure up his soul from the Sonnets, cannot escape the retribution inseparable from his task. This probing in the Sonnets after their author's story is so deeply perplexed an enterprise as to engross the whole energy of them that essay it : so that none bent on digging up the soil in which they grew has had time to count the blossoms they put forth. Some even (as Gervinus) have been altogether blinded by the sweat of their labour, holding that the ' Sonnets, æsthetically considered, have been over-estimated ' (Shakespeare, *Commentary*, 452). He writes much of Shakespeare's supposed relation to Southampton ; but ' for the elegancy, facility, and golden cadence of poetry, *caret*.' Yet we know from Meres and others that Shakespeare impressed his contemporaries, during a great part of his life, not only as the greatest living dramatist, but also as a lyrical poet of the first rank. Thus in 1598 Richard Barnefield, after praising Spenser, Daniel, and Drayton : —[1]

> ' And *Shakespeare* thou, whose hony-flowing Vaine
> (Pleasing the World) thy Praises doth obtaine.

---

[1] ' *A Remembrance of some English Poets* : Poems in Divers Humors,' printed with separate title-page at the end of ' *The Encomion of Lady*

> Whose *Venus* and whose *Lucrece*, (sweet, and chaste)
> Thy Name in fame's immortall Booke have plac't
> Live ever you, at least in Fame live ever :
> Well may the Body dye, but Fame dies never ' :

and thus John Weever in 1599 (*Epigrammes in the Oldest Cut and Newest Fashion*) :—

> ' Honie-tong'd Shakespeare, when I saw thine issue,
>   I swore Apollo got them and none other,
> Their rosie-tainted features cloth'd in tissue,
>   Some heaven-born goddesse said to be their mother ;
> Rose-checkt *Adonis* with his amber tresses,
>   Fair fire-hot *Venus* charming him to love her,
> Chaste *Lucretia*, virgine-like her dresses,
>   Prowd lust-stung Tarquine seeking still to prove her. . . .'

Now, these tributes were paid at a time when lyrical poetry was the delight of all who could read English. In one year (1600) three famous anthologies were published—*England's Helicon*, that is, *England's Parnassus*, and *Belvedere, or the Garden of the Muses* ; and, something more than a year later, the author of the *Returne from Parnassus* writes this of Shakespeare, when he reaches him in his review of the poets whose lyrics were laid under contribution for the *Belvedere* :—

> INGENIOSO. William Shakespeare.
> JUDICIO. Who loves Adonis' love, or Lucre's rape,
>   His sweeter verse containes hart robbing life,
>   Could but a graver subject him content,
>   Without loves foolish languishment.

Discounting somewhat from the academical asperity of his judgment, you find Shakespeare still regarded well into the seventeenth century [1] as a love poet whose siren voice could steal men's hearts.

Pecunia,' 1598. Michael Drayton in his *Matilda*, 1594-1596, after referring to Daniel's *Rosamond*, refers to Shakespeare's *Lucrece*. It is interesting to note that the reference is cut out of all subsequent editions.

[1] Dated by Arber.

In gauging the æsthetic value of a work of art we cannot always tell ' how it strikes a contemporary ' ; and, even when we can, it is often idle to consider the effect beside maturer judgments. But when, as in the case of these Poems, later critics have scarce so much as concerned themselves with æsthetic value, we may, unless we are to adventure alone, accept a reminder of the artist's intention from the men who knew him, who approved his purpose, and praised his success. To Francis Meres, living among poets who worshipped Beauty to the point of assigning a mystical importance to its every revelation through the eye, it was enough that Shakespeare, like Ovid, had wrought an expression for that worship out of the sound and the cadence of words, contriving them into harmonies haunted by such unexplained emotion as the soul suffers from beautiful sights. We need not set Meres as a critic beside, say, Hazlitt. But when Hazlitt quarrels with the Narrative Poems because they are not realistic dramas, and when Gervinus takes the Sonnets for an attempt at autobiography, baulked only by the inherent difficulty of the Sonnet form, it may be profitable to reconsider the view of even the euphuist Meres. Still, none can be asked to accept that view without some warning of the risk he runs. To maintain, with Meres, that Shakespeare's Poems, including the Sonnets, are in the first place lyrical and elegiac, is to court a hailstorm of handy missiles. Hazlitt —who, to be sure, would none of Herrick—denounced the Narrative Poems for ' ice-houses ' ; and Coleridge's ingenious defence—that their wealth of picturesque imagery was Shakespeare's substitute for dramatic gesture—is almost as damaging as Hazlitt's attack.   The one states, the other implies, that they were awkward attempts at Drama, mere essays at the form in which the author was afterwards to find his vocation.   And when we come to the Sonnets, the view of Meres, and of all who agree with Meres, draws a hotter fire : not only from those who push the personal theory to its extreme conclusion, treating the Sonnets as private letters written to assuage emotion with scarce a thought for art, but also from those who vigorously deny that any Sonnet can be lyrical.   Yet the hazard must be faced; for the *Venus*, the *Lucrece*, and the *Sonnets* are, each one, in the first place lyrical and elegiac.   They are concerned chiefly with the delight and the pathos of Beauty, and they reflect this inspiration in their forms : all else in them, whether of personal experience or contemporary art, being mere raw material and conventional trick, exactly as important to these works of Shakespeare as the existence of quarries at Carrara and the inspiration from antique marbles newly discovered were to the works of Michelangelo.   It is easy to gauge the relative importance in Shakespeare's work between his achievement as an artist and his chances as a man.   For the relative importance is measured by the chasm which sunders his work from the work of contemporaries labouring under like conditions; and if his Sonnets have little in common with Constable's, his narrative verse has still less in common with (say) Marston's *Pygmalion*.

Unless this view be admitted there is no excuse for linking the Narrative Poems with the Sonnets: we can take down the Plays, or study, instead of the Sonnets, such conclusions upon Shakespeare's passionate experience as the commentator has been able to draw. And many of us do this, yielding to the bias of criticism deflected from its proper office by pre-occupation with matters outside the mood of æsthetic delight. But the mistake is ours, and the loss, which also is ours, is very great. The nature of it may be illustrated from that which comes upon the many who shrink from reading the earliest of Shakespeare's Plays, or read it only in search of arguments against his authorship. Starting from the improbable conjecture, that the character of an author may be guessed from the incidents he chooses to handle, critics have either alluded to *Titus Andronicus* with an apology, or have denied it to be Shakespeare's.[1] But, read without prejudice or without anxiety to prove that Shakespeare could not have chosen the theme of Mutilation for the spring of unspeakable pathos, the play in no wise ' reeks of blood,' but, on the contrary, is sweet with the fragrance of woods and fields, is flooded with that infinite pity whose serene fountains well up within the walls of an hospital. It is true that Lavinia suffers a worse fate than Philomela in Ovid's tale ; that her tongue is torn out, lest it should speak her wrong ; that her hands are cut off, lest they should write it. But mark the *treatment* of these worse than brutalities. Thus speaks Marcus of her hands (ii. 4) :—

> ' Those sweet ornaments,
> Whose circling shadows Kings have sought to sleep in,
> And might not gain so great a happiness
> As have thy love.'

---

[1] Dowden, *Shakespeare, His Mind and Art*, pp. 54, 55. Gerald Massey, *Shakespeare's Sonnets and His Private Friends*, p. 851. Halliwell-Phillipps, *Outlines*, i. 79.

And again :—

> ' O, had the monster seen those lily hands
> Tremble, like aspen-leaves, upon a lute,
> And make the silken strings delight to kiss them,
> He would not then have touched them for his life ! '

And of her tongue (iii. 1) :—

> ' O, that delightful engine of her thoughts,
> That blabb'd them with such pleasing eloquence,
> Is torn from forth its pretty hollow cage
> Where, like a sweet melodious bird, it sung
> Sweet varied notes, enchanting every ear.'

Who can listen to these lines or to those which tell
how

> ' Fresh tears
> Stood on her cheeks, as doth the honey-dew
> Upon a gather'd lily almost wither'd,'

and yet conclude that ' if any portions of the Play
be from his hand, it shows that there was a period
in Shakespeare's authorship when the Poet had not
yet discovered himself ' ?   In the same scene, hark
to the desolate family :—

> ' Behold our cheeks
> How they are stain'd, as meadows yet not dry
> With miry slime left on them by a flood ' :—

and consider that daughter's kiss which can avail
her father nothing :—

> ' Alas, poor heart, that kiss is comfortless
> As frozen water to a starved snake.'

These passages are stamped with the plain sign-
manual of Shakespeare : not the creator who, living
in the world, fashioned Hamlet and Falstaff and
Lady Macbeth, but the lyrical poet, bred in Arden
Forest, who wrote *Romeo and Juliet* and *Love's
Labour's Lost*, the *Midsummer Night's Dream* and

the *Two Gentlemen of Verona,* the *Venus* and the *Lucrece,* and the *Sonnets.* They are of that sweet and liquid utterance, which conveys long trains of images caught so freshly from Nature that, like larks in cages, they seem still to belong to the fields and sky.

Our loss is great indeed if an impertinent solicitude for Shakespeare's morals, an officious care for his reputation as a creator of character, lead us to pass over *Titus Andronicus,* or to lend, in the other early plays, a half-reluctant ear to his ' enchanting song ' and his succession of gracious images. But that loss, great as it is in the Plays, is greater and more gratuitous in the Poems, which belong to the same phase of his genius, and yield it a more legitimate expression. The liquid utterance by every character of such lovely imagery as only a poet can see and seize may be, and is most often, out of place in a drama : since it delays the action, falsifies the portraiture, and carries the audience from the scene back to the Playwright's boyhood in the Warwickshire glades. But in a poem it is the true, the direct, the inevitable revelation of the artist's own delight in Beauty. And it is too much to ask of those who drink in this melody without remorse from the Plays, that they shall sacrifice the Poems also to the fetish of characterisation, or shall mar their enjoyment of the Sonnets with vain guesses at a moral problem, whose terms no man has been able to state. Let those, who care for characterisation only, avoid the Poems and stick to the Plays : even as they neglect Chaucer's *Troilus* for his *Prologue* to *The Canterbury Tales.* Each must satisfy his own taste ; but, if there be any that dwell overfondly (as it seems to others) on the sweetness of Shakespeare's earlier verse, let them remember that he too dwelt with a like fondness on Chaucer's long lyric of romantic love. The *Troilus* must certainly have been a part of Shakespeare's life, else he could never have written the opening to the Fifth Act of his *Merchant of Venice* :—

> ' The moon shines bright ; in such a night as this
> When the sweet wind did gently kiss the trees
> And they did make no noise, in such a night
> Troilus methinks mounted the Troyan walls
> And sigh'd his soul toward the Grecian tents
> Where Cressid lay that night.'

He had stood with the love-sick Prince through that passionate vigil on the wall, and had felt the sweet wind ' increasing in his face.'   And if Shakespeare, ' qui après Dieu créa le plus,' found no cause in the *Prologue* for slighting the *Troilus*, surely we, who have created nothing, may frankly enjoy his Poems without disloyalty to his Plays ?

Of course, to the making of these Poems, as to the making of every work of art, there went something of the author's personal experience, something of the manner of his country and his time ; and these elements may be studied by a lover of Poetry.   Yet only that he may better appreciate the amount superadded by the Poet.   The impression which the artist makes on his material, in virtue of his inspiration from Beauty, and of his faculty acquired in the strenuous service of Art, must be the sole object and reward of artistic investigation.   For the student of history and the lover of art are bound on diverse quests.   The first may smelt the work of art in his crucible, together with other products of contemporary custom and morality, in order to extract the ore of historic truth.   But for the second to shatter the finished creations of art in order to show what base material they are made of—surely this argues a most grotesque inversion of his regard for means and end ? To ransack Renaissance literature for parallels to Shakespeare's verse is to discover, not Shakespeare's art but, the common measure of poetry in Shakespeare's day ; to grope in his Sonnets for hints on his personal suffering is but to find that he too was a man, born into a world of confusion and fatigue. It is not, then, his likeness as a man to other men, but his distinction from them as an artist, which concerns the lover of art. And in his Poems we find that distinction to be this : that through all the vapid enervation and the vicious excitement of a career which drove some immediate forerunners down most squalid roads to death, he saw the beauty of this world both in the pageant of the year and in the passion of his heart, and found for its expression the sweetest song that has ever triumphed and wailed over the glory of loveliness and the anguish of decay.

II

To measure the amount in these Poems which is due to Shakespeare's art, let us consider the environment and accidents of his life, and then subtract so much as may be due to these. He was born [1] at the very heart of this island in Stratford-on-Avon, a town in the ancient Kingdom of Mercia—the Kingdom of the Marches—whose place-names still attest the close and full commingling of Angle with

[1] Among many sources of information let me acknowledge my special indebtedness to Professor Dowden, Mr. Robert Bell, and above all, the late Thomas Spencer Baynes. (*Shakespeare Studies.* Longmans, Green and Co., 1894.)

Celt.[1]   And he was born—April 22nd, or 23rd, 1564—
full eighty years after Bosworth Field, by closing the
Middle Age, had opened a period of national union at
home, and had made room and time for a crowd of
literary and artistic influences from abroad.   He
was, therefore, an Englishman in the wider extension of that inadequate term ; and he lived when
every insular characteristic flared up in response to
stimulants from the Renaissance over-sea.   For
nationality is not fostered by seclusion, but dwindles,
like a fire, unless it be fed with alien food.   By
parentage he was heir to the virtues and traditions of diverse classes.   His mother, Mary Arden,
daughter of a small proprietor and ' gentleman of
worship,' could claim descent from noble stocks,
and that in an age when good blood argued a tradition of courtesy among its inheritors as yet unprized
by other ranks.   But, though something of Shakespeare's gentleness and serenity may be traced to
his mother's disposition, it is—with Shakespeare as
with Dickens [2]—the father, John, who strikes us
the more sharply, with the quainter charm of a
whimsical temperament.   John was the eldest son
of Richard, tenant of a forest farm at Snitterfield,
owned by Robert Arden of Wilmcote, the aforesaid
' gentleman of worship.'   But John had a dash of
the adventurer, and dreamed of raising the family
fortunes to a dignity whence they had declined.[3]   So
he left the little farm behind him in 1551, and, shifting his base of operations some three or four miles to

---

[1] Cf. the Rev. Stopford Brooke's *History of Early English Literature*,
and T. S. Baynes, who quotes J. R. Green and Matthew Arnold.

[2] The parallel was noted first—but only in talk—by the late R. L.
Stevenson.   He was keenly alive (I am told) to its possibilities, which,
indeed, are encouraging enough.

[3] Griffin Genealogy. *Times*, October 14, 1895.

Stratford, he there embarked his capital of hope in a number of varied enterprises : [1] with such success, that in six years he could pretend to the hand of Mary Arden, the heiress of his father's landlord. Like Micawber, he counted on ' something turning up ' in a market town ; and, although his career was marked from the very outset by a happy-go-lucky incuriousness,[2] at first he was not disappointed. He becomes a burgess, or town-councillor, probably at Michaelmas 1557, High Bailiff in 1568, Chief Alderman in 1571 ; purchasing house property, and making frequent donations to the poor. His high heart and his easy good-nature won him wealth and friends ; but they landed him at last in a labyrinth of legal embarrassments, so that the family history becomes a record of processes for debt, of mortgages and sales of reversionary interests. In 1578 he obtains relief from one-half of the aldermanic contribution to military equipment ; and, again, he is altogether excused a weekly contribution of fourpence to the poor. In the same year he mortgages his estate of the Asbies for forty pounds, and his sureties are sued by a baker for his debt of five pounds. In 1579 he sells his interest in two messuages at Snitterfield for four pounds. In 1586 his name is removed from the roll of Aldermen because he ' doth not come to the halles when they are warned, nor hath done for a long time.' And in 1592 his affairs have sunk to so low an ebb that

[1] He is described in the register of the Bailiff's Court for 1556 as a ' glover,' but according to tradition he was also a butcher, wool-stapler, corn-dealer, and timber-merchant.

[2] He was fined in 1552 for not removing the household refuse which had accumulated in front of his house, and in 1558 for not keeping his gutter clean. Some argue, but not very plausibly, that every record or tradition which they hold derogatory to Shakespeare or his father, is to be referred to others of the same name.

—curiously enough—with Fluellen and Bardolph for companions in misfortune, he 'comes not to church for fear of process for debt.' [1]   Yet poverty and sorrow neither tamed his ambition nor sealed up his springs of sentiment.   Through the lean years he persists in appealing to the Heralds' College for a

[1] Some have held this plea a pretext to cover recusancy : and, from Malone downwards, the best authorities have conjectured in John Shakespeare one of the many who at that time had no certitude of, perhaps no wish for, a definite break and a new departure in religion.   The Rev. T. Carter has argued (*Shakespeare, Puritan and Recusant*, 1897), that John Shakespeare *and William*, were Puritans.   Such conscription of the dead to the standards of religious factions may well seem unnecessary in any case.   Applied to the Poet of All Time, it is repugnant and absurd. As to John, Mr. Carter's contention is found to rest on certain entries in the municipal accounts of Stratford-on-Avon.   These show that images were defaced by order of the Town Council in the year 1562-3, and that vestments were sold in 1571.   Now, John Shakespeare filled a small office during the first, and the important post of Chief Alderman during the second, of these two years.   In order to gauge how nearly such transactions may point to every member of the Town Council, who did not repudiate them, having been a Puritan, it is necessary to consider the attitude of most Englishmen towards questions of ritual at that time.   According to Green and other received authorities it was an attitude of uncertainty. ' To modern eyes,' Green writes (*History of the English People*, ii. 308), ' the Church under Elizabeth would seem little better than a religious chaos.' After ten years of her rule ' the bulk of Englishmen were found to be "utterly devoid of religion," and came to church " as to a May game." '   It is therefore difficult or, as I hold, impossible to determine from the action of individuals upon questions of ritual, and still more so from their in-action, whether they were Puritans, loyal supporters of the last new State Religion, or Church-Papists, viz. :—those who conformed in public and heard mass at home.   But apart from such points, which can hardly be determined, Mr. Carter puts himself out of court on two broad issues. (1) He makes John a Puritan, and chronicles his application for coat-armour (p. 177) without comment.   Contrast ' Lenvoy to the Author ' by Garter Principall King of Armes, prefixed to Guillim's *Display of Heraldrie*, 1610 :—

> ' *Peevish* Preciseness, *loves no* Heraldry,
> Crosses *in Armes, they hold* Idolatry. . . .
> *Shortly no difference twixt the* Lord *and* Page.

> *Honours*, Recusants ' (*i.e.* puritan recusants) ' *doe so multiply*,
> *As* Armes, *the* Ensignes *of* Nobility,
> *Must be laid downe ; they are too glorious*
> *Plaine idle shewes, and superstitious :*
> Plebeian *basenesse doth them so esteeme.*

grant of arms ; [1] and in 1579, being reduced to the straitest expedients, he still pays an excessive sum for the bell at his daughter's funeral. It was not altogether from Shakespeare's own experience, but also, we may think, from boyish memories of this kindly and engaging Micawber that he was afterwards to draw his unmatched pictures of thriftless joviality. From him, also, Shakespeare may well have derived his curious knowledge of legal procedure and of the science of heraldry, for his father contested some sixty lawsuits, and applied, at least three times, for coat-armour. But the father, if he squandered

" Degrees *in bloud, the steps of pride and scorne,*
All Adam's *children, none are Gentle borne :*
Degrees *of state, titles of* Ceremony : "
Brethren *in* Christ, *greatnesse is* tyranny :
O impure Purity *that so doth deeme !* '

and Guillim's own opinion :—' the *swans purity* is too *Puritanicall,* in that his featters and outward appearance he is all white, but inwardly his body and flesh is very blacke.' (2) He omits the introduction of stage plays into Stratford under John Shakespeare's auspices, and asserts (p. 189) that ' Puritans of the days of Elizabeth had not the abhorrence of the stage which the corruptions of Charles II.'s reign called forth.' Let me quote the Corporation of London in 1575 :—' To play in plague-time increases the plague by infection : to play out of plague-time calls down the plague from God ' (Fleay, *History of the Stage,* p. 47) :—and William Habington, a devout Catholic, writing in 1634, when Prynne had just lost his ears for attacking Players in *Histrio-mastix* :—

' Of this wine should *Prynne*
Drinke but a plenteous glasse, he would beginne
A health to *Shakespeare's* ghost.'

Castara, Part ii., *To a Friend.*

Mr. Carter's attempt to incarcerate Shakespeare in the ' prison-house of Puritanism ' rests on too slender a basis to stand unless buttressed by new, and not very convincing, accounts of the principal movements and characters of the time. For example, he makes James I. a hero of Puritanism, in the face of his declarations :—' A Scottish Presbytery as well fitteth with Monarchy as God and the Devil,' and his threat against the Puritans : —' I will make them conform, or I will harry them out of the land ! '
[1] Conceded in 1596 and extended in 1599. Some dispute this. But the arms of 1596 appear on Shakespeare's monument. Cf. the drafts of Grants of Coat-Armour proposed to be conferred on John Shakespeare, from original MSS. preserved at the College of Arms. (Halliwell-Phillipps, *Outlines*, ii. pp. 56, 61.)

his inheritance, left him an early love and understanding of the stage. ' The best companies in the
Kingdom constantly visited Stratford during the
decade of Shakespeare's active youth from 1573 to
1584 ' [1] : thanks, I cannot but think, to the taste and
instigation of Shakespeare's sire ; for we first hear
of stage plays during the year in which he was High
Bailiff, or Mayor, and we know that, during his
year of office, he introduced divers companies to the
town, and, doubtless, in accordance with custom,
inaugurated their performances in the Guild-hall.

From the known facts of John Shakespeare's extraction and career we may infer the incidents of his
son's boyhood : the visits to the old home at high
seasons of harvest and sheep-shearing; the sports
afield with his mother's relations ; the convivial
gatherings of his father's cronies ; and certain days
of awe-struck enchantment when the Guild-hall resounded to the tread and declamation of Players.
But in the first years all these were incidental to the
regular curriculum of Stratford Grammar-School—
still to be seen in the same building over the Hall.
Fortunately we know what that curriculum was,
and a bound is set to speculation on the nature and
extent of the schooling Shakespeare had.   From the
testimony of two forgotten books,[2] Mr. Baynes has
pieced together the method of teaching in use at
grammar-schools during the years of Shakespeare's
pupilage ; and his theory is amply and minutely con-

---

[1] Baynes, p. 67.

[2] John Brinsley's *Ludus literarius, or Grammar Schoole,* 1612 (Brinsley
was master of the Ashby-de-la-Zouche Grammar-School for 16 years), and
Charles Hoole's *A New Discovery of the old Art of Teaching Schoole,* etc.
This book, though of later date—Hoole was born in 1610—has its own
interest ; since the author was head-master of a school at Rotherham
closely resembling the Stratford School in ' its history and general features.'
—(Baynes.)

firmed by many passages in the Plays.[1] Shakespeare
went to school at seven, and, after grinding at Lily's
Grammar, enjoyed such conversation in Latin with
his instructors as the Ollendorfs of the period could
provide. The scope and charm of these 'Confabu-
lationes pueriles' may be guessed from his sketch
in *Love's Labour's Lost* :—

> SIR NATHANIEL. ' Laus Deo, bone intelligo.'
> HOLOPHERNES. ' Bone ! bone for bene. Priscian a little
>   scratched ; 'twill serve.'
> SIR NATHANIEL. ' Videsne quis venit ? '
> HOLOPHERNES. ' Video et gaudeo.' [2]

And from Holophernes his ' Fauste precor. Old
Mantuan, old Mantuan ! who understandeth thee
not, loves thee not,' we may infer that the pupil did
not share the pedagogic admiration for the Eclogues
of the monk, Mantuanus.[3]

But when, with Æsop's fables, these in their
turn had been mastered, the boy of twelve and
upwards was given his fill of Ovid, something less
of Cicero, Virgil, Terence, Horace, and Plautus,
and, perhaps, a modicum of Juvenal, Persius, and
Seneca's tragedies ; and of these it is manifest, from

---

[1] Baynes, *Shakespeare's Studies*, pp. 147-249 : ' *What Shakespeare Learnt
at School.*'

[2] I preserve Theobald's emendation.   In one of the manuals, ' *Familiares
Colloquendi Formulae in usum Scholarum concinnatae*,' Mr. Baynes has
found, ' Who comes to meet us ?   *Quis obviam venit ?*   He speaks false
Latin, *Diminuit Prisciani caput*; 'Tis barbarous Latin, *Olet barbariem.*'
Cf. Holofernes :—' O, I smell false Latin, ' dunghill ' for unguem.'

[3] From Michael Drayton's epistle in verse to Henry Reynolds—*Of
Poets and Poesy*—1627, we gather that his poetic aspirations survived the
same youthful ordeal :—

> ' For from my cradle (you must know that) I
> Was still inclined to noble Poesie ;
> And when that once *Pueriles* I had read,
> And newly had my Cato construéd. . . .
> And first read to me honest *Mantuan*.'

R

the Poems and the early Plays,[1] that Ovid left by far the most profound impression in Shakespeare's mind. But his studies were cut short. At fourteen [2] he was taken from school, doubtless to assist his father amid increasing difficulties, and we have a crop of legends suggesting the various callings in which he may have laboured to that end.[3] None of these legends can be proved, but none is impossible in view of his father's taste for general dealing and of the random guidance he is likely to have given his son. After four and a half years of such hand-to-mouth endeavour, sweetened, we may guess, by many a holiday in the forest and derelict deer-park at Fulbrook,[4] Shakespeare, in December 1582, being yet a lad of eighteen, married Anne Hathaway, his senior by eight years, daughter to the tenant of Shottery Farm. This marriage may, or may not, have been preceded in the summer by a betrothal of legal validity: [5] his eldest child, Susannah, was born in May 1583. But in either case the adventure was of that romantic order which is justified by success alone, and such success must have seemed doubtful when twins were born in February 1585. About this period of youth, ' when the blood 's lava and the pulse a blaze,' may be grouped the legends of the drinking-match between rival villages at Bidford, and of the deer-slaying resented by Sir Thomas Lucy.

[1] Cf. in particular *Love's Labour 's Lost* and *Titus Andronicus*.

[2] Rowe, 1709.

[3] Rowe makes him a dealer in wool, on the authority of information collected by Betterton ; Aubrey (before 1680) a school-master, and elsewhere a journeyman butcher, which is corroborated by the Parish Clerk of Stratford, born 1613. To Malone's conjecture, that he served in an Attorney's office, I will return.

[4] The property of an attainted traitor, ' sequestered, though not administered by the Crown.'—Baynes, as above, p. 80.

[5] Mr. Halliwell-Phillipps argues that it was. There is no evidence either way.

Mr. Baynes places this latter exploit at Fulbrook ; and, if he be right, Sir Thomas's interference was unwarranted, and may have been dictated by Protestant bigotry against Shakespeare for his kinship with the Ardens of Parkhall, who stood convicted of a plot against the Queen's life.[1] We know little of these years ; but we know enough to approve Shakespeare's departure in search of fortune. For at Stratford, frowned on by the mighty and weighed down with the double burden of a thriftless father and his own tender babes, there was nothing for him but starvation.

III

To London, then, he set out on some day between the opening of 1585 and the autumn of 1587, looking back on a few years of lad's experience and forward to the magical unknown. And to what a London ! Perhaps the first feature that struck him, re-awaking old delights, was the theatres on both banks of Thames. It may even be that he rode straight to one of these houses—(one built by James Burbage, himself a Stratford man)—and that, claiming the privilege of a fellow-townsman, he enrolled himself forthwith in the company of the Earl of Leicester's players.[2] It is likelier than not ; for Burbage can hardly have built, not this later structure but, *the* ' Theater,' twenty years earlier, for a first home of the drama in London, without receiving the congratulations, perhaps the advice, of Shakespeare's

[1] Certain indications, each slight in itself, taken together point to some sympathy on Shakespeare's part with the older faith. The Rev. Richard Davies in notes on Shakespeare, made before the year 1708, says ' he dyed a Papist.'

[2] Baynes. Fleay holds that Shakespeare joined the company at Stratford and travelled with it to London.

father, in those old prosperous aldermanic days, when every strolling company might claim a welcome from the Mayor of Stratford ; and the probability is increased by the presence of two other Stratford men, Heminge and Greene, in the same company. In Blackfriars, also, and near the theatres, stood the shop of Thomas Vautrouillier, publisher, and here Shakespeare found another acquaintance: for Richard Field served the first six years of his apprenticeship (1579-1585) with Vautrouillier, and Richard was the son of ' Henry ffielde of Stratford uppon Aven in the countye of Warwick, tanner,' whose goods and chattels had once, we know, been valued by the Poet's father and two other Stratfordians.[1] Now, about the time of Shakespeare's advent to London, Richard Field married Jaklin, the daughter or widow [2] of Vautrouillier, and succeeded to the *émigré's* business. The closeness of the connection is confirmed by our knowledge that Field printed the first three editions of *Venus* (1593, 1594, 1596) and the first *Lucrece* (1594). But Field also printed Puttenham's *Arte of English Poesie* (1589), and, in ' a neat brevier Italic,' fifteen books of Ovid's *Metamorphoses*. In 1595, again, he printed his fine edition, the second,[3] of North's *Plutarch*, following it up with others in 1603, 1607, 1612. Without companioning Mr. William Blades [4] so far as to infer that Shakespeare worked as a printer with Field, we

---

[1] *Dict. Nat. Biog.* Richard Field. Arber, transcript, ii. 93.

[2] In 1588 he married, says Ames, ' Jaklin, d. of Vautrollier ' (*Typographical Antiquities*, ed. Herbert, ii. 1252) and succeeded him in his house 'in the Black Friers, neer Ludgate.' Collier quotes the marriage register —R. Field to Jacklin, d. of Vautrilliam 12 Jan. 1588. It is stated, however, in a list of master-printers included in the ' Stationers' Register ' (transcript, iii. 702) that Field married Vautrouillier's widow, and succeeded him in 1590.

[3] The first was published by Vautrouillier in 1579.

[4] *Shakespere and Typography*, 1877.

cannot miss the significance of his friend's having
given to the world the Latin poem which left so deep
an impression on Shakespeare's earlier lyrical verse,
and that English translation from Amyot's *Plutarch*,
out of which he quarried the material of his Greek
and Roman plays.

When Shakespeare came to London, then, he found
in Blackfriars a little colony of his fellow-townsmen
caught up in the two most pronounced intellectual
movements of that day : the new English Drama
and the reproduction, whether in the original or in
translation, of classical masterpieces. We know
nothing directly of his life during the next five years.
There is the tradition that he organised shelter and
baiting for the horses of the young gallants, who
daily rode down to the Theatres after their midday
meal ; and there is the tradition that he paid one
visit to Stratford every year.[1] Yet it is easy to
conjecture the experience of a youth and a poet
translated from Warwickshire to a London rocking
and roaring with Armada-patriotism and the literary
fervour of the ' university pens.' All the talk was
of sea-fights and new editions : Drake and Lyly,
Raleigh and Lodge, Greene and Marlowe and
Grenville were names in every mouth. The play-
houses were the centres, and certain young lords
the leaders, of a confused and turbulent movement
appealing with a myriad voices to the lust of the
eye and the pride of life. In pure letters Greene's
Menaphon (1589), Lodge's *Rosalynd* [2] (1590), were
treading on the heels of Lyly's later instalments of
Euphues ; and Sidney's *Arcadia*,[3] long known in

---

[1] Aubrey (before 1680).
[2] Where Shakespeare found the germ of *As You Like It*.
[3] Begun 1580, published 1590.

MS., was at last in every hand.   The first three
books of *The Faery Queen* were brought over from
Ireland, and were published in the same year.
Poetry, poetical prose, and, for the last sign of a
literary summer, even criticism of the aim and art
of poetry—as Webb's *Discourse of English Poetrie*
(1586), Puttenham's *Arte of English Poesie* (1589),
and Sidney's *Apologie for Poetrie* [1]—all kept pouring
from the press.   But the Play was the thing that
chiefly engaged the ambition of poets, and took the
fancy of young lords.   The players, to avoid the
statute which penalised their profession, were enrolled as servants of noblemen, and this led, directly,
to relations, founded on their common interest,
between the patron who protected a company and
the poet who wrote for it.   Indirectly it led to much
freedom of access between nobles who, though not
themselves patrons, were the friends or relatives of
others that were, and the leading dramatists and
players.   Noblemen are associated with Poets, *i.e.*
Playwrights, in contemporary satires.   In Ben
Jonson's *Poetaster*, for example, Cloe, the wife of a
self-made man, asks, as she sets out for the Court :
' And will the Lords and the Poets there use one
well too, lady ? '   These artistic relations often
ripened into close personal friendships : Ben Jonson,
for example, left his wife to live during five years as
the guest of Lord Aubigny ; [2] and Shakespeare's
friendships with Southampton and William Herbert
are so fully attested as to preclude the omission of
all reference to their lives from any attempt at

---

[1] Not published till 1595, but written perhaps as early as 1581.

[2] Esme Stewart, Lord Aubigny, Duke of Lennox (cf. Jonson's *Epigrams*,
19, and the dedication of *Sejanus*).   ' Five years he had not bedded with
her, but had remained with my lord Aulbany,' *Drummond's Conversations*,
13, quoted by Fleay.

reconstituting the life of Shakespeare. Doubtless they arose in the manner I have suggested. In 1599 [1] we read ' the Lord Southampton and Lord Rutland came not to the Court ; the one doth very seldom ; they pass away the time in London, merely in going to plays every day ' ; and from Baynard's Castle to the Blackfriars Theatre was but a step for Pembroke's son, William Herbert, ' the most universally beloved and esteemed of any man of his age.' [2] Shakespeare wrote to Southampton :—' The love I dedicate to your lordship is without end ' ; [3] and we know, apart from any inference deduced from the Sonnets, that William Herbert also befriended our poet. His comrades dedicated the Folio (1623) after his death to William Herbert and his brother Philip, as ' the most incomparable paire of brethren,' in memory of the favour with which they had ' prosequuted ' both the Plays ' and their Authour living.' Shakespeare was the friend of both Southampton and Herbert ; and in his imagination, that mirror of all life, the bright flashes and the dark shadows of their careers must often have been reflected.

IV

Southampton was scholar, sailor, soldier, and lover of letters. [4] Born in 1573, he graduated at sixteen as a Master of Arts at St. John's College, Cambridge. [5]

[1] Letter from Rowland White to Sir Robert Sidney. Rowe, on the authority of Sir William Davenant, states that Southampton once gave Shakespeare £1000. The story, if it be true, probably refers to an investment in the Blackfriars Theatre.

[2] Clarendon.   [3] Dedication of *Lucrece*.

[4] ' Qui in primo aetatis flore praesidio bonarum literarum et rei militaris scientia nobilitatem communit, ut uberiores fructus maturiore aetate patriae et principi profundat.'—Camden's *Britannia*, 8vo, 1600, p. 240.

[5] Southampton was admitted a student in 1585 (æt. 12). Note that Tom Nash, who in after years ' tasted the full spring ' of Southampton's

At twenty-four he sailed with Essex as captain of the *Garland*, and, attacking thirty-five Spanish galleons with but three ships, sank one and scattered her fellows. And for his gallantry on shore in the same year (1597), he was knighted in the field by Essex before Villa Franca, ere ' he could dry the sweat from his brows, or put his sword up in the scabbard.' [1] Now, in 1598 Essex was already out of favour with the Queen—she had been provoked to strike him at a meeting of the Council in July ; but he was popular in London, and had come, oddly enough, to be looked on as a deliverer by Papists and Puritans both. In April 1599 he sailed for Ireland, accompanied by Lord Southampton ; and we need not surmise, for we know, how closely Shakespeare followed the fortune of their arms. In London, ' the quick forge and working-house of thought,' Shakespeare weaves into the chorus to the Fifth Act of his *Henry V.* a prophetic picture of their victorious return :—

> ' Were now the general of our gracious empress,
> As in good time he may, from Ireland coming,
> Bringing rebellion broachéd on his sword,
> How many would the peaceful city quit
> To welcome him ! '

The play was produced in the spring of that year, but its prophecy went unfulfilled. Essex failed where so many had failed before him ; and, being censured by the Queen, replied with impertinent complaints against her favours to his political opponents, Cecil, Raleigh, and that Lord Cobham who had two years

liberality (*Terrors of Night*, 1594) matriculated at the same College in 1582, and ever cherished its memory :—' Loved it still, for it ever was and is the sweetest nurse of knowledge in all that university ' (*Lenten Stuff*).

[1] Gervase Markham, *Honour In Its Perfection*, 4to, 1624.

earlier taken umbrage at Shakespeare's *Henry IV.*[1]
In September he returned suddenly from a futile
campaign, and on Michaelmas Eve, booted, spurred,
and bespattered, he burst into the Queen's chamber,
to find her with ' her hair about her face.' [2] He was
imprisoned and disgraced, one of the chief causes
of Elizabeth's resentment being, as she afterwards
alleged, 'that he had made Lord Southampton
general of the horse contrary to her will.' [3] For
Southampton was already under a cloud. He had
presumed to marry Elizabeth Vernon without await-
ing the Queen's consent, and now, combining the
display of his political discontent with the indulgence
of his passion for the theatre, he, as I have said, is
found avoiding the Court and spending his time in
seeing plays. The combination was natural enough,
for theatres were then, as newspapers are now, the
cock-pits of political as of religious and literary contention. Rival companies, producing new plays,
or ' mending ' old ones each month, and almost each
week, were quick to hail the passing triumphs, or
to glose the passing defeats of their chosen causes.
Whilst high-born ladies of the house of Essex besieged the Court clad in deep mourning,[4] and the
chances of his being forgiven were canvassing among
courtiers wherever they assembled, Dekker in *Patient
Grissel* (1599), Heywood in his *Royal King and Loyal
Subject,*[5] hinted that probation, however remorseless,

[1] *Infra.*

[2] Rowland White to Sir Robert Sidney, Michaelmas day, 1599.

[3] *Ibid.*, 25th October 1599.   [4] Rowland White, *passim.*

[5] I venture to date this play 1600, although printed much later, on the
following grounds :—(1) It was published with an apology for the number
of its ' rhyming lines,' which pleaded that such lines were the rage at the
date of its first production, though long since discarded in favour of blank
verse and ' strong lines.' The plea would hardly tally with a later date.
(2) The allusion to Dekker's *Phaethon*, produced 1598, and re-written for
the Court, 1600, points to Heywood's play having been written whilst

might be but the prelude to a loftier honour.   Now,
just at this time there occurs a strange reversal in
the attitudes of the Court and the City towards the
Drama.   One Order of Council follows another,[1]
enjoining on the Mayor and Justices that they shall
limit the number of play-houses; but the City authorities, as a rule most Puritanical, are obstinately
remiss in giving effect to these decrees.   Mr. Fleay
attributes this waywardness to a jealous vindication
of civic privileges : I would rather ascribe it to
sympathy with Essex, ' the good Earl.'   The City
authorities could well, had they been so minded,
have prevented the performance of *Richard II.*, with
his deposition and death, some ' forty times ' in open
streets and houses, as Elizabeth complained ; [2] and,
indeed, it is hard to account for the Queen's sustained
irritation at this drama save on the ground of its
close association with her past fears of Essex.[3]

Dekker's, referred to also in Jonson's *Poetaster*, 1601, was attracting
attention.   In *Poetaster*, iv. 2, Tucca calls Demetrius, who is Dekker,
Phaethon.   (3) The passage of Heywood's play in which this allusion
occurs is significant :—

> ' PRINCE.   The Martiall 's gone in discontent, my liege.
> KING.   Pleas'd, or not pleas'd, if we be England's King,
>   And mightiest in the spheare in which we move,
>   Wee 'll shine along this *Phaethon* cast down.'

This trial of the Marshal, who is stripped of all his offices and insignia,
seems moulded on the actual trial of Essex in June 1600, as described by
Rowland White in a letter to Sir Robert Sidney of June 7th, 1600 :—' The
poore Earl then besought their Honors, to be a meane unto her Majestie
for Grace and Mercy ; seeing there appeared in his offences no Disloyalty
towards Her Highness, but Ignorance and Indiscretion in hymself.   I
heare it was a most pitifull and lamentable sight, to see hym that was the
Mignion of Fortune, now unworthy of the least Honor he had of many ;
many that were present burst out in tears at his fall to such misery.'   A
writer (probably Mr. R. Simpson) in *The North British Review*, 1870, p. 395,
assigns Heywood's play to 1600.

    [1] June 22, 1600.   March 10, 1601.   May 10, 1601.   December 31, 1601.
Quoted by Fleay.
    [2] Nichols, iii. 552.
    [3] Cf. Elizabeth to Harrington :—' By God's Son I am no Queen ; this
man is above me.'

Months after the Earl's execution, she exclaimed to
Lambard :—' I am Richard the Second, knowe yee
not that ? ' [1]   And we have the evidence of Shakespeare's friend and colleague, Phillips, for the fact
that *Richard II.* was performed by special request of
the conspirators on the eve of their insane rising [2]
(February 7, 1601)—that act of folly, which cost
Essex his head and Southampton his liberty during
the rest of Elizabeth's reign.

But if Shakespeare's colleagues, acting Shakespeare's Plays, gave umbrage to Essex's political
opponents in *Henry IV.*, applauded his ambition in
Henry V., and were accessories to his disloyalty in
Richard II., there were playwrights and players
ready enough to back the winning side. Henslowe,
an apparent time-server, commissioned Dekker to
re-write his *Phaethon* for presentation before the
Court (1600), with, it is fair to suppose, a greater
insistence on the presumption and catastrophe of the
' Sun's Darling ' ; and Ben Jonson, in his *Cynthia's
Revels* (1600), put forth two censorious allusions to
Essex's conduct. Indeed the framework of this
latter play, apart from its incidental attacks on other
authors, is a defence of ' Cynthia's ' severity. Says
Cupid (i. 1) :—' The huntress and queen of these
groves, Diana, in regard of some black and envious
slanders hourly breathed against her for divine
justice on Actæon . . . hath . . . proclaim'd a
solemn revels, which (her godhead put off) she will
descend to grace.' The play was acted before

---

[1] Halliwell-Phillipps, *Outlines*, ii. 359. Lambard, August 1601, had
opened his *Pandecta Rotulorum* before her at the reign of Richard II.

[2] ' Examination of Augustyne Phillypps servant unto the Lord Chamber-
leyne, and one of his players,' quoted by Halliwell-Phillipps, *Outlines*, ii.
360. Phillips died, 1605, leaving by will ' to my fellow William Shakespeare, a thirty shillings piece of gold.'

Elizabeth, and contains many allusions to the
' Presence.'   After the masque, Cynthia thanks the
masquers (v. 3) :—

> ' For you are they, that not, as some have done,
>   Do censure us, as too severe and sour,
>   But as, more rightly, gracious to the good ;
>   Although we not deny, unto the prouu,
>   Or the profane, perhaps indeed austere :
>   For so Actæon, by presuming far,
>   Did, to our grief, incur a fatal doom. . . .
>   Seems it no crime to enter sacred bowers
>   And hallow'd places with impure aspect.'

In 1600, such lines can only have pointed to Essex-
Actæon's mad intrusion into the presence of a Divine
Virgin.   In 1601 if, as some hold, these lines were a
late addition, the reference to Essex's execution was
still more explicit.

We know that Essex had urged the Scotch King,
our James I., to enforce the recognition of his claim
to the succession by a show of arms,[1] and that James
' for some time after his accession considered Essex
a martyr to his title to the English crown.' [2]   Mr.
Fleay points out [3] that ' Lawrence Fletcher, comedian
to His Majesty,' was at Aberdeen in October 1601,
and that Fletcher, Shakespeare, and the others in
his company, were recognised by James as his players
immediately after his accession (1603).[4]   The title-
page of the first *Hamlet* (1603 : entered in the
Stationers' Registers, July 26, 1602) puts the play
forward ' as it hath beene diverse times acted by
his Highnesse servants in the Cittie of London ;
as also in the two Universities of Cambridge and
Oxford, and *elsewhere*.'   Mr. Fleay, therefore, to my

[1] *Queen Elizabeth*, E. S. Beesley.
[2] *Criminal Trials*, L. E. K. i. 394 ; quoted by Fleay.
[3] *History of the Stage*, 136.
[4] The licence is quoted by Halliwell-Phillipps in full, *Outlines*, ii. 82.

thinking, proves his case : [1] that Shakespeare's company was travelling in 1601 whilst Ben Jonson's *Cynthia* was being played by the children of the Chapel. In the light of these facts it is easy to understand the conversation between Hamlet and Rosencrantz, Act ii. 2, which, else, is shrouded in obscurity :—

> ' HAMLET. What players are they ?
>
> ROSENCRANTZ. Even those you were wont to take such delight in, the tragedians of the *City*.
>
> HAMLET. How chances it they travel ? Their residence, both in reputation and profit, was better both ways.
>
> ROSENCRANTZ. I think their *inhibition* comes by means of the late *innovation*.
>
> HAMLET. Do they hold in the same estimation they did when I was in the City ? are they so followed ?
>
> ROSENCRANTZ. No, indeed they are not.
>
> HAMLET. How comes it ? Do they grow rusty ?
>
> ROSENCRANTZ. Nay, their endeavour keeps in the wonted pace ; but there is, sir, an *eyrie of children*, little eyases that cry out on the top of question and are most *tyrannically* clapped for 't : these are now the fashion, and so berattle the common stages—so they call them—that many wearing rapiers are afraid of goose-quills, and dare scarce come thither. . . . Faith, there has been much to do on both sides, and the nation holds it no sin to tarre them to controversy ; there was for a while no money bid for argument unless the poet and the player went to cuffs on the question. . . .[2]
>
> HAMLET. Do the boys carry it away ?
>
> ROSENCRANTZ. Ay, that they do. my lord ; Hercules and his load too.' [3]

---

[1] Mr. Sidney Lee (*Dict. Nat. Biog.* ' Shakespeare ') objects that there is nothing to indicate that Fletcher's companions in Scotland belonged to Shakespeare's company. This hardly touches the presumption raised by the fact that ' Fletcher, *Comedian to His Majesty*,' *i.e.* to James as King of Scotland in 1601, was patented with Shakespeare, Burbage, and others, as the ' King's servants ' on James's accession to the English throne in 1603.

[2] See *infra* on the personal attacks in *Cynthia's Revels* and *Poetaster.*

[3] *I.e.* the Globe Theatre.

The collection of such passages ; Shakespeare's professed affection for Southampton ; his silence when so many mourned the Queen's death, marked (as it was) by a contemporary : all these indications tend to show that Shakespeare shared in the political discontent which overshadowed the last years of Elizabeth's reign. But it is safer not to push this conclusion, and sufficient to note that the storms which ruined Essex and Southampton lifted at least a ripple in the stream of Shakespeare's life.[1]

V

To turn from Southampton to Shakespeare's other noble patron, is to pass from the hazards of war and politics to the lesser triumphs and disasters of a youth at Court. Many slight but vivid pictures of Herbert's disposition and conduct, during the first two years of his life at Court, are found in the intimate letters of Rowland White to Herbert's uncle, Sir Robert Sidney. ' My Lord Harbert '—so he invariably styles him—' hath with much a doe brought his Father to consent that he may live at *London*, yet not before next spring.' This was written 19th April 1597, when Herbert was but seventeen. During that year a project was mooted between Herbert's parents and the Earl of Oxford for his marriage with Oxford's daughter, Bridget Vere, aged thirteen.[2] It came to nothing by reason of her tender years, and Herbert, in pursuance of a promise extracted from a father confined by illness

[1] I shall not pursue the further vicissitudes of Southampton's adventurous career, for the last of Shakespeare's Sonnets was written almost certainly before the Queen's death or soon after.

[2] Mr. Tyler, *Shakespeare's Sonnets*, p. 45, quotes the Rev. W. A. Harrison and the original letters, discovered by him, which prove the existence of this abortive contract.

to his country seat, came up to town, and thrust into the many-coloured rout, with all the flourish and the gallantry, and something also of the diffidence and uneasiness, of youth. You catch glimpses of him : now, a glittering figure in the medley, watching his mistress, Mary Fitton, lead a masque before the Queen, or challenging at the Tournay in the valley of Mirefleur [1]—an equivalent for Greenwich, coined for the nonce, since both place and persons must be masked after the folly of the hour ; and again you find him sicklied with ague and sunk in melancholy— the Hamlet of his age, Gardiner calls him—seeking his sole consolation in tobacco.

I cannot refrain from transcribing Rowland White's references in their order, so clean are the strokes with which he hits off Herbert, so warm the light he sheds on the Court that surrounded Herbert. 4th August 1599 :—' My lord Harbert meanes to follow the camp and bids me write unto you, that if your self come not over, he means to make bold with you and send for *Bayleigh* '—Sir Robert Sidney's charger—' to Penshurst, to serve upon. If you have any armor, or Pistols, that may steede him for himself only, he desires he may have the Use of them till your own Return.' 11th August 1599 :— ' He sent to my lady '—(' Sidney's sister, Pembroke's mother ')—' to borrow *Bayleigh*. She returned this Answer, that he shall have it, but conditionally, that if you come over or send for yt to Flushing he may restore yt, which he agrees to.' 18th August 1599 : —' My Lord Harbert hath beene away from Court these 7 Daies in *London*, swagering yt amongest the Men of Warre, and viewing the Maner of the Musters.'

---

[1] This name belongs to 1606 ; in 1600, however, he also jousted at Greenwich.

8th September 1599 :—' My lord Harbert is a continuall Courtier, but doth not follow his Business with
that care as is fitt ; he is to cold in a matter of such
Greatness.'   12th September 1599 :—' Now that my
lord Harbert is gone, he is much blamed for his cold
and weak maner of pursuing her Majestie's Favor,
having had so good steps to lead him unto it.   There
is want of spirit and courage laid to his charge, and
that he is a melancholy young man.'   September 13,
1599 :—' I hope upon his return he will with more
lisse [1] and care undertake the great matter, which
he hath bene soe cold in.' [2]   On the 20th September
1599, White perceives ' that Lord Nottingham would
be glad to have Lord Harbert match in his house '—
i.e. marry his daughter.   This, then, is the second
project of marriage entertained on Herbert's behalf.
On Michaelmas Day, White describes Essex's return,
and you gather from many subsequent letters how
great was the commotion caused by his fall.   ' The
time,' he writes, September 30th, ' is full of danger,'
and 11th October :—' What the Queen will determine with hym is not knowen ; but I see litle
Hope appearing of any soddain liberty.'   Meanwhile
Herbert steers clear of the eddies, and prosecutes his
cause with greater energy.   Whilst Southampton is
a truant at the play, ' My lord Harbert ' (11th
October) ' is at Court, and much bound to her
Majestie for her gracious Favor, touching the
Resignation of the office of Wales.'   Herbert, indeed, seems to have been favoured by all the Court
faction, including even Sir Robert Cecil, the chief

---

[1] Fr. *liesse* = gaiety.
[2] About this time his father underwent an operation for the stone, and,
if he had died under it, his place in Wales would have gone to the Earl of
Worcester or the Earl of Shrewsbury.   Herbert was to secure the reversion
to himself.

enemy of Essex and, therefore, of Southampton. November 24, 1599 :—' My lord Harbert is exceedingly beloved at Court of all men.' And 29th November 1599, ' 9000 (Herbert) is very well beloved here of all, especially by 200 (Cecil) and 40 who protest in all places they love him.' In the same letter, ' 9000 (Herbert) is highly favoured by 1500 (the Queen) for at his departure he had access unto her, and was private an Houre ; but he greatly wants advise.' On 28th December 1599, we find him sick with ague, and again, 5th January 1600 :— ' My Lord Harbert is sick of his tertian ague at Ramesbury.' On the 12th January 1600 we have the first notice of Mary Fitton :—' Mrs. Fitton is sicke, and gone from Court to her Father's.' 19th January 1600 :—' My lord Harbert coming up towards the Court, fell very sicke at Newberry, and was forced to goe backe again to Ramisbury. Your pies,' White continues, exhibiting the solicitude of uncle and mother alike for the young courtier, ' were very kindly accepted there, and exceeding many Thankes returned. My Lady Pembroke desires you to send her speedely over some of your excellent Tobacco.' [1] 24th January 1600 : — Herbert has ' fallen to have his ague again, and no hope of his being here before Easter.' 26th January 1600 :— He complains ' that he hath a continuall Paine in his Head, and finds no manner of ease but by taking of Tobacco.' The mother's care extended even to the lady, Mary Fitton, whom her son was soon to love—supposing, that is, that he did not love her already. 21st February 1600 :—' My lady goes often to my Lady Lester, my Lady Essex and my Lady

---

[1] Tobacco was first introduced by Nicot as a sovereign remedy against disease.

Buckhurst, where she is exceeding welcome ; she
visited Mrs. Fitton, that hath long bene here sicke
in London.' But her son was soon to recover.
26th February 1600 :—' My lord Harbert is well
again ; they all remove upon Saturday to Wilton
to the races; when that is ended, my Lord Harbert
comes up.' 22nd March 1600 :—' My lord Harbert
is at Court and desires me to salute you very kindly
from him. I doubt not but you shall have great
comfort by him and I believe he will prove a great
man in Court. He is very well beloved and truly
deserves it.'

But some of the love he won brought danger in
its train. The next two references, describing the
marriage of Mistress Anne Russell to ' the other Lord
Herbert,' viz., Lord Worcester's son, picture a
masque in which Mrs. Fitton played a conspicuous
part before the eyes of her young lover. 14th June
1600 :—' There is a memorable mask of 8 ladies ;
they have a straunge Dawnce newly invented ; their
attire is this : Each hath a skirt of cloth of silver, a
rich wastcoat wrought with silkes, and gold and
silver, a mantell of Carnacion Taffete cast under the
Arme, and there Haire loose about their shoulders,
curiously knotted and interlaced. These are the
maskers, My Lady Doritye, Mrs. Fitton, Mrs. Carey,
Mrs. Onslow, Mrs. Southwell, Mrs. Bes Russell, Mrs.
Darcy and my lady Blanche Somersett. These 8
daunce to the musiq Apollo bringes, and there is a
fine speech that makes mention of a ninth,'—of
course the Queen—' much to her Honor and Praise.'
The ceremony was ' honored by Her Majestie's
Presence,' and a sennight later we hear how all
passed off. 23rd June 1600 :—' After supper the
maske came in, as I writ in my last ; and delicate it

was to see 8 ladies soe pretily and richly attired.
Mrs. Fitton leade, and after they had donne all their
own ceremonies, these 8 Ladys maskers choose 8
ladies more to daunce the measures. Mrs. Fitton
went to the Queen, and wooed her to daunce ; her
Majesty asked what she was ; *Affection,* she said.
Affection ! said the Queen. *Affection* is false. Yet
her Majestie rose and daunced.' . . . ' The bride was
lead to the Church by Lord Harbert,' and ' the Gifts
given that day were valewed at £1000 in Plate and
Jewels at least.' Nine months later Mrs. Fitton
bore Herbert an illegitimate child ; but meanwhile
he pursued his career as a successful courtier.
8th August 1600 :—' My lord Harbert is very well
thought of, and keapes company with the best and
gravest in Court, and is well thought of amongst
them.' The next notice, in the circumstances as we
know them, is not surprising. 16th August 1600 :—
' My lord Harbert is very well. I now heare litle of
that matter intended by 600 (Earl of Nottingham)
towards hym, only I observe he makes very much
of hym ; but I don't find any Disposition at all in
this gallant young lord to marry.'

With the next we come to Herbert's training for
the tournament, and gather something of his relations
with the learned men whom his mother had collected
at Wilton to instruct him in earlier years. Mr.
Sandford had been his tutor, sharing that office, at
one time, with Samuel Daniel, the poet and author
of the *Defence of Rhyme.* 26th September 1600 :—
' My Lord Harbert resolves this yeare to shew
hymselfe a man at Armes, and prepared for yt ; and
because it is his first tyme of runninge, yt were good
he came in some excellent Devize, I make it known
to your lordship that if you please to honor my lord

Harbert with your advice ; my feare is, that Mr.
Sandford will in his Humor, persuade my lord to
some pedantike Invention.' Then, 18th October
1600 :—' My lord Harbert will be all next weeke at
Greenwich, to practice at Tylt. He often wishes
you here. Beleve me, my lord, he is a very gallant
Gentleman and, indeed, wants such a Frend as you
are neare unto him.' Again, 24th October 1600 :—
' Lord Harbert is at Greenwich practicing against the
Coronation (?) ' ; and, 30th October 1600 :—' My
lord Harbert is practicing at Greenwich, I sent him
word of this ; he leapes, he dawnces, he singes, he
gives cownterbusses, he makes his Horse runne with
more speede ; he thanckes me, and meanes to be
exceeding merry with you this winter in Baynard's
Castel, when you must take Phisicke.' The rest is
silence ; for Rowland White, the intimate, the
garrulous, is succeeded in the Sidney Papers by duller
correspondents, who attend more strictly to affairs
of state, and the issue of Herbert's intrigue is learned
from other sources. But before I draw on them, let
me set Clarendon's finished picture of Herbert [1] by
the side of these early thumb-nails :—' He was a man
very well bred, and of excellent parts, and a graceful
Speaker upon any subject, having a good proportion
of Learning, and a ready Wit to apply it, and enlarge
upon it : of a pleasant and facetious humour, and a
disposition affable, generous, and magnificent. . . .
Yet his memory must not be Flatter'd, that his
virtues, and good inclinations may be believ'd ; he
was not without some allay of Vice, and without
being clouded with great Infirmities, which he had
in too exorbitant a proportion. He indulged to
himself the Pleasures of all kinds, almost in all

---

[1] *History of the Rebellion*, ed. 1705, vol. i. book i. p. 57.

excesses. To women, whether out of his natural
constitution, or for want of his domestick content
and delight (in which he was most unhappy, for he
paid too dear for his Wife's Fortune, by taking her
Person into the bargain) he was immoderately given
up.   But therein he likewise retain'd such power,
and jurisdiction over his very appetite, that he was
not so much transported with beauty, and outward
allurements, as with those advantages of the mind,
as manifested an extraordinary wit, and spirit, and
knowledge, and administred great pleasure in the
conversation. To these he sacrificed Himself, his
precious time, and much of his fortune. And some,
who were nearest his trust and friendship, were not
without apprehension, that his natural vivacity, and
vigour of mind begun to lessen and decline by those
excessive Indulgences.' In time he filled nearly all
the greater offices of the Court, and ' died of an
Apoplexy, after a full and chearful supper,' in 1630,
leaving no children from his marriage, but a debt of
£80,000 on his estate.[1]

I have lingered over William Herbert, who, excepting Southampton, received more dedicatory verses
from poets, who were also playwrights, than any
other noble of his time ; for, whether or not he was
the ' only begetter ' of Shakespeare's Sonnets, he
was certainly Shakespeare's friend, and one of the
brightest particles in the shifting kaleidoscope of
Court and Stage. Though now one company and
now another was *inhibited*, the Court and Theatre
were never in closer contact than during the last
years of Elizabeth's reign, when at Christmas and
Twelfth Night a play was almost invariably acted
by request ' in the Presence.' Two companies of

[1] *Court and Times of Charles I.*, ii. 73.

players were the servants of the highest officers at
the Court, the Lord Chamberlain and the Lord
Admiral.   And the Lord Admiral was that Earl of
Nottingham who ' made very much ' of Herbert and
desired him for a son-in-law.[1]   The Theatre was
dignified by the very trick of majesty, and the Court
transfigured by the spirit of masquerade.   Davies
tells of Shakespeare in a ' Kingly part,' picking up a
glove let drop by Gloriana's self, with the gag :—

> ' And though now bent on this high embassy,
>   Yet stoop we to take up our cousin's glove.'

The tradition that Shakespeare played these parts
is persistent, and I cannot doubt that his allusion to
himself was obvious to his audience when he puts
into Hamlet's mouth these words :—' He that plays
the King shall be welcome ; his majesty shall have
tribute of me.' [2]

It is almost certain that Mary Fitton, the Queen's
Maid of Honour, was on intimate terms with the
players in the Lord Chamberlain's (Shakespeare's)
Company ; for Kempe, who played the Clown's part,
seems to have dedicated to her the account of his

---

[1] We have a pretty picture of his kindness to Herbert's little cousin in
another letter of Rowland White to Sir R. Sidney.   April 26th, 1600 :—
' All your children are in Health, the 3 greater, and litle Mr. Robert, were
at Court, and in the Presence at St. George's Feast, where they were much
respected.   I brought up Mr. Robert, when the Knights were at dinner ;
who plaied the wagg soe pretily and boldly that all tooke Pleasure in him,
but above the rest, my lord Admirall, who gave him sweet meats and he
prated with his Honor beyond measure.'

[2] Personal allusions were the sauce of every play.   Cf. Jonson's *Cynthia's
Revels* (1600), Act v. 2 :—

' Amorphus. Is the perfume rich in this jerkin ?
   Perfumer. Taste, smell ; I assure you, sir, pure benjamin, the only
            spirited scent that ever awaked a Neapolitan nostril.'

Jonson is constantly called ' Benjamen ' (Bengemen) in Henslowe's *Diary*.

famous *Morris to Norwiche*,[1] as he writes, ' to shew
my duety to your honourable selfe, whose favour
(among other bountifull frends) makes me (despight
of this sad world) judge my hart corke and my
heeles feathers.'   Such an intimacy is intrinsically
probable from her relations with Herbert, who
' prosecuted Shakespeare with his favour,' from the
custom of the age, and above all from her own
fantastic disposition.   Elsewhere you read [2] that
' in the tyme when that Mrs. Fytton was in great
favour, and one of her Majestie's maids of honor (and
during the tyme yt. the Earle of Pembroke [3] favoured
her), she would put off her head tire and tucke upp
her clothes, and take a large white cloak, and march
as though she had bene a man to meete her lover,
William Herbert.'   The inspiration of Shakespeare's
laughter-loving heroines in doublet and hose need
not, then, have come exclusively from boys playing
in women's parts.[4]

But there are shadows in the hey-day pageantry
of this Court which borrowed the trappings and
intrigues of the Stage, and something of its tragedies
also.   In 1601 Southampton is arrested, and Essex
dies on the scaffold for the criminal folly of the
Rising.   In the same spring William Herbert is
disgraced and imprisoned, because Mary Fitton is

---

[1] Entered at Stationers' Hall, 22nd April 1600.   The dedication, it is
true, gives ' Anne,' almost certainly in error, for Mary Fitton.   Anne, so
far as we know, was never a Maid of Honour, and can hardly have been
one in 1600, since she had married Sir John Newdigate in 1585.   See W.
Andrews, *Bygone Cheshire*, p. 150.   He quotes the Rev. W. A. Harrison.

[2] In a document (assigned by Mr. Tyler after a pencil note on it to
Oct. 1602).   *Domestic Addenda*, Elizabeth, vol. xxxiv.   Mary Fitton
suffered from hysteria (*Gossip from a Muniment Room*, 1897, p. 27).

[3] Herbert succeeded, 1601.

[4] Marston.   *Sat.* ii. (1598) :—

' What sex they are, since strumpets breeches use,
And all men's eyes save Lynceus can abuse.'

to bear him a child, and he ' utterly renounceth all
marriage.' [1]   In truth 'twas a dare-devil age of large
morals and high spirits.   Sir Nicholas l'Estrange

[1] Mr. Tyler (*Shakespeare's Sonnets*, 1890, p. 56) quotes (1) the postscript
of a letter, February 5, 1601, from Sir Robert Cecil to Sir George Carew :
—' We have no news but that there is a misfortune befallen Mrs. Fitton,
for she is proved with child, and the Earl of Pembroke, being examined,
confesseth a fact, but utterly renounceth all marriage.   I fear they will
both dwell in the Tower awhile, for the Queen hath vowed to send them
thither ' (*Calendar of Carew MSS.*).   (2) A letter in the Record Office
from Tobie Matthew to Dudley Carleton, March 25, 1601 :—' I am in
some hope of your sister's enlargement shortly, but what will happen
with the Erle I cannot tell ' (W. E. A. Axon in William Andrews' *Bygone
Cheshire*, 1895).   In 1606(?) Mary's mother writes :—' I take no joye to
heer of your sister, nore of that boy, if it had pleased God when I did hear
her, that she hade bene beried, it hade saved me from a gret delle of sorow
and gryffe, and her ffrom shame, and such shame as never have Cheshyre
Woman ; worse now than evar, wright no more of her.'—*Ibid.*   Tyler
quotes a document of the late Rev. F. C. Fitton copied by his father
(b. 1779) from a MS. by Ormerod, author of the *History of Cheshire*, containing this entry :—

Capt. Lougher =	Mary Fitton =	Capt. Polwhele
1st husband	Maid of Honour had	2nd husband
	one bastard by Wm.	
	E. of Pembroke, and	
	two bastards by Sir	
	Richard Leveson, Kt.	

This entry is confirmed, though the order of Mary Fitton's marriages is
reversed, by an extract, communicated by Lord de Tabley to the Rev.
W. A. Harrison, from ' a very large (elephant) folio of *Cheshire Genealogies*
with coloured arms, thus :—

Sir Edward ffitton
of Gawesworth

Captaine =	Mary =	Captaine	This Mary Fitton had by Will.
Lougher	ffitton	Polewheele	Herbert Earle of Pembroke a
2 husb.	mayd of	i. husband	bastard. And also by Sir
	honour		Richard Lusan she had two
			bastard daughters.'

Some years later Mary's mother writes to her daughter Anne that Pole-
whele ' is a veri knave, and taketh the disgrace off his wyff and all her
ffryndes to make the world thynk hym worthy of her and that she des-
sarved no better.'   Also about 1606-7 Mary's aunt, wife of Sir Francis
Fitton, denounces her niece as ' the vyles woman under the sun.'   Mary
was baptized at Gawesworth, June 24, 1578, so that her age was 22-23
in March 1601.   Cf. also Lady Newdigate-Newdegate's *Gossip from a
Muniment Room*, 1897.

reports that when Sir William Knollys lodged ' at Court, where some of the ladyes and maydes of Honour us'd to friske and hey about in the next room, to his extreme disquiete a nights, though he often warned them of it ; at last he getts in one night at their revells, stripps off his shirt, and so with a payre of spectacles on his nose and Aretine in his hand, comes marching in at a posterne door of his owne chamber, reading very gravely, full upon the faces of them.'   He enjoyed his joke : ' for he fac'd them and often traverst the roome in this posture above an houre.'   As the coarse web of Elizabethan embroidery shows beneath the delicate ornament and between the applied patches of brilliant colour, so in the manners of Elizabeth's Court does a texture, equally coarse, run visibly through the refinements of learning and the bravery of display.   Even in the amusements of the Queen, who read Greek and delighted in Poetry, do we find this intermingling of the barbarous, of the ' Gothic ' in the contemptuous application of that byword, and also of that un-conscious humour which we read into archaic art. ' Her Majesty is very well,' writes Rowland White (12th May 1600) ; ' this Day she appointes to see a *Frenchman* doe Feates upon a Rope, in the Conduit Court.   To-morrow she hath commanded the Beares, the Bull and the Ape, to be baited in the Tiltyard. Upon Wednesday she will have solemne Dawncing.' An archaic smile is graven on the faces above the ruff of this Renaissance Cynthia, and our Ninth Muse is also our ' Good Queen Bess,' own daughter to ' Bluff King Hal.'   Sometimes she proceeded somewhat drastically to adjust her several diver-sions :—' On 25th July 1591 the Privy Council wrote to the Lord Mayor directing the suppression

of plays on Sundays and on Thursdays, because it
interfered with bear-baiting, which was maintained
for Her Majesty's pleasure, if occasion require.' [1]
This singular ground was but one, and certainly the
least, of many, for interfering with the Theatres.
They shut automatically whenever the number of
plague-cases reached a statutory limit ; and they
were closed, I have surmised, for political reasons,
and also, more than once, for handling religious controversies.

VI

Soon after Shakespeare's advent, the Martin
Marprelate controversy, begun in 1588, overflowed
from the press [2] to the stage.[3]   Shakespeare, without
doubt, saw Martin, the pseudonymous *persona* of the
Reformers, caricatured by their antagonists, with
a cock's comb, an ape's face, a wolf's belly, and a
cat's claws,[4] the better to scratch the face of
Divinity ; [5] he also saw ' blood and humour ' taken
from him, on the very boards,[6] perhaps, of the
theatre in which he played.   These astounding products of religious intolerance, coupled with the pre-
vailing taste for mountebank bear-fighting, led to the
staying of all plays in the City by the Lord Mayor
(Harte) at the instance of Lord Walsingham [7] acting

[1] Fleay : from Chalmers's *Apology*, p. 379.

[2] The pamphlets are alluded to by Shakespeare. Nash, in *Strange
News*, etc., January 12, 1593, p. 194, mentions Lyly's *Almond for a Parrot*,
and bids Gabriel (Harvey) *respice funem.* Cf. *Comedy of Errors*, iv. 4 :—
   Dro. E. Mistress, *Respice funem*, or rather, the prophecy like the parrot,
      ' Beware the rope's end.'—FLEAY.

[3] Before August 1589. Arber, *Introduction to Martin Marprelate.*
Fleay, *History of the Stage*, p. 92.

[4] Lyly's *Pap with a Hatchet*, about September 1589.—Arber.

[5] Nash, *Pasquil's Return*, October 1589.

[6] Nash, *Countercuffe to Martin Junior*, August 1589.

[7] Fleay.

on representations from Tilney, Master of the Revels.
The Admiral's players and Lord Strange's—*i.e.*
Shakespeare and his colleagues—were summoned
and inhibited. But Lord Strange's company con-
tumaciously shifted its venue, and played that
afternoon at the Cross Keys ; so two of the players
were committed to the Counter and prohibited till
further orders.[1] On the death of Ferdinando Lord
Strange, Shakespeare and his colleagues joined the
Chamberlain's Company.[2] And, in July 1597, they,
with other companies, were again in difficulties, probably of a like origin. The Privy Council, acting on
a letter from the Lord Mayor, directed the Justices
of Surrey and Middlesex ' nerest to London ' to
prohibit all plays ' within London or about the city,'
and to ' pluck down ' the theatres : alleging ' the
lewd matters handled on the stage ' as the first
ground for such action.[3] The city fathers had complained that the theatres tempted their apprentices
to play truant ; but the ' matters handled on the
stage ' must have counted for as much, or more, in
fostering their puritanical opposition.

High among the causes of offence to the ultra-
protestant faction at this time, I must reckon the

[1] Lyly, *Pap with a Hatchet*, September 1589 :—' Would these comedies
(against Martin) might be allowed to be played that are penned.'—Fleay,
The English Drama, ii. 39.

[2] Mr. Fleay, in his Index lists of Actors, places Shakespeare in Leicester's
Company, 1587-9 ; in Lord Strange's, 1589-93 ; in the Chamberlain's,
1594-1603. From his list of Companies it appears that on the death of
Henry Carey, Lord Hunsdon, July 22, 1596, who had been Chamberlain
since 1585, George Carey, Lord Hunsdon, took over the Company under
his own name until, on the 27th April 1597, he succeeded Lord Chamberlain Brook, who died the 5th of the preceding March. He kept on the
Company as Chamberlain from then till 1603.

[3] Halliwell, *Illustrations*, p. 21, quoting ' Registers of the Privy Council.'
On the death of Lord Chamberlain Brook (cf. Note [2]) and succession of
George Carey, Lord Hunsdon, this action was annulled, and his players
took possession of the Curtain.

name first given to the Sir John Falstaff of Shakespeare's *Henry IV.*—viz., Sir John Oldcastle ; for
Sir John Oldcastle, Lord Cobham, had died a
Protestant martyr, burned for Lollardy by Henry v.
Some traces of this initial offence survive in the revised version, published in quarto, the first part in
1598, the second in 1600.   Thus (Part I. i. ii.) :—

> ' FALSTAFF.   And is not my hostess of the tavern a most sweet
>   wench ?
> PRINCE.   As the honey of Hybla, my old lad of the Castle.'

In Part II. i. ii. line 113 the Quarto, instead of the
Fal. given later in all the Folios, prefixes *Old.* to
Falstaff's speech.[1]   In ii. iii. 2 Shallow is made to
say :—' Then was Jack Falstaff, now Sir John, a boy
and Page to Thomas Mowbray, Duke of Norfolk '—
a post actually filled by the historical Oldcastle.[2]
In the Epilogue to Part II. the old name is explicitly
withdrawn :—' Falstaff shall die of a sweat, unless
already a' be killed with your hard opinions ; for
Oldcastle died a martyr, and this is not the man.'
The whole transaction is set forth by Fuller in a
passage which I have not seen quoted.[3]   In his life
of John Fastolfe, Knight, he writes :—' To avouch
him by many arguments valiant, is to maintain that
the sun is bright, though since the *Stage* hath been
over bold with his memory, making him a *Thra-
sonical Puff*, and emblem of *Mock-valour*.   True it

---

[1] Theobald concluded that ' the play being printed from the Stage
manuscript, Oldcastle had been all along alter'd into Falstaff, except in
this single place, by an oversight, of which the printers not being aware,
continued the initial traces of the original name.'   Malone rejects this
conclusion; but the evidence against him is decisive.

[2] Boas, *Shakspere and his Predecessors*, 1896, p. 260.

[3] *The History of the Worthies of England*, published posthumously by
Fuller's son, 1662.   This passage in the account of Norfolk must have
been written less by a great deal than forty years after Shakespeare's
death.

is Sir *John Oldcastle* did first bear the brunt of the one, being made the *make-sport* in all plays for a *coward*. It is easily known out of what *purse* this black *peny* came. The *Papists* railing on him for a *Heretick*, and therefore he must also be a *coward*, though indeed he was a *man* of *arms*, *every inch of him*, and as valiant as any in his age. Now as I am glad that *Sir John Oldcastle* is *put out*, so I am sorry that Sir *John Fastolfe* is *put in*, to relieve his memory in this base service, to be the *anvil* for every *dull wit* to strike upon. Nor is our Comedian [1] excusable by some alteration of his name, writing him Sir *John Falstafe* (and making him the *property* of *pleasure* for King *Henry* the fifth, to abuse) seeing the *vicinity* of sounds intrench on the memory of *that worthy Knight*, and few do heed the *inconsiderable difference* in spelling of their name.'

But the matter does not end here. Shakespeare's name appears on the title-page of another play, also published in quarto in the same year, 1600 :—

' *The first part*
of the true and hono-
rable history, of the life of
Sir John Old-castle, the good
Lord Cobham.
As it hath bene lately acted by the Right
honorable the Earle of Notingham
Lord High Admirall of England
his servants.
Written by William Shakespeare
London, printed for T. P.
1600.'

Now Shakespeare did not write this play,[2] and his name only appears on certain copies. It has,

---

[1] Shakespeare, without a doubt. Cf. Fuller's account of him, *infra*.

[2] We know from Henslowe's *Diary* that it was written by M(ichael) D(rayton), A(nthony) M(onday), Hathway and Wilson, who were paid in

accordingly, been urged that his name was added to
enhance the value of a pirated edition.   Yet I find
it hard to believe that any one can have hoped to
palm off such a play as Shakespeare's.   It was
written for and acted by the rival Company (the
Admiral's) during the run of Shakespeare's *Henry
IV.*, abnormally prolonged during several years, off
and on, by the popularity of this very character.
It is also, in fact and on the face of it, a protestant
pamphlet, written specifically in reply to Shakespeare's abuse of Oldcastle's name.   This is apparent
from the Prologue, the significance of which has not,
I believe, been noted :—

> ' The *doubtfull Title* (Gentlemen) prefixt
> Upon the Argument we have in hand,
> May breed suspence, and wrongfully disturbe
> The peacefull quiet of your settled thoughts.
> To stop which scruple, let this breefe suffice.
> *It is no pamper'd Glutton we present,*
> *Nor aged Counsellor to youthful sinne ;*
> But one, whose vertue shone above the rest,
> A valiant martyr, and a vertuous Peere,[1]
> In whose true faith and loyalty exprest
> Unto his Soveraigne, and his Countries weale :
> We strove to pay that tribute of our love
> Your favours merit : let *faire Truth be grac'd*
> *Since forg'd invention former time defac'd.*'

The villain and principal character of the Play,
which follows to ' grace fair truth,' is a Priest who
turns highwayman for his leman's sake, robs the

full, £10, October 16, 1599, with a gift of 10s. for the first playing in
November.—Fleay, *History of the Stage*, p. 108.

[1] The astounding inaccuracy of Mr. Carter (*Shakespeare: Puritan and
Recusant*) may be illustrated as above from this handling of this subject.
He attributes this line to Shakespeare, and gives it to the *Merry Wives* !
In the same paragraph, p. 144, he gives the early use of the name *Oldcastle* to the *Merry Wives* instead of *Henry IV.*, and the phrase, ' Oldcastle
died a martyr, and this is not the man,' also to the *Merry Wives* instead
of to the *Epilogue. II. Henry IV.*

King in a scene inverted from Prince Hal's escapade,
is discovered, in dicing against him, through staking
a stolen angel which the King had marked, commits
murder, and is finally hanged in chains.   The
addition of Shakespeare's name to a missile so
violently retorted against his handiwork may well
be but an insolent device, for which there are many
analogues in the controversial amenities of the
time.[1]

VII

If there be dark shadows in the life of the Court,
there are shadows, also dark enough, in the other
brilliant world of letters.   Greene starves in a
garret (September 1592).   Marlowe, his *Hero and
Leander* yet unpublished, is stabbed to death in
a tavern brawl (1593).   And, apart from the squalid
tragedy of their deaths, these great men of letters
were literary Mohocks in their lives.   There are
few parallels to the savage vindictiveness of the
Marprelate controversy, and the men who could
wield such weapons were ever ready to lay them with
amazing truculence about the shoulders of any new
adventurer into the arena of their art.   Shakespeare
came in for his share of the bludgeoning from the
outset.   The swashing blows of Tom Nash, in his
address ' To the Gentlemen students of both Universities ' (prefixed to Greene's *Menaphon*, 1589),[2]
whistled suspiciously near his head and must, at
least, have been aimed at some of his new colleagues.[3]

---

[1] *E.g.* Jonson having attacked Dekker in *The Poetaster*, a play into
which he introduces himself as Horace, Dekker retorted in *Satiromastix* by
lifting one of Jonson's characters, Tucca, the better to rail at Jonson,
again under his self-chosen name of Horace.

[2] Dated by Ed. Arber.

[3] *Ibid.* ' It is a common practice now a daies amongst a sort of shifting
comparisons, that runne through every arte and thrive by none, to leave

And they are but a part of the general attack delivered by the ' University pens ' upon the actors and
authors of the new Drama :—' Who (mounted on
the stage of arrogance) think to outbrave better
pens with the swelling bombast of a bragging blank

the trade of noverint (*i.e.* attorney) whereto they were borne, and busie
themselves with the indevors of Art, that could scarcelie latinise their
necke-verse (to claim benefit of clergy) if they had neede ; yet English
Seneca read by candle night yeeldes manie good sentences, as *Bloud is a
beggar*, and so foorth ; and if you intreate him faire on a frostie morning,
he will affoord you whole *Hamlets*, I should say handfuls of tragical
speaches.' Mr. Arber has argued that this passage does not refer to
Shakespeare, (1) because *his* play of *Hamlet* was not yet written, (2) because
it applies only to translators. On the other hand (1) the earlier *Hamlet*
referred to here and in Dekker's *Satiromastix*, was acted by Shakespeare's
colleagues, and may have been retouched by him before he produced the
two versions attributed to his authorship—if indeed the Quarto of 1603
can be called a separate version, and be not a pirated edition made from
shorthand notes. (2) Although the whole passage refers to translators,
this and other incidental remarks are clearly directed against the new
drama. *Titus Andronicus* is ascribed by Mr. Dowden to the preceding
year, and is said by Baynes to reflect the form of Seneca's later plays.
Out of four plays acted by Shakespeare's company, June 3-13, 1594, three
bear the titles of plays afterwards ascribed to him, viz. *Andronicus,
Hamlet, The Taming of the Shrew* (Fleay, *History of the Stage*, p. 97). Many
other plays with titles afterwards borne by plays indubitably rewritten
by Shakespeare, were acted even earlier. Fleay and Dowden agree sub-
stantially in placing *Love's Labour's Lost, Love's Labour Won (Much Ado
about Nothing), Comedy of Errors, Romeo and Juliet, Two Gentlemen of
Verona*, three parts of *Henry VI., All's well that ends well, Troylus and
Cressida, The Jealous Comedy (Merry Wives of Windsor)*, and *Twelfth
Night* in the early years, 1588-1593. Without even considering the date
at which Shakespeare may be called sole author of a play (for that is a
wholly different question), we may infer that his practice of adding touches
to the stock MSS. of his company was one which grew with the popular
success attending it. If that be so, an attack in 1589 on a play, afterwards appropriated to Shakespeare, cannot be said to miss him.

The extensive habit of anonymity and collaboration in the production
of plays shows that they were regarded simply as the property of the
company, and were paid in full when the authors received their fee. The
profits were shared : cf. Tucca to Histrio, the *impresario*, after the
exhibition of acting by his two boys:—' Well, now fare thee well, my
honest penny-biter : commend me to seven shares and a half, and remember to-morrow. If you lack a service—(*i.e.* a patron whose service
should protect against the statute)—you shall play in my name, rascals ;
but you shall buy your own cloth, and I 'll have two shares for my countenance.' It was a matter of business, and remained so until the fame
of certain authors led to publication. Drayton's Plays of which he was
sole author have all perished.

verse.' ' Players avant '[1] was their war-cry ; and, when Greene himself utters it, he does not leave the reference in doubt. In a *Groat's Worth of Wit Bought with a Million of Repentance* (1592) he warns Marlowe, Peele, and Lodge, his particular friends in the fraternity of ' ballet-makers, pamphleteers, press-haunters, boon pot-poets, and such like,'[2] to beware of players :—' Those puppets, who speak from our mouths, those anticks garnisht in our colours. . . . Yes,' he goes on, ' trust them not ; for there is an upstart crow, beautified in our feathers, that, with his *tiger's heart wrapt in a player's hide*,[3] supposes he is as well able to bombast out a blank verse as the best of you, and being an absolute *Johannes fac totum*, is, in his own conceit, the only Shakescene in a country.'

You find the same attitude towards players in *The Return from Parnassus*.[4] Acting is the ' basest trade ' (iv. 5), and again (v. 1) :—

' Better it is mongst fiddlers to be chiefe,
Than at plaiers trenchers beg reliefe.'

Such is the conclusion of the two Scholars in the play after exhausting every expedient to win a livelihood by their learning. They go on to attack ' those glorious vagabonds,'

' That carried earst their fardels on their backes,'

grudging them their ' coursers,' and ' Sattan sutes '[5] ' and pages,' since

' With mouthing words that better wits had framed,
They purchase lands, and now Esquires are made.'

---

[1] From a poem by Thomas Brabine, gent. ; also appended to Greene's *Menaphon*.   [2] Lodge : cf. W. Raleigh, *The English Novel*.
[3] A line parodied from the 3rd *Henry VI.* : ' Recently revised, if not originally written, by Shakespeare.'—Baynes, 105.
[4] Acted by the students of St. John's College, Cambridge.
[5] ' Satin suits ' is one of the catchwords in the duel between Jonson and Dekker.—*Infra.*

The last shot must surely have been aimed at Shakespeare, who had procured a grant of arms for his father in 1599, and had purchased 107 acres of arable for £320 in 1602. But the date of this Play is uncertain : Mr. Arber argues for January in that year, and this would cast doubt on the reference. On the other hand, Burbage and Kempe, Shakespeare's colleagues, are introduced in their own persons (iv. 5), when Kempe thus trolls it off :—' Few of the University pen plaies well, they smell too much of that writer *Ovid*, and that writer *Metamorphosis*, and talke too much of *Proserpina* and *Juppiter*. Why, heres our fellow Shakespeare puts them all downe, I and Ben Jonson too. O, that Ben Jonson is a pestilent fellow, he brought up Horace giving the Poets a pill,[1] but our fellow *Shakespeare* hath given him a purge that made him beray his credit.' Controversy has raged round this passage ; but it seems certain (*a*) that, in common with the whole scene, it is an ironical reflection on the ignorance and the social success of the players ; and (*b*) that it refers to Dekker's *Satiromastix* or *The Untrussing of the Humorous Poet*. This play, in which Dekker retorted upon *The Poetaster*, was published in 1602 ; but, of course, it had before been presented ' publickly by the Lord Chamberlaine his servants, and privately by the Children of Paules.' [2]

VIII

Of more importance than all the ' paper warres in Paules Church-yard ' was this famous campaign fought out upon the stage—the Poetomachia [3] in

---

[1] Viz., in *The Poetaster*, v. i.   [2] Title-page.
[3] Dekker's address ' *To the World* ' prefixed to *Satiromastix*.

which Dekker and Jonson were protagonists. As distinguished from the onslaught of the ' university pens,' it was a civil war, involving most of the leading playwrights and actors. It raged for years; [1] we know that Shakespeare must have been in the thick of it ; and if it be impossible to say for certain on which side he was ranged, it is easy to hazard a guess.

Of his attitude towards Jonson we know little. There is the tradition that he introduced him to the stage ; there is the fact that he acted in his plays— in *Every Man in His Humour*, 1598, immediately before the Poetomachia, and in *Sejanus*, 1604, soon after it ; there is Fuller's account of the ' wit combats' between them ; [2] there is the tradition that

---

[1] Jonson, as the Author, in the ' Apology,' appended to *The Poetaster* :—

> ' Three years
> They did provoke me with their petulant styles
> On every stage.'

[2] *The History of the Worthies of England, endeavoured by Thomas Fuller, D.D.* Published, unfinished, by ' the author's orphan, John Fuller,' in 1662. From its bulk we may judge that it occupied many years of Thomas Fuller's life, so that it brings his account of Shakespeare fairly close to the date of his death (1616), and well within the range of plausible tradition. I quote the whole passage for its quaintness :—' William Shakespeare was born at Stratford on Avon in this county (Warwick) in whom three eminent Poets may seem in some sort to be compounded. 1. *Martial* in the *warlike* sound of his Sur-name (whence some may conjecture him of a *Military extraction*), *Hasti-vibrans* or *Shake-speare*. 2. *Ovid*, the most *naturall* and *witty* of all Poets, and hence it was that Queen *Elizabeth* coming into a Grammar-school made this extempore verse :—

" *Persius a Crab-staffe, Bawdy* Martial, Ovid *a fine Wag.*"

3. Plautus, who was an exact Comædian, yet never any scholar, as our *Shake-speare* (if alive) would confess himself. Adde to all these, that though his Genius generally was *jocular*, and inclining him to *festivity*, yet he could (when so disposed) be *solemn* and *serious*, as appears by his Tragedies, so that *Heraclitus* himself (I mean if secret and unseen) might afford to smile at his Comedies, they were so *merry*, and *Democritus* scarce forbear to smile at his Tragedies, they were so *mournfull*.

' He was an eminent instance of the truth of that Rule, *Poeta non fit, sed nascitur*, one is not *made*, but *born* a Poet. Indeed, his learning was very little, so that as *Cornish diamonds* are not polished by any lapidary,

Shakespeare entertained Jonson and Drayton at Stratford on the eve of his death.[1]   Against these proofs of good-fellowship there is the conjecture,[2] founded on Kempe's speech quoted above, that Shakespeare had a hand in the production of Dekker's *Satiromastix* [3] and, perhaps, played William Rufus in it.   Of Jonson's attitude towards Shakespeare we know more, but the result is ambiguous. We have the two poems in *Underwoods*—the second, surely, the most splendid tribute ever paid by one poet to another ?   But, then, we have Jonson's conversations with Drummond of Hawthornden, in which he spared Shakespeare as little as any, laying down that he 'wanted art and sometimes sense.' We have, also, the strong tradition that Jonson treated Shakespeare with ingratitude.   This may have sprung from the charge of malevolence preferred against Jonson, so he tells us himself, by Shakespeare's comrades (*Discoveries* : 'De Shakspeare nostrat.').   'I remember,' he says, 'the players have often mentioned it as an honour to Shakspeare, that in his writing (whatsoever he penned) he never blotted out a line.   My answer hath been, Would he had blotted a thousand, which they thought a male-

but are pointed and smoothed even as they are taken out of the Earth, so *nature* itself was all the *art* which was used upon him.

'Many were the *wit-combates* betwixt him and *Ben Johnson*, which two I behold like a *Spanish great Gallion*, and an *English man of War* ; Master Johnson (like the former) was built far higher in learning, *Solid*, but *Slow* in his performances.   *Shake-spear* with the *English-man of War*, lesser in *bulk*, but lighter in *sailing*, could turn with all tides, tack about and take advantage of all winds, by the quickness of his Wit and Invention.   He died Anno Domini 16 . . . and was buried at *Stratford* upon *Avon*, the Town of His Nativity.'

[1] Shakespeare, Drayton, and Ben Jonson 'had a merry meeting, and itt seems drank too hard, for Shakespeare died of a feaver there contracted.' —*Diary* of Ward, Vicar of Stratford, bearing the date 1662.

[2] T. Tyler and R. Simpson.

[3] Acted by his Company, the Lord Chamberlain's.

volent speech.' In this passage we probably have Jonson's settled opinion of Shakespeare, the artist and the man. He allows ' his excellent phantasy, brave notions and gentle expressions wherein he flowed,' but, he qualifies, ' with that facility, that sometimes it was necessary he should be stopped.' He admits that ' his wit was in his own power,' but adds :—' Would the rule of it had been so too, many times he fell into those things could not escape laughter.' As arrogant as men (and scholars) are made, Jonson found some of Shakespeare's work ' ridiculous ' ; but he was honest, and when he says, ' I loved the man, and do honour his memory, on this side idolatry, as much as any,' we must believe him. But we are not to infer with Gifford that Drummond misrepresented Jonson, or that Jonson, during the Poetomachia, did not trounce Shakespeare for rejecting, with success, the Jonsonian theory of the Drama.

Gifford, to minimise the authority of Drummond's report, denounces that Petrarchan for a ' bird of prey ' ; but his whole apology for Ben Jonson is a piece of special pleading too violent and too acerb to command much confidence. He is very wroth with the critics of the eighteenth century, who had scented an attack on Shakespeare in the Prologue to Jonson's *Every Man in His Humour*. But what are the facts ? The Play, in which Shakespeare had acted (1598), is published (1600) without the Prologue. A revised version is published with the Prologue in 1616, but, as Mr. Fleay has proved [1] from internal references to the ' Queen ' and ' Her Majesty,' that version must also have been acted before Elizabeth's death (1603), and he adds an

---

[1] *The English Drama*, vol. i. p. 358.

ingenious argument for assigning its production to
the April of 1601.[1]   In the added Prologue Jonson
denounces the ' ill customs of the age ' in neglecting
the Unities.   He ' must justly hate' to 'purchase'
the 'delight' of his audience by the devices of those
who

> ' With three rusty swords,
> And help of some few foot and half-foot words,
> Fight over York and Lancaster's long jars,
> And in the tyring house bring wounds to scars.'

With his usual complacency :—

> ' He rather prays you will be pleas'd to see
> One such to-day, as other plays should be ;
> Where neither chorus wafts you o'er the seas,' etc. etc.

Without referring these two gibes specifically to
Shakespeare's *Henry VI.* ii. and iii., and *Henry V.*
(although the second describes what the chorus in
Henry V. was actually doing at the time [2]), or the
remaining lines to other plays from his hand, it is
clear that the whole tirade is an attack in set terms
on the kind of play which Shakespeare wrote, and
which the public preferred before Jonson's.[3]   The
attack is in perfect accord with Jonson's reputation
for militant self-sufficiency, and, if he made friends

---

[1] iii. 2, Bobadil says :—' To-morrow 's St. Mark's day.'   It appears
from Cob's complaint that the play was acted on a Friday.   Cf. Jonson's
Bartholomew Fair, 1614 :—' Tales, Tempests and such like drolleries.'

[2] Fleay, *ibid.*

[3] Cf. the copy of verse by Leonard Digges (*floruit* 1617-1635) ' evidently
written,' says Halliwell-Phillipps, ' soon after the opening of the second
Fortune Theatre in 1623 :—

> ' Then some new day they would not brooke a line,
> Of tedius (though well laboured) *Cataline,*
> *Sejanus* was too irksome ; they prize the more
> Honest Iago, or the jealous Moore.

He goes on to say that Jonson's other plays, *The Fox* and *The Alchemist,*
even when acted ' at a friend's desire . . . have scarce defrai'd the seacole
fire ' ; when ' let but Falstaffe come,' Hal, Poins, or ' Beatrice and Bene-
dicke,' and ' loe, in a trice the cock-pit, galleries, boxes, all are full.'

again with Shakespeare, he also made friends again with Marston. Dekker wrote thus of him :—' 'Tis thy fashion to flirt ink in every man's face ; and then to crawle into his bosome.' [1]

In the Poetomachia Dekker and Marston were the victims of Jonson's especial virulence, which spared neither the seaminess of an opposite's apparel nor the defects in his personal appearance ; but it is hard to say whether they or he began it.   Drummond in his *Conversations* attributes the beginning of Jonson's quarrel with Marston to Marston's having ' represented him on the stage in his youth given to venery ' ;   and in Dekker's *Patient Grissel* (1599), in which Chettle had a hand, Emulo may be Jonson ; for the taunt at his thin legs :—' What 's here ? laths ! Where 's the lime and hair, Emulo ? ' :—is of a piece with innumerable jests at the expense of Jonson's scragginess,[2] and his early work at bricklaying.   Jonson, at any rate, did not reserve his fire till 1601, though in his apology to *The Poetaster* he suggests that he did :—

> ' Three years
> They did provoke me with their petulant styles
> On every stage.'

It was in 1599 that he began the practice of staging himself and his fellows : himself as a high-souled critic, his fellows as poor illiterates whose foibles it was his duty to correct. As Asper in *Every Man out of His Humour* (1559), as Crites [3] in *Cynthia's Revels* (1600), as Horace in *The Poetaster* (1601), he professes a lofty call to reform the art and manners of his age. This was too much for rivals in a profession in any case highly competitive, and rendered the

---

[1] *Satiromastix.*   [2] He got fat in later life.
[3] Criticus in an earlier version.

more precarious by the capricious inhibition of the
Companies for which its members wrote. It was
hard when their own men were ' travelling ' [1] or
idle, on account of the Plague or for having offended
the authorities, to be lampooned by ' the children
of the Chapel ' playing Jonson's pieces before the
Queen. And at last in *Satiromastix* (1602), Dekker
gave as good as he got, through the mouth of the
Tucca he had borrowed from Jonson :—' No, you
starv'd rascal, thou 't bite off mine eares then, thou
must have three or foure suites of names, when like
a lousie Pediculous vermin th'ast but one suite to
thy backe ; you must be call'd *Asper*, and *Criticus*,
and *Horace*, thy tytle 's longer in reading than the
stile a the big Turkes : Asper, Criticus, Quintus,
Horatius, Flaccus.'

Between the opening in 1599 and the end in
1602, the wordy war never relaxes. Jonson staged
Marston in *Every Man out of His Humour* (1599)
as Carlo Buffone : [2]—' a public, scurrilous and profane jester . . . a good feast-hound and banquet-
beagle,' whose ' religion is railing and his discourse
ribaldry ' ; and, in *Satiromastix*, Dekker suggests
that Jonson-Horace, if at a tavern supper he ' dips
his manners in too much sauce,' shall sit for a penalty
' a th' left hand of *Carlo Buffon*.' Jonson-Crites in
Cynthia's Revels (1600) attacks Hedon-Dekker and
Anaides-Marston (iii. 2) :—

> ' The one a light, voluptuous reveller,
> The other a strange, arrogating puff,
> Both impudent and arrogant enough.'

Dekker retorts by quoting the lines in *Satiromastix* ;

---

[1] *E.g.* Shakespeare's Company in 1601.—Fleay.
[2] Fleay rejects this attribution, but he is alone in his opinion.

while Marston parodies them in *What You Will.*[1] In
The Poetaster (1601) Jonson-Horace administers pills
to Demetrius Fannius-Dekker and Crispinus [2] (or
Cri-spinas or Crispin-ass)-Marston, so that they vomit
on the stage such words in their vocabulary as
offended his purist taste. Dekker in *Satiromastix*,
' untrusses the Humorous poet,' *i.e.* tries Horace-
Jonson, and condemns him to wear a wreath of
nettles until he swears, among other things, not to
protest that he would hang himself if he thought any
man could write Plays as well as he ; not ' to exchange compliments with Gallants in the Lordes
roomes, to make all the house rise up in Armes, and
to cry that 's Horace, that 's he, that 's he, that 's
he, that pennes and purges Humours and diseases ' ;
nor, when his ' playes are misse-likt at Court,' to
' crye Mew like a Pusse-cat,' and say he is glad to
' write out of the Courtier's Element.' In all these
Plays acute literary criticism is mingled with brutal
personal abuse. Thus, for sneering at seedy clothes
and bald or singular heads,[3] Horace is countered with
his bricklaying and his coppered ' face puncht full
of oylet-holes, like the cover of a warming pan.' One
might hastily infer that Jonson was the life-long
enemy at least of Dekker and Marston. Yet it was
not so. Dekker had collaborated with him on the

[1] Published 1607, ' written shortly after the appearance of *Cynthia's
Revels.*' A. H. Bullen. Introduction to Works of John Marston, 1887.
Acted 1601.—Fleay.

[2] Juvenal's ' Ecce iterum Crispinus '—a notorious favourite of Domitian.

[3] *Tucca.* ' Thou wrongst heere a good honest rascall Crispinus, and a
door varlet Demetrius Fannius (brethren in thine owne trade of Poetry);
thou sayst Crispinus' sattin dublet is reveal'd out heere, and that this
penurious sneaker is out of elboes.'—*Satiromastix.*

Sir Vaughan. ' Master Horace, Master Horace . . . then begin to
make your railes at the povertie and beggarly want of hair.' Follows a
mock heroic eulogy of hair by Horace, thirty-nine lines in length.—*Ibid.*

Tucca. ' They have sowed up that broken seame-rent lye of thine that
Demetrius is out at Elbowes, and Crispinus is out with sattin.'—*Ibid.*

eve of these hostilities,[1] though for the last time. Marston's shifting alliances are merely bewildering : the very man whom he libels at one time he assists, at another, in libelling a third. Outraged (you would think) by Jonson's reiterated onslaughts, and conscious of equally outrageous provocation and retort, in 1604 he plasters *Sejanus* with praise ; but next year, after the failure of that Play, he hits it, so to say, when it is down.[2] Between the two pieces of attention he collaborates with Jonson and Chapman in producing *Eastward Ho*.[3] He, certainly, was no friend to Shakespeare ;[4] for when *The Metamorphosis of Pigmalion*, his ' nasty ' copy of *Venus and Adonis*—the epithet is his own—failed as a plagiarism, he had the impudence (*Scourge of Villainy*, vi.) to declare it a parody, written to note

> ' The odious spot
> And blemish that deforms the lineaments
> Of modern Poesy's habiliments.'

Yet he must have sided with Shakespeare now and then. As we shall see.

[1] Dekker and Jonson are paid for ' *Page of Plymouth*, Aug. 20 and Sept. 2, 1599. Dekker, Jonson, and Chettle for *Robert 2, King of Scots*,' Sept. 3, 15, 16, 27, 1599.—Henslowe's *Diary*, quoted by Fleay.

[2] Preface to *Sophonisba* :—' Know that I have not laboured in this poem to tie myself to relate anything as an historian, but to enlarge everything as a poet. To transcribe authors, quote authorities and translate Latin prose orations into English blank verse, hath, in this subject, been the least aim of my studies ' :—an obvious blow at *Sejanus*.

[3] In which Warton (*History of English Poetry*, iv. 276, ed. 1824) discovers many ' satirical parodies ' of Shakespeare. Gifford replies ; but Gertrude's parody of Ophelia's song, iii. 2, is a hard nut for the apologist, not to insist on the name—Hamlet—given to a footman who is accosted by Potkins with a ' S'foot, Hamlet, are you mad ? '

[4] He harps on one of Shakespeare's lines :

> ' A man, a man, a kingdom for a man.'
> The first line of Sat. vii. *The Scourge of Villainy* (1598).
> ' A fool, a fool, a fool, my coxcomb for a fool.'
> *Parasitaster.*
> ' A boat, a boat, a full hundred marks for a boat.'
> *Eastward Ho.*

But amidst the welter and confusion of this em-
broilment, it is possible to discern, if not a clear-cut
line between opposed forces, at least a general
grouping about two standards.   There was the tribe
of Ben, with Jonson for leader, and Chapman for
his constant,[1] Marston for his occasional, ally.   And,
to borrow the war-cries of 1830, there was opposed
to this Classical army a Romantic levy, with Shakespeare, Dekker, and Chettle among its chiefs.
Where much must be left to surmise, we know that
Chettle once went out of his way to befriend Shakespeare, apologising handsomely for Greene's onslaught in *A Groat's Worth of Wit*, and contrasting
him favourably with Marlowe ; and that Dekker,
as we gather from Kempe's speech in *The Returne
from Parnassus*, found Shakespeare an ally in his
war against Jonson.[2]   We know, too, from Henslowe's *Diary*, that Dekker and Chettle collaborated
in April and May 1599, on a play called *Troilus and
Cressida*,[3] and, from the Stationers' Registers, that
a play with that name was acted by the Lord
Chamberlain's servants (Shakespeare's Company)
on February 7, 1603.   May we not have herein the
explanation of Shakespeare's *Troilus*, in which he

---

[1] Jonson in his Conversations with Drummond said that ' he loved
Chapman.'   They were imprisoned together for satirising James First's
Scotch Knights in *Eastward Ho*, but Chapman turned in his old age.   One
of his latest poems arraigns Ben for his overweening arrogance.

[2] Some find an allusion to this in Jonson's dialogue acted, only once,
at the end of *The Poetaster* in place of an Author's apology, which the
Authorities had suppressed :—

> ' What they have done 'gainst me,
> I am not moved with : if it gave them meat
> Or got them clothes, 'tis well ; that was their end,
> Only amongst them, I am sorry for
> *Some better natures,* by the rest so drawn
> To run so vile a line.'

[3] *Trojelles and Cressida.*   Also in *Patient Grissel*, October 1599.

caricatures the manners and motives of everybody in the Greek (*i.e.* the Classic) tents ? [1] This play and the allusions to rival poets in the Sonnets are the two deepest mysteries of Shakespeare's work. But if we accept the division of forces which I have suggested, a gleam of light may fall on both. It is reasonable to suppose that Shakespeare, who habitually vamped old Plays, took the Dekker-Chettle play for the staple of his own ; and, if he did, the satirical portions of his *Troilus and Cressida,* so closely akin to the satire of *Satiromastix,* may be a part of Dekker's attack on Chapman, Jonson, and Marston. Chapman's *Shield of Achilles* and his ' *Seaven Bookes of the Iliades of Homere, Prince of Poets* ' [2] appeared in 1598, the year before the Dekker-Chettle *Troilus,* and were prefaced by arrogant onslaughts, repeated again and again, upon ' apish and impudent braggarts,' [3] men of ' loose capacities,' ' rank riders or readers who have no more souls than bur bolts ' : upon all, in short, who prefer ' *sonnets* and lascivious ballads ' before ' Homerical poems.' [4]   If this suggestion be ac-

---

[1] Shakespeare's Play was published in 1609, *apparently* in two editions : (1) with ' As it was acted by the King's Majestie's servants at the Globe (the title of Shakespeare's Company after 1603) ; and (2) with a preface stating that the Play had never been ' Stal'd with the Stage.' But the two editions are ' absolutely identical,' even the Title-page being printed from the same forme.—*Preface to Cambridge Shakespeare,* vol. vi. This mystification does not affect the overmastering presumption that Shakespeare's Play, published in 1609, and acted by his company between 1603-1609, was the Play, or a re-written version of the Play, acted by his Company in 1603. The presumption that the 1603 Play was founded on that of Dekker and Chettle is also strong. Dekker's *Satiromastix* was played by Shakespeare's Company in 1601.

[2] Books 1, 2, and 7-11 inclusive. The copy in the British Museum bears the autograph, ' Sum Ben Jonsonii.'

[3] Preface to the Reader. Folio.

[4] ' To the Understander,' *Shield of Achilles.* His deepest concern is lest he should be thought a ' malicious detractor of so admired a poet as Virgil.' —*Epistle dedicatory to the Earl Marshal, Ibid.*

cepted, we have Shakespeare, a Trojan, abetting the Trojan Dekker against Chapman, an insolent Greek. Shakespeare's play, and Dekker's of 1599, if, as I have surmised, it was the sketch which Shakespeare completed, were founded, ultimately, on the mediæval romance into which the French Trouvère, Benoit de Sainte-Maure, first introduced the loves of Troilus and Briseida, *Roman de Troie* (1160)— afterwards imitated by Boccaccio, Guido delle Colonne, Chaucer and Caxton (*Recuyell of the Histories of Troy*).[1] In this traditional story, adapted to flatter a feudal nobility, which really believed itself the seed of Priam, Hector is the hero, treacherously murdered by Achilles. In *Lucrece* there is no attack on the Greeks, but Dekker, who calls London Troynovant (*Seven Deadly Sins*, 1607), and the Romantic School generally, resented the rehabilitation of Homer's credit—Chaucer had called him a liar—involving, as it did, the comparative disgrace of their hero : all the more that the new glorification of the Greeks came from arrogant scholars, who presumed on their knowledge of the Greek language to rail at the ignorance and to reject the art of their contemporaries and predecessors. That Shakespeare did so abet Dekker against Chapman is a theory more in harmony with known facts than Gervinus' guess that Shakespeare, chagrined by the low moral tone of Homer's heroes, felt it incumbent on him to travesty their action. Minto and Mr. Dowden find in Chapman the rival poet of Shakespeare's Sonnets—(I should prefer to say one of the rival poets)—and this falls in with the

---

[1] Ker, *Epic and Romance*, p. 378, traces Shakespeare's ' dreadful sagittary' (*Troilus and Cressida*, v. v. 14) back to Benoit's ' Il ot o lui un saietaire Qui moult fu fels et deputaire.'

theory. The banter of Ben Jonson (Ajax) in the
Play is more obvious, and pushes, even beyond
reasonable supposition, the view, which I submit,
that much of Shakespeare's version was written by
him during the Poetomachia.   Many of the plainest
attacks and counterbuffs of that war are in the
Epilogues and Prologues to the Plays involved in it.
The Speaker of the Epilogue to *Cynthia* (1600) will
not ' crave their favour ' of the audience, but will
' only speak what he has heard the maker say ' :—

> ' By God 'tis good, and if you like 't, you may.'

As Envy descends slowly, in the Introduction to *The
Poetaster* (1601), the Prologue enters ' hastily in
armour,' and replies to censures provoked by this
bragging challenge :—

> ' If any muse why I salute the stage
> An *armed* Prologue ; know, 'tis a dangerous age,
> Wherein who writes, had need present his scenes
> Forty-fold proof against the conjuring means
> Of base detractors and illiterate apes. . . .
> Whereof the allegory and hid sense
> Is, that a well erected *confidence*
> Can fright their pride and laugh their folly hence.
> Here now, put case our author should once more,
> Swear that his play was good ; he doth implore
> You would not argue him of arrogance.'

Marston's Epilogue, added, I imagine, to his *Antonio
and Mellida* [1] (1601), says :—' Gentlemen, though I
remain an *armed* Epilogue, I stand not as a *peremptory challenger of desert*, either for him that composed the Comedy, or for us that acted it ' ; and, at
the lips of the Prologue to Shakespeare's *Troilus*,
the jest runs on—

---

[1] It is satirised in *The Poetaster* (1601) ; so that both may have been on
the boards together.

> ' Hither am I come
> A Prologue *arm'd*, but not in *confidence*
> Of Author's pen or actor's voice. . . .'

I venture to call this Prologue Shakespeare's, for other lines in it, as those on the Trojan Gates :—

> ' With massy staples,
> And corresponsive and fulfilling bolts ' :—

are to me *audibly* his.[1]   Shakespeare, I hold, wrote this Prologue, and wrote it while the Prologue to *The Poetaster* was still a fresh object for ridicule.[2] That Thersites in Shakespeare's *Troilus* stood for Marston can hardly be doubted.   When Agamemnon says ironically (I. iii. 72) :—

> ' We are confident
> When rank Thersites opes his *mastic* [3] jaw
> We shall hear music ' :—

the allusion to Marston, who had signed himself ' Therio*mastix* ' to the prose *Envoy* of his *Scourge of Villainy*, is patent.[4]   More: apart from this

---

[1] Mr. Fleay, *Chronicles of the English Drama*, ii. 190, holds the authorship of the Prologue very doubtful.   But this is a question not of evidence but of ear.

[2] Fleay, *Ibid.*, i. 366 :—' Whoever will take the trouble to compare the description of Crites (Jonson) by Mercury in *Cynthia's Revels*, ii. 1, with that of Ajax by Alexander in *Troilus and Cressida*, i. 2, will see that Ajax is Jonson.'   But he is inconsistent.   *Ibid.*, ii. 189 :—' The setting up of Ajax as a rival to Achilles shadows forth the putting forward of Dekker by the King's men to write against Jonson his *Satiromastix*,' so that Ajax = Dekker, Achilles = Jonson.   This inconsistency does not invalidate his conclusion that rival playwrights are satirised, and in many other passages of *Troilus*, the ' guying ' of the Greek Commander by Patroclus to amuse Achilles (I. iii. 140-196) :—

> ' And with ridiculous and awkward action
> Which, Slanderer, he imitation calls,
> He pageants us ' :—

and the ' guying ' of Ajax by Thersites (undoubtedly Marston) also to amuse Achilles (III. iii. 266-292), are not to be explained unless as portions easily recognisable at the time of the general ' guying ' in the Poetomachia.

[3] Rowe suggested *mastiff*; Boswell *mastive*.

[4] Fleay, again inconsistently, refers this line to Dekker, *History of the Stage*, 106, and to Marston, *Chronicle of the English Drama*, i. 366.

punning taunt there is no parallel for the foul railing of Thersites' every speech outside the persistent blackguardism of Marston's *Satires* and *Scourge of Villainy.*

Did Shakespeare join elsewhere with his own hand in the Poetomachia ?   The question arises when we reflect that the Plays contributed to it by Jonson, Marston, and Dekker fairly bristle with personalities : recognised by the key which Dekker supplied in *Satiromastix.*   Of all Shakespeare's characters, Pistol is the one in which critics have especially scented a personal attack;   and some have thought that Marlowe was the victim.   But Marlowe never wrote as Pistol is made to speak ; whilst Marston generally, and particularly in the Satire (*Scourge* vi.) to which I have already alluded, writes in the very lingo of the Ancient.͂   Urging that his 'nasty' *Pigmalion* was in truth but a reproach upon *Venus and Adonis*, he says, and the accent is familiar :—

> ' Think'st thou that genius that attends my soul,
> And guides my fist to scourge magnificos,
> Will deign my mind be rank'd in Paphian shows ? ' :—

Indeed, when we remember the ' wit combats ' at the Mermaid, in which these pot companions and public antagonists—Carlo Buffone cheek by jowl with Asper—rallied each other on their failings, and Jonson's anecdote [1] that he had once ' beaten Marston and taken his *pistol* from him,' it is pleasant to imagine that the name of Shakespeare's scurrilous puff was the nickname of Jonson's shifty ally.[2]   For in considering this wordy war, it is necessary to re-

---

[1] Drummond's *Conversations.*

[2] Jonson comments on some such adventure in his *Epigrams,* LXVIII.— On Playwright :—

> ' Playwrit convict of public wrongs to men,
> Takes *private beatings*, and begins again.

member that the fight was, in the main, a pantomime
' rally,' in which big-sounding blows were given and
returned for the amusement of the gallery.   Captain
Tucca, the character borrowed from *The Poetaster* to
set an edge on Dekker's retort, speaks the Epilogue
to *Satiromastix*, and begs the audience to applaud
the piece in order that Horace (Jonson) may be
obliged to reply once again.   Half in fun and half in
earnest did these ink-horn swash-bucklers gibe each
other over their cups, and trounce each other on the
boards.   Yet behind all the chaff and bustle ' of
that terrible Poetomachia lately commenced between
Horace   the   Second   and   a   band   of   lean-witted
poetasters,' [1] there was a real conflict of literary
aims ; and in that conflict Shakespeare took the part
of the Romantics, upon whose ultimate success the
odds were, in Dekker's nervous phraseology, ' all
Mount   Helicon   to   Bun-hill.' [2]   Without   seeking
further to distinguish the champions, it is sufficient
to know that Shakespeare was an actor and a playwright throughout the alarums and excursions of
these paste-board hostilities, whose casualties, after
all, amounted but to the ' lamentable merry murdering of Innocent Poetry.' [3]

> Two kinds of valour he doth shew at once ;
> Active in 's brain, and passive in his bones.'

The Quarto of Shakespeare's *Henry V.* was published in 1600.   Pistol is
beaten in it, as Thersites is beaten in *Troilus.*   Pistol uses the fustian word
' exhale ' ;   so does Crispinus in *Poetaster* (noted by Fleay).   Pistol's
' Fetch forth the lazar kite of Cresides kinde ' is reminiscent of *Troilus,*
produced the year before.   Pistol's ' What, have we Hiren here ' is a mock
quotation from an early play of which Marston makes use more than once.

[1] Address ' To the World ' prefixed to *Satiromastix.*   The author thanks
Venusian Horace for the ' good words '—detraction, envy, snakes, adders,
stings, etc.—which he gives him.   They are taken from the Prologue to
The Poetaster.   [2] ' To the World ' prefixed to *Satiromastix.*

[3] Dekker, Epilogue to *Satiromastix.*   In the thick of the fray, 1601,
Jonson, Chapman, Marston, and Shakespeare each contributed a poem
on *The Phœnix and the Turtle* to Robert Chester's *Love's Martyr* !

IX

In examining the relation between the lyrics which Shakespeare wrote and the environment of his life, it was impossible to overlook this controversy which must have lasted longer and bulked larger than any other feature in that life.[1] For Shakespeare, the man, was in the first place an actor and a playwright bound up in the corporate life of the Company to which he belonged. We are apt to reconstruct this theatric world, in which he had his being, fancifully : from his Plays rather than from the Plays of his contemporaries, and from the few among his Plays which are our favourites, just because they differ most widely from theirs. But his world of everyday effort and experience was not altogether, as at such times it may seem to us, a garden of fair flowers and softly sighing winds and delicate perfumes, nor altogether a gorgeous gallery of gallant inventions : it was also garish, strident, pungent ; a Donnybrook Fair of society journalists, a nightmare of Gillray caricature. ' A Gentleman,' you read, ' or an honest Citizen, shall not sit in your pennie-bench Theatres with his squirrel by his side cracking nuttes ; nor sneake into a Taverne with his Mermaid ; but he shall be satyr'd, and epigram'd upon, and his humour must run upo' the Stage : you 'll ha *Every Gentleman in 's humour*, and *Every Gentleman out on 's humour.*' [2] Shakespeare tells the

---

[1] The *Venus* and *Lucrece* were written, of course, years before the Poetomachia ; but, unless we accept the improbable view that Shakespeare brought his *Venus* with him from Stratford, both were written under conditions to which the Poetomachia gives a clue.

[2] Dekker's *Satiromastix*. In his address ' *To the World*,' he instances Captain Hannam as the living prototype taken for *Tucca* by Jonson. In the earlier Marprelate plays (*circa* 1589) Nash's antagonist, Gabriel Harvey, was put on the stage. Aubrey, before 1680, wrote that ' Ben Jonson and he (Shakespeare) did gather humour of men dayly wherever they came.'

same story, when he makes *Hamlet* say of the
players:—'They are the abstract and brief chronicles
of the time : after your death you were better to
have a bad epitaph than their ill report while you
live.' [1] Note that he speaks of the actors, not the
playwrights : though much of their satire turned on
size of leg, scantness of hair, pretensions to gentility
and seediness of apparel in well-known individuals
veiled under transparent disguises. Far more obvious even than such lampooning was the actors'
' guying ' of persons and types which we see reflected
in *Troilus* [2] and enacted in *Cynthia's Revels*. The
actor playing Crites (v. 3) takes off every trick of
speech and gesture in the person whom he caricatures, for, says Hedon :—' Slight, Anaides, you
are mocked ' ; and again, in the Induction, one of
the three children who play it borrows the Prologue's
cloak, and mimics, one after another, the gallants
who frequent the theatre ; so that here is the
' genteel auditor ' to the life, with his ' three sorts of
tobacco in his pocket,' swearing—' By this light '—
as he strikes his flint, that the players ' act like so
many wrens,' and, as for the poets—' By this
vapour '—that ' an 'twere not for tobacco the very
stench of them would poison ' him.

We can picture from other sources both the conditions of Shakespeare's auditors and the upholstering
of his stage. Dekker,[3] describing ' how a gallant
should behave himself at a playhouse,' writes of the
groundling who masked the view of the 'prentices :—

[1] *Hamlet*, II. ii. 501. Fleay, *History of the Stage*, p. 160 :—' 1601, May
10, the Council writes to the Middlesex Justices complaining that the
players at the Curtain represent on the stage under obscure manner, but
yet in such sort as all the hearers may take notice both of the matter and
the persons that are meant thereby ' : certain gentlemen that are yet alive.
[2] I. iii. 140-196. III. iii. 266-292. Cf. *supra*.
[3] *Gull's Horn-Book*.

'But on the very rushes where the comedy is to dance, yea, under the state of Cambyses himself, must our feathered estridge, like a piece of ordnance, be planted valiantly (because impudently) beating down the mews and hisses of the opposed rascality.' The dignity of 'Cambyses state' may be guessed from Henslowe's list [1] of grotesque properties— 'Serberosse (Cerberus') three heads ; Ierosses (Iris') head and rainbow ; 1 tomb of Dido ; 1 pair of stairs for Fayeton (Phaethon) and his 2 leather antic's coats' and 'the city of Rome (!).' The gallant in gorgeous apparel, his jerkin 'frotted' with perfumes, 'spikenard, opoponax, ænanthe,' [2] the 'Court-mistress' in 'Satin cut upon six taffetaes,' the 'prentice and harlot viewed these plays, farced with scurrilous lampoons, and rudely staged on rushes, through an atmosphere laden with tobacco and to an accompaniment of nut-cracking and spitting. This was Shakespeare's shop, the 'Wooden O' into which he crammed

'the very casques
That did affright the air at Agincourt,' [3]

and in which, year after year, he won fame and wealth and rancorous envy from defeated rivals.

We catch a last note of detraction, in *Ratseis' Ghost* (1605-6), wherein the phantom hightobyman advises a strolling Player to repair to London :— 'There thou shalt learn to be frugal (for players were never so thrifty as they are now about London), and to feed upon all men ; to let none feed upon thee ; to make thy hand a stranger to thy pocket, thy heart slow to perform thy tongue's promise ; and when thou feelest thy purse well lined, buy thee

[1] Quoted by Fleay, *History of the Stage*, 114.
[2] *Cynthia's Revels*.   [3] Chorus to *Henry V.* i.

some place of lordship in the country, that, growing
weary of playing, thy money may then bring thee
to dignity and reputation : then thou needest care
for no man ; no, not for them that before made thee
proud when speaking their words on the stage.'
' Sir, I thank you,' quoth the Player, ' for this good
council : I promise you I will make use of it, for I
have heard, indeed, of some that have gone to
London very meanly and have come in time to be
exceeding wealthy.' It is significant, almost con-
clusive, to know that Shakespeare's name appeared
on the roll of the King's Players for the last time in
1604 and that in 1605 he purchased an unexpired
term (thirty years) in the lease of tithes both great
and small, in Stratford : thus securing an addition
to his income equal to at least £350 [1] a year of our
money.

X

Behind this life of business, on and for the stage,
Shakespeare, as the friend of young noblemen, saw
something of the Court with its gaiety and learning
and display, ever undermined by intrigue, and sometimes eclipsed by tragedy.   He was impeded in his
art by controversies between puritans, churchmen,
and precisians, and exercised in his affection for those
who to their own ruin championed the old nobility
against the growing power of the Crown.   As a loyal
citizen of London, he must have grieved at her sins
and diseases, over which even Dekker, the railing
ruffler of *Satiromastix*, wailed at last in the accents
of a Hebrew prophet :—' O *London*, thou art great
in glory, and envied for thy greatness ; thy Towers,
thy Temples, and thy Pinnacles stand upon thy

[1] Baynes.

head like borders of fine gold, thy waters like frindges
of silver hang at the hemmes of thy garments.
Thou art the goodliest of thy neighbours, but the
prowdest, the welthiest, but the most wanton.
Thou hast all things in thee to make thee fairest,
and all things in thee to make thee foulest ; for thou
art attir'd like a Bride, drawing all that looke upon
thee, to be in love with thee, but there is much harlot
in thine eyes ' . . . so ' sickness was sent to breathe
her unwholesome ayres into thy nosthrills, so that
thou, that wert before the only Gallant and Minion
of the world, hadst in a short time more diseases
(than a common harlot hath) hanging upon thee ;
thou suddenly becamst the by-talke of neighbors,
the scorne and contempt of Nations.' [1]   Thus Dekker
in 1606 ; and, in the next year, Marston, who
equalled him in blatant spirits and far excelled him
in ruffianism, left writing for the Stage, and entered
the Church !

These are aspects of Shakespeare's environment
which we cannot neglect in deciding how much or
how little of his lyrical art he owed to anything but
his own genius and devotion to Beauty.   Least of
all may we first assume that his art reflects his environment, and then, inverting this imaginary
relation, declare it for the product of a golden age
which never existed.   Yet, thanks to modern
idolatry of naked generalisations, it is the fashion
to throw Shakespeare in with other fruits of the
Renaissance, acknowledging the singularity of his
genius, but still labelling it for an organic part of a
wide development.   And in this development we
have been taught to see nothing but a renewal of
life and strength, of truth and sanity, following on

[1] *The Seven Deadly Sins of London* (1606).

the senile mystifications of an effetc Middle Age.
The theory makes for a sharp definition of contrast ;
but it is hard to find its justification either in the facts
of history or in the opinions of Shakespeare's contemporaries, who believed that, on the contrary,
they lived in an epoch of decadence. In any age
of rapid development there is much, no doubt, that
may fitly be illustrated by metaphors drawn from
sunrise and spring ; but there are also aspects akin
to sunset and autumn. The truth seems to be that
at such times the processes of both birth and death
are abnormally quickened. To every eye life becomes more coloured and eventful daily ; but it
shines and changes with curiously mingled effects :
speaking to these of youth and the hill-tops, and to
those of declension and decay.

In 1611 Shakespeare withdrew to Stratford-on-
Avon.[1] Of his life in London we know little at first
hand. But we know enough of what he did ;
enough of what he was said to have done ; enough of
the dispositions and the lives of his contemporaries ;
to imagine very clearly the world in which he worked
for some twenty-three years. He lived the life of a
successful artist, rocked on the waves and sunk in
the troughs of exhilaration and fatigue. He was
befriended for personal and political reasons by
brilliant young noblemen, and certainly grieved over
their misfortunes. He was intimate with Southampton and William Herbert, and must surely
have known Herbert's mistress, Mary Fitton. He
suffered, first, rather more than less from the jealousy
and detraction of the scholar-wits, the older Uni-

---

[1] Baynes argues that he left London in 1608. He ceased writing for
the stage in 1611, and disposed of his interest in the Globe and Blackfriars
Theatres probably in that year.

versity pens, and then, rather less than more, from the histrionic rivalry of his brother playwrights. He was himself a mark for scandal,[1] and he watched the thunder clouds of Politics and Puritanism gathering over the literature and the drama which he loved.[2]   Yet far away from the dust and din of these turmoils he bore the sorrows, and prosecuted the success of his other life at Stratford.   His only son, Hamnet, died in 1596.   His daughter, Susannah, married, and his mother, Mary Arden, died in 1608, and in the same year he bestowed his name on the child of an old friend, Henry Walker.   Through all these years, by lending money and purchasing land, he built up a fortune magnified by legend long after his death.   And in the April of 1616 he died himself, as some have it, on his birthday.   He ' was bury'd on the north side of the chancel, in the great Church at Stratford, where a monument is plac'd on the wall.   On his grave-stone underneath is :—

> " Good friend, for Jesus' sake, forbear
> To dig the dust inclosed here.
> Blest be the man that spares these stones,
> And curst be he that moves my bones." ' [3]

This slight and most imperfect sketch, founded mainly on impressions brought away from the study

[1] Sir W. Davenant boasted that he was Shakespeare's son :—' When he was pleasant over a glass of wine with his most intimate friends ' (Aubrey's *Lives of Eminent Persons*. Completed before 1680). Cf. Halliwell-Phillipps' *Outlines*, ii. 43. And there is that story of the trick the poet played on Burbage : which might hail from the *Decameron*. See John Manningham's *Diary*, 13th March 1601-2.

[2] Warton, *Hist. of Eng. Poetry* (1824), iv. 320. ' In 1599 . . . Marston's *Pygmalion*, Marlowe's *Ovid*, the *Satires* of Hall and Marston, the epigrams of Davies and the Caltha poetarum, etc., were burnt by order of the prelates, Whitgift and Bancroft. The books of Nash and Harvey were ordered to be confiscated, and it was laid down that no plays should be printed without permission from the Archbishop of Canterbury, nor any ' English Historyes ' (novels ?) without the sanction of the Privy Council.'

[3] Rowe, 1709.

of many noble portraits, is still sufficient to prove
how little the Poems owe, even remotely, to the
vicissitudes of an artist's career.   Of the wild wood-
land life in Arden Forest, of boyish memories and of
books read at school, there is truly something to be
traced in echoes from Ovid and in frequent illustrations drawn from sport and nature.   But of the later
life in London there is little enough, even in the
Sonnets that tell of rival poets and a dark lady, and
nothing that points so clearly to any single experience as to admit of definite application.   For in
Shakespeare's Poems, as in every great work of art,
single experiences have been generalised or, rather,
merged in the passion which they rouse as a height
and a pitch of sensitiveness immeasurable in contrast
with its puny origins.   The volume and the intensity
of an artist's passion have led many to believe that
great artists speak for all mankind of joy and sorrow.
But to great artists the bliss and martyrdom of man
are of less import, so it seems, than to others.   The
griefs and tragedies that bulk so largely in the lives
of the inapt and the inarticulate are—so far as we
may divine the secrets of an alien race—but a small
part of the great artist's experience : hardly more,
perhaps, than stimulants to his general sense of the
whole world's infinite appeal to sensation and
consciousness.

XI

Shakespeare's Poems are detached by the perfection of his art from both the personal experience
which supplied their matter and the artistic environment which suggested their rough-hewn form.   Were
they newly discovered, you could tell, of course, that
they were written in England, and about the end of

the Sixteenth Century : just as you can tell a Flemish
from an Italian, a Fourteenth from a Sixteenth
Century picture ; and every unprejudiced critic
has said of the Sonnets that they ' express Shakespeare's own feelings in his own person.' [1] That is
true. But it is equally true, and it is vastly more
important, that the Sonnets are not an Autobiography. In this Sonnet or that you feel the
throb of great passions shaking behind the perfect
verse ; here and there you listen to a sigh as of a
world awakening to its weariness. Yet the movement and sound are elemental : they steal on your
senses like a whisper trembling through summer-
leaves, and in their vastness are removed by far from
the suffocation of any one man's tragedy. The
writer of the Sonnets has felt more, and thought
more, than the writer of the *Venus* and the *Lucrece* ;
but he remains a poet—not a Rousseau, not a
Metaphysician—and his chief concern is still to
worship Beauty in the imagery and music of his
verse. It is, indeed, strange to find how much of
thought, imagery, and rhythm is common to *Venus
and Adonis* and the *Sonnets*, for the two works could
hardly belong by their themes to classes of poetry
more widely distinct—(the first is a late Renaissance
imitation of late Classical Mythology ; the second
a sequence of intimate occasional verses)—nor could
they differ more obviously from other poems in the
same classes. Many such imitations and sequences
of sonnets were written by Shakespeare's contem-

[1] Mr. Dowden :—' With Wordsworth, Sir Henry Taylor, and Mr. Swin-
burne ; with François-Victor Hugo, with Kreyssig, Ulrici, Gervinus, and
Hermann Isaac ; with Boaden, Armitage Brown, and Hallam ; with
Furnivall, Spalding, Rossetti, and Palgrave, I believe that Shakespeare's
Sonnets express his own feelings in his own person.' So do Mr. A. E.
Harrison and Mr. Tyler.

poraries, but among them all there is not one poem
that in the least resembles *Venus and Adonis*, and
there are but few sonnets that remind you, even
faintly, of Shakespeare's. And just such distinctions
isolate *The Rape of Lucrece*. By its theme, as a
romantic story in rhyme, it has nothing in common
with its two companions from Shakespeare's hand ;
but it is lonelier than they, having indeed no fellow
in Elizabethan poetry and not many in English
literature. Leaving ballads on one side, you may
count the romantic stories in English rhyme, that
can by courtesy be called literature, upon the fingers
of one hand.   There are but two arches in the bridge
by which Keats and Chaucer communicate across the
centuries, and Shakespeare's *Lucrece* stands for the
solitary pier.   Yet, distinct as they are from each
other in character, these three things by Shakespeare
are closely united in form by a degree of lyrical
excellence in their imagery and rhythm which severs
them from kindred competitors : they are the first
examples of the highest qualities in Elizabethan
lyrical verse.   No poet of that day ever doubted
that ' poesie dealeth with *Katholon*, that is to say
with the universall consideration,' [1] or that of every
language in Europe their own could best ' yeeld the
sweet slyding fit for a verse.' [2]   But in these three
you find the highest expression of this theory and
this practice alike : a sense of the mystery of Beauty
profound as Plato's, with such a golden cadence as
no other singer has been able to sustain.

XII

Venus and Adonis was published in 1593, the year
of Marlowe's death, and was at once immensely

[1] Sidney, *Apologie for Poetrie*.   [2] *Ibid.*

popular, editions following one hard upon another,
in 1594, 1596, 1599, 1600, and (two editions) 1602.
Shakespeare dedicated his poem to Lord Southampton, and called it ' the first heir of his invention.'
There is nothing remarkable in his choice of a metre
—the ' staffe of sixe verses ' (ab ab cc) ; for four years
earlier Puttenham (?) had described it (*The Arte of
English Poesie*, 1589) as ' not only *most usual*, but
also very pleasant to th' eare.' We need not, then,
suppose that Shakespeare borrowed it exclusively
from Lodge. He may have been guided in his
choice. For Lodge had interwoven a short allusion
to *Adonis*' death into his *Scylla's Metamorphosis*,
also published in 1589 and written in this staff of six.
But Lodge's melody is not Shakespeare's :—

> ' Her dainty hand addressed to claw her dear,
> Her roseal lip allied to his pale cheek,
> Her sighs, and then her looks, and heavy cheer,
> Her bitter threats, and then her passions meek :
> How on his senseless corpse she lay a-crying,
> As if the boy were then but now a-dying ' :—

and, indeed, Shakespeare's poem is, in all essentials,
utterly unlike Lodge's *Scylla*, Marlowe's unfinished
Hero and Leander, Drayton's *Endymion and Phœbe*,
and Chapman's *Ovid's Banquet of Sense*. Still less
does it resemble the earlier adaptations from Ovid's
Metamorphoses, as Thomas Peend's ' *Salmacis and
Hermaphroditus* ' (1565) :—

> ' Dame Venus once by Mercurye
> Comprest, a chylde did beare,
> For beauty farre excellyng all
> That erst before hym weare.'

It borrows from, or lends to, Henry Constable's
Sheepheard's Song scarce a phrase,[1] and the same

---

[1] *The Sheepheard's Song of Venus and Adonis.* First published in
England's Helicon, 1600 : it may have been written before Shakespeare's

may be said still more emphatically of its relation to Spenser's five stanzas[1] on ' The Love of *Venus* and her Paramoure,' and to Golding's Ovid.   Briefly, it has nothing to do either with studious imitations of the Classics or with the ' rhyme doggerel ' that preceded them, for it throws back to the mediæval poets' use of Ovid : to Chrétien de Troyes, that is, the authors of the *Roman de la Rose*, and Chaucer, who first steeped themselves in the *Metamorphoses*, and then made beautiful poems of their own by the light of their genius in the manner of their day. Sometimes you may trace the extraction of an image in Shakespeare's verse back and up the mediæval tradition.   Thus (Sonnet CXIX.) :—

> ' What potions have I drunke of syren teares
> Distill'd from lymbecks.'

Thus Chaucer (*Troilus*, iv.) :—

> ' This Troilus in tearës gan distill
> As licour out of allambick full fast.'

And thus the *Roman de la Rose* (l. 6657) :—

> ' Por quoi donc en tristor demores ?
> Je vois maintes fois que tu plores.
> Cum alambic sus alutel.'

Adonis.   The bare theme, which is not to be found in Ovid, of Venus's vain soliciting and of Adonis's reluctance, is alluded to in Marlowe's *Hero and Leander* :—

> ' Where Venus in her naked glory strove
> To please the careless and disdainful eyes
> Of proud Adonis, that before her lies ' :—

and in Robert's Greene's pamphlet, *Never Too Late* (1590) :—

> ' Sweet *Adon*, dar'st not glance thine eye
> (*N'oseres vous, mon bel amy ?*)
> Upon thy Venus that must die ?
> *Je vous en prie*, pitty me :
> *N'oseres vous, mon bel*, mon bel,
> *N'oseres vous, mon bel amy ?*

[1] *Faerie Queene*, iii. 1, 34-38.

But with greater frequency comes the evidence of
Shakespeare's loving familiarity with Ovid whose
effects he fuses : taking the reluctance of Adonis
from *Hermaphroditus* (*Metamorphoses*, iv.) ; the
description of the boar from Meleager's encounter
in viii. ; and other features from the short version
of *Venus and Adonis* which Ovid weaves on to the
terrible and beautiful story of Myrrha (x.).[1] In all
Shakespeare's work of this period the same fusion of
Ovid's stories and images is obvious. Tarquin and
Myrrha are both delayed, but, not daunted, by
lugubrious forebodings in the dark ; and *Titus
Andronicus*, played for the first time in the year
which saw the publication of *Venus and Adonis*,
is full of debts and allusions to Ovid. Ovid, with
his power of telling a story and of eloquent discourse,
his shining images, his cadences coloured with assonance and weighted with alliteration ; Chaucer, with
his sweet liquidity of diction, his dialogues and
soliloquies—these are the ' only true begetters ' of the
lyric Shakespeare. In these matters we must allow
poets to have their own way : merely noting that
Ovid, in whom critics see chiefly a brilliant man of
the world, has been a mine of delight for all poets
who rejoice in the magic of sound, from the dawn
of the Middle Ages down to our own incomparable
Milton.[2] His effects of alliteration :—

' Corpora Cecropidum pennis pendere putares ;
    Pendebant pennis. . . .
    Vertitur in volucrem, cui stant, in vertice cristae ' :—

---

[1] Cf. *Le Roman de la Rose*. Chap. cvii. follows the order of Ovid's
Tenth Book, passing from Pygmalion to ' Mirra ' and adding ll. 21992, ' Li
biaus *Adonis* en fu nés.'

[2] Mackail on ' Milton's Debt to Ovid ' (*Latin Literature*, 142.) Cf. Ker,
Epic and Romance, 395.

his gleaming metaphors, as of Hermaphroditus after his plunge :—

> ' In liquidis translucet aquis ; ut eburnea si quis
> Signa tegat claro, vel candida lilia, vitro ' :—

are the very counterpart of Shakespeare's manner in the Poems and the Play which he founded in part on his early love of the *Metamorphoses*.

But in *Titus Andronicus* and in *Venus and Adonis* there are effects of the open air which hail, not from Ovid, but from Arden :—

> ˙ The birds chant melody on every bush ;
> The snake lies rolled in the cheerful sun ;
> The green leaves quiver with the cooling wind,
> And make a chequer'd shadow on the ground ':—

Thus the Play (ii. 3), and thus the Poem :—

> ' Even as the wind is hush'd before it raineth . . .
> Like many clouds consulting for foul weather.'

Indeed in the Poem, round and over the sharp portrayal of every word and gesture of the two who speak and move, you have brakes and trees, horses and hounds, and the silent transformations of day and night from the first dawn till eve, and through darkness to the second dawn so immediately impressed, that, pausing at any of the cxcix. stanzas, you could almost name the hour.   The same express observation of the day's changes may be observed in *Romeo and Juliet*.   It is a note which has often been echoed by men who never look out of their windows, and critics, as narrowly immured, have denounced it for an affectation.   Yet a month under canvas, or, better still, without a tent, will convince any one that to speak of the stars and the moon is as natural as to look at your watch or an almanack.   In the *Venus* even the weather changes. The Poem opens soon after sunrise with the ceasing of a shower :—

> ' Even as the sun with purple colour'd face,
>   Had ta'en his last leave of the weeping morn.'

But by the LXXXIXth Stanza, after a burning noon, the clouds close in over the sunset. ' Look,' says Adonis :—

> ' The world's comforter with weary gate
> His day's hot task hath ended in the west,
> The owl (night's herald) shrieks, 'tis very late,
> The sheep are gone to fold, birds to their nest,
> And coal-black clouds, that shadow heaven's light,
> Do summon us to part and bid good-night.'

The next dawn is cloudless after the night's rain :—

> ' Lo here the gentle lark, weary of rest,
> From his moist cabinet mounts up on high,
> And wakes the morning, from whose silver breast
> The sun ariseth in his majesty ;
> Who doth the world so gloriously behold,
> That cedar tops and hills seem burnisht gold.'

Beneath these atmospheric effects everything is clearly seen and sharply delineated :—

> ' The studded bridle on a ragged bough
> Nimbly she fastens.'

And when the horse breaks loose :—

> ' Some time he trots, as if he told the steps.'

Then the description of a hunted hare (Stanzas CXIV.-CXVIII.) :—

> ' Sometimes he runs along a flock of sheep
> To make the cunning hounds mistake their smell. . . .
>
> By this poor Wat far off upon a hill
> Stands on his hinder legs with listening ear. . . .
> Then shalt thou see the dew-bedabbled wretch
> Turn and return, indenting with the way ;

Each envious briar his weary legs doth scratch,
Each shadow makes him stop, each murmur stay ' :—

howbeit a treasure of observation, is no richer than that other of the hounds which have lost their huntsman :—

' Another flap-mouth'd mourner, black and grim,
Against the welkin, vollies out his voice,
Another and another, answer him,
Clapping their proud tails to the ground below,
Shaking their scratch-ears, bleeding as they go.'

The illustrations from nature :—

' As the dive-dapper peering through a wave
Who being lookt on, ducks as quickly in . . .

As the snail whose tender horns being hit
Shrinks backward in his shelly cave with pain ' :—

are so vivid as to snatch your attention from the story ; and when you read that ' lust ' feeding on ' fresh beauty '

' Starves and soon bereaves
As caterpillars do the tender leaves,'

the realism of the illustration does violence to its aptness. It is said that such multiplicity of detail and ornament is out of place in a classic myth. But Shakespeare's Poem is not a classic myth. Mr. Swinburne contrasts it unfavourably with Chapman's *Hero and Leander*, in which he finds ' a small shrine of Parian sculpture amid the rank splendour of a tropical jungle.' Certainly that is the last image which any one could apply to *Venus and Adonis*. Its wealth of realistic detail reminds you rather of the West Porch at Amiens. But alongside of this realism, and again as in Mediæval Art, there are wilful and half-humorous perversions of nature.

When Shakespeare in praise of Adonis' beauty says
that

> ' To see his face, the lion walked along
> *Behind some hedge*, because he would not fear him,'

or that

> ' When he beheld his shadow in the brook,
> The fishes spread on it their golden gills,'

you feel that you are still in the age which painted
St. Jerome's lion and St. Francis preaching to the
birds.   But you feel that you are half way into
another.   The poem is not Greek, but neither is it
Mediæval : it belongs to the debatable dawntime
which we call the Renaissance.   There is much in it
of highly charged colour and of curious insistence on
strange beauties of detail ; yet, dyed and dædal as
it is out of all kinship with classical repose, neither
its intricacy nor its tinting ever suggests the Aladdin's
Cave evoked by Mr. Swinburne's Oriental epithets :
rather do they suggest a landscape at sunrise.   There,
too, the lesser features of trees and bushes and knolls
are steeped in the foreground with crimson light, or
are set on fire with gold at the horizon ; there, too,
they leap into momentary significance with prolonged
and fantastic shadows ; yet overhead, the atmosphere is, not oppressive but, eager and pure and
a part of an immense serenity.   And so it is in
the Poem, for which, if you abandon Mr. Swinburne's illustration, and seek another from painting,
you may find a more fitting counterpart in the
Florentine treatment of classic myths : in Botticelli's
Venus, with veritable gold on the goddess's hair and
on the boles of the pine trees, or in Piero di Cosima's
Cephalus and Procris, with its living animals at gaze
before a tragedy that tells much of Beauty and

nothing of Pain. Shakespeare's Poem is of love, not death ; but he handles his theme with just the same regard for Beauty, with just the same disregard for all that disfigures Beauty. He portrays an amorous encounter through its every gesture ; yet, unless in some dozen lines where he glances aside, like any Mediæval, at a gaiety not yet divorced from love, his appeal to Beauty persists from first to last ; and nowhere is there an appeal to lust. The laughter and sorrow of the Poem belong wholly to the faery world of vision and romance, where there is no sickness, whether of sentiment or of sense. And both are rendered by images, clean-cut as in antique gems, brilliantly enamelled as in mediæval chalices, numerous and interwoven as in Moorish arabesques ; so that their incision, colour, and rapidity of development, apart even from the intricate melodies of the verbal medium in which they live, tax the faculty of artistic appreciation to a point at which it begins to participate in the asceticism of artistic creation. ' As little can a mind thus roused and awakened be brooded on by mean and indistinct emotion, as the low, lazy mist can creep upon the surface of a lake while a strong gale is driving it onward in waves and billows ' :—thus does Coleridge resist the application to shift the avenue of criticism on this Poem from the court of Beauty to the court of Morals, and upon that subject little more need be said. How wilful it is to discuss the moral bearing of an invitation couched by an imaginary Goddess in such imaginative terms as these :—

> ' Bid me discourse, I will inchant thine eare,
> Or like a Fairie, trip upon the greene,
> Or like a Nymph, with long disheveled heare,
> Daunce on the sands, and yet no footing seene ! '

As well essay to launch an ironclad on ' the foam of perilous seas in fairylands forlorn.'

When Venus says, ' Bid me discourse, I will inchant thine ear,' she instances yet another peculiar excellence of Shakespeare's lyrical art, which shows in this Poem, is redoubled in *Lucrece*, and in the Sonnets yields the most perfect examples of human speech :—

> ' Touch but my lips with those fair lips of thine,
> Though mine be not so fair, yet are they red. . . .
>
> Art thou ashamed to kiss ?   Then wink again,
> And I will wink, so shall the day seem night. . . .'

These are the fair words of her soliciting, and Adonis's reply is of the same silvery quality :—

> ' If love have lent you twenty thousand tongues,
> And every tongue more meaning than your own,
> Bewitching like the wanton mermaid's songs,
> Yet from mine ear the tempting tune is blown. . . .'

And, as he goes on :—

> ' Lest the deceiving harmony should run
> Into the quiet closure of my breast ' :—

you catch a note prelusive to the pleading altercation of the Sonnets. It is the discourse in *Venus and Adonis* and *Lucrece* which renders them discursive. And indeed they are long poems, on whose first reading Poe's advice, never to begin at the same place, may wisely be followed. You do well, for instance, to begin at Stanza cxxxvi. in order to enjoy the narrative of Venus' vain pursuit : with your senses unwearied by the length and sweetness of her argument. The passage hence to the end is in the true romantic tradition : Stanzas cxl. and cxli. are as clearly the forerunners of Keats as cxliv. is the child of Chaucer. The truth of such

art consists in magnifying selected details until
their gigantic shapes, edged with a shadowy iridescence, fill the whole field of observation. Certain
gestures of the body, certain moods of the mind,
are made to tell with the weight of trifles during
awe-stricken pauses of delay. Venus, when she is
baffled by ' the merciless and pitchy night,' halts

> ' amazed as one that unaware
> Hath dropt a precious jewel in the flood,
> Or stonisht as night wanderers often are,
> Their light blown out in some mistrustfull wood.'

She starts like ' one that spies an adder ' ; ' the
timorous yelping of the hounds appals her senses ' ;
and she stands ' in a trembling extasy.'

Besides romantic narrative and sweetly modulated
discourse, there are two rhetorical tirades by Venus
—when she ' exclaimes on death ' [1] :—

> ' Grim grinning ghost, earth's-worme, what dost thou meane
> To stifle beautie and to steale his breath,' etc. :—

and when she heaps her anathemas on love :—

> ' It shall be fickle, false and full of fraud,
> Bud, and be blasted in a breathing while ;
> The bottome poyson, and the top ore-strawed
> With sweets, that shall the truest sight beguile,
> The strongest bodie shall it make most weake,
> Strike the voice dumbe, and teach the foole to speake ' :—

and in both, as also in Adonis's contrast of love and
lust :—

> ' Love comforteth, like sunshine after raine,
> But lust's effect is tempest after sunne,
> Love's gentle spring doth always fresh remaine,
> Lust's winter comes ere summer halfe be donne ;
> Love surfets not, lust like a glutton dies :
> Love is all truth, lust full of forged lies ' :—

---

[1] I retain the early spelling, as something of the rhetorical force depends
on the sounds it suggests.

you have rhetoric, packed with antithesis, and
rapped out on alliterated syllables for which the only
equivalent in English is found, but more fully, in
the great speech delivered by Lucrece.[1] The seed
of these tirades, as of the dialogues and the gentle
soliloquies, seems derived from Chaucer's *Troilus
and Criseyde* ; and in his *Knight's Tale* (1747-1758)
there is also a foreshadowing of their effective
alliteration, used—and this is the point—not as an
ornament of verse, but as an instrument of accent.
For example :—

> ' The helmës they to-hewen and to-shrede ;
> Out brest the blood, with sternë stremës rede.
> With mighty maces the bonës they to-breste ;
> He thurgh the thikkeste of the throng gon threste,' etc.

This use of alliteration by Shakespeare, employed
earlier by Lord Vaux :—

> ' Since death shall dure till all the world be waste ' [2] :—

and later by Spenser [3] :—

> ' Then let thy flinty heart that feeles no paine,
> Empierced be with pitiful remorse,
> And let thy bowels bleede in every vaine,
> At sight of His most sacred heavenly corse,
> So torne and mangled with malicious forse ;
> And let thy soule, whose sins His sorrows wrought,
> Melt into teares, and grone in grieved thought ' :—

is not to be confused with ' the absurd following of
the letter amongst our English so much of late
affected, but now hist out of Paules Church yard ' ; [4]
for it does not consist in collecting the greatest
number of words with the same initial, but in letting

---

[1] In denunciation of Night, Opportunity, and Time (764-1036).
[2] *Paradise of Dainty Devices*, 1576.
[3] *An Hymne of Heavenly Love* (September 1596).
[4] Campion, *Observations in the Art of English Poesy*, 1602.

the accent fall, as it does naturally in all impassioned speech, upon syllables of cognate sound. Since in English verse the accent is, and by Shakespeare's contemporaries was understood to be, ' the chief lord and grave Governour of Numbers,' [1] this aid to its emphasis is no less legitimate, and is hardly less important, than is that of rhyme to metre in French verse : we inherit it from the Saxon, as we inherit rhyme from the Norman ; both are essential elements in the poetry built up by Chaucer out of the ruins of two languages. But Shakespeare is the supreme master of its employment : in these impassioned tirades he wields it with a naked strength that was never approached, in the Sonnets with a veiled and varied subtilty that defies analysis. There are hints here and there in the *Venus* of this gathering subtilty :—

> ' These blew-vein'd violets whereon we leane
> Never can blab, nor know not what we meane . . .
>
> Even as a dying coale revives with winde . . .
>
> More white and red than doves and roses are.'

But apart from the use of cognate sounds, which makes for emphasis without marring melody, in many a line there also lives that more recondite sweetness, which plants so much of Shakespeare's verse in the memory for no assignable cause :—

> ' Scorning his churlish drum and ensinge red. . . .
>
> Dumbly she passions, frantikely she doteth. . . .
>
> Showed like two silver doves that sit a billing. . . .
>
> Leading him prisoner in a red-rose chaine. . . .

---

[1] S. Daniel's *Defence of Ryme*, 1603 :—' Though it doth not strictly observe long and short sillables, yet it most religiously respects the accent.' —*Ibid.* Cf. Sidney's *Apologie* :—' Wee observe the accent very precisely.'

> Were beautie under twentie locks kept fast,
> Yet love breaks through and picks them all at last. . . .
>
> O learne to love, the lesson is but plaine
> And once made perfect never lost again.'

Herein a cadence of obvious simplicity gives birth to an inexplicable charm.

I have spoken of Shakespeare's images, blowing fresh from the memory of his boyhood, so vivid that at times they are violent, and at others wrought and laboured until they become conceits. You have ' No fisher but the ungrown fry forbears,' with its frank reminiscence of a sportsman's scruple ; or, as an obvious illustration, ' Look how a bird lies tangled in a net ' ; or, in a flash of intimate recollection :—

> ' Like shrill-tongu'd tapsters answering everie call,
> Soothing the humours of fantastique wits ' :—

the last, an early sketch of the ' Francis ' scene in *Henry IV.*, which, in quaint juxtaposition with ' cedar tops and hills ' of ' burnisht gold,' seems instinct with memories of John Shakespeare and his friends, who dared not go to church. **But,** again, you have conceits :—

> ' But hers (eyes), which through the crystal tears gave light,
> Shone like the Moone in water seen by night ' ;

' A lilie prison'd in a gaile of snow ' ; and ' Wishing her cheeks were gardens ful of flowers So they were dew'd with such distilling showers.' But, diving deeper than diction, alliteration, and rhythm : deeper than the decoration of blazoned colours and the labyrinthine interweaving of images, now budding as it were from nature, and now beaten as by an artificer out of some precious metal : you discover beneath this general interpretation of Phenomenal Beauty, a gospel of Ideal Beauty, a confession of

faith in Beauty as a principle of life.   And note—
for the coincidence is vital—that these, the esoteric
themes of *Venus and Adonis,* are the essential themes
of the *Sonnets.*   In Stanza XXII. :—

> ' Fair flowers that are not gathered in their prime
> Rot and consume themselves in little time ' :—

and in Stanzas XXVII., XXVIII., XXIX., you have the
whole argument of Sonnets I.-XIX.   In Stanza
CLXXX. :—

> ' Alas poore world, what treasure hast thou lost,
> What face remains alive that 's worth the viewing ?
> Whose tongue is musick now ?   What canst thou boast,
> Of things long since, or any thing insuing ?
> The flowers are sweet, their colours fresh, and trim,
> But true sweet beautie liv'd, and di'de with him ' :—

you have that metaphysical gauging of the mystical
importance of some one incarnation of Beauty
viewed from imaginary standpoints in time, which
was afterwards to be elaborated in Sonnets XIV.,
XIX., LIX., LXVII., LXVIII., CIV., CVI.   And in Stanza
CLXX. :—

> ' For he being dead, with him is beautie slaine,
> And beautie dead, blacke Chaos comes again ' :—

you have the succinct *credo* in that incarnation of an
Ideal Beauty, of which all other lovely semblances
are but ' shadows ' and ' counterfeits,' which was
to find a fuller declaration in Sonnets XXXI. and LIII.,
and XCVIII.

But in Shakespeare's Poems the beauty and
curiosity of the ceremonial ever obscure the worship
of the god ; and, perhaps, in the last stanza but one,
addressed to the flower born in place of the dead
Adonis and let drop into the bosom of the Goddess
of Love, you have the most typical expression of

those merits and defects which are alike loved and
condoned by the slaves of their invincible sweetness :—

> ' Here was thy father's bed, here in my brest,
> Thou art the next of blood, and 'tis thy right,
> So in this hollow cradle take thy rest,
> My throbbing hart shall rock thee day and night ;
> There shall not be one minute in an houre
> Wherein I will not kiss my sweet love's floure.'

Here are conceits and a strained illustration from the
profession of law ; but here, with these, are lovely
imagery and perfect diction and, flowing through
every line, a rhythm that rises and falls softly, until,
after a hurry of ripples, it expends itself in the three
last retarding words.

XIII

The Rape of Lucrece was published in 1594, and
was dedicated in terms of devoted affection to Lord
Southampton. It was never so popular as the
Venus, yet editions followed in 1598, 1600, 1607,
1616, 1624, and 1632 [1] ; and its subsequent neglect
remains one of the enigmas of literature. It is
written in the seven-lined stanza borrowed by
Chaucer from Guillaume de Machault, a French
poet, whose talent, according to M. Sandras [2] was
' essentiellement lyrique.' The measure, indeed, is
capable of the most heart-searching lyrical effects.
Chaucer chose it, first for his *Compleint unto Pité* and,
more notably, for his *Troilus and Criseyde* ; in 1589
Puttenham (?) had noted that ' his meetre Heroicall
is very grave and stately,' and was ' most usuall
with our auncient makers ' ; Daniel had used it for

---

[1] Two others of 1596 and 1602 have been cited but never recovered.
[2] *Étude sur G. Chaucer,* 1859.

his *Rosamund,* published four years before *Lucrece,*
Spenser for his *Hymnes,* published the year after.
The subject lay no further than the form from
Shakespeare's hand.   He took it from Ovid's *Fasti.*[1]
Mr. Furnivall has argued that he may also have read
it in Livy's brief version of the tragedy, or in *The
Rape of Lucrece,* from William Painter's *The Palace
of Pleasure* (1566), where, he notes, ' Painter is but
Livy, with some changes and omissions.'   Warton,
History of English Poetry (1824, iv. 241-2), cites ' A
ballet the grevious complaynt of Lucrece,' 1568 ; ' A
ballet of the death of Lucreessia,' 1569 ; and yet
another of 1576.   He adds :—' Lucretia was the
grand example of conjugal fidelity throughout the
Gothic Ages.'   That is the point.   Shakespeare took
the story from Ovid, with the knowledge that
Chaucer had drawn on the same source for the Fifth
Story in his *Legend of Good Women,* just as Chaucer
had taken it from Ovid, with the knowledge that its
appositeness had been consecrated before 1282 in
chapter L. of *Le Roman de la Rose* :—

> ' Comment Lucrece par grant ire
> Son cuer point, derrompt et dessire
> Et chiet morte terre adens,
> Devant son mari et parens.'

And Shakespeare must certainly have been familiar
with the allusion to it in North's *Plutarch,* as with
the passage in Sidney's *Apologie,* where a painting of
Lucrecia is imagined to illustrate the art of those
who are ' indeed right Poets ' as distinguished from
the authors of religious or of moral and metaphysical verse.   This passage, save where it suffers
from the constraint of an apologetic attitude, stands
still for a sound declaration of the ethics of art ; and

[1] Book ii. 721 *et seq.*

in Shakespeare's day, when such questions were canvassed as freely as in our own, it may well have determined his choice.

But speculation on the literary origins of a poem is idle when the poem is in itself far worthier attention than all the materials out of which it has been contrived—the more so when of these the literary origins are the most remote and the least important. Shakespeare, indeed, owes more to the manner of Chaucer's *Troilus* than to the matter of his *Lucretia*, or of its original in Ovid.   For in treating that story the two poets omit and retain different portions : Chaucer, on the whole, copying more closely paints on a canvas of about the same size, whereas Shakespeare expands a passage of 132 lines into a poem of 1855.   Chaucer omits Ovid's note rendered by Shakespeare's

> ' Haply that name of chaste unhap'ly set
> This bateless edge on his keen appetite.'

He also omits Lucretia's unsuspecting welcome of Tarquin, making him ' *stalke* ' straight into the house ' ful theefly.'   Shakespeare retains the welcome, and reserves the phrase, 'Into the chamber wickedly he *stalks*,' for a later incident.   On the other hand, Chaucer renders the passage, ' Tunc quoque jam moriens ne non procumbat honeste, respicit,' some what quaintly :—

> ' And as she fel adown, she cast her look
> And of her clothës yit she hedë took,
> For in her falling yit she haddë care
> Lest that her feet or swichë thing lay bare ' :—

and Shakespeare omits it.   Both keep the image of the lamb and the wolf, together with Lucretia's *flavi capilli*, which are nowhere mentioned by Livy.

In the *Lucrece*, as in the *Venus*, you have a true development of Chaucer's romantic narrative ; of the dialogues, soliloquies, and rhetorical bravuras which render Books IV. and V. of his *Troilus* perhaps the greatest romance in verse. And yet the points of contrast between the *Lucrece* and the *Venus* are of deeper interest than the points of comparison, for they show an ever-widening divergence from the characteristics of Mediæval romance. If the *Venus* be a pageant of gesture, the *Lucrece* is a drama of emotion. You have the same wealth of imagery, but the images are no longer sunlit and sharply defined. They seem, rather, created by the reflex action of a sleepless brain—as it were fantastic symbols shaped from the lying report of tired eyes staring into darkness ; and they are no longer used to decorate the outward play of natural desire and reluctance, but to project the shadows of abnormal passion and acute mental distress. The Poem is full of nameless terror, of ' ghastly shadows ' and ' quick-shifting antics.' The First Act passes in the ' dead of night,' with ' no noise ' to break the world's silence ' but owls' and wolves' death-boding cries,' nor any to mar the house's but the grating of doors and, at last, the hoarse whispers of a piteous controversy. The Second shows a cheerless dawn with two women crying, one for sorrow, the other for sympathy. There are never more than two persons on the stage, and there is sometimes only one, until the crowd surges in at the end to witness Lucrece's suicide. I have spoken for convenience of ' acts ' and a ' stage,' yet the suggestion of these terms is misleading. Excepting in the last speech and in the death of Lucrece, the Poem is nowhere dramatic : it tells a story, but at each situation the Poet pauses to survey and to illustrate the romantic and emotional values of the relation between his characters, or to analyse the moral passions and the mental debates in any one of them, or even the physiological perturbations responding to these storms and tremors of the mind and soul. When Shakespeare describes Tarquin's stealthy approach :—

' Night wandering weazels shriek to see him there ;
They fright him, yet he still pursues his fear ' :—

or Lucrece shrinking from the dawn :—

' Revealing day through every cranny spies
And seems to point her out where she sits weeping ' :—

or Collatine's attempt at railing when he is inarticulate with wrath :—

' Yet some time " Tarquin " was pronounced plain
But through his teeth, as if the name he tore ' :—

his method is wholly alien from the popular methods of our own day. Yet would they be rash who condemned it out of hand.

The illustration of gesture, and of all that passes in the mind, by the copious use of romantic imagery constitutes an artistic process which is obviously charged with sensuous delight, and is in its way not less realistic than the dramatic method which has superseded it. The hours of life, which even ordinary men and women expend in selfish sensation and a fumbling, half-conscious introspection, far outnumber the hours in which they are clearly apprized of eventful action and speech between themselves and their fellows ; and in men of rarer temperament life often becomes a monodrama. The dramatic convention is also but a convention with its own limitations, staling by over-practice into the senseless rallies of a pantomime or the trivial symbols of a meagre psychology. The common-place sayings and doings of the puppets are meant by the author to suggest much ; and, when they are duly explained by the critics, we may all admire the reserved force of the device. But it remains a device. In the romantic narratives of Chaucer, Shakespeare, and Keats, with their imaginative illustrations of the mind's moods and their imagina- tive use of sights and sounds accidental to moments of exacerbated sensation, you have another device which portrays, perhaps more truly, the hidden mysteries of those temperaments whose secrets are really worth our guessing. It is at least worth while to watch an artist, who has shown the inevitable acts and words of any one man in any one situation, at work within upon the accompanying sequence of inevitable sensations and desires. And sometimes, too, from the analysis of emotion in the *Lucrece* you catch a sidelight on the more subtle revelation in the Sonnets :—

> ' O happiness, enjoy'd but of a few,
> And if possest, as soon decayed and done
> As is the morning's silver melting dew
> Against the golden splendour of the sun !
>
> The aim of all is but to nurse the life
> With honour, wealth, and ease in waning age ;
> And in this aim there is such thwarting strife
> That one for all or all for one we gage ;
> As life for honour in fell battle's rage ;
> Honour for wealth ; and oft that wealth doth cost
> The death of all, and all together lost.
>
> What win I if I gain the thing I seek ?
> A dream, a breath, a froth of fleeting joy,
> Who buys a minute's mirth to wail a week
> *Or sells eternity to get a toy ?* '

Vanitas vanitatum! Besides this philosophy of pleasure, there is also a pathos in *Lucrece* which is nowise Mediæval. The Poem is touched with a compassion for the weakness of women, which is new and alien from the trouvère convention of a knight who takes pity on a damsel :—

> ' Their gentle sex to weep are often willing ;
> Grieving themselves to guess at others' smarts,
> And then they drown their eyes, or break their hearts . . .
>
> Though men can cover crimes with bold stern looks,
> Poor women's faces are their own fault's books.'

Then let

> ' No man inveigh against the withered flower,
> But chide rough winter that the flower hath kill'd :
> Not that devour'd, but that which doth devour
> Is worthy blame.'

But in spite of so much that is new in the *Lucrece*, there is no absolute break between it and the *Venus* : the older beauties persist, if they persist more sparsely, among the fresh-blown. As ever in Shakespeare's earlier work, there are vivid impressions of things seen :—

> ' You mocking birds, quoth she, your tunes entomb
> Within your hollow swelling feather'd breasts . . .
>
> Ay me ! the bark peel'd from the lofty pine,
> His leaves will wither, and his sap decay . . .
> As lagging fouls before the Northern blast.
>
> As through an arch the violent roaring tide
> Outruns the eye that doth behold his haste,
> Yet in the eddy boundeth in his pride
> Back to the strait that forced him on so fast ' . . .

Illustrations are still drawn from sport :—

> ' Look, as the full fed hound or gorged hawk
> Unapt for tender smell or speedy flight.' . . .

There are, as ever, conceits :—

> ' Without the bed her other fair hand was,
> On the green coverlet ; whose perfect white
> Showed like an April daisy on the grass . . .'

> ' And now this pale swan in her watery nest
> Begins the sad dirge of her certain ending ' :—

and there are, as I have said, tirades of an astonishing rhetorical force, passages which, recited by an English Rachel, would still bring down the house. As the denunciations of Night :—

> ' Blind muffled bawd ! dark harbour of defame !
> Grim cave of death ! whispering conspirator ' :—

of Opportunity :—

> ' Thy secret pleasure turns to open shame,
> Thy private feasting to a public fast,
> Thy smoothing titles to a ragged name :
> Thy sugard tongue to bitter wormwood tast :
> Thy violent vanities can never last ' :—

and of Time :—

> ' Eater of youth, false slave to false delight,
> Base watch of woes, sin's pack-horse, vertue's snare ' :—

whose glory it is :—

> ' To ruinate proud buildings with thy hours
> And smear with dust their glitt'ring golden towers . . .
> To feed oblivion with decay of things.'

The form of these tirades is repeated from the *Venus*, but their music is louder, and is developed into a greater variety of keys, sometimes into the piercing minors of the more metaphysical Sonnets :—

> ' Why work'st thou mischief in thy pilgrimage ?
> Unless thou could'st return to make amends.
> One poor retiring minute in an age
> Would purchase thee a thousand thousand friends. . . .
>
> Thou ceaseless lackey to eternity ! '

Y

This last apostrophe is great ; but that in *Lucrece* there should be so many of the same tremendous type, which have escaped the fate of hackneyed quotation, is one of the most elusive factors in a difficult problem :—

> ' Pure thoughts are dead and still
> While Lust and Murder wake to stain and kill. . . .
>
> His drumming heart cheers up his burning eye. . . .
>
> Tears harden lust, though marble wears with raining. . . .
>
> Soft pity enters at an iron gate. . . .
>
> Unruly blasts wait on the tender spring,
> Unwholesome weeds take root with precious flowers,
> The adder hisses where the sweet birds sing,
> What virtue breeds, iniquity devours.'

These, for all their strength and sweetness, might conceivably have been written by some other of the greater poets.   But these :—

> ' And dying eyes gleam'd forth their ashy lights. . . .
>
> 'Tis but a part of sorrow that we hear :
> Deep sounds make lesser noise than shallow fords,
> And sorrow ebbs, being blown with wind of words. . . .
>
> O ! that is gone for which I sought to live,
> And therefore now I need not fear to die. . . .
>
> For Sorrow, like a heavy hanging bell,
> Once set on ringing with his own weight goes ' :—

these, I say, could have been written by Shakespeare only.   They may rank with the few which Arnold chose for standards from the poetry of all ages ; yet by a caprice of literary criticism they are never quoted, and are scarce so much as known.

XIV

The fate of Shakespeare's Sonnets has been widely different from the fate of his Narrative Poems.   The *Venus* and the *Lucrece* were popular at once, and ran through many editions : the Sonnets, published in 1609, were not reprinted until 1640, and were then so effectually disguised by an arbitrary process of interpolation, omission, rearrangement, and misleading description as to excite but little attention, until in 1780 Malone opened a new era of research into their bearing on the life and character of Shakespeare.   Since then the tables have been turned.   For while the *Venus* and the *Lucrece* have been largely neglected, so many volumes, in support of theories so variously opposed, have been written on this aspect of the Sonnets, that it has become impossible even to sum up the contention except by adding yet another volume to already overladen shelves.

The controversy has its own interest ; but that interest, I submit, is alien from, and even antagonistic to, an appreciation of lyrical excellence.   I do not mean that the Sonnets are ' mere exercises ' written to ' rival ' or to ' parody ' the efforts of other poets.   Such curiosities of criticism are born of a nervous revulsion from conclusions reached by the more confident champions of a ' personal theory ' ; and their very eccentricity measures the amount of damage done, not by those who endeavour, laudably enough, to retrieve a great lost life, but by those who allow such attempts at biography to bias their consideration of poems which we possess intact.   If, indeed, we must choose between critics, who discover an autobiography in the Sonnets, and critics, who find in them a train of poetic exhalations whose airy iridescence never reflects the passionate colours of this earth, then the first are preferable. At least their theory makes certain additions which, though dubious and defective, are still additions to our guesses at Shakespeare the man ; whereas the second subtracts from a known masterpiece its necessary material of experience and emotion. But we need not choose : the middle way remains of accepting from the Sonnets only the matter which they embody and the form which they display.

Taking them up, then, as you would take up the *Lucrece* or another example of Shakespeare's earlier work, there is nothing to note in their metrical form but the perfection of treatment by which Shakespeare has stamped it for his own. They were immediately preceded by many sonnet-sequences : by so many, indeed, that Shakespeare could hardly have taken his place at the head of his lyrical contemporaries without proving that he, too, could write sonnets with the best of them. Sidney's *Astrophel and Stella* (written 1581-84) had been published in 1591— (when Tom Nash was constrained to bid some other ' Poets and Rimers ' to put out their ' rush candles,' and bequeath their ' crazed quaterzayns ' to the chandlers—for ' loe, here hee cometh that hath broek your legs ')—with the sonnets of ' sundry other noblemen and gentlemen ' appended, among them twenty-eight by S(amuel) and D(aniel), nineteen of which were afterwards reprinted in his *Delia* ; the next year H(enry) C(onstable) published twenty, afterwards reprinted in his *Diana* ; in 1593 B. Barnes published *Parthenophil and Parthenope*, containing a hundred and four (besides madrigals, odes, and eclogues) ; and in 1594 W. Percy, to whom this gathering had been dedicated, riposted in twenty, ' to the fairest Cœlia,' which touch the nadir of incompetence.   But in the same memorable year three other sequences appeared, whose excellence and fame rendered an attempt in this form almost obligatory upon any one claiming to be a poet : H(enry) C(onstable)'s *Diana*, with ' divers quatorzains of honourable and learned personages,'—notably, eight by Sidn'ey, afterwards appended to the Third Edition of the *Arcadia* ; Samuel Daniel's *Delia*, consisting of fifty-five ; [1] and Michael Drayton's *Idea's Mirrour*, fifty-one strong, augmented to fifty-nine in 1599 and eventually (1619) to sixty-three.   Then in 1595 Spenser published his *Amoretti* (written 1592(?)), and in 1596 R. L(inche) his *Diella* and B. Griffin his *Fidessa*.   I name these last because an example from R. Linche :—

> ' My mistress' snow-white skin doth much excell
> The pure soft wool Arcadian sheep do bear ' :—

will show what inept fatuity co-existed with the highest flights of Elizabethan verse ; and because the third number in *Fidessa* [2] was reprinted by Jaggard in the *Passionate Pilgrim* (1599), together with other pieces stolen from Shakespeare and Barnefield.   The publication of such a medley attests the well-known fact that Elizabethan sonnets were handed about in MS. for years among poetical cliques, and, as W. Percy complains, ' were committed to the Press ' without the authors' knowledge, although ' concealed . . . as things privy ' to himself.[3]   It is also worth noting that the Elizabethans I have named,

---

[1] Nineteen of which had appeared, cf. *supra*.

[2] Griffin was almost certainly one of Shakespeare's connections by marriage. See ' Shakespeare's Ancestry,' *The Times*, Oct. 14, 1895.

[3] W. Percy to the Reader.

who signed their sonnet-sequences sometimes only
with initials, often transfigured them by additions,
omissions, and rearrangings prior to republication ;
and this was especially the practice of Daniel and
Drayton, whose sonnets, it so happens, offer the
closest points of comparison to Shakespeare's.   That
two of Shakespeare's should have been published
with the work of others in 1599, and afterwards, with
slight variations, as units in a fairly consecutive
series, is quite in the manner of the time.   There is
no mention of *Delia* in all the twenty-eight appended
by Daniel to *Astrophel and Stella* [1] ; but nineteen of
these were interpolated into the later sequence, which
bears her name, yet mentions it in thirteen only out
of fifty-five.   To glance at Drayton's *Idea* is to be
instantly suspicious of another such mystification.
The proem begins :—

> ' Into these loves, who but for Passion looks,
>   At this first sight here let him lay them by ' :—

and the author goes on to boast that he sings
' fantasticly ' without a ' far-fetched sigh,' an ' Ah
me,' or a ' tear.'   Yet the sixty-first in the completed
series (1619) is that wonderful sob of supplication for
which Drayton is chiefly remembered :—

> ' Since there 's no help, come, let us kiss and part ! '

Only by the use of the comparative method can we
hope to recover the conditions under which sonnets
were written and published in Shakespeare's day.
A sidelight, for instance, is thrown on the half good-
natured, half malicious rivalry between the members
of shifting literary cliques, from the fact that Shakespeare, Chapman, Marston, and Jonson all con-

---

[1] Sonnet XIII. opens thus :—

> ' My *Cynthia* hath the waters of mine eyes.'

tributed poems on the Phœnix to Rob. Chester's *Love's Martyr* (1601),[1] and that sonnets on the same subject occur in Daniel's additions to *Astrophel* (Sonnet III.), and in Drayton's *Idea* (Sonnet XVI.). All six poets are suspected, and some are known, to have been arrayed from time to time on opposed sides in literary quarrels ; yet you find them handling a common theme in more or less friendly emulation. I fancy that many of the coincidences between the Sonnets of Shakespeare and those of Drayton, on which charges of plagiarism have been founded, and by whose aid attempts have been made to fix the date of Shakespeare's authorship, may be explained more probably by this general conception of a verse-loving society divided into emulous coteries. Mr. Tyler adduces the conceit of ' eyes ' and ' heart ' in Drayton's XXXIII. (Ed. 1599), and compares it to Shakespeare's XLVI. and XLVII. (1609) ; but it appears in Henry Constable. Again, he instances Drayton's illustration from a ' map ' in XLIII. [2] ; and, perhaps by reason of the fashionable interest in the New World, the image was a common one : Daniel employs it in his *Defence of Ryme*. And if Drayton, in this sonnet, ' strives to eternize ' the object of his affection in accents echoed by Shakespeare, Daniel does the like in his L. :—

> ' Let others sing of Knights and Palladins
> In aged accents, and untimely words,' etc. :—

with a hit at Spenser that only differs in being a hit from Shakespeare's reference in CVI. :—

> ' When in the chronicle of wasted time
> I see descriptions of the fairest wights
> And beauty making beautiful old rhyme
> In praise of ladies dead and lovely Knights.'

---

[1] See Note IV. on *The Sonnets*.   [2] Ed. 1599 = XLIV. of 1619.

Of course it differs also in poetic excellence ; yet many chancing on Daniel's later line :—

' Against the dark and Time's consuming rage ' ;—

might mistake it for one by the mightier artist. Drayton, like Shakespeare, upbraids someone, whom he compares to the son—and the sex is significant— ' of some rich penny-father,' for wasting his ' Love ' and ' Beauty,' which Time must conquer, ' on the unworthy ' who cannot make him ' survive ' in ' immortal song.' [1] And the next number sounds familiar, with its curious metaphysical conceit of identity between the beloved one and the poet who sings him.[2] If any one had thought it worth his while to investigate the biographical problems of Drayton's obviously doctored *Idea*, he would have found nuts to crack as hard as any in Shakespeare's Sonnets.   It is best, perhaps, to take Sidney's advice, and to ' believe with him that there are many misteries contained in Poetrie, which of purpose were written darkely.'   At any rate, the ironic remainder of the passage throws a flood of light on the extent to which the practice of *immortalising* prevailed :—' Believe ' the poets, he says, ' when they tell you they will make you immortal by their verses,' for, thus doing, ' your name shall flourish in the Printers' shoppes ;   thus doing, you shall bee of kinne to many a poetical preface ;   thus doing, you shall be most fayre, most rich, most wise, most all, you shall dwell upon superlatives.' [3]

Shakespeare's Sonnets, then, belong to a sonneteering age, and exhibit many curious coincidences with the verse of his friends and rivals.   But his true

[1] Sonnet x. Ed. 1619.   [2] Cf. Shakespeare's XXXIX., XLII., LXII.
[3] Sidney, *Apologie*.

distinction in mere metrical form, apart from finer subtleties of art, consists in this : that he established the quatorzain as a separate type of the European Sonnet ; he took as it were a sport from the garden of verse, and fixed it for an English variety. The credit for this has been given to Daniel ; but the attribution cannot be sustained. For Daniel sometimes hankered after the Petrarchan model, though in a less degree than any other of Shakespeare's contemporaries : he travels in Italy,[1] contrasts his Muse with Petrarch's,[2] imitates his structure,[3] and strains after feminine rhymes. Shakespeare alone selected the English quatorzain, and sustained it throughout a sonnet sequence.[4] Even the merit of invention claimed for Daniel must be denied him. When Shakespeare makes Slender say [5] :—' I had rather than forty shillings I had my book of songs and sonnets here ' :—he refers to *Tottel's Miscellany*, published in 1557. But the numbers by the Earl of Surrey in that anthology were written many years earlier, and in the Eighth of his Sonnets there printed, you will find as good a model for Shakespeare's form as any in Daniel's *Delia* :—

> Set me whereas the sunne doth parche the grene
> Or where his beames do not dissolve the yse :
> In temperate heate where he is felt and sene :
> In presence prest of people madde or wise.
> Set me in hye, or yet in lowe degree :
> In longest night, or in the shortest daye :
> In clearest skye, or where clowdes thickest be :
> In lusty youth, or when my heeres are graye.

---

[1] *Delia*, XLVII., XLVIII.   [2] *Ibid.*, XXXVIII.
[3] *Ibid.*, XXXI. and XXXIII. and X. of the Sonnets appended to *Arcadia*.
[4] Sidney and Drayton frequently copy French and Italian models. Spenser's linked quatrains are neither sonnets nor quatorzains : they represent an abortive attempt to create a new form.
[5] *Merry Wives of Windsor*, i. I.

> Set me in heaven, in earth or els in hell,
> In hyll, or dale, or in the fomyng flood :
> Thrall, or at large, alive where so I dwell :
> Sicke or in health : in evyll fame or good.
> > Hers will I be, and onely with this thought
> > Content my selfe, although my chaunce be nought.[1]

The theme is borrowed from Petrarch ; but the form is Surrey's, who used it in nine out of his fourteen sonnets, and essayed the Petrarchan practice in but one.   By this invention he achieved a sweetness of rhythm never attained in any strict imitation of the Italian model until the present century.   His sonnet is the true precursor of Shakespeare's, and it owes—directly—little more than the number of its lines to France and Italy : being founded on English metres of alternating rhymes, with a final couplet copied by Chaucer from the French two centuries before.

The number of sonnet-sequences published in the last decade of the Sixteenth Century, during which Shakespeare lived at London in the midst of a literary movement, raises a presumption in favour of an early date for his Sonnets, published in 1609 ; and this presumption is confirmed by the publication of two of them in *The Passionate Pilgrim* (1599). We know from CIV. that three years had elapsed since he first saw the youth to whom the earlier Sonnets were addressed ; and the balance of internal evidence, founded whether on affinities to the plays or on references to political and social events affecting Shakespeare as a dramatist and a man,[2] points to the years 1599-1602 as the most probable period

---

[1] ' Form and favour ' in Shakespeare's Sonnet CXXV., ' golden tresses ' in his LXVIII. may also be echoes of Surrey.

[2] Cf. Sonnet LXVI. :—' And art made tongue-tied by authority ' :— with the edict of June 1600, inhibiting plays and playgoers.

for their composition.[1] Further confirmation of an
almost decisive character has been adduced by Mr.
Tyler.[2] But I pass his arguments, since they are
based, in part, on the assumption that the youth in
question was William Herbert ; and, although Mr.
Tyler would, as I think, win a verdict from any
jury composed and deciding after the model of Scots
procedure, his case is one which cannot be argued
without the broaching of many issues outside the
sphere of artistic appreciation.

XV

Had Shakespeare's Sonnets suffered the fate of
Sappho's lyrics, their few surviving fragments would
have won him an equal glory, and we should have
been damnified in the amount only of a priceless
bequest. But our heritage is almost certainly intact : the Sonnets, as we find them in the Quarto of
1609, whether or not they were edited by Shakespeare, must so far have commanded his approval
as to arouse no protest against the form in which
they appeared. It would have been as easy for him
to reshuffle and republish as it is impossible to
believe that he could so reshuffle and republish, and
no record of his action survive. Taking the Sonnets,
then, as published in their author's lifetime, you discover their obvious division into two Series :—in the
First, one hundred and twenty-five, closed by an
Envoy of six couplets, are addressed to a youth ;
in the Second, seventeen out of twenty-eight are
addressed to the author's mistress, and the others

---

[1] See Note III. on *The Sonnets*.
[2] Introduction to the ' Shakespeare Q., No. 30 ' and *Shakespeare's
Sonnets*. London, D. Nutt, 1890.

comment, more or less directly, on her infidelity and on his infatuation. Most critics—indeed all not quixotically compelled to reject a reasonable view— are agreed that the order in the First Series can scarce be bettered ; and that within that Series certain Groups may be discerned of sonnets written at the same time, each with the same theme and divided by gaps of silence from the sonnets that succeed them. There is also substantial agreement as to the confines of the principal Groups ; but between these there are shorter sequences and even isolated numbers, among which different critics have succeeded in tracing a greater or lesser degree of connection. The analogy of a correspondence, carried on over years between friends, offers perhaps the best clue to the varying continuity of the First Series. There, too, you have silences which attest the very frequency of meetings, with silences born of long absence and absorption in diverse pursuits ; there, too, you have spells of voluminous writing on intimate themes, led up to and followed by sparser communications on matters of a less dear importance. The numbers seem to have been chronologically arranged ; and, that being so, the alternation of continuous with intermittent production shows naturally in a collection of poems addressed by one person to another at intervals over a period of more than three years.

There are seven main groups in the First Series :—

Group A, I.-XIX. :—The several numbers echo the arguments in *Venus and Adonis,* Stanzas XXVII.- XXIX. They are written, ostensibly, to urge marriage on a beautiful youth, but, essentially, they constitute a continuous poem on Beauty and Decay. That is the subject, varied by the introduction of two subsidiary themes; the one, philosophic, on immortality conferred by breed :—

> ' From fairest creatures, we desire increase
> That thereby beauty's *Rose* might never die ' :—

the other, literary, on immortality conferred by verse :—

> ' My love shall in my verse ever live young.'

This line is the last of the sonnet which serves as an envoy to the Group. Here follow Sonnets XX.-XXI., XXII., XXIII.-XXIV., XXV. : occasional verses written, playfully or affectionately, to the youth who is now dear to their author. In giving the occasional sonnets I bracket only those which are obviously connected and obviously written at the same time.

Group B, XXVI.-XXXII. :—A continuous poem on absence, dispatched, it may be, in a single letter, since it opens with a formal address and ends in a full close. In this group there are variations on the disgust of separation and the solace of remembered love ; but it is a poem and not a letter—turning each succeeding emotion to its full artistic account.

Group C, XXXIII.-XLII. :—The first of the more immediately personal garlands. The writer's friend has wronged him by stealing his mistress's love. The counterpart to this group, evidently written on the same theme and at the same time, will be found in the Second Series (CXXXIII.-CXLIV.), addressed in complaint to the writer's mistress, or written in comment on her complicity in this wrong. The biographical interest of this Group has won it an undeserved attention at the expense of others. Many suppose that all the Sonnets turn on this theme, or, at least, that the loudest note of passion is here sounded. But this is not so. Of all ten three

at the most can be called tragic.   These are XXXIV.—
but it arises out of the lovely imagery of XXXIII.,
XXXVI., but it ends :—

> ' I love thee in such sort
> As thou being mine, mine is thy good report ' ;

and XL., but it ends :—' Yet we must not be foes.'
XXXIII. is indeed beautiful, but the others return to
the early theme of mere immortalising, or are expressed in abstruse or playful conceits which make
it impossible to believe they mirror a soul in pain.
They might be taken for designed interpolations,
did they not refer, by the way, to a sorrow, or misfortune, not to be distinguished from the theme of
their fellows.   Knowing what Shakespeare can do to
express anguish and passion, are we not absurd to
find the evidence of either in these Sonnets, written,
as they are, on a private sorrow, but in the spirit of
conscious art ?

> ' If my slight Muse do please these curious days
> The pain be mine, but thine shall be the praise.'—XXXVIII.

Here follow XLIII., XLIV.-XLV., XLVI.-XLVII.-XLVIII.,
XLIX., L.-LI., LII., connected or occasional pieces on
mere absence.   Then LIII.-LIV., and LV. return to the
theme of immortalising.   The first two are steeped
in Renaissance platonism ;   while the last (as Mr.
Tyler has shown) does but versify a passage in
which Meres quotes Ovid and Horace (1598) :   it
seems to be an Envoy.

  Group D, LVI.-LXXIV. :—The Poet writes again
after silence :—' Sweet love, renew thy force.'   The
first three are occasioned by a voluntary absence of
his friend ;   but that absence, unexpectedly prolonged, inspires a mood of contemplation which,
becoming ever more and more metaphysical, is by

much removed from the spirit of the earlier poem on absence (*Group B,* XXVI.-XXXII.) with its realistic handling of the same theme. In LIX. the poet dwells on the illusion of repeated experience, and speculates on the truth of the philosophy of cycles :—

> ' If there be nothing new, but that which is
> Hath been before, how are our brains beguiled.'

In LX. he watches the changing toil of Time :—

> ' Like as the waves make towards the pebbled shore
> So do our minutes hasten to their end.'

In LXI. he gazes into the night at the phantasm of his absent friend, and thus leads up to a poem in three parts (LXII.-LXV., LXVI.-LXX., LXXI.-LXXIV.) on Beauty that Time must ruin, on the disgust of Life, and on Death. These nineteen numbers, conceived in a vein of melancholy contemplation, are among the most beautiful of all, and are more subtly metaphysical than any, save only CXXIII., CXXIV., CXXV. There follow LXXV., LXXVI., LXXVII.

Group E, LXXVIII.-LXXXVI., is the second of a more immediate personal interest. It deals with rival poets and their meretricious art—especially with one Poet who by ' the proud full sail of his great verse ' has bereft the writer of his friend's admiration. The nine are written in unbroken sequence and are playful throughout, suggesting no tragedy.

But in *Group F,* LXXXVII.-XCVI., the spirit of the verse suddenly changes : the music becomes plangent, and the theme of utter estrangement is handled with a complete command over dramatic yet sweetly modulated discourse. The Group is, indeed, a single speech of tragic intensity, written in elegiac verse more exquisite than Ovid's own. Here the First Series is most obviously broken, and XCVII.

xcviii.-xcix. emphasise the break. They tell of
two absences, the first in late summer (xcvi.), the
second in the spring. They are isolated from the
Group which precedes, and the Group which follows
them, and they embrace an absence extending, at
least, from early autumn in one year to April in the
next. The first is of great elegiac beauty, the second
of curious metaphysical significance ; the third seems
an inferior, perhaps a rejected, version of the second.

Group G, c.-cxxv., opens after a great silence :—
' Where art thou, Muse, that thou forget'st so long ' :
—and the poet develops in it a single sustained attack
on the Law of Change, minimising the importance of
both outward chances and inward moods. Once
more taking his pen, he invokes his Muse (c.) ' to be
a satire to Decay,' to bring contempt on ' Time's
spoils,' and to ' give fame faster than Time wastes
Life.' True, he argued against this in *Group E* :
deprecating (lxxxii.) ' strained touches of rhetoric '
when applied to one ' truely fair ' and, therefore,
' truely sympathized ' by ' true plain words ' :
maintaining (lxxxiii.) that silence at least did not
' impair beauty,' and disparaging (lxxxv.) ' comments of praise richly compiled.' But now he puts
this same defence into the mouth of his Muse, making
her argue in turn (ci.) that Truth and Beauty, which
both ' depend on ' his Love, need no ' colour ' and
no ' pencil ' since ' best is best, if never intermixed.'
Yet he bids her ' excuse not silence so,' since it lies
in her to make his love ' outlive a guilded tomb,'
and ' seem long hence as he shows now.' In this
Group, as in earlier resumptions, the music is at
first imperfect. But it soon changes, and in cii.
the apology for past silence is sung in accents sweet
as the nightingale's described. There are marked

irregularities in the poetic excellence of the Sonnets :
which ever climbs to its highest pitch in the longer
and more closely connected sequences.   This is the
longest of all : a poem of retrospect over a space
of three years to the time when ' love was new, and
then but in the spring.'   In its survey it goes over
the old themes with a soft and silvery touch : Beauty
and Decay, Love, Constancy, the Immortalising of
the Friend's beauty conceived as an incarnation of
Ideal Beauty viewed from imaginary standpoints in
Time.   And interwoven with this rehandling, chiefly
of the themes in the First and Fourth Groups, is
an apology (CIX.-CXII., CXVII.-CXX., CXXII.) for a
negligence on the Poet's part of the rites of friendship, which he sets off (CCC.) against his Friend's
earlier unkindness :—' *That you were once unkind,
befriends me now.*'   This apology offers the third, and
only other, immediate reference to Shakespeare's
personal experience ; and, on these sonnets, as on
those which treat of the Dark Lady and the Rival
Poet, attention has been unduly concentrated.   They
seem founded on episodes and moods necessarily
incidental to the life which we know Shakespeare
must have led.   To say that he could never have
slighted his art as an actor :—

> ' Alas, 'tis true I have gone here and there
> And made myself a motley to the view . . .
>
> My nature is subdued
> To what it works in like the dyer's hand ' :—

and then to seek for far-fetched and fantastic in-
terpretations is to evince an ignorance, not only of
the obloquy to which actors were then exposed, and
of the degradations they had to bear, but also of
human nature as we know it even in heroes.

Wellington is said to have wept over the carnage at Waterloo; the grossness of his material often infects the artist, and 'potter's rot' has its analogue in every profession. This feeling of undeserved degradation is a mood most incident to all who work, whether artists or men of action : an accident, real but transitory, which obliterates the contours of the soul, and leaves them intact, as a fog swallows the Town without destroying it.

In cxxi. there is a natural digression from this personal apology to reflections cast on Shakespeare's good name. In cxxii. the apology is resumed with particular reference to certain tablets, the gift of the Friend, which the Poet has bestowed on another. He takes this occasion to resume the main theme of the whole group by pouring contempt on ' dates ' and ' records ' and ' tallies to score his dear love ' : the tablets, though in fact given away, are still ' within his brain, full charactered, beyond all date even to Eternity.' Thus does he lead up directly to the last three sonnets (cxxiii., cxxiv., cxxv.), which close this ' Satire to Decay,' and with it the whole series (i.-cxxv.). They are pieces of mingled splendour and obscurity in which Shakespeare presses home his metaphysical attack on the reality of Time ; and the difficulty, inherent in an argument so transcendental, is further deepened by passing allusions to contemporary events and persons, which many have sought to explain, with little success. Here follows an Envoy of six couplets to the whole Series.

The Second Series shows fewer traces of design in its sequence than the First. The magnificent cxxix. on ' lust in action ' is wedged between two : one addressed to Shakespeare's mistress and one descriptive of her charm ; both playful in their fancy.

CXLVI. to his soul, with its grave pathos and beauty, follows on a foolish verbal conceit, written in octo-syllabic verse ; while CLIII. and CLIV. are contrived in the worst manner of the French Renaissance on the theme of a Greek Epigram.[1] But the rest are, all of them, addressed to a Dark Lady whom Shake-speare loved in spite of her infidelity, or they com-ment on the wrong she does him. It cannot be doubted that they were written at the same time and on the same subject as the sonnets in Group C, XXXIII.-XLII., or that they were excluded from that group on any ground except that of their being written to another than the Youth to whom the whole First Series is addressed. Like the numbers in Group C, they are alternately playful and pathetic ; their diction is often as exquisite, their discourse often as eloquent. But sometimes they are sardonic and even fierce :—

> ' For I have sworn thee fair and thought thee bright,
> Who art as black as hell, as dark as night.'

XVI

The division of the Sonnets into two Series and a number of subsidiary Groups springs merely from the author's actual experiences, which were the occasions of their production, and from the order in time of those experiences. But the poetic themes suggested by such experiences and their treatment by Shakespeare belong to another sphere of con-sideration. They derive — not from the brute chances of life which, in a man not a poet, would have suggested no poetry, and, to a poet not Shake-speare, would have dictated poetry of another

[1] Dowden, 1881.

character and a lesser perfection, but—from Shakespeare's inborn temperament and acquired skill, both of selection and execution.   These poetic themes are comparatively few in number, and recur again and again in the several Groups.   Some are more closely connected with the facts of Shakespeare's life ; others embody the general experience of man ; others, again, detached, not only from the life of Shakespeare but, from the thought of most men, embody the transcendental speculations of rare minds which, at certain times and places—in Socratic Athens and in the Europe of the Renaissance —have commanded a wide attention.   Follows a tabulation.

(1) Themes personal to Shakespeare :—

> *His Friend's Error.*   Group C, XXXIII.-XLII., XCIV.-XCVI., CXX. CXXXIII.-CXXXV.
> *The Dark Lady.*   Group C, and the Second Series, CXXVII.-CLII.
> *His Own Error.*   XXXVI., CX., CXII., CXVII.-CXXII.
> *His Own Misfortune.*   XXV., XXIX., XXXVII., CXI.
> *The Rival Poets.*   XXI., XXXII., Group E, LXXVIII.-LXXXVI., and (as I hold) LXVII., LXVIII., LXXVI., and CXXV.

That there were more Rival Poets than one is evident from LXXVIII. 3 :—

> ' Every alien pen hath got my use,
> And under thee their poesy disperse ' :—

and from LXXXIII. 12 :—

> ' For I impair not beauty, being mute
> When others would give life.'

And among these others who still sing, while the Poet is himself silent, two are conspicuous :—

> ' There lives more life in one of your fair eyes
> Than *both your poets* can in praise devise.'

(2) Themes which embody general experience :—

Love.   XX.-XXXII., XXXVII., XLIII.-LII., LVI., LXIII., LXVI.,
 LXXI., LXXII., LXXV., LXXXVII.-XCII., XCVI., CII., CV., CXV.-
 CXVI.
Absence.   Group B, XXVI.-XXXI., XXXIX., XLIII.-LII., LVII.,
 LVIII., XCVII., XCVIII.
Beauty and Decay.   Group A, I.-XIX., XXII., LXXVII.

At times this Theme is treated in a mood of contemplation remote from general experience—as in
LIV., LV., LX., LXIII.-LXV.,—and, thus handled, may
serve, with two Themes, derived from it :—

Immortality by Breed.   I.-XIV., XVI., XVII.
Immortality by Verse.   XV., XVII.-XIX., XXXVIII., LIV., LV.,
 LX., LXV., LXXIV., LXXXI., C., CI., CVII. :—

for a transition to (3) Themes which are more
abstruse and demand a more particular examination.

Identity with his Friend :—

xx.   ' My glass shall not persuade me I am old
        So long as youth and thou are of one date. . . .

        For all that beauty that doth cover thee
        Is but the seemly raiment of my heart. . . .'

xxxix.   ' What can mine own praise to mine own self bring ?
          And what is 't but mine own when I praise thee ? . . .

xlii.   ' But here 's the joy : my friend and I are one. . . .'

lxii.   ' 'Tis thee, myself, that for myself I praise,
         Painting my age with beauty of thy days. . . .'

cxxxiii.   ' Me from my self thy cruel eye hath taken
            And my next self (his friend) thou harder hast
            ingrossed ' . . .

cxxxiv.   ' My self I 'll forfeit, so that other mine
            Thou wilt restore.'

The conceit of Identity with the person addressed is
but a part of the machinery of Renaissance Platonics

derived, at many removes, from discussions in the Platonic Academy at Florence. Michelangelo had written in 1553 :—' If I yearn day and night without intermission to be in Rome, it is only in order to return again to life, which I cannot enjoy without the soul ' [1]—viz., his friend.

The Idea of Beauty.

In XXXVII. ' That I . . . by a part of all thy glory live ' is a ' *Shadow*,' cast by his Friend's excellence, which yet ' doth such *substance* give ' that ' I am not lame, poor, nor despised.' In XXXI. all whom the Poet has loved and ' supposed dead '—' love and all Love's loving parts '—are not truly dead, ' but things removed that hidden in there lie '—viz.—in the Friend's bosom :—

> ' Their images I lov'd I view in thee,
> And thou, all they, hast all the all of me.'

The mystical confusion with and in the Friend of all that is beautiful or lovable in the Poet and others is a development from the Platonic theory of the IDEA OF BEAUTY : the eternal type of which all beautiful things on earth are but shadows. It is derived by poetical hyperbole from the Poet's prior identification of the Friend's beauty with Ideal Beauty. The theory of Ideal Beauty was a common feature of Renaissance Poetry throughout Europe. Du Bellay had sung it in France fifty years before Shakespeare in England :—

> ' Là, O mon âme, au plus haut ciel guidée,
> Tu y pourras recognoistre l'idée
> De la beauté qu'en ce monde j'adore.'

We need not infer that Shakespeare studied Du Bellay's verse or the great *corpus* of Platonic poetry

[1] J. A. Symonds's translation.

in Italy. Spenser, who translated some of Du Bellay's sonnets at seventeen, had touched the theory in his *Hymne of Heavenly Beautie* (1596) :—

> ' More faire is that (heaven), where those *Idees* on hie
> Enraungèd be, which *Plato* so admired ' :—

and had set it forth at length in his *Hymne in Honour of Beautie* (1596) :—

> ' *What time this world's great Workmaister* did cast
> To make all things such as we now behold,
> It seems that he before his eyes had plast
> A goodly Paterne. . . .
>
> That wondrous Paterne . . .
> Is perfect *Beautie*, which all men adore. . . .
>
> How vainely then do ydle wits invent,
> That *Beautie* is nought else but mixture made
> Of colours faire. . . .
>
> Hath white and red in it such wondrous powre,
> That it can pierce through th' eyes unto the hart . . .?
>
> That *Beautie* is not, as fond men misdeeme,
> An outward shew of things that only seeme. . . .
>
> But that faire lampe . . .
> . . . is heavenly born(e) and cannot die,
> Being a parcell of the purest skie. . . .
>
> Therefore where-ever that thou doest behold
> A comely corpse, with beautie faire endewed,
> Know this for certaine, that the same doth hold
> A beauteous soul. . . .'

Mr. Walter Raleigh has pointed out to me that Spenser and Shakespeare must have been familiar with Hoby's translation of Baldassare Castiglione's *Il Cortegiano*, published in 1561.[1] Indeed Spenser in his *Hymne in Honour of Beautie* does but versify

---

[1] ' *The Courtyer* of Count Baldessar Castilio divided into foure bookes. Very necessary and profitable for yonge Gentilmen and Gentilwomen abiding in Court, Palaice or Place, done into Englyshe by Thomas Hoby. Imprinted at London by Wyllyam Seres at the signe of the Hedghogge,

the argument of Hoby's admirable Fourth Book.
'Of the *beawtie*,' Hoby writes, 'that we meane,
which is onlie it that appeereth in bodies, and
especially in the face of man . . . we will terme it
an influence of the heavenlie bountifulness, the whiche
for all it stretcheth over all thynges that be created
(like the light of the Sonn) yet when it findeth out a
face well proportioned, and framed with a certein
livelie agreement of severall colours, and set forth
with lightes and shadowes, and with an orderly
distance and limites of lines, thereinto it distilleth
itself and appeereth most welfavoured, and decketh
out and lyghtneth the subject, where it shyneth with
a marveylous grace and glistringe (like the sonne
beames that strike against a beautifull plate of fine
golde wrought and sett with precyous jewelles).'

In Hoby's exposition the beauty of the human face
is the best reflector of the Heavenly Beauty which,
like the sunlight, is reflected from all things—from
the 'world,' the 'heaven,' the 'earth,' the 'sun,'
the 'moon,' the 'planets'—from 'fowls,' 'trees,'
'ships,' 'buildings' — even from the 'roof of
houses': so that 'if under the skye where there
falleth neyther haile nor rayne a mann should builde
a temple without a reared ridge, it is to be thought,
that it coulde have neyther a sightly showe nor any
beawtie. Beeside other thinges therefore, it giveth
great praise to the world, in saying that it is
beawtifull. It is praised, in sayinge, the beawtifull
heaven, beawtifull earth, beawtifull sea, beawtifull
rivers, beawtifull•wooddes, trees, gardeines, beawtifull cities, beawtifull churches, houses, armies. In
conclusion this comelye and holye beawtie is a

1561.' Cf. 'Adieu, my true court-friend: farewell my dear Castilio':—
where *Malevole* addresses *Bilioso*.—Marston's *The Malcontent*, i. i. 302.

wonderous settinge out of everie thinge. And it may be said that *Good and beautifull* be after a sort one selfe thinge, especiallie in the bodies of men : of the beawtie whereof the nighest cause (I suppose) is the beawtie of the soule : the which as a partner of the right and heavenlye beawtie, maketh sightly and beawtifull what ever she toucheth.' Plato's theory of Beauty had been ferried long before from Byzantium to Florence, and had there taken root, so that Michelangelo came to write :—

> ' Lo, all the lovely things we find on earth,
>   Resemble for the soul that rightly sees
>   That source of bliss divine which gave us birth :
> Nor have we first-fruits or remembrances
>   Of heaven elsewhere. Thus, loving loyally,
>   I rise to God, and make death sweet by thee.' [1]

And from Italy young noblemen, accredited to Italian courts or travelling for their pleasure, had brought its influence to France and England. So you have Spenser's *Hymne* ; Drayton harping on *Idea* [2] ; and Barnfield (1595) apostrophising the sects :—

> ' The Stoicks thinke (and they come neere the truth)
>   That vertue is the chiefest good of all,
>   The Academicks on *Idea* call.'

Shakespeare must have read Spenser's *Hymn* and Hoby's *Courtyer*, in which Plato, Socrates, and

---

[1] J. A. Symonds's translation. The great body of Platonic poetry did not pass without cavil even in Italy, for thus does the Blessed Giovenale Ancina state the defence and his reply :—' Mi rispose per un poco di scudo alla difesa, non esser cio tenuto ivi per lascivo, ne disonesto amore, se ben vano, e leggiero, ma *Platonico*, civile, modesto, con simplicità, e senza malitia alcuna, e per consequente poi honesto, gratioso, e comportabile. Al che sogginusi io subito, non amor *Platonico*, nò, ma si ben veramente *Plutonico*, civè Satanico, e Infernale.' *Nuove Laudi Ariose della Beatissima Virgine.* Rome. 1600.

[2] On the title-page of *The Shepherd's Garland*, 1593 ; *Ideas Mirrour*, 1594, etc.

Plotinus are all instanced : the phrase — *genio Socratem* — applied to him in the epitaph on his monument attests his fondness for Platonic theories ; he was conversant with these theories, and in the Sonnets he addressed a little audience equally conversant with them ; it is, therefore, not surprising that he should have borrowed their terminology. In some sonnets he does so, but the *Sonnets* are not, therefore, as some have argued, an exposition of Plato's theory or of its Florentine developments. Shakespeare in certain passages does but lay under contribution the philosophy of his time just as, in other passages, he lays under contribution the art and occupations of his time, and in others, more frequently, the eternal processes of nature. His *Sonnets* are no more a treatise of philosophy than they are a treatise of law. So far, indeed, is he from pursuing, as Spenser did pursue, a methodical exposition of the Platonic theory that he wholly inverts the very system whose vocabulary he has rifled. The Friend's beauty is no longer Hoby's ' plate of fine gold,' which reflects Eternal Beauty more brilliantly than aught else. For a greater rhetorical effect it becomes in Shakespeare's hand itself the very archetypal *pattern* and *substance* of which all beautiful things are but *shadows*.[1]

In I. the Poet urges the youth to marry, ' That thereby Beauty's *Rose* might never die ' :—

> XIV. ' *Truth* and *Beauty* shall together thrive
> If from thy self to store thou would'st convert :
> Or else of thee this I prognosticate,
> Thy end is *Truth's* and *Beauty's* doom and date.'

---

[1] ' Shadow ' (Lat. *umbra*) was the term of art in Renaissance Platonism for the Reflection of the Eternal Type. Giordano Bruno discoursed in Paris ' *De Umbris Idearum.*'

XIX. His is ' Beauty's *pattern* to succeeding men.'

LIII. ' What is your *substance*, whereof are you made
That millions of strange *shadows* on you tend ?
Since every one hath, every one, one shade,
And you, but one, can every *shadow* lend.'

The beauty of Adonis is such a *shadow,* so is the
beauty of Helen: the ' spring of the year . . . doth
shadow of your beauty show . . . and you in every
blessed shape we know. In all external grace you
have some part.' And in XCVIII. ' The lily's white,
the deep vermilion in the rose ' are :—

' But figures of delight, drawn after you, you *pattern* of
all those,'

' As with your *shadow* I with these did play.'

The Truth of Beauty.

The theme of the IDEA OF BEAUTY, of his friend's
beauty as the incarnation of an eternal type, is often
blended with another metaphysical theme—THE
TRUTH OF BEAUTY, *e.g.* in XIV. (*supra*). LIV.:—*Truth*
is an ornament which makes ' *Beauty* ' seem more
beauteous. Here the Poet seems to equivocate on
the double sense, moral and intellectual, of our word
Truth, comparable to the double sense of our word
Right, if, indeed, this be altogether a confusion of
thought arising from poverty of language, and not
a mystical perception by poets of some higher
harmony between the Beautiful, the Good, and the
True. Goethe wrote :—*Das Schöne enthält das Gute* ;
and Keats :—

' Beauty is Truth, Truth Beauty, that is all
Ye know on earth and all ye need to know.'

Many hold this for madness, but if that it be, it has
been a part of the ' divine madness ' of poets since

they first sang—' the most excellent of all forms of enthusiasm (or possession) ' ; [1] and Shakespeare, when he handles the TRUTH OF BEAUTY, does so almost always with but a secondary allusion, or with no allusion at all, to his Friend's constancy. He argues that the IDEA OF BEAUTY, embodied in his Friend's beauty, of which all other beautiful things are but shadows, is also Truth : an exact coincidence with an ' eternal form ' to which transitory present-ments do but approximate.   Plato wrote :—' Beauty alone has ' any such manifest image of itself : ' so that it is the clearest, the most certain of all things, and the most lovable,' [2] and Shakespeare (*Lucrece*, ll. 29-30) :—

> ' Beauty itself doth of itself persuade
> The eyes of men without an orator.'

Thus, in LXII., the Poet looks in the glass and thinks :—

> ' No face so gracious is as mine,
> No shape so *true*, no *truth of such account*.'

And why is his shape so *true* and the *truth* of it so important ?   Because, reverting to the theme of *Identity*, his shape is that of the Friend's beauty :—

> ' 'Tis thee (myself) that for myself I praise,
> Painting my age with *beauty* of thy days. . . .'

Again in CI. :—

> ' O Truant Muse, what shall be thy amends
> For thy neglect of *truth* in *beauty* dyed ?
> Both *truth* and *beauty* on my love depends.'

And the Poet makes his Muse reply :—

> ' *Truth* needs no colour with his colour fixt,
> *Beauty* no pencil *beauty's truth* to lay :
> But best is best, if never intermixt.'

---

[1] Plato's *Phædrus*. *Plato and Platonism*, Pater, 156.   [2] *Ibid.*, 158.

False Art Obscures the Truth of Beauty.

In this last passage the Poet resumes an argument, put forward in earlier numbers, that the beauty of his Friend, being true, can only suffer from ' false painting ' and ' ornament.' While so defending Beauty, which is Truth, from the disfigurement of false ornament, Shakespeare compares the false art of the Rival Poets, who also sing his Love, with the common practices of painting the cheeks [1] and wearing false hair [2] :—

> XXI. ' So is it not with me as with that Muse,
> Stirred by a painted beauty to his verse,
> Who heaven itself for *ornament* doth use,
> And every fair with his fair doth rehearse. . . .
> O let me *true* in love but *truly* write,
> And then believe me my love is as *fair*
> As any mother's child.'

In LXVII. all these themes are brought together :—

> ' Why should *false painting* immitate his cheek
> And steal dead seeing of his living hue ?
> Why should poor *Beauty* indirectly seek
> Roses of *shaddow*, since his Rose is *true* ? '

In LXVIII. ' His cheek is the map of days out-worn, before the golden tresses of the dead . . . were

---

[1] Cf. Richard Barnfield, *The Complaint of Chastitie*, 1594. An obvious echo of the tirades in Shakespeare's *Lucrece*. He writes of many :—

> ' Whose lovely cheeks (with rare vermillion tainted)
> Can never blush because their faire is painted.'

> ' O faire-foule tincture, staine of Women-kinde,
> Mother of Mischiefe, Daughter of Deceate,
> False traitor to the Soule, blot to the Minde,
> Usurping Tyrant of true Beautie's seate ;
> Right Coisner of the eye, lewd Follie's baite,
> The flag of filthiness, the sinke of Shame,
> The Divell's dey, dishonour of thy name.'

[2] Cf. Bassanio's speech, *Merchant of Venice*, iii. 2 :—' The world is still deceived by ornament.'

shorn away . . . to live a second life on second head ' :—

> ' And him as for a map doth nature store
> To shew *false art* what Beauty was of yore.'

Here ' false art ' cannot refer, at any rate exclusively, to the actual use of fucuses and borrowed locks, for when the theme is resumed (LXXXII.), the illustration of ' gross painting ' is directly applied to the ' false art ' of the Rival Poets :—

> ' When they have devized
> What strained touches Rhetoric can lend,
> Thou, *truly fair*, were *truly* sympathised
> In *true* plain words, by thy true telling friend.
> And their *gross painting* might be better used
> Where cheeks need blood, in thee it is abused.'

LXXXIII. continues :—

> ' I never saw that you did *painting* need,
> And therefore to your fair no *painting* set. . . .
> Their lives more life in one of your fair eyes
> Than both your *Poets* can in *praise* devize.'

And in LXXXIV. :—

> ' Who is it that says most, which can say more
> Than this rich praise, that you alone are you.'

This ' false painting ' is the ' false art ' of the Rival Poets in LXXXV., their ' praise richly compiled,' their ' golden quill ' and ' precious phrase by all the Muses filed.'

Imaginary Standpoints in Time.

The Poet views this *Ideal Beauty* of his friend from *Imaginary Standpoints in Time.* He looks back on it from an imaginary future (CIV.), and tells the ' Age unbred, Ere you were born was Beauty's summer dead.' He looks forward to it from the past, and,

the descriptions of the fairest wights in the Chronicle
of wasted Time (CVI.) shew him that

> 'Their antique pen would have exprest
> Even such Beauty as you master now.'

So all their ' praises are but prophesies.'   Sometimes,
with deeper mysticism, he all but accepts the *Illusion
of Repeated Experience* for a truth of Philosophy.
' If there be nothing new, but that which is, hath
been before ' (LIX.), then might ' Record with a backward look

> Even of five hundred courses of the sun
> Show me your image in some antique book.'

For his Friend's beauty is more than a perfect type
prophesied in the past : it is a re-embodiment of
perfection as perfection was in the prime :—

LXVII.   ' O, him she (Nature) stores, to show what wealth she
  had
  In days *long since* before these last so bad . . .'

LXVIII.   ' And him as for a map doth Nature store
  To shew false art what Beauty was *of yore.*'

The Unreality of Time.

Since this Ideal Beauty is true, is very Truth, it is
independent of Time, and eternal ; it, with the love it
engenders, is also independent of accident, and is
unconditioned :—

CVII.   ' Eternal love in love's fresh case
  Weighs not the dust and injury of age,
  Nor gives to necessary wrinkles place,
  But makes antiquity for aye his page . . .'

CXVII.   ' Love 's not Time's fool, though rosy lips and cheeks
  Within his bending sickle's compass come.'

Thus does the whole Series culminate in an *Attack
on the Reality of Time.*—CXXIII., CXXIV., CXXV. are

obscure to us ; yet they are written in so obvious a sequence, and with so unbroken a rhythmical swing, as to preclude the idea of extensive corruption in the text.   They must once have been intelligible.   Some attempts at elucidation have been made by fixing on single words, such as ' state ' (CXXIV. 1) and ' canopy ' (CXXV. 1), and then endeavouring to discover an allusion to historical events or to the supposed nobility of the person to whom the verses were addressed.   But these attempts dissemble the main drift of the verses' meaning, which is clearly directed, at least in CXXIII. and CXXIV., against the reality and importance of Time.   In C., which opens this Group (C.-CXXV.), the Poet has bidden his Muse to ' make Time's spoils despised everywhere.'   In CXVI. he has declared that Love is an eternal power, of a worth unknown, but immeasurably superior to the accidents of Time.   In LIX. he has urged that even our thoughts may be vain repetitions of a prior experience :—

> ' If there be nothing new, but that which is
> Hath been before, how are our brains beguiled
> Which labouring for invention bear amiss,
> The second burthen of a former child ? '

And here, in a magnificent hyperbole, he asserts that ' pyramids ' (1, 2) built up by Time with a might which is 'newer' by comparison with his own change-lessness, are, for all their antiquity, but ' new dress-ings ' of sights familiar to ante-natal existence :—

> ' Our dates are brief and therefore we admire
> What thou dost foist upon us that is old.'

So far there is fairly plain sailing, but the ensuing Lines 7, 8, constitute a real crux :—

> ' And rather make them born(e) to our desire
> Than think that we before have heard them told ' :

Assuming these lines to refer to 'what' Time 'foists
upon us,' the second implies that we ought to
recognise the old things foisted upon us by Time
for objects previously known, but that we 'prefer
to regard them as really new'—as just 'born'—
(Tyler), and 'specially created for our satisfaction'
(Dowden). The explanation is not satisfactory,
though probably the best to be got from the assumed
reference. But (1) this reference of 'them' to
'what' followed by a singular 'that is,' can hardly
be sustained grammatically, and (2) it scarce makes
sense. Shakespeare cannot have intended that we
admire things for their age while 'we regard them
as really new.' I suggest that the plural 'them'
refers grammatically to the plural 'dates,' and that
the word usually printed 'born'[1] in line 7 had
best be printed 'borne' as it is in the Quarto[2]
(='bourn'). We make our brief dates into a bourn
or limit to our desire (cf. 'confined doom,' CVII. 4)
instead of recollecting that 'we have heard them
told' (=reckoned) 'before.' There is but a colon in
the Quarto after line 8. And the third Quatrain
continues to discuss dates (=registers, line 9, and
records, line 11). In line 11 Shakespeare denies the
absolute truth both of Time's records and the witness
of our senses :—

> For thy records and what we see doth lie.'

The sonnet, in fact, does but develop the attack of the
one before it (CXXII.), in which he declares that the
memory of his Friend's gift 'shall remain beyond all
date even to Eternity ; that such a 'record' is better
than the 'poor retention' of tablets ; and that he
needs no ' " tallies " to " score " his dear love.'

---

[1] Printed so first by Gildon, and accepted by subsequent editors.
[2] Borne (French), and in Hamlet, Folio 1623 and Quarto.

In cxxiv. line 1:—' If my dear love were but the child of *State* ' :—' State ' may contain a secondary allusion (as so often with Shakespeare) to the dignity of the person addressed ; but its primary meaning, continuing the sense of the preceding sonnet, and indeed of all the numbers from c., is ' condition ' or ' circumstance.' (Cf. ' Interchange of *state* and *state* itself confounded to decay,' lxiv. ; and ' Love's great *case* ' in cviii.). If his Love were the child of circumstance it might be disinherited by any chance result of Fortune ; but on the contrary, ' it was builded far from *accident*.' And ' *accident*,' as were ' *case* ' and ' *State*,' is also a term of metaphysic : his Love belongs to the absolute and unconditioned, to Eternity and not to Time. In developing the idea of mutations in fortune, Shakespeare glances aside at some contemporary reverse in politics or art which we cannot decipher. It may have been the closing of the Theatres, the censorship of Plays, the imprisonment of Southampton or of Herbert. No one can tell, nor does it matter, for the main meaning is clear : namely, that this absolute Love is outside the world of politics, which are limited by Time, and count on leases of short numbered hours ; but in itself is ' hugely politic,' is an independent and self-sufficing State. In the couplet :—

> ' To this I witness, call the fools of time
> Which die for goodness, who have lived for crime ' :—

some find an allusion to the merited execution of Essex, popularly called ' the good Earl.' But the probability is that Shakespeare sympathised with Essex and those of the old nobility who were jealous of the Crown. And, again, it is simpler to take the lines as a fitting close to the metaphysical disquisi-

> Anon permit the basest clouds to ride
> With ugly rack on his celestial face,
> And from the forlorn world his visage hide,
> Stealing unseen to west with this disgrace. . . .

LXXIII. ' In me thou see'st the twilight of such day
> As after sunset fadeth in the west ;
> Which by and by black night doth take away
> Death's second self, that seals up all the rest.'

Taine insists, perhaps too exclusively, on the vivid imagery of Shakespeare's verse ; Minto and Mrs. Meynell, perhaps too exclusively, on the magic of sound and association which springs from his unexpected collocation of words till then unmated. The truth seems to lie in a fusion of the two theories. When Shakespeare takes his images from nature, the first excellence is predominant ; the second, when he takes them from the occupations of men.

Often, in the Sonnets, he illustrates his theme with images from *Inheritance*,[1] or *Usury*,[2] or the *Law* ; [3] and then his effects are rather produced by the successful impressment of technical terms to the service of poetry than by the recollections they revive of legal processes :—

> ' When to the *sessions* of sweet silent thought
> I *summon* up remembrance of things past.'

---

[1] I. ' tender heir.' II. ' by succession.' IV. ' legacy ' ; ' bequest.'

[2] IV. ' usurer.' VI. ' usury ' ; ' loan.' XXXI. ' tears ' are ' interest of the dead.'

[3] XIII. lease ; determination. XVIII. lease ; date. XXX. sessions ; summon. XLVI. defendant's plea ; title ; impannelled ; quest ; tenants ; verdict. XLIX. ' And this my hand against myself uprear,' viz., in taking an oath. LXXIV. arrest ; trial. LXXXVII. charter ; bonds ; determinate ; patent ; misprision ; judgment. CXX. fee ; ransoms. CXXVI. audit ; quietus, ' a technical term for the acquittance which every Sheriff (or accountant) receives on selling his account, at the Exchequer.' The frequency of these terms in the Sonnets and Plays led Malone to conclude that Shakespeare must at one time have been an attorney. If so, we may the better believe that Ben Jonson intended Ovid for Shakespeare in *The Poetaster*, i. I. ;—' Poetry ! Ovid, whom I thought to see the pleader,

Among such occupations he draws also upon
Journeys (L.) ; *Navigation* (LXXX., LXXXVI., CXVI.) :—

> ' O, no ! it is an ever-fixed mark (sea-mark)
> That looks on tempests and is never shaken ;
> It is the star to every wandering bark ' :—

Husbandry (III.) ; *Medicine* (CXVIII.) ; *Sieges* (II.) :—

> ' When forty winters shall *besiege* thy brow
> And dig deep *trenches* in thy beauty's *field* ' :—

and a *Courtier's Career* (VII., CXIV.) :—

> XXXIII. ' Full many a glorious morning have I seen
> *Flatter* the mountain-tops with *sovereign* eye. . . .'

> XXV. ' Great princes' *favourites* their fair leaves spread
> But as the marygold at the sun's eye ' :—

and this last was of a more striking application than
now in the days of Elizabeth or James. He draws
also on the arts of *Painting* (frequently), of *Music*
(VIII., CXXVIII.), of the *Stage* (XXIII.) ; on the *Dark
Sciences* :—

> XV. ' Whereon the stars in secret influence comment.'

> CVII. ' The mortal moon hath her eclipse endured,
> And the sad augurs mock their own presage '—

> XIV. ' Not from the *stars* do I my judgement pluck,
> And yet, methinks, I have *Astronomy* ' (Astrology) :—

so *prognosticating* from his friend's ' eyes ' ; on
Alchemy (XXXIII.), and *Distillation* (VI., LIV.) :—

> V. ' Then were not summer's *distillation* left
> A liquid prisoner pent in walls of glass. . . .'

> CXIX. ' What *potions* have I drunk of Syren tears
> *Distill'd* from lymbecks (alembics) foul as hell within.'—

When, as in these examples, he takes his illustrations
from professions and occupations, or from arts and

became Ovid the play-maker ! ' *Ibid*, ' *Misprize* ! ay, marry, I would
have him use such words now. . . . He should make himself a style out
of these.' And *passim*.

sciences, his magic, no doubt, is mainly verbal ; but it springs from immediate perception (as in the case of annual and diurnal changes), when his images are taken from subtler effects of sensuous appreciation, be it of *Shadows* ; of the *Transparency* of *Windows* (III., XXIV.) ; of *Reflections in Mirrors* (III., XXII., LXII., LXXVII., CIII.), or of *Hallucinations in the Dark* :—

> XXVII. ' Save that my soul's imaginary sight
> Presents their shaddow to my sightless view,
> Which, like a jewell hung in ghastly night,
> Makes black night beauteous. . . .'

> XLIII. ' When in dead night thy fair imperfect shade
> Through heavy sleep on sightless eyes doth say ! '

> LXI. ' Is it thy will thy image should keep open
> My heavy eyelids to the weary night ? '

And this source of his magic is evident also, when, as frequently, he makes use of *Jewels* (XXVII., XXXIV., XLVIII., LII., LXV., XCVI.) ;—*Apparel* (II., XXVI., LXXVI.) ;—the *Rose* (I., XXXV., LIV., LXVII., XCV., XCIX., CIX.) ;—the *Grave* (I., IV., VI., XVII., XXXI., XXXII., LXXI., LXXII., LXXVII., LXXXI.) ;—*Sepulchral Monuments* (LV., LXXXI., CVII.) ;—the *Alternation of Sunshine with Showers* (XXXIII., XXXIV.) ;—the *Singing of Birds* (XXIX.), and their *Silence* (XCVII., CII.). *Realism* is the note of these imaginative perceptions, as it is when he writes :—

> XXXIV. ' 'Tis not enough that through the cloud thou break
> To dry the rain on my storm-beaten face. . . .'

> XXIII. ' As an imperfect actor on the Stage,
> Who with his fear is put beside his part. . . .'

> L. ' The beast that bears me, tired with my woe
> Plods dully on. . . .'

> LX. ' Like as the waves make towards the pebbled shore. . . .'

LXXIII. ' When yellow leaves, or none, or few do hang
            Upon those boughs ' :—

when he instances the '*Dyer's Hand*' (CXI.) and the
' *crow that flies in heaven's sweetest air* ' (LXX.)—a
clue to carrion—or when he captures a vivid scene of
nursery comedy :—

> CXLIII. ' Lo, as a careful housewife runs to catch
>   One of her feather'd creatures broke away,
>   Sets down her babe, and makes all swift despatch
>   In pursuit of the thing she would have stay ;
>   Whilst her neglected child holds her in chase,
>   Cries to catch her whose busy care is bent
>   To follow that which flies before her face,
>   Not prizing her fair infant's discontent.'

In all such passages the magic springs from imaginative observation rather than from unexpected verbal
collocutions.   And, while this observation is no less
keen, the rendering of it no less faithful, than in the
earlier Lyrical Poems, *Conceits*, though still to be
found, are fewer :—*e.g.*, of the *Eye and Heart* (XXIV.,
XLVI., XLVII.) ; of the *Four Elements*—earth, air, fire,
water (XLIV., XLV.) ; and of the *taster to a King*
(CXIV.).

XVIII

ELOQUENT DISCOURSE.—On the other hand the
ELOQUENT DISCOURSE of the earlier Poems becomes
the staple of the *Sonnets* and their highest excellence.
It is for this that we chiefly read them :—

> XXXVI. ' Let me confess that we two must be twain
>   Although our undivided loves are one. . . .'

> XL. ' Take all my loves, my love, yea, take them all ;
>   What hast thou then more than thou hadst be-
>   fore ? . . .'

> CXXXIX. O call me not to justify the wrong
>   That thy unkindness lays upon my heart. . . .'

CXL. 'Be wise as thou art cruel ; do not press
        My tongue-tied patience with too much disdain ;
        Lest sorrow lend me words, and words express
        The manner of my pity-wanting pain.
        If I might teach thee wit, better it were,
        Though not to love, yet, love to tell me so. . . .
        For if I should despair, I should grow mad,
        And in my madness might speak ill of thee.'

The last, addressed to the Dark Lady, are, it may
be, as eloquent as any addressed to the Youth, but
they lack something of those others' silvery sadness :—

LXXI. 'No longer mourn for me when I am dead,
        Than you shall hear the surly sullen bell,
        Give warning to the world that I am fled
        From this vile world, with vilest worms to dwell :
        Nay, if you read this line, remember not
        The hand that wrote it ; for I love you so,
        That I in your sweet thoughts would be forgot,
        If thinking of me then should make you woe.
        O, if, I say, you look upon this verse
        When I perhaps compounded am with clay,
        Do not so much as my poor name rehearse,
        But let your love even with my life decay ;
            Lest the wise world should look into your moan.
            And mock you with me after I am gone.

LXXII. 'O, lest the world should task you to recite
        What merit lived in me that you should love.
        After my death, dear love, forget me quite,
        For you in me can nothing worthy prove ;
        Unless you would devise some virtuous lie,
        To do more for me than mine own desert,
        And hang more praise upon deceaséd I
        Than niggard truth would willingly impart :
        O, lest your true love may seem false in this,
        That you for love speak well of me untrue,
        My name be buried where my body is,
        And live no more to shame nor me nor you.
            For I am sham'd by that which I bring forth.
            And so should you, to love things nothing worth.

xc. ' Then hate me when thou wilt ; if ever, now ;
Now while the world is bent my deeds to cross,
Join with the spite of fortune, make me bow,
And do not drop in for an after-loss :
Ah ! do not when my heart hath scap'd this sorrow,
Come in the rearward of a conquer'd woe ;
Give not a windy night a rainy morrow,
To linger out a purpos'd overthrow.
If thou wilt leave me, do not leave me last,
When other petty griefs have done their spite ;
But in the onset come ; so shall I taste
At first the very worst of fortune's might ;
     And other strains of woe, which now seem woe,
     Compar'd with loss of thee will not seem so.'

XIX

VERBAL MELODY.—The theme of xc. is a sorrow
which has, I suppose, been suffered, at one time or
another, by most men: it is hackneyed as dying.
Yet the eloquence is peerless. I doubt if in all
recorded speech such faultless perfection may be
found, so sustained through fourteen consecutive
lines. That perfection does not arise from any
thought in the piece itself, for none is abstruse ; nor
from its sentiment, which is common to all who love,
and suffer or fear a diminution in their love's return ;
nor even from its imagery, though the line, ' Give not
a windy night a rainy morrow ' holds its own against
Keats's ' There is a budding morrow in midnight,'
which Rossetti once chose for the best in English
poetry. It arises from perfect verbal execution :
from diction, rhythm, and the just incidence of
accentual stresses enforced by assonance and alliteration. The charm of Shakespeare's verbal surprises
—e.g., ' a lass unparalleled,' ' multitudinous seas,'
instanced by Mrs. Meynell—once noted, is readily
recognised, but much of his Verbal Melody defies

analysis.   Yet some of it, reminding you of Chaucer's
' divine liquidness of diction, his divine fluidity of
movement ' :—[1]

> ' Feel I no wind that soúneth so like peyne
>   It séith " Alás ! why twýnned be we tweýne " ' :—

or of Surrey :—

> ' The gólden gíft that nature did thee gëve
>   To fasten frendes, and fede them at thy will
>   With form and favour, taught me to beléve
>   How thou art máde to shew her gréatest skill :—

may be explained by that absolute mastery he had
over the rhythmical use of our English accent.
Mr. Coventry Patmore has justly observed [2] that
' the early poetical critics '—notably Sidney and
Daniel—' commonly manifest a much clearer dis-
cernment of the main importance of rhyme and
accentual stress, in English verse, than is to be found
among later writers.'   And this because, as he goes
on to say, ' the true spirit of English verse appears
in its highest excellence in the writings of the poets
of Elizabeth and James.'   If we neglect *Quantity*,
that is to say the duration of syllables, whose sum
makes up an equal duration for each line—and we
must neglect it, for, except in the classical age of
Greece, and of Rome in imitation of Greece, no
language observes so constant a quantity for its
syllables as to afford a governing element in verse—
we find in English verse *Rhyme* and *Accentual Stress*
or *Ictus*.   Now, *Rhyme*, but falteringly nascent in
Folk-song before his day, was fully acclimatised by
Chaucer from French, which has no emphatic
accents, at a time when French was the natural
tongue of the cultured in England.   In a language

[1] Matthew Arnold.   [2] *Essay on English Metrical Law.*

without emphatic accents, or exact quantity, Rhyme was, and Rhyme is, a necessity to mark off and enforce the only constant element, viz., *Metre* or the number of syllables in each line.   But in the homely and corrupt English of Chaucer's day, and side by side with the Court poetry, another poetry persisted, which was based exclusively upon the accentual stresses natural to northern languages.   And it persisted down even to Shakespeare's day.   We find so curious and artful a metrist as Dunbar pursuing both traditions :—Chaucer's rhymed ' staff of seven ' and the unrhymed, alliterative verse of *Piers Plowman*.   Dunbar died, *c*. 1513 (as some think, at Flodden).   But after his voice was silenced we have a contemporary poem on the battle—*Scottish Field* [1] :—

> There were girding forth of guns, with many great stones ;
> Archers uttered out their arrows and eagerly they shotten ;
> They proched us with spears and put many over ;
> That the blood outbrast at their broken harness.
> There was swinging out of swords, and swapping of heads,
> We blanked them with bills through all their bright armour,
> That all the dale dinned of the derf strokes :—

and editions of *Piers Plowman* were published in 1551 and 1561, showing a continuous appreciation of our indigenous but archaic mode.   In that mode the major accents fall on syllables either consonantal or of cognate sound.   This was no device of mere artifice : the impassioned speech of any Englishman becomes charged with stresses so heavy as to demand syllables of kindred sound on to which they may fall, and the demand is met unconsciously, since otherwise the weight of the accent would interrupt and

---

[1] Cited by Ker with the reference :—Ed. Robson, Chetham Society, 1855, from the Lyme MS. ; ed. Furnivall and Hales, *Percy Folio Manuscript*, 1867.

shatter the flow of discourse. The heavy beat at the end of a French line and the heavy accents in an English line must be met and supported in the first case by Rhyme, in the second, by syllables similarly produced. Shakespeare, in the Sonnets, whilst revelling in the joy of Rhyme, handed down from the French origin of English verse and confirmed by the imitation of Italian models, also turned the other and indigenous feature of English verse to the best conceivable advantage. No other English poet lets the accent fall so justly in accord with the melody of his rhythm and the emphasis of his speech, or meets it with a greater variety of subtly affiliated sounds.

This may be illustrated from any one of the more melodious and, therefore, the more characteristic Sonnets. Take the First :—

1. From *f*airest *C*rea*t*ures we desi*r*e in*c*re*a*se
2. That thereby beauty's *R*ose might never *D*ie
3. But as the *R*i*p*er should by *T*ime de*c*ease
4. His *t*ender he*ir* might b*ear* his memory.
5. But thou con*tr*acted to thine own *bright eyes*
6. Feed'st thy light's *f*lame with se*lf*-substantial *f*uel
7. Making a *f*amine where a*b*undance *lies,*
8. Th*y*self thy *f*oe to thy sweet self *too* c*r*uel
9. Th*ou* that art n*ow* the world's fresh ornament
10. And *o*nly he*r*ald to the *g*audy spri*ng*
11. With*in* thine own *b*ud *b*uriest thy content
12. And *t*ender ch*ur*l mak'st w*a*ste in ni*gg*arding
13. P*i*ty the w*or*ld or else this *g*lutton *be*
14. To *eat* the world's due by the *g*rave and *thee* :—

and you observe (1) the use of kindred sounds, of alliteration or of assonance or of both, to mark the principal stresses in any one line :—*E.g.,* line 1, *C*reatures and in*c*rease, where both are used ; line 3, *R*iper and T*i*me ; line 4, *he*ir and b*ear* ; line 5, con*tra*cted and *bright*; line 9, T*hou* and *now* :—and (2), and this is most characteristic, the juxtaposition of assonantal sounds where two syllables consecutive, but in separate words, are accented with a marked pause between them :—*E.g.*, line 5, br*ight* e*yes* ; line 8, *too* cr*uel* ; line 11, b*u*d b*u*riest; line 12, m*ak'*st w*a*ste. Mr. Patmore points out [1] that ' ordinary English phrases exhibit a great preponderance of emphatic and unemphatic syllables in consecutive couples,' and our eighteenth century poets, absorbed in Metre and negligent of varied Rhythm, traded on this feature of our tongue to produce a number of dull iambic lines by the use of their banal trochaic epithets, ' balmy,' ' mazy,' and the rest. Shakespeare constantly varies his Rhythm in the Sonnets, and frequently by this bringing of two accented syllables together, with a pause between. But, when he does so, he ensures a correct delivery by affiliating the two syllables in sound, and prefixing to the first a delaying word which precludes any scamping of the next ensuing accent :—*E.g.* ' own ' before ' bright eyes ' ; ' self ' before ' too cruel ' ; ' churl ' before ' mak'st waste.' Cf. ' Earth ' before ' sings hymns ' in XXIX. 12 ; and XV. 8, ' and *wear their brave state* out of memory.'

It is by this combination of Accent with Rhyme that Shakespeare links the lines of each quatrain in his Sonnets into one perfect measure. If you except two—' Let me not to the marriage of true minds,' and ' The expense of spirit in a waste of shame '—you find that he does not, as Milton did afterwards, build up his sonnet, line upon line, into one monumental whole : he writes three lyrical quatrains, with a pronounced pause after the second

[1] *Essay on English Metrical Law.*

and a couplet after the third. Taking the First
Sonnet once more, you observe (3) the binding together of the lines in each quatrain by passing on a
kindred sound from the last, or most important,
accent in our line to the first, or most important,
in the next :—*E.g.* from 2 to 3, from D*ie* to R*i*per
by assonance ; from 3 to 4, from *T*ime to *T*ender by
alliteration ; from 6 to 7, from *F*uel to *F*amine ;
from 7 to 8, from *F*amine . . . *lies* to Th*y*self . . .
*F*oe ; from 9 to 10, from *Or*nament to H*er*ald ; from
11 to 12, from con*tent* to *tend*er ; from 13 to 14, from
be to *eat*.   Cf. LX., lines 6, 7 :—

> ' *Cr*awls to maturity wherewith being *cr*own'd
> *Cr*ooked eclipses 'gainst his glory fight.'

and CVIII. 9, 10 :—

> ' So that eternal love in love's fresh *case*
> *Weighs* not the dust.'

In a Petrarchan sonnet any such assonance, if it
embraced the rhyme, would prove a blemish, but
in the Shakespearian quatorzain it is a pleasant and
legitimate accessory to the general binding together
of the quatrain.   Most subtle of all is the pent-up
emphasis brought to bear on *Rose* in I. 2—a word
not easily stressed—by the frequency of R's in the
first line and their absence till *Rose* is reached in the
second.   (4) For a further binding together of the
quatrain the Rhyme, or last syllable, though not
accented, is often tied by assonance to the first
syllable, though not accented, of the next line :—
E.g. I. lines 3, 4, dec*ease*—H*is* ; lines 7, 8, l*ies*—
th*ys*elf ; lines 10, 11, Spr*ing*—*with*in, lines 12, 13,
niggard*ing*—*Pi*ty.   Shakespeare's effects of alliteration, apart from this use of them for the binding

2 B

together of the quatrain, are at some times of astonishing strength :—

> LXV. 7, 8. ' When rocks impregnable are not so *stout*
> Nor *gates* of *steel* so *strong* but Time decays ' :—

and at others of a strange sweetness :—

> IX. 5. ' The *world will* be thy *widow* and still *weep*.'

Again, at others he uses the device antithetically in discourse :—

> XXXIX. 10. ' Were it not thy *sour leisure* gave *sweet leave* ' :—

and his rhythm is at all times infinitely varied :—

> XIX. 14. ' My love shall in my verse *ever* live long. . . .'
>
> XXXIII. 7. ' And from the *forlorn world* his visage hide. . . .'
>
> LXXXVI. 4. ' Making their *tomb* the *womb* wherein they grew. . . .'
>
> XI. 10. ' Harsh, featureless, and rude, *barrenly* perish.'

Apart from all else, it is the sheer beauty of diction in Shakespeare's Sonnets which has endeared them to poets. The passages, which I have quoted to other ends, must abundantly have proved this. Yet let me add these :—

> V. 5, 6. ' For never-resting time leads summer on
> To hideous winter, and confounds him there.'
>
> XVII. 7-12. ' The age to come would say, This Poet lies,
> Such heavenly touches ne'er touch'd earthly faces.
> So should my papers, yellowed with their age,
> Be scorn'd, like old men of less truth than tongue,
> And your **true** rights be termed a poet's rage,
> And stretchéd metre of an antique song.'
>
> XVIII 1-4. ' Shall I compare thee to a summer's day ?
> Thou art more lovely and more temperate :
> Rough winds do shake the darling buds of May
> And summer's lease hath all too short a date.'

XLVIII. 10, 11. 'Save where thou art not, though I feel thou art
Within the gentle closure of my breast.'

LIV. 5, 6. 'The canker-blooms have all as deep a die
As the perfuméd tincture of the roses.'

LX. 9, 10. 'Time doth transfix the flourish set on youth,
And delves the parallels in beauty's brow.'

LXIV. 5, 6. 'When I have seen the hungry ocean gain
Advantage on the kingdom of the shore.'

LXV. 1-4. 'Since brass, nor stone, nor earth, nor boundless sea,
But sad mortality o'ersways their power,
How with this rage shall beauty hold a plea,
Whose action is no stronger than a flower ?'

LXXXIX. 8. 'I will acquaintance strangle, and look strange.'

XCIV. 9, 10. 'The summer's flower is to the summer sweet,
Though to itself it only live and die.'

XCVII. 1-4. 'How like a winter hath my absence been,
From thee, the pleasure of the fleeting year !
What freezings have I felt, what dark days seen !
What old December's bareness everywhere.'

XCVII. 12-14. 'And thou away, the very birds are mute :
Or, if they sing, 'tis with so dull a cheer,
That leaves look pale, dreading the winter's near.'

XCVIII. 9 10. 'Nor did I wonder at the lily's white,
Nor praise the deep vermilion in the rose.'

CV. 1. 'Let not my love be call'd idolatry.'

CXXXII. 5, 6. 'And truly not the morning sun in heaven
Better becomes the gray cheeks of the East.'

CXLII. 5, 6. 'Or, if it do, not from those lips of thine
That have profaned their scarlet ornaments.'

CXLVI. 13, 14. 'So shalt thou feed on death, that feeds no men,
And death once dead, there's no more dying then.'

XX

It matters nothing to Art that Titian may have painted his Venus from the Medici's wife : Antinous gave the world a Type of Beauty to be gazed at without a thought of Hadrian. But the case is not altered when the man who rejoices or suffers is also the man who labours and achieves. It matters nothing to Art that Luca Signorelli painted the corpse of his beloved son, and it is an open question if Dante loved indeed a living Beatrice. Works of perfect Art are the tombs in which artists lay to rest the passions they would fain make immortal. The more perfect their execution, the longer does the sepulchre endure, the sooner does the passion perish. Only where the hand has faltered do ghosts of love and anguish still complain. In the most of his Sonnets Shakespeare's hand does not falter. The wonder of them lies in the art of his poetry, not in the accidents of his life ; and, within that art, not so much in his choice of poetic themes as in the wealth of his IMAGERY, which grows and shines and changes : above all, in the perfect execution of his VERBAL MELODY. That is the body of which his IMAGERY is the soul, and the two make one creation so beautiful that we are not concerned with anything but its beauty.

P.S.—Let me here acknowledge my great debt to Mr. W. E. Henley for his constant help in the writing of this Essay. But for his persuasion I should never have attempted a task which, but for his encouragement, I could never have accomplished.

ELIZABETHAN ADVENTURE
IN ELIZABETHAN LITERATURE

ELIZABETHAN ADVENTURE
IN ELIZABETHAN LITERATURE

'CHERISH Marchandise, keep the Admiraltie.' I lit
on this line in *The Libell*, little book, that is, ' on
England's policie,' a rugged poem interpolated by
Hakluyt into his famous *Voyages* (1599). The advice
was, and is, so obviously sound that none need insist
on its soundness; and it hit my fancy on another
score. It occurs in a poem which, else, is one lament
over the decadence of England's sea-power; and
that lament is wedged into the classic story of
England's earliest and greatest achievements by sea.
But such intrusion of counsel, of regret, of fore-
boding, into a contemporary record of the golden
age of expansion struck a note not unfamiliar. A
like incongruity is still, to-day, the dominant feature
of our national attitude towards national endeavour.
A like lament sings wailing in our ears.

I should mock the mighty dead did I compare the
last quarter of the nineteenth with the last quarter
of the sixteenth century. There can be no comparison; but there is similarity—in miniature. Mr.
Chamberlain has told us that ' we live in interesting
times '; Mr. Goschen, that we have two hundred
and fifty effective ships of war; and, from South
Africa, from East and West Africa, from the Nile,
from the Yukon valley, from the Indian frontier,
from the China seas, there is one story of expansion

and of risk. The hopes and fears of our kinsmen over-sea loom magnified in the daily press. Nor is there refuge in literature ; books on the Colonies are but collected journalism, blue-books but edited despatches. Men of action have their work, men of letters their art ; but there is no apparent relation between the two.

So I turn to Elizabethan literature and dip at hazard here and there, to strike the track of Elizabethan adventures. They did great things, and their contemporaries wrote great books. Let us, then, dive into these Elizabethan books, and let us see to what extent and in what fashion they mirror the deeds of the Elizabethan adventures. In them we can study the relation of literature to national expansion, and the aspects of that relation may prove suggestive, even encouraging. At any rate the study of it may serve for an anodyne to suspense.

Taking up this relation, then, the first thing that strikes is the portentous volume of the adventure, and the portentous volume of the literature, which may fairly be called Elizabethan. The second is the narrowness of the area within which the two overlap. The gigantic output of Elizabethan authors is not, as one might have supposed, mainly concerned with the prodigious deeds of Elizabethan adventurers. Indeed, in dramatic and lyrical poetry, which form the chief features of Elizabethan literature, it is only here and there that you discover a transient allusion to the national ferment which carried all kinds and conditions of men to the uttermost parts of the earth.

Yet when Shakespeare left the glades of Warwickshire he came, as I have said elsewhere, to a ' London rocking and roaring with Armada enthusiasm.' The

names of poets and playwrights were, no doubt, on
every tongue—Lyly and Lodge, Marlowe and Spenser
—but the air was ringing, too, with the names of
adventurers—of Raleigh, and Drake, and Grenville.
An acute critic has argued that the literature of any
epoch portrays, not the immediate needs and actions
of an age, but its aspirations towards those experiences which are most remote from its own.   Thus,
in our own age, which, in the main, is one of peace
and industry, we have the novel and the ballad of
adventure.   Men who spend their lives at desks,
when they take a holiday into the region of romance,
seek for relaxation in the terror of a shipwreck or
the shambles of a battlefield.   This theory is confirmed by a study of Elizabethan verse.   It is all
but grotesque to find such a man as Sir Walter
Raleigh masquerading in poetry as a shepherd, and
piping alternate ditties with Edmund Spenser on
what they were pleased to call an ' oaten reed.'   But
it is not, on second thoughts, inexplicable.   To the
war-worn and sea-weary, who had pierced the
tangles of Brazil, threaded the icebergs of Labrador,
and affronted the batteries of Cadiz, the Arcadia of
convention, with its ' soft white wool Arcadian sheep
do bear ' and its flageolets tied up with ribbands,
offered the most welcome, because the most complete, contrast.   It was, of all men in the world, Sir
Philip Sidney who wrote ' Arcadia ' and the most
moving sequence of love sonnets, next to Shakespeare's, which we have in English.

   Having noted the huge volume of what I may
call ' Arcadian ' verse, we may now note, outside
that volume, and even within it, allusions here and
there which can only be appreciated when they are
referred to the enterprises that occupied so many

Elizabethans.   In the sonnets of Shakespeare, Daniel, Drayton, Constable, and others, there are frequent allusions to 'maps.'   In Shakespeare's *Twelfth Night*, you read of 'more lines than is in the new map with the augmentation of the Indies.'   Now maps did not then 'summon up remembrance' of dull hours in a schoolroom : they were associated in men's minds with the latest attempt at co-ordinating the latest theory of the world's configuration, born of the latest voyage beyond unknown seas ; so that then maps thrilled with adventure and speculation and mystery.   And, again, in Elizabethan poetry and, more particularly, in Shakespeare's Plays, you have powerful descriptions of storms at sea.   Pericles, with his wife dying in childbirth on the weltering ship, addresses the cyclone :—

> 'Thou stormest venomously,
> Wilt thou spit all thyself ?   The seaman's whistle
> Is as a whisper in the ear of death
> Unheard.'

In *Troilus and Cressida* you have

> 'the dreadful Spout
> Which shipmen do the Hurricano call.'

In *The Tempest*, amid much else of wonderful description, Ariel is asked

> 'Hast thou, Spirit,
> Perform'd to point the tempest that I bade thee ?'

He answers

> 'To every article.
> I boarded the King's ship : now on the beak,
> Now in the waist, the deck, in every cabin,
> I flamed amazement : Sometime I'd divide,
> And burn in many places ; on the topmast,
> The yards, and bowsprit, would I flame distinctly,
> Then meet and join.'

But that description of a now familiar phenomenon of electricity is taken from Elizabethan accounts of Magellan's first voyage round the world. I shall quote from *Purchas his Pilgrimes*, published in 1625 ; but, in this instance, based on Eden's translation of Pigafetta's Journal ; and Eden published in 1577, say ten years before Shakespeare came to town. Thus it runs in *Purchas* : ' Here were they in great danger by Tempest : But as soone as the three Fires, called Saint Helen, Saint Nicholas, and Saint Clare, appeared upon the Cables of the Ships, suddenly the tempest and furie of the Windes ceased.' I cannot doubt that Shakespeare drew on this account of Magellan's voyage for his *Tempest*, for on the very next page in *Purchas* we come upon Setebos, Caliban's god. You read that four Giants, so the story ran, that is to say four savages of lofty stature, were shackled by a stratagem, and that ' when they saw how they were deceived, they roared like Bulls, and cryed upon their great Devill *Setebos*, to helpe them.' I shall insist later on a closer connection between Elizabethan prose and Elizabethan adventure ; but, reverting now to poetry, you find in Shakespeare several allusions to Indians and the Indies. ' O America, the Indies,' for example, in *The Comedy of Errors*, an early play ; and, again, in *The Tempest*, ' They will not give a doit to relieve a lame beggar when they will lay out ten to see a dead Indian.' A similar reference to an Indian, as the feature of a show, will be found in *Henry VIII*.

In that play, one of the latest by Shakespeare—most of it, indeed, and the passage which I shall quote, being by Fletcher—you have a wider declaration, not of the instruments and accidents, the 'maps' and 'tempests' of discovery, but of the spirit working in men's minds which drove them to expand the Empire. It was written some years after James I. came to the throne, but, since the last act shows the christening of Elizabeth, a prophecy of the only safe kind, namely, one written after the event, is placed in the mouth of Cranmer :—

> ' When Heaven shall call her from this cloud of darkness . . .
> . . . . . . Peace, plenty, love, truth, terror,
> That were the servants to this chosen infant,
> Shall then be his (James's) and like a vine grow to him :
> Wherever the bright sun of Heaven shall shine,
> The honour and the greatness of his name
> Shall be, and make new nations : he shall flourish,
> And, like a mountain cedar, reach his branches
> To all the plains about him.   Our children's children
> Shall see this and bless heaven.'

It cannot be said that James did much to promote colonisation ; indeed, he hampered the Virginian settlers at every turn : but it is true that the seed of new nations was then sown, far-scattered by the spirit of expansion.

The passage may be paralleled from Shakespeare's contemporary, Daniel :—

> ' Who in time knows whither we may vent
>   The treasures of our tongue ?   To what strange shores
> This gain of our best glory shall be sent
>   T' enrich unknowing nations with our stores ?
> What worlds, in th' yet unforméd Occident,
>   May 'come refined with th' accents that are ours ? '

In an earlier poet, Christopher Marlowe, Shakespeare's master, you find the same theme of expansion put into the mouth of *Tamburlaine the Great*.   Dying, he calls out :—

> ' Give me a map ; then let me see how much
> Is left for me to conquer all the world,
> That these, my boys, may finish all my wants.'

And the stage direction follows (*one brings him a map*). This insistence on ' maps,' the Spanish touch in the word ' Hurricano,' the frequent confusion of America with India, all to be noted in these allusions to adventure scattered through Elizabethan verse, are signs of the time and indices to current opinion. There is such another in one of Shakespeare's sonnets, the 116th, which we admire for its mingled splendour and obscurity. He writes of love :—

> ' O no ! It is an ever-fixéd mark
> That looks on tempests and is never shaken ;
> It is the star to every wandering bark
> Whose worth 's unknown, although his height be taken.'

Here, ' mark ' clearly means a ' sea-mark,' or beacon, but the reference to the star, presumably the North Star, has proved a stumbling block to critics. Yet some light is shed upon it by recalling that the English versions of Spanish discoveries, by Eden, Hakluyt, and Lock were new books when Shakespeare wrote. For in those versions the disappearance of the North Star, when you sail far enough South, and the variation of the compass from it, when you sail 'far enough West, constituted themes for wonder and mysterious awe. Even in Purchas' account of Columbus' first voyage, published so late as 1625, you read : ' On the fourteenth day of September he first observed the variation of the Compas, which no man till then had considered, which every day appeared more evident.' These shiftings of the Pole Star which, until then, had been the one thing stable in a world of change, gave rise to the wildest speculations. Elsewhere, you find the most frantic attempts to account for such apparent changes by assumptions that the world bore the shape not of an apple, but of a pear, or that the earth was in parts piled up in protuberances of gigantic elevation. America was to them, truly, a new world, as new as the planet Mars would be to us ; and the spirit in which it was regarded in relation to the Pole Star may be gauged from a passage in Peter Martyr, written, no doubt, in 1516, but only Englished by Eden during Shakespeare's lifetime : ' We ought therefore certainely to think ourselves most bound unto God, that in these our times it hath pleased him to reveale and discover this secrete in the finding of this new worlde, whereby wee are certaynely assured, that *under our Pole Starre* '—mark that ' our '—' and under the Æquinoctiall line, are most goodly and ample regions.'

The third thing, then, which strikes as you note the insistence on ' maps,' the confusion of India with America, the awe inspired by new stars, and the wonderful tales reported by Othello of

> ' Anthropophagi and men whose heads
> Do grow beneath their shoulders,'

is the recent origin, the novelty, the consequent mystery of the enterprises on which Elizabethan Adventurers embarked. And these impressions were of course heightened by the fact that the English, with few exceptions, were the latest in this field of adventure, and that the accounts of earlier discoveries had but recently been translated out of Spanish and Latin into the English tongue. To understand this, we must trace the sequence of nautical discovery. The first praise must be given to the Portuguese, who were first, because they first ' trusted the compass,' ' the touched Needle,' which Purchas writes, ' is the soule of the Compasse, by

which every skilfull Mariner is emboldened to compasse the whole body of the Universe.   Let the
Italians,' he goes on ' have their praise for Invention :
the praise of Application thereof to these remote
Discoveries is due to the Portugals, who first began
to open the Windowes of the World, to let it see it
selfe.'   Again, ' the Loadstone,' he writes, ' was the
Lead-Stone, the very seed and ingendring stone of
Discoverie.'

Now nobody wanted to discover America.   They
wanted to reach India by sea, to reach Cathay, or
China, and Cipango ; a fabulous island of fabulous
wealth, whose image seems to have been formed,
partly from Plato's legend of the island Atlantis ;
partly, perhaps, from rumours of Japan brought
over land, from mouth to mouth, by Oriental
traders, who had never been further than China, and,
since the adventure of Marco Polo, never so far.
Mr. Fiske's admirable book, *The Discovery of America*
and the old maps which he reproduces in it, show that
Columbus and Amerigo Vespucci both died without
a suspicion that they had discovered America.
They, and others after them for years, practically,
omitted the extent of the Pacific from their conception of the Globe, even as they contracted the extent
of Asia eastwards.   Where they did, as matter of
fact, find America, they expected to find China, and,
in the South Sea, the great Island, Cipango.   They
are always searching for Cipango, the court of the
Great Khan, or the Land of Ophir.

Some idea of the pace of these discoveries, and of
the resulting confusion and difficulty of assimilation,
may be gauged from the fact that Europeans (setting
the report of Herodotus on one side) crossed the
Equator for the first time only in 1472, by creeping

down the coast of Africa. Remembering that, we can realise the audacity of Columbus twenty years later. We can understand the murmurs of his men at what seemed madness, and was in fact the project of a ' dreamer, dreaming greatly.' The story is too well known to bear repetition, even in Elizabethan English. I merely note that at Cuba ' he went on land, thinking it to be Zipango ' (Purchas). Omitting for the moment John Cabot, we come next to Amerigo Vespucci, a Florentine, who served both Spain and Portugal. He made four voyages between 1497-1504, and did, in fact, discover the continent of South America, sailing along the coast of Brazil as far south as latitude 34°. But, like Columbus, he died without knowing this. Even on the map of Ptolemy, dated 1540, the New World was still an island in the South Sea—' Novus Orbis, the Atlantic Island which they call Brazil and America.' Gerard Mercator was the first, in 1541, to trace America with some approximation to its real shape, printing AME in large type on the north, and RICA on the south lobe of that continent. In 1531, Vasco Nunez de Balboa, and not Cortes, as Keats' famous Sonnet would lead us to suppose, gazed at the Pacific for the first time from a peak in Darien. I omit the conquests of Mexico and Peru by Cortes and Pizarro, only to insist on one point in respect of these discoveries, namely, that all lands discovered, or discoverable, in the New World, had been made over in anticipation to Castille, and consequently to Spain, by a Bull of Alexander VI., in 1493 ; and on a second, namely, that neither Catholic France nor Protestant England ever acquiesced in that papal injunction. The ' animadversions on the said Bull,' to be read in *Purchas his Pilgrimes* are long, and, in parts, too

vigorous for modern quotation.   But the conclusion
is in the right spirit of the Elizabethan adventurers.
Purchas, after praising the French and Henry VII.
for rejecting it, apostrophises his king, James I. :—
' And long, long may his Majestie of Great Brittaine
spread his long and quiet Armes to the furthest East
and remotest West, in the gainefull Traffiques, in the
painefull Discoveries, in the Glorious and Christian
Plantations of his Subjects (maugre such Bugbeare,
Bull-beare bellowings) . . . all Arts and Religions
concurring into one Art of Arts, the Truth of Religion, and advancing of the Faith, together with the
glory of his Name, and splendour of his State, the
love of his People, the hopes of his Royal Posteritie
to the last of Ages.   Amen.   Amen.'   That has the
true Elizabethan ring about it, though written some
years after Gloriana's death.

A truer title of Spain to our respect is, that she
sent out Magellan with the first expedition which
accomplished the circumnavigation of the world ;
an exploit which can never be paralleled, unless, in-
structed by Mr. Wells, we should invade the planet
Mars.   We know every incident of that voyage—
and so did Shakespeare—from Eden's translation of
Pigafetta's journal, upon which Purchas founded his
later narration.   The story regains its freshness when
you read it in the first English translation of a sur-
vivor's narrative.   The Patagonian giants, one of
whom was ' very tractable and pleasant,' while
another ' declared by signs, that if they made any
more Crosses, Setebos would enter into his body, and
make him burst.'   ' The stars about the South Pole
. . . gathered together, which are like two Clouds,
one separate a little from another and somewhat
dark in the midst,' that is to say, the gap in the stellar

heaven still called Magellan's Cloud; the inevitable
Cipango, always found because always sought; the
Cannibals; ' the sea full of weeds and herbes'; 'the
bats as bigge as eagles' that 'are good to be eaten,
and of taste much like a Henne'; all these observations restore the sense of actuality, and the sense of
the marvellous. But I must condense the pleasing
tale. Magellan—Fernando de Magellanes in Spanish
—sailed with five ships on September 20, 1519, and
two hundred and fifty men, of whom one was English. The next winter, at Port Saint Julian, three
of his ships mutinied. Undaunted, he boarded one,
killing its captain, and now, with three to two in his
favour, he attacked the others. A grim monument of
that strife is noted by Fiske, when he comes to Drake's
voyage round the world. Magellan sailed again
with the spring, in August, 1520, to find the opening
to the Straits, now named after him, on October 21.
In the strait, which is some three hundred miles in
length, one of his ships stole away and back to Spain.
He took five weeks in passing the strait. His men
might murmur, but Magellan answered that he
would go on if he had to eat the leather off his ship's
yards. Eden, followed by Purchas, reports that
' when the Capitayne Magalianes was past the
Strayght, and sawe the way open to the other mayne
sea, he was so gladde thereof that for joy the teares
fell from his eyes.' But the most trying, because the
least expected, experience was still before him.
They counted on Cipango and Cathay; but, you
read, ' they sayled three moenths and twentie days
before they saw any land : and, having by this time
consumed all their Bisket and other Victuals, they
fell into such necessitie that they were inforced to
eate . . . skinnes and pieces of leather, which were

foulded about certaine great Ropes of the shippes.'
Thus did Magellan justify his word. At last they
made the Philippines, and knew that they had
accomplished the greatest exploit of navigation.
But Magellan himself was never again to see Europe.
In the spirit of a crusader he converted one tribe to
Christianity, and then led it to war against a neigh-
bour king. In this contest he was killed on April 27,
1521. His followers vacated and burnt one out of
the three remaining ships ; a second was driven back
to the Moluccas ; and the last, with forty-seven
hands, made for the Cape of Good Hope ; rounded
it on May 16, 1522, and crossed the equator on
June 8, only fifty years after it had been crossed for
the first time from the north by Santarem and
Escobar. At the Cape Verde Islands thirteen hands,
who had landed, were arrested and imprisoned
by the Portuguese. The remainder, being called on
to surrender, stretched every stitch of canvas, and,
after eight more weeks of the ocean, on September 6,
the thirtieth anniversary of the day on which
Columbus weighed anchor for Cipango, the *Victoria*
sailed into the Guadalquivir, and eighteen gaunt
survivors, out of two hundred and fifty men,
landed to tell the strangest story ever told by man
to men.

Such were the exploits of Spain ! ' What way
soever,' you read, ' the Spaniards are called, with a
beck only, or a whispering voice, to anything rising
above water, they speedily prepare themselves to
fly, and forsake certainties under the hope of more
brilliant success.'

And now for the French. The French entered into
competition with the Spaniards for the commerce
and soil of the New World as early as in 1504. In

Hakluyt's Voyages, that great Elizabethan bible of adventure, you have Varazzano's account, to his employer, Francis I., in 1524, of his discovery of Florida. There he found a ' courteous and gentle people '—' vines growing naturally, which, growing up, tooke holde of the trees as they do in Lombardie,' and people ' clad with the feathers of fowles of divers colours.' These and other accounts were translated out of French by Richard Hakluyt (iii. 36) and presented to Sir Walter Raleigh. In Hakluyt, also, you may read the discoveries made in Canada by Jacques Cartier in 1535. Here we come for the first time upon Montreal (Mont Réal in French), Mount Roiall in Hakluyt's English. And we look back along the vista of years over the protracted rivalry between France and England in Canada, which was to end only with the death of Wolfe on the Heights of Abraham. But France, torn by the throes of expiring feudalism and the new miseries of religious war, could not support the enterprise she had undertaken. Yet there is a lesson to be learnt from her. When Jesuits and Calvinists had carried their strife into New France beyond the Atlantic, and when merchants grudged the necessary expense for the construction of a fort, the French Viceroy, Champlain (1620), uttered a memorable saying: ' It is not best to yield to the passions of men ; they sway but for a season ; it is a duty to respect the future.' So he built the castle of St. Louis on its ' commanding cliff.' Those words were spoken fifty years after the English entered the field against France and Spain ; but they remain a good counsel for Imperialists to our own day—' It is a duty to respect the future.' From the French, the English learned to look forward to centuries still in the womb of Time ;

from the Spaniards, to follow 'a beck only, or a whispering voice,' and ' to fly and forsake certainties under the hope of more brilliant success.' As our own poet of Empire, Rudyard Kipling, has sung in our own day :—

'Came the whisper, came the Vision, came the Power with
    the Need,
Till the Soul that is not man's soul was lent us to lead.'

And now we must consider how the English came to lead.   There was a false dawn of enterprise under Henry VII., but it did not develop into refulgent glory until Elizabeth had mounted the throne.   Still it must be noted as an earnest of the splendour to be.   The whole story may be read in the great work published in 1599 by the Rev. Richard Hakluyt, a friend of the adventurers, whose being thrilled with their strangely mingled inspiration of religious fervour and imperial audacity.   Recollect, let me say it again, that the English were not seeking America as we know it, but West India.   And, since Spain was seeking India and Cathay by a south-west, England, from the beginning, with one brief interlude, sought those fabulous lands by a north-west, passage.   In 1497, the very year in which Vespucci discovered (without knowing it) the continent of South America, and five years after Columbus had discovered the Islands of the West Indies, Henry VII. gave John Cabot, a native of Venice and a resident in Bristol, licence ' to take sixe English ships in any haven or havens of the realme of England . . . to seeke out, discover, and finde whatsoever isles, countreys, regions, or provinces of the heathen and infidels whatsoever they be, and in what part of the world soever they be, which before this time had been un-

known to all Christians.' That was his answer to
the Pope's bull. So you read that ' John Cabot, a
Venetian, and his sonne Sebastian (with an English
fleet, set out from Bristoll), discovered land which
no man before that time had attempted, on the 24
of June, about five of the clock early in the morning.
This land he called Prima Vista, that is to say, First
Scene.' I need not go into the thorny question of
the son's, Sebastian's, credibility in his narrative
of subsequent discoveries which he alleges himself
to have made. His veracity has been impeached by
Sir Clements Markham ; but, since Vespucci was at
one time similarly accused, I must hope that, in the
case of Sebastian Cabot also, the error may be
ultimately traced, not to his lying, but to the in-
accurate application of geographical names in his
own writings and the writings of his early commentators. The real importance of Sebastian's
writings, whether truthful or not, is that, years later,
they inspired the Elizabethan adventurers.

Under Henry VIII. you find traces of sporadic
attempts to follow up the achievement of the Cabots,
but they did not amount to much. We read that
Henry was ' exhorted with very weighty and substantial reasons, to set forth a discovery even to the
North Pole,' and we know that two ships sailed for
St. John and Newfoundland in 1527. In 1536 an
expedition ended in ' extreme famine,' so that ' our
men eate one another,' upon which the captain stood
up and ' made a notable oration, containing, howe
much these dealings offended the Almightie, and
quoted the Scriptures from first to last, what God
had in cases of distresse done for them that called
upon Him, and told them that the power of the
Almighty was then no lesse than in al former time

it had bene.'   A brave and pious man, whom we may well remember !

But the ideas of the English upon geography during the first half, and more, of the sixteenth century, were still confused.   They went groping in different directions, encountering strange and terrible experiences.   Robert Tomson, a merchant of Andover, was imprisoned in Mexico between 1556-1558.   Others were turned back by ice and fog from the endeavour towards the North-West.   So, still failing to apprehend the size of the globe, both as to the extent of Asia and of the Pacific, they tried to reach India and Cathay by a north-east passage, north of Russia.   In 1553 Sir Hugh Willoughby and Richard Chancellor set out, in that direction, on a ' voyage intended for the discoverie of Cathay and divers other regions, dominions, islands, and places unknowen.'   The expedition was fitted out by ' Master Sebastian Cabota (Cabot), Esquire, and Governour of the mysterie and companye of the Marchant Adventurers of the citie of London.'   The tragic end of an adventure thus founded upon equal parts of ignorance and daring has furnished one of the most striking of all these striking scenes.   The two ships were separated by foul weather.   We have, first, Chancellor's account, with its surmise as to the fate of his comrades :—' But if it be so, that any miserable mishap have overtaken them, if the rage and furie of the sea have devoured these good men, or if as yet they live, and wander up and downe in strange countreys, I must needs say they were men worthy of better fortune, and if they be living, let us wish them safetie and a good returne : but if the crueltie of death hath taken holde of them, God send them a Christian grave and sepulchre.'   Their end was strange and moving beyond Chancellor's surmise. We have the last words of Sir Hugh Willoughby in his own hand. They run thus :— ' Seeing the year farre spent, and also very evill wether, as frost, snow, and haile, as though it had been the deepe of winter, we thought best to winter there. Wherefore we sent out three men south-south-west, to search if they could finde people, who went three dayes journey, but could finde none : after that we sent other three Westward foure daies journey, which also returned without finding any people. Then sent we three men south-east three daies journey, who in like sort returned without finding of people, or any similitude of habitation.' That is all :—' the rest is silence,' for these notes were found a year or more after, under the frozen hand of Sir Hugh Willoughby, sitting frozen in his cabin, with all his Company, singly and in groups, frozen in different parts of the ship. On the margin of Willoughby's journal you read the brief record, ' In this haven they died.'

I pass over the earlier voyages of John Hawkins, to Guinea and thence to the West Indies with cargoes of negroes. It was he who started the slave trade, but we must not judge another age by the standard of to-day. Hawkins, recording a storm, could set down that ' Almighty God would not suffer His elect to perish ' ; and I cannot doubt his good faith. But, passing over these voyages to the West Coast of Africa, I come to the time when the seed sown by Sebastian Cabot in his writings began to sprout in the minds of the Elizabethan adventurers. Sir Humphrey Gilbert, Raleigh's half-brother by an earlier marriage, had read and considered Sebastian's narratives, and he had also considered Willoughby's death, and much else which to us seems amazingly beside the mark — as passages from Homer and Plato ; mediæval legends of savages cast up on the ' coast of Germany,' wherever that may have been, and the navigations of ' Ochther ' in the time of King Alfred.   And out of this strange compost of truth and legend he framed his famous discourse ' to prove a passage by the north-west to Cathaia.'   This discourse was written in 1576 ; its author must be considered the prime mover of the Adventurers, and his pamphlet conclusively shows how slight was the knowledge, how dark the counsels, of the men who, in truth, made the world what it is to-day.   Fantastic, wrong-headed, obstinate, reckless, but brave beyond report and belief, it was Sir Humphrey Gilbert and his school—Raleigh, Drake, Hawkins, Frobisher, Davis, Cavendish—who made the New World, in the full extension and intention of that phrase : the New World, not only of America, but of freedom in thought and of expansion in civilisation.   They cast the bread of civilisation on the waters, content that posterity should see it return after three centuries.

Humphrey Gilbert ends his discourse with these words ; ' Desiring you hereafter never to mislike with me, for the taking in hande of any laudable and honest enterprise ; for if through pleasure or idlenesse we purchase shame, the pleasure vanisheth, but the shame remaineth for ever, and therefore, to give me leave without offence, alwayes to live and die in this minde.   That he is not worthy to live at all, that for feare, or danger of death, shunneth his countrey's service, and his own honour ; seeing death is inevitable, and the fame of vertue immortall. Wherefore in this behalfe, *Mutare vel timere sperno* '

—' I scorn to change or to be afraid.' You will see that in his death he lived up to that lofty device.

It was Sir Humphrey Gilbert who fired the imagination of Queen Elizabeth and of his half-brother, Sir Walter Raleigh, who, in his turn, inspired others and equipped more expeditions at his own charges than any other of the Adventurers. Humphrey Gilbert published his treatise in 1576, and, in the same year, Martin Frobisher set out on his first voyage to the North-West for the search of the Strait or Passage to China. He was, you read in Hakluyt, ' determined and resolved with himself to make full proofe thereof, and to accomplish or bring true certificate of the truth, or else never to returne againe, knowing this to be the onely thing of the world that was left yet undone, whereby a notable minde might be made famous and fortunate.' Queen Elizabeth waved to him as he dropped down the Thames. He made two other voyages in the same direction during the next two years, 1577-78, and, in the fanciful manner of the day, he called the ice-bound land of frost which he discovered, Meta Incognita, that is the ' Unknown Goal.' The reports are all of ice. ' The force of the Yce so great, that not onely they burst and spoyled the foresaid provision, but likewise so raised the sides of the ships, that it was friteful to behold, and caused the hearts of many to faint.' And again, ' We came by a marveilous huge mountaine of Yce, which surpassed all the rest that ever we saw ; for we judged it to be neere fourscore fathomes above water . . . and of compasse about halfe a mile.' They were bewildered by icebergs and mists, ' getting in at one gap and out at another.' Later, in 1585-6, you have the two voyages of John Davis 'for the discoverie of the North-west Passage.' Nothing could daunt them from their dream of Cathay. But the reports are the same :—' the shoare beset with yce a league off into the sea, making such yrksome noyse, as that it seemed to be the true patterne of desolation, and after the same our Captaine named it, The Land of Desolation.'

Sir Humphrey Gilbert's discourse was the prime motor of these forlorn hopes ; yet his desperate expectation of reaching China by the North-West issued in practical advantage—the foundation of the colony of Virginia by his greatest pupil, Raleigh. Before I touch upon that, I will give you Sir Humphrey's end, not unworthy of his motto, ' Mutare vel timere sperno.' He sailed for the last time in 1583. Frobisher had brought back a few stones in which the ' mineral men ' detected gold. So Elizabeth put her private money into the speculation, and, with but two more years of his licence or charter to run, Sir Humphrey sailed for the Arctic El Dorado, now realised, after three centuries, in Klondyke. They made the Orkneys ' with a merrie wind.' But the expedition proved disastrous. On his return, Sir Humphrey would not leave his little frigate, the *Squirrel*, of ten tons, for the larger *Golden Hinde*, and this is what befell, in the words of an eyewitness : ' I will hasten to the end of this tragedie, which must be knit up in the person of our Generall ; and as it was God's ordinance upon him, even so the vehement persuasion and entreatie of his friends could nothing availe to divert him from a wilful resolution of going through in his frigate. . . . This was his answer : " I will not forsake my little company going homeward, with whom I have passed so

many stormes and perils." . . . Men which all their
lifetime had occupied the sea, never saw more outrageous seas. . . . Munday, the ninth of September,
in the afternoone, the Frigat was neere cast away,
oppressed by waves, yet at that time recovered ;
and giving foorth signes of joy, the Generall, sitting
abaft with a booke in his hand, cried out to us in the
Hinde (so oft as we did approach within hearing),
" we are as neere to heaven by sea as by land."
Reiterating the same speech, well beseeming a
souldier, resolute in Jesus Christ, as I can testifie he
was.   The same Monday night, about twelve of the
clock, or not long after, the Frigat being ahead of us
in the *Golden Hinde*, suddenly her lights were out,
whereof as it were in a moment we lost the sight, and
withall our watch cryed, the Generall was cast away,
which was too true ; for in that moment the Frigat
was devoured and swallowed up by the sea.   Yet
still we looked out all that night, and ever after,
untill we arrived upon the coast of England.'   *Mutare
vel timere sperno :* he would not change his ship, and
he was ready to die.

Sir Walter Raleigh took up his brother's work.
He was born in 1552, and went to Oriel College,
in later years the Alma Mater of another empire-
builder, Cecil Rhodes.   But in 1569, Raleigh went
to France, and fought for the Huguenots under
Coligny.   Persuaded, as I have said, by Sir
Humphrey Gilbert, he took up exploration and
fitted out the expedition of 1576.   He directed these
distant endeavours largely from the Court, and from
Ireland, where he commanded a company in 1579.
But his heart was in discovery and colonisation.
Undeterred by Sir Humphrey's failure and death, in
the next year he joined, with another brother, Sir

Adrian Gilbert, and a merchant, Sandeman, a company called 'The Colleagues of the Fellowship for the Discovery of the North-west Passage.' He sent John Davis out on that quest, and about the same time he sent out his kinsman, Richard Grenville, to maintain his darling project, the Colony of Virginia. Between whiles, you find him entertaining the poet Spenser in Ireland. Spenser describes the visit thus :—

> ' Whom when I askéd from what place he came,
>   And how he hight ? himself he did ycleep
> The Shepheard of the Ocean by name,
>   And said he came far from the main sea deep.'

I cannot follow out the vicissitudes of Raleigh's career, but, keeping to my text, I may give some references to him in Elizabethan literature. His search for that Will-o'-the-wisp, El Dorado in Guiana, was acclaimed by a poet, probably Chapman, in these strains :—

> ' Guiana whose rich feet are mines of gold,
> Whose forehead knocks against the roof of stars,
> Stands on her tip-toe at fair England looking,
> Kissing her hand, bowing her mighty breast,
> And every sign of all submission making
> To be her sister and the daughter both
> Of our most sacred maid.'

There is much else to the same sanguine and delusive purpose :—

> ' And there do palaces and temples rise
>   Out of the earth to kiss th' enamoured skies.'

Sir Walter's own account of that expedition fills many pages of Hakluyt. To show his self-gathered resolution, I will quote one passage : ' I sent Captaine Whiddon the yeere before to get what knowledge he could of Guiana, and the end of my journey at this time was to discover and enter the same, but my intelligence was far from truth, for the country is situate above 600 English miles further from the sea, then I was made believe it had bin, which afterward understanding to be true by Berreo, I kept it from the knowledge of my Company, who else would never have been brought to attempt the same : of which 600 miles I passed 400, leaving my ships so farre from mee at ancker in the sea, which was more of desire to performe that discovery, then of reason, especially having such poore and weake vessels to transport ourselves in.'

I know not where you will find a calmer account of a more dogged endeavour in pursuit of a vainer phantasmagoria.   But Raleigh's day of days was at the sack of Cadiz in 1596.   It was Raleigh who overbore the timid counsels of Lord Thomas Howard, crying out to Lord Essex, ' Entramos ! Entramos ! ' a permission so acceptable to the gallant young Earl, that he threw his hat into the sea for sheer joy. Then Raleigh betook him to his ship, and led the van under the batteries and right into the harbour. When his vessel, shattered by shot, was on the point of sinking, he left it to enter Essex's ship, and, though wounded severely by a splinter, had himself carried on shore and lifted on to a horse, to charge with Essex against the Spanish army.   Of the sea-fight Hakluyt says :—' What manner of fight this was, and with what courage performed, and with what terror to the beholder continued, where so many thundering tearing peeces were for so long a time discharged, I leave it to the Reader to thinke and imagine.'   Of the charge on shore, he tells us :—
' The time of the day was very hot and faint, and the way was all of dry deepe slyding sand in a manner,

and beside that, very uneven. . . . But the most famous Earle, with his valiant troupes, rather running in deede in good order, then marching, hastened on them with such unspeakable courage and celerity, as within one houres space and lesse, the horsemen were all discomforted and put to flight, their leader being strooken downe at the very first encounter, whereat the footmen being wonderfully dismayed and astonished at the unexpected manner of the Englishmen's kinde of such fierce and resolute fight, retyred themselves with all speed possible that they could.'

We know the story of Sir Walter Raleigh but too well; his cruel imprisonment, his more cruel liberation to save his life by accomplishing the impossible, and his most cruel execution on a warrant signed fifteen years earlier.   He knew all that is to be known of success and failure, of Courts and treachery, of sea-fights and assaults on cities, of treasure islands, and tempests, and long marches in tangled forests. And just because he knew these things so nearly, he has written beautiful verse in praise of their opposites :—

> ' Heart-tearing cares and quiv'ring fears,
>   Anxious sighs, untimely tears,
>   Fly, fly to Courts,
>   Fly to fond worldlings' sports ;
>   Where strained sardonic smiles are glosing still,
>   And Grief is forced to laugh against her will,
>   Where Mirth's but mummery,
>   And sorrows only real be.'

The man who was killed for not finding El Dorado wrote :—

> ' Go let the diving negro seek
>   For gems hid in some forlorn creek ;

We all pearls scorn,
But what the dewy morn
Congeals upon each little spire of grass,
Which careless Shepherds beat down as they pass ;
And gold ne'er here appears,
Save what the yellow Ceres wears.'

Sir Walter sought his rest in Arcadia ; but he only found it on the scaffold. Old and racked with ague, he mounted the steps easily ; for his prayer that the fit might not shake him before his peers and the crowd was granted. And he made his dying speech with inimitable grace and animation. Then, asking to be shown the axe, ' I prithee,' said he, ' let me see it. Dost thou think I am afraid of it ? ' So taking it in his hand, he kissed the blade, and passing his finger lightly along the edge, said to the Sheriff, ' 'Tis a sharp medicine, but a sound cure for all diseases.' A few minutes later, when the headsman hesitated, he partially raised his head from the block, and called aloud in the old voice of command : ' What dost thou fear ? Strike, man ! '

I have no space in which to give the accounts of Sir Richard Grenville's voyages, and the story of his death on the *Revenge* is well known. But it has been something altered in modern versions to suit modern taste. His real reason for declining to turn about is given by Raleigh :—' Sir Richard utterly refused to turn from the enemy, alleging that he would rather choose to die than to dishonour himself, his country, and Her Majesty's ship.' We must take the Adventurers as they were. Sir Richard died and doomed his ship and company, not to save the wounded, but, as Mr. David Hannay makes plain, on the point of honour. It was his rule of life never to turn his back on the Spaniards, and he saw no reason for changing it when it involved his death. This appears from the full report of his dying speech. ' Here die I, Richard Grenville, with a joyful and a quiet mind, for that I have ended my life as a good soldier ought to do, who has fought for his country, Queen, religion, and honour.   Wherefore my soul joyfully departeth out of this body, and shall always leave behind it an everlasting fame of a true soldier, who hath done his duty as he was bound to do.   But the others of my company have done as traitors and dogs, for which they shall be reproached all their lives, and leave a shameful name for ever.'

I have left Sir Francis Drake to the last, and can now but touch upon him.   He set himself grimly down to the work of capturing Spanish treasure ships, although England was at peace with Spain, upon the ground, which he held sufficient, that the Spaniards imprisoned and executed Englishmen. That, and the pretence of Spain to exclusive dominion in South America, seemed to him to constitute a state of war more truly than of peace.   He grasped what Carlyle calls ' the essential veracity' of the situation.   So he acted accordingly, and became the terror of Spain, the ' dragon,' according to the Spanish poet, ' or old serpent' of the Apocalypse. In Hakluyt you catch a vivid glimpse of him on his first voyage, climbing a tree above the jungle in order to see the Pacific.   And there is the wonderful story of his—the second—circumnavigation of the globe. He sailed November 15, 1577.   When he reached Port St. Julian you read, ' We found a gibbet standing upon the maine, which we supposed to be the place where Magellan did execution upon some of his disobedient and rebellious company.' The skeleton had hung there for more than fifty

years. On the homeward track they passed the
Cape of Good Hope, and you read, ' This Cape is a
most stately thing, and the fairest Cape we saw in
the whole circumference of the earth. . . . We
arrived in England,' so the record ends, ' the third
of November, 1580, being the third yeere of our departure.' I must omit with regret all reference to the
defeat of the Spanish Armada, to which Drake contributed, perhaps, more than any other. He sailed
for the last time with John Hawkins in 1595, and
both of these great commanders died during the
voyage. Their deaths are simply recorded in
Hakluyt : ' And that night came up to the easter-
most end of S. John, where Sir John Hawkins departed this life.' That, and no more. And so, too,
with Drake : ' On the 28 at 4 of the clocke in the
morning our Generall Sir Francis Drake departed this
life, having beene extremely sicke of a fluxe, which
began the night before to stop on him. He used
some speeches at or a little before his death, rising
and apparelling himselfe, but being brought to bed
againe within one houre died.' What would we not
give for those unreported speeches ! But that is the
end.

Willoughby had died ' congealed and frozen ' in
the North some twenty years before, Raleigh was
to die on the scaffold some twenty years after, the
great epoch of Elizabethan adventure ; and how
short that epoch was ! Drake, Hawkins, Frobisher,
Grenville, Humphrey were all dead, and, save
Frobisher, who was carried on shore to die, all were
sunk in shotted hammocks beneath the seas they had
mastered within twenty years. The glorious life of
the Adventurers was crowded into the brief compass
of but two decades. They set out late in the day

with little knowledge, but with much hope and with boundless courage. Their El Dorados vanished in thin air ; but they founded the British Empire of the sea. And their names shall be remembered and loved so long as the English tongue is spoken in the land they were never to see again, and in many other lands where it is also spoken, thanks, in the first place, to them.

SIR WALTER SCOTT

SIR WALTER SCOTT

My Lord Provost and Gentlemen,—Any man rising to propose 'The Memory of Sir Walter Scott' in any gathering must needs be abashed. Should he keep to the beaten path, Charity herself could but say with Dr. Johnson that his speech ' contains much that is true and trite.' Should he digress from the obvious, Justice must add with the sage, ' and much that is original and ridiculous.' But when, as now, a speaker born south of the Tweed stands confronted by ' The Edinburgh Walter Scott Club ' ; when, as to-night, your President, less fortunate in that capacity than twelve of his predecessors, can claim no bond of nativity with you and the subject of your loving reverence ; why then, gentlemen, he can only reflect that you are wholly responsible for the aberration of your choice, and claim acquittal for his conduct of the case, ' If '—as Sir Walter was so fond of quoting—' If, so he be in that concatenation accordingly.'

Not for me the privileged nonchalance of my predecessors ! Of, say, Mr. Haldane, with his easy ' In this Our dining-room, restrained from the criticism of . . . outsiders, we may let Ourselves go a little about Ourselves.' From that point of view your President is an outsider. But I make no apology for intrusion. From any other point of view, and there are many, I may say to you with Plutarch's old soldier who found a solitary freedman performing the funeral rites of Pompey the Great, 'O Friend . . . thou shalt not have all this honour alone . . . to bury the only and most famous captain of the Romans.' From any other point of view, I expostulate with Byron :—

> Scotland ! Still proudly claim thy native bard,
> And be thy praise his first and best reward,
> Yet not with thee alone his name should live,
> But own the vast renown a world can give.

My concatenation is œcumenical. But do not be alarmed. Of the many points of view from which the memory of Sir Walter Scott may be regarded, I shall occupy only three.

There is one, remote indeed from the world's renown because intimate to any man born a Briton, which I cannot ignore. To the Briton, aware of his natal prerogatives, there are few better than this : that Walter Scott may be, first a living part of his childhood, and then the entertainer of his youth, before he becomes the companion of riper years. I remember vividly my delight on discovering the story of *Rob Roy*, when reading that wonderful book for the third time at the age of eleven. The earlier attempts had been breathless plunges into seas of incomprehensible dialect ; 'adventures of a diver' hazarded to snatch the pearls of freebooting. At eleven I was still rather shy of 'Diana Vernon.' Later on I fell in love with her, like the rest of you, and, after further reperusals, came at last to such an appreciation of 'Andrew Fairservice' as may be vouchsafed to a Briton who is not a Scot.

But consider the subtle and complex charm of Scott's novels to any man who savours them in maturity after looting them as a boy ; to any man

who recalls the young companions with whom he
impersonated their characters, ' all now,' in Scott's
phrase, ' all now sequestered or squandered'—working
at large in the far ranges of the Empire, or toiling
each in his tunnel at home.　Any such, though born a
generation after Scott died, can truly say with Scott's
friend, Lady Louisa Stuart, ' They awaken in me
feelings I could hardly explain to another.　They
are to me less like books than like letters one treasures
up, pleasant yet mournful to the soul, and I cannot
open one of them without a thousand recollections.'
That is one point of view.

　Yes ; but turn the page in the *Letters* (i. 49) for
Scott's reply to his friend, and you read—in the
language of courteous formality which belonged to
his time and in no way justifies the absurd charge
of undue deference to rank sometimes preferred
against him—' I am very glad your Ladyship found
the tales in some degree worth your notice.　It cost
me a terrible effort to finish them, for between
distress of mind and body I was unfit for literary
composition.　But in justice to my booksellers I was
obliged to dictate while I was scarce able to speak for
pain.'　Thus, in the one year 1819, at the age of
48, did Scott give to Scotland and the world, in seven
volumes, *The Bride of Lammermoor, The Legend of
Montrose,* and *Ivanhoe.*　And thus he fought on for
thirteen more years, showering forth volumes each
one of which was received with ecstasy by Europe ;
but, for himself, toiling and suffering, yet gentle and
undaunted, through ruin due to the fault of others,
through bereavement through fear—the only fear
he knew—lest increasing illness should destroy that
magic faculty by which he was determined to vindi-
cate a chivalrous point of honour and to safeguard

the home on which his human affections were set. That, gentlemen, is another point of view. From it we may contemplate, not the story-teller who entranced our boyhood, nor the singer of Romance, nor the delineator of character, nor the patriot who revealed Scotland to herself as another Normandy of high-born hearts, nor the essayist, nor the biographer, nor the captain in a world-wide literary movement ; but simply, a Man ; a man so brave, so kind, so sensible, that he encourages our manhood and knocks the nonsense out of us all.

What a man ! Think of his magnanimity. He, of all men, wrote the only generous criticism on the Third Canto of *Childe Harold* (1816) at a moment when the world, for reasons, good, bad, and idiotic, united to crush the rival who had eclipsed his poetic fame. His criticism was generous. But it was just. Generosity as a rule is more true than detraction. What can be sounder than this, ' Almost all (his) characters . . . are more or less Lord Byron himself, and yet you never tire of them. It is the same set of stormy emotions acting on the same powerful mind . . . it is the same sea dashing on the same rocks, yet presented to us under such a variety of appearance that they have all the interest of novelty.' When Byron dies in 1824, it is Scott, the Bayard without reproach, who writes, ' I have been terribly distressed at poor Byron's death. In talents he was unequalled, and his faults were those rather of a bizarre temper . . . than any depravity of disposition. He was devoid of selfishness, which I take to be the basest ingredient in the human composition.'

If that was his attitude towards the rival who had beaten him in poetry, so was it towards the partner

who had ruined him in business. In the shock of
the crash that levelled the whole edifice of his hopes,
he can say, ' To nourish angry passions against a man
whom I really liked, would be to lay a blister on my
own heart.'

Think of his sterling sense. He liked an artist
to be ' a right good John Bull, bland and honest and
open, without any . . . nonsensical affectation.'
' Having observed,' he writes, ' how very unhappy
literary persons are made (not to say ridiculous into
the bargain) by pitching their thoughts and happiness on popular fame,' I ' resolved to avoid at least
that error.' Some recent contributors to a literary
correspondence may be pained to hear that Scott
cared for popularity only as a means to supporting
his family and paying twenty shillings in the pound.
For that he would work ' at the rate of £24,000 a
year,' checked only by this saving reflection—' but
then we must not bake buns faster than people have
appetite to eat them.'

He loved individual liberty. No cobbler, if he
had his way, should lose his stall to facilitate street
improvements. That was before the days of the
London County Council.

But turn from that to his public patriotism.
When things were not going too well with our armies,
and Joanna Baillie despaired to him of our country's
future : ' I detest croaking,' says he ; ' if true, it is
unpatriotic, and if false, worse. . . . My only ambition,' he goes on, ' is to be remembered, if remembered at all, as one who knew and valued national
independence, and would maintain it in the present
struggle to the last man and the last guinea, tho'
the last guinea were my own property, and the last
man my own son.'

The claims of individual liberty and public patriotism have blinded some men to the nicest scruples of personal honour. But they never blinded Scott. ' If,' he writes, ' I were capable in a moment of weakness of doing anything short of what my honour demanded, I would die the death of a poisoned rat in a hole, out of mere sense of my own degradation.' No wonder that he fought on ! Refusing a touching offer of help with the observation, ' There is much good in the world, after all. But I will involve no friend, either rich or poor. My own right hand shall do it.' It is not as if he liked labour. He loathed it. So he recalls his ' flourishing plantations,' and exclaims, ' . . . *Barbarus has segetes*, I will write my finger-ends off first.'

The morning rays of youthful enterprise faded out from the ' sober twilight ' in which he laboured. But he is never gloomy. On the contrary, he illumines his solitude with beams of the mellowest humour and flashes of delightful wit. It is we who are sad ; not he ; haranguing ' Madam Duty ' and calling her the plainest word in the English language. And, as Swinburne has pointed out, now that we have the *Journal*, we need no longer be sad. For we see him as he was, gay and buoyant to the last ; not tortured by Fortune, as we thought, but rounding on the fickle goddess with the merriest quips, until weariness and suffering wring from him the first faltering note—' I often wish I could lie down and sleep without waking. But I will fight it out, if I can.' And he just could. Death released him in the moment of victory. He was wont, in his modesty, to disparage the writer by comparison with the soldier. But Wolfe did not die more gloriously on the Heights of Abraham. And when he died we are glad to know that ' every newspaper in Scotland and many in England had signs of mourning usual on the ' death ' of a king.' His royal soul passed on its way from a sorrowing nation. If there can be an epic in the intimate prose of one man's private letters and journal, the *Journal and Letters* of Sir Walter Scott are an epic of the British home.

I have touched on the redoubled delight which the novels can give to any man who has read them as a boy. I have dwelt on the part which Scott himself played as a man. He was a great man. But was he a great artist ? That is my third point of view. If we are to consider him fairly from that point of view, we must strip from his works the glamour reflected on them, both from our own early associations, and from our present knowledge of the personality which he was at such pains to dissemble.

What did he accomplish as an artist ? What effects of his art endure ? We must face these questions in an artistic age, when so few achieve anything memorable, and so many assert that the mighty dead lacked finish. Scott ' gives himself away ' to the apostles of precious sterility. Let us make that admission. But let us also make the corresponding claim. He gives himself away in harvests. He was not, all allow, ' a barren rascal,' and we need not review the amount of his work. But neither, all must concede, was he a punctilious creator. ' His literary life ' resembled, he tells us, ' the natural life of a savage ; absolute indolence interchanged with hard work.' And we know, again from him, that he cheerfully ended the second volume of a novel without ' the slightest idea how the story was to be wound up to a catastrophe.' In

what sense, then, was he a great artist, or as we hold
in this Club, one of the greatest ?   Scott could turn
a phrase with precision when he pleased ;   none
better.   But let us go deeper.

A great artist, interpreting mankind to men, and
reconciling man to his lot, does one of two things ;
and the greatest do both.   He either bequeathes a
vast completed monument to posterity, or else he
invents a new method as a guide to future endeavour.
Scott's claim under the first head is not in dispute.
Let us establish his claim under the second head ;
his claim to have invented a method that was both
new and dynamic.

To do that I will put a competent and impartial
witness into the box.   I am too ignorant to be competent, too enamoured to be impartial.

I put Nassau Senior into the box.   I have by me
his reviews of the novels conveniently collected from
the *Quarterly*, and bound in one volume.   To read
them is to look back at the immediate impression
made by the novels on a critic, competent, impartial,
even I may say hostile.   Senior, educated at Eton,
and distinguished at Oxford, belongs, in terms of the
conflict between ' Classics and Romantics,' distinctly
to the Classical tradition, and is apt enough to behave ' in that concatenation accordingly.'   He writes
in 1821, seven years after *Waverley* was published,
still in ignorance of its authorship so complete, that
he notes an heraldic error committed by the ' unknown ' in *Ivanhoe*, and, turning to *Marmion*,
wonders at the coincidence of ' a similar mistake in
his great rival, Sir Walter Scott.'   And this is what
he says—or rather what ' we ' say, for he never
relaxes the august plural of Gifford's critical engine :—
' We shall never forget the disappointment and list-

lessness with which in the middle of a watering-place long vacation WE tumbled a new, untalked-of, anonymous novel out of the box which came to Us from Our faithless librarian, filled with substitutes for everything WE had ordered. . . . WE opened it, at hazard, in the second volume, and instantly found Ourselves, with as much surprise as Waverley . . . in the centre of the Chevalier's court. Little did WE suspect while we wondered who this literary giant might be, that seven years after, WE should be reviewing so many more of his volumes.' Senior looks back once again, in 1824, to the wonderful day on which he first read *Waverley* in the seaside lodging-house, ' little aware that the work which was delighting us was to form an epoch in the literary history of the world.' My hostile Classical witness gives abundant testimony to the novelty and force of Scott's art.

Its immediate effect was no less evident to all non-critical contemporaries. A Hungarian tradesman pointed out the bust of ' le sieur Valtere Skote ' as the portrait of ' l'homme le plus célèbre en l'Europe.' Dr. Walsh, travelling from Constantinople to England, found the fame of Scott's works at every stage from the frontier of Christendom. But let us consider the moment at which Scott produced this effect.

It was in 1814, the year of the Congress of Vienna, that Scott, ' rummaging in the drawers of an old cabinet,' found the mislaid MS. of *Waverley*, and ' took the fancy of finishing it.' He did finish the last two volumes in the course of three summer weeks, and writes, ' I had a great deal of fun in the accomplishment of this task, though I do not expect that it will be popular in the South, as much of the

humour, if there be any, is local, and some of it even
professional.'　Yet it is odds to-day that the name
of Waverley is familiar to as many as the names of
Castlereagh or Metternich.

Scott produced this effect at the climax of a series
of political convulsions which had wracked the diplomacy and shattered the armies of Europe.　Blood
enough had been spilled.　And now ink was to be
spilled.　For that one book did more than any other
to precipitate the controversy between Classics and
Romantics.　And Scott did more than any other
writer to give impulse and area to the Romantic
School.

By what method, we may ask, did he make the
Chevalier interesting in 1814 not only to Senior, my
Classical witness, but to nations who knew nothing
of Scottish manners, and cared little enough, I
dare say, for an abortive effort to retrieve one lost
crown, prosecuted in an age almost forgotten by
men who had seen the crowns of all Europe redis-
tributed, by the Revolution, by Napoleon, and the
Congress ?

Let us look at his method.　*Waverley, Guy Manner-
ing, Redgauntlet* are written, as Scott himself tells us,
round the professional knowledge of a lawyer with
a predilection for lawlessness.　Their origins are of
the driest.　Never did such irritating grains of sand
excite the production of such pearls.　These cannot
be accidents of Scott's temperament and vocation.
We cannot explain him as a literary oyster.　Indeed,
the image is inadequate.　They are not pearls, but,
rather, gems bespeaking design.　Senior tries to
explain the method of their execution.　He addresses
himself to a new harmony in literature, and seeks to
account for its charm.　He notes that the author

SIR WALTER SCOTT   433

of *Waverley* painted two classes : beggars and
gipsies, sovereigns and their favourites, ' the very
lowest and the very highest ranks of society,' better
' than that rank to which he must himself belong.'
And asks how the author came to copy more correctly
what he knew imperfectly, than what he knew well ?
After canvassing the question, backwards and for-
wards, he concludes that portraits partly imagined
may be more true than portraits wholly observed ;
and so affirms that Scott, by employing both imagination and observation in conjunction, had indeed
discovered a new method which saved him from two
dangers : the danger ' of losing general resemblance
in too close a copy of individuals with whom he was
intimate,' and the further danger ' of introducing
effort . . . over-colouring and caricature . . . in his
endeavour to render striking . . . representations
of the well known.' Now those are the errors of
Realism. Senior saw that it was a mistake, by
focussing the obvious, to belie general experience
widely imagined ; and a greater mistake to make
the obvious grotesque in order to redeem it from
dulness.

Scott avoided these two errors to which realism
is prone. But he did far more, which was not
apparent to a Classic making reluctant concessions
to a Romantic. Senior gets at half the truth of
Scott's new departure, but only at half.

In order to get at the whole truth ; in order to
understand the magnitude of Scott's innovation, we
must consider the condition of literature at the
moment when he rummaged in the drawers of that
old cabinet.

Scott's complete achievement is still obscured to
us by the conflict between Classics and Romantics.

2 E

Nor is that strange. The din and dust of the conflict puzzled even the protagonists engaged in it. You have Goethe declaring ' The Classic is health, the Romantic disease.' And you have Victor Hugo, dubbed, like Scott, a leader of the Romantics, denying the existence of the conflict and even the meaning of the terms. Hugo asserts, in 1824, that the two battle-cries—*les deux mots de guerre*—have no meaning unless, indeed, ' Classic ' meant only literature of an earlier epoch, and Romantic only literature that had developed with the nineteenth century.

But that will not do. The romantic movement, and the conflict, were each of them real enough. And two qualifications must be added. In the first place, the romantic movement derived from a date far anterior to 1800, from Macpherson's *Ossian* (1761-63), Walpole's *Castle of Otranto* (1764), and Bishop Percy's *Reliques* (1765). The movement then migrated to Germany, and became fantastic. It returned to Britain and became gruesome. In the second place, the conflict was not a straight issue between Classics and Romantics. That is why Hugo and others misunderstood what they were fighting about. The conflict was more truly a triangular turmoil between Classics, Romantics, and Realists. It was launched by Classics on the monstrous developments to which romantic and realistic methods had been pushed. The Classics were making reprisals on both, and Scott defeated those reprisals by combining the two.

Romance founded on imagination, and Realism founded on observation, are the primary methods by which the mind seeks to express the need of the heart. The classic method is a secondary mode.

It can be, and had been, applied alike to the Romantic
and the Realistic. Throughout the eighteenth
century the classic mode had selected and polished
until the element of wonder had disappeared from
literature's image of life. The romantic image,
classically treated, had become, as it were, a statue
in a nobleman's park. The realistic image, classically treated, had become, as it were, any party of
nobodies—'buddies,' I think, you call them in
Scotland—seated round a table, and applying
delicate seismometers to every tremor, however
faint, with which the heart responds to any fact,
however trivial. This was too dull; yes, and too
false to life, in which wonder is the most constant
element. After smoothing the romantic into the
inane, it had to be galvanised into the diabolic. After
sweetening the realistic with sentiment, it had to be
salted with satire. The passion for wonder revived,
and was gratified. It was indulged till the Romantic
School, developing into the School of Horror, turned
their statue into a hobgoblin; and the Realistic
School, developing into a School of Scandal, turned
their 'nobodies' into high-tobymen and demi-reps.
Each tried to tickle or shock. The romance of
Ossian was exaggerated to the gruesome by Monk
Lewis. The realism of Defoe was spiced to the
satirical; delightfully by the incomparable Jane
Austen, and outrageously by ruder hands. Peacock,
whose *Maid Marian* appeared in 1819 with *Ivanhoe*,
combines both extravagances in the satirical-
fantastic.

It is here that Scott intervenes with momentous
effect and enduring results. He eschewed, as Senior
noted, the excesses of the Realists. But he also
eschewed the excesses of the Romantics. He re-

jected the fantastic from romance, and the cynical
from realism. His huge performance was to hark
back to the first springs of each, at the moment when
the Classics declared war on the enormities to which
both were committed.

Scott stepped back—so to say—to embrace a
wider panorama of humanity and, from a position
of artistic detachment, painted what he saw, tinged
by the aerial perspective of wonder. His image of
life is the ' verissima, dulcissima imago ' ; true, but
not trite ; sweet, but not false ; wonderful, but not
inhuman. He made an epoch in literature by
creating romantic-realism ; by clothing actuality
with atmosphere ; by striking a richer chord from
notes of human experience, which till then had been
sounded singly.

No doubt he was lucky—like all conquerors. He
happened to have loved the old romantic poetry, and
imitated it admirably in his early poems. He
happened to have understood the new realistic
prose, and explained Defoe's method in his famous
analysis of Mrs. Veal's apparition ' the next day after
her death.'   So, in 1814, he trained the two into one
channel, and drew off their united power from the
welter of literary cross-currents. He produced a
pure stream of literary energy. And that stream
flowed for fifty years and more, turning the mills of
many movements even outside literature ; of the
Oxford movement in religion ; the Young England
movement in politics, and the Morris-Rossetti movement in art.

His achievement as an artist is that he appealed
to the general feelings of mankind by truth, wonder,
and charm.

Perhaps his strangest charm is woven by his unexpected reconciliations—of the lawyer and outlaw, of the servant and master, of the Jacobite and Hanoverian, of Scotland and England, of 'Time long past' and 'To-day.'

By these reconciliations, by searching for hidden chords of human experience, he feels his way to the supreme reconciliation of man to man's destiny. That is the work, often unconscious, of great masters. But for their magical counterpoint the present would be all to each of us ; ' an apex,' Pater calls it, ' between two hypothetical eternities ' ; a naked note, so poignant that it pierces. As Landor puts it, ' The present, like a note of music, is nothing but as it appertains to what is past and what is to come.' But how few among writers, classic, romantic, or realistic, have shown this by their art. Walter Scott is of those few. He extracted secrets from oblivion to endow what is with the mystery of what has been ; and, so, puts us in case to expect the future. He strikes a full chord upon the keys of time. It is only the greatest musicians of humanity, who thus exalt the present by fealty to the past, and make it a herald of eternal harmonies.

He leads us through the maze of time and seems to hold a clue. We wander with him, and we wonder with him, till we believe with him that the labyrinth of man's fate must lead some whither worth our seeking.

And he made light of all this. But for necessity that clamped him to the desk till his pen dropped from a dying hand, he would have bade farewell to his task with a Sidney's

Splendidis longum valedico nugis.

Yet his radiant trifles are the regalia of his native

land, and symbols of a suzerainty that still influences the literature of Europe. That is much. But there is more. His worth as a man excels his work as an author. It is an example of valour to all men, in all lands, for ever.